Practical Social Investigatio

Qualitative and Quantitative Methods in Social Research

0

12

Practical Social Investigation
Qualitative and Quantitative Methods in Social Research

Christopher J Pole
Department of Sociology, University of Leicester

and

Richard Lampard
Department of Sociology, University of Warwick

Prentice
Hall

An imprint of **Pearson Education**

Harlow, England · London · New York · Reading, Massachusetts · San Francisco · Toronto · Don Mills, Ontario · Sydney
Tokyo · Singapore · Hong Kong · Seoul · Taipei · Cape Town · Madrid · Mexico City · Amsterdam · Munich · Paris · Milan

Pearson Education Limited
Edinburgh Gate
Harlow
Essex CM20 2JE

and Associated Companies throughout the world

Visit us on the World Wide Web at:
www.pearsoneduc.com

_____

First published 2002

ISBN 0 136 16848 5

British Library Cataloguing-in-Publication Data
A catalogue record for this book is available from the British Library

Library of Congress Cataloging-in-Publication Data
Pole, Christopher J. (Christopher John), 1959–
      Practical social investigation: qualitative and quantitative methods in social research /
   Christopher J. Pole and Richard Lampard.
         p.   cm.
      Includes bibliographical references and index.
      ISBN 0-13-616848-5
      1. Social sciences–Research–Methodology.   I. Lampard, Richard.   II. Title.

   H62.P576 2002
   300'.7'2–dc21   2001021348

   10   9   8   7   6   5   4   3   2   1
   05   04   03   02   01

Typeset in 9.5/13pt Giovanni book by 35
Printed by Ashford Colour Press Ltd, Gosport

For Lizzie and Charlotte (C.P.)

In Memory of Pooter and Wub (R.L.)

Contents

Preface and acknowledgements

The origins of this book lie in our experiences of teaching social research methods (to undergraduates, postgraduates and others), and also in our shared view that both qualitative and quantitative approaches have important roles to play in social research. From our perspective there is consequently a need for a research methods text which does justice to both approaches. Arguably there are already edited texts in existence which satisfy this need, but such texts can sometimes be rather fragmentary, and we hope that this book, written by two authors who have each used both approaches, succeeds in treating the approaches in a more integrated and coherent way.

This book is intended to be useful to students who are carrying out empirical research, regardless of whether they are doing so in the context of a taught course or to provide the raw material for a project report or dissertation. The emphasis is thus on research practice rather than on the philosophy of social research, though the book encourages the reader to reflect on the implications of the research techniques that she or he uses for the nature and meaning of her or his research findings.

In our experience, undergraduates, postgraduates and fully fledged researchers in the field of social studies all typically have gaps in their knowledge of social research methods. Hence, while this book is intended to be accessible to novice researchers at undergraduate level, much of its content will be of equal interest (or perhaps even greater interest) to postgraduates. (Perhaps the hallmark of a good social research methods text is that it is bought by first-year undergraduates who are still referring to it during and beyond their doctoral studies.) Of course, addressing such gaps in researchers' knowledge will sometimes stretch beyond the scope of our book, but we hope that the references that we have made to more detailed material will address some of these more specific needs.

We now turn to the structure of the book. The first chapter considers what research is, why it is done, and what forms of knowledge it generates. The second chapter focuses on the planning and design of research studies. The book then moves on to data-collection issues, with the third chapter focusing on the issue of sampling, in both its quantitative and qualitative forms. The fourth chapter looks at the collection of data via various forms of observation, whereas the fifth chapter focuses specifically on the survey method. The sixth chapter discusses aspects of interviewing.

Not all social research involves the generation of new data, and the seventh chapter focuses on the use of existing data in the form of documents, official statistics and survey datasets. In the eighth and ninth chapters attention turns to qualitative and quantitative forms of data analysis, though data analysis is an ongoing process which is consequently also referred to in the earlier, data-collection-orientated chapters. The tenth chapter considers the sometimes neglected topic of writing about research, and the eleventh and final chapter brings together material from the earlier chapters, within a holistic consideration of the research process built around two example projects. Supplementary material includes a glossary at the back of the book, and a companion set of web pages on the Internet (see the note that follows this Preface).

Finally, we would like to acknowledge the contributions made to the development of this book by a range of people. The students whom we have taught at the Universities of Leicester and Warwick (and elsewhere) have obviously had a profound impact on the ways in which we think and talk about research methods. In addition, various colleagues have worked on projects upon which this book draws as examples; we would therefore like to thank Angela Bolton, Bob Burgess, John Hockey, Phil Mizen, Marlene Morrison, Mo Padfield, Kay Peggs, Ian Procter and Annemarie Sprokkereef. We are grateful to Duncan Gallie and to Roger Jowell of SCPR (now the National Centre for Social Research) for permission to make available the sub-sets of survey data. The encouragement and support of Christina Wipf-Perry of Prentice Hall and of Matthew Smith of Pearson Education during the preparation of the book were invaluable, and we would also like to acknowledge the helpful comments of some anonymous reviewers. We, of course, must take the blame for the book's many imperfections.

We are grateful to the following for permission to reproduce copyright material: Financial Times Limited for the headline "New rules push up crime figures" © *Financial Times* 13 October 1999; Guardian Newspapers Limited for the headline "Crime still falling but at a slower rate" published in *The Guardian* 13 October 1999; Telegraph Group Limited for the headline "Statistics shake-up shows rise in crime" by David Millward published in *The Daily Telegraph* 11 October 1999; and Times Newspapers Limited for the headlines "Violent crime figures set to soar" published in *The Times* 11 October 1999, and "Violent crime falling for first time in years" published in *The Times* 13 October 1999.

The views expressed in this book are those of the authors. They do not represent the views of any of their previous co-authors or researchers, or of any of the bodies involved in funding the research from which examples have been drawn throughout the text.

Note on the book's companion web pages

Sub-sets of data from two social surveys can be downloaded via the Internet from web pages corresponding to this book. These web pages also contain material which allows the reader to replicate the statistical analyses presented in Chapter 9, assuming that he or she has access to the statistical software package SPSS for Windows. Links to the web pages can be found on the publisher's website and authors' homepages; the pages are currently located at http://www.warwick.ac.uk/~syrdr/psi/.

One of the sub-sets of data originates from the main survey of the 1986 Social Change and Economic Life Initiative (SCELI) main (Work Attitudes and Histories) survey. This initiative was funded by the Economic and Social Research Council. The second sub-set originates from the 1991 British Social Attitudes Survey (carried out by Social and Community Planning Research (SCPR), which has since been renamed the National Centre for Social Research). Academic users can obtain the full set of data from each of these surveys from the Data Archive at the University of Essex (http://www.data-archive.ac.uk/).

This book is not sponsored or approved by SPSS, and any errors are in no way the responsibility of SPSS. SPSS is a registered trademark, and all references in the text of this book to SPSS products are to the trademarks of SPSS Inc. SPSS Screen Images © SPSS Inc. For further information contact: SPSS UK Ltd., First Floor, St Andrews House, West Street, Woking GU21 1EB, UK.

Windows and PowerPoint are registered trademarks of the Microsoft Corporation. Minitab is a registered trademark of Minitab Inc. GLIM is a registered trademark of The Royal Statistical Society. NUD*IST is a registered trademark of Qualitative Solutions and Research Pty Ltd. The Ethnograph is a registered trademark of Qualis Research Associates. Filofax is a registered trademark of Filofax UK.

Chapter 1   Introducing social investigation: what is research and why do we do it?

Introduction

The concern of this opening chapter and of this book as a whole, is with research as an activity. We are concerned with the process, procedures, theories and practicalities of doing research. The style we shall adopt, therefore, is an active style which seeks to take the reader through the various stages of social research, not in an uncritical, step-by-step way which assumes that research is always neat and tidy, but in a way that shows that research can be challenging, confusing, frustrating but above all very rewarding.

Our starting point is one which assumes that research is undertaken for a reason. The reasons may be many and varied. For example, we may be required to do a piece of research as part of a degree course, or we may be asked to do a piece of research for an organisation or a group that we belong to, looking into specific aspects of their work. We may choose to do research because of long-standing curiosity about a particular topic, or we may do some research in advance of a journey or some other kind of important event. Whilst the specific reasons for the research may vary, in all cases the basic reason remains the same.

> Quite simply, we do research because we want to find something out. Or, put more 'scientifically', we want to gather more knowledge about a particular topic.

We can dress research up in all kinds of scholarly language, but ultimately, the reason for it is:

> to know more at the end of it than we did at the beginning.

Reducing research to such a simple characterisation is useful as it cuts away some of the mystique which surrounds it. In addition, by talking about gathering knowledge or finding out, we emphasise the importance of the research process, of actually doing research. If we know more about a particular topic after doing the research than we did before it, then the research process, the doing of it, must be the important bit.

However, at another level, characterising research in such a simplistic way may mean that we by-pass some of its important aspects. For example, seeing research merely as a means of finding things out may be accurate, but it does not provide us with an understanding of the way in which research is done, or of the relationship between the way it is done and the knowledge which it produces. Neither does it tell us much about the different kinds of research that we might do or the different kinds of knowledge that they can produce.

On the other hand, by starting in such a simple way we can gradually build up to more complex questions about the nature of the knowledge that research yields and the relationship between this and the research tools that are deployed in order to generate the knowledge. However, in order to understand how to do research we first need to know what research is. Let us begin, therefore, by asking this most basic question.

What is research?

Whilst we may see research quite simply as a means of finding out or acquiring more knowledge, we should also see it as doing something special. When we talk about knowledge in the context of social research we refer to attempts to know things in a way which goes beyond description, anecdote or common sense. This is not to decry description, anecdotes or common sense, since they all have an important contribution to make to what we know about the world and how we know it, but in research terms we are looking for a kind of knowledge which is more enduring and more universal than that which applies only to particular events or situations. More formally, by conducting research, the researcher is attempting to make a contribution to his/her field of enquiry and, consequently, to what we know about the social world.

This attempt to get to know more about the social world has been characterised in many different ways: as a journey (Delamont, 1992), as fun (Schratz and Walker, 1995), as being nosy (Blaxter *et al.*, 1996), as something approaching an art form (Wolcott, 1995), or even as akin to slaughtering a pig (Eco, 1988, cited in Schratz and Walker, 1995).

Each of these definitions refers to a process. The suggestion is that, in order to make a successful journey, slaughter a pig, practise an art form or be nosy, there are a number of specific procedures that we must undertake. In addition, the journey, the slaughter, the art and being nosy imply change. We have travelled from one place to another, we have meat products (though at the cost of the life of the pig), we possess an artefact or the experience of creating art, or we know more about a particular situation. The implication is that by undertaking these diverse activities we move from one situation

to another and, presumably, our lives (though not those of the pig or, for that matter, vegetarians) are better for it. They, like research, are seen to be worthwhile activities.

However, while analogies of this kind may make us think constructively about the nature of research, they can take us only so far. Moreover, some analogies may confuse more than they enlighten. To pursue any meaningful discussion of research and the research process we need to move from general characterisations and analogies to definitions which dispense with the imagery and get to the heart of what research involves.

Drawing on a number of sources which have influenced the ways in which we have thought about and practised research over the years, including other texts, lectures and above all our experience of doing research, we offer the following definition:

> Research is a careful search, capable of withstanding close examination, for information which can be used to produce or enhance knowledge.

The intention here is to emphasise a number of things:

- Research is a process.
- Research has to be planned and well thought through.
- Information or data on their own do not necessarily constitute knowledge.
- Research has to be able to stand up to challenges from those who may wish to question or discredit its methods and the findings which are generated by the application of those methods.

In more technical language, we are saying that research is a process whereby we seek knowledge about a given phenomenon which is valid and reliable. By this we mean that we need to be confident that the methods used in the research are sound and that the knowledge produced is well grounded in the data which have been collected. Taking this down to the bare essentials once more, we are saying that research is about the search for knowledge.

In offering our own definition of research in this 'active' way we are well aware that we open ourselves up to challenges and disagreement. We welcome this, and as this is a book about 'doing' we hope to encourage thought, debate and argument right from the start. By thinking about and challenging definitions of research we will hopefully become more familiar with what it is and also see ways of enhancing the definition and of thinking critically about approaches to doing research.

In saying that research is about finding or about producing knowledge we assume either that knowledge is there to be discovered or that it is something which is created by the research process. This is an important distinction which introduces the notion of different kinds of knowledge. We will return to this idea in more detail later in this introductory chapter and elsewhere in the book. However, at this early stage, where we are considering approaches to research, it may be useful to start to consider how different approaches to research can produce different kinds of knowledge.

Approaches to research

Having suggested that there may be different kinds of knowledge it would also seem logical to suggest that different kinds of knowledge are linked to different kinds of research. For example, we are all no doubt familiar with depictions of the eccentric scientist conducting research with steaming flasks and test tubes; similarly we may all have been stopped in the street and asked questions by a person with a clipboard intent on discovering our views on a particular product; likewise we will have read or heard of opinion polls, particularly around general election times, which report on the popularity of political parties. We will also be aware of research in a slightly less obvious way as we go about our everyday lives: for instance, if we watch a TV documentary, especially of the 'fly on the wall' variety,

or see a film or read a book, or travel in a car or use a piece of household equipment.

All of these depictions, practices and products make use of research. The point that we wish to make is that we live our lives surrounded by research, using things that are the fruits of research. Moreover, we also conduct our own research as part of everyday life, in order to make decisions and to take action based on those decisions. Some of these decisions may be very important, even life changing. For example, before we apply for a job or a place at university, or buy a house or a car, we engage in a form of research by gathering information from various sources, evaluating and analysing this information, accepting some as more important than others, rejecting some as unreliable or irrelevant. Eventually, on the basis of our endeavours, we come to a conclusion and make the decision upon which we will base our action. Similarly, a form of research often underpins more trivial or mundane activities. For example, even the weekly or daily act of food shopping involves research, as we decide what we need to buy in order to cook the evening meal and from which store(s) this is best purchased.

In terms of our definition of research, all of these instances involve a careful search for information which will provide us with knowledge about a particular situation. On the basis of this information we take action. To take appropriate action, we need to be sure that the information has been collected carefully and thoughtfully. We can then have confidence in the actions that we take based upon it.

In many of the everyday situations described above we carry out and use research without thinking about it. It forms part of our lives. However, if we do stop to think about the activities that we engage in and the kinds of information that we base our decisions and actions on, then it becomes obvious, very quickly, that we use different kinds of information upon which to base our decisions and actions and that these different kinds of information are collected by different methods.

Let us return to our earlier examples to illustrate the point. The eccentric scientist is likely to be conducting an experiment with the test tubes and chemicals, perhaps measuring the effect of a particular process or procedure; the market researcher is looking for opinions on a particular product; the film maker or author may draw together information from a variety of sources in order to make their film or book seem realistic or true to life; and before deciding which university to apply to, we will doubtless read the prospectus, look at its position in the 'league tables' of university performance and visit the university on an open day. In each of these situations information is being collected but it is being collected in different ways and, moreover, the kinds of information being collected are also quite different.

For example, the scientist is likely to generate numerical information which gives precise measurements about different aspects of the experiment. The market researcher may write down the things people say to him/her, or he/she may tick appropriate pre-specified boxes which provide the best summary of the answers given. Alternatively, he/she may tape-record your voice as you express your opinions. In researching your university choice you may have obtained written information from the prospectus, acquired other published material from a particular department and, on the basis of an interview or an open day, you will have your own observations of the university. You may also have had the chance to ask questions of members of staff or current students, so you will be able to draw on a variety of information sources.

With the examples above we have begun to identify different kinds of information. Some is numerical, some is text-based, some is based on observation and therefore visual, whilst some is verbal, taken from conversations or interviews. For the purpose of understanding research and the research process, we can begin to classify the information further in a way which begins to tell us something about its nature. To start with, let us call the information 'data'. By using this term we give it a more dynamic quality by implying that we are going to analyse and draw conclusions from it. We may also begin to think about the origin of the data. Were the data collected at first hand by the researcher from those who are the focus of the research? If so we would call this **primary** data. Or were they collected in a sort of second-hand way, where the researcher is more distant from those who are the focus of the research? For example, research based on official statistics or the analysis of text would fall into this category. In such cases, we would call the data **secondary** data.

We may also find it useful to think about the data in terms of two broad categories: qualitative or quantitative. By quantitative we refer to data which are numerical and based on counting or enumerating. These may be measurements or scores attributed to particular things. By qualitative we refer to data which seek to convey the essence or the quality of the experience. These may include speech, observations, written text or pictures. Although these two categories are used for sorting data into separate and different types, there are some forms of data which fall into both categories or between the two. For example, certain kinds of interviews may be tightly structured, sticking to a pre-determined schedule (see Chapter 6). So whilst the data they collect are based on speech they are counted and turned into numerical measurements of the given phenomena. Nevertheless, despite possible ambiguities, the distinction between qualitative and quantitative data remains useful in thinking about research and what we hope it will achieve.

In using different approaches to our research and collecting different kinds of data, we may be hoping to say different things, to address different questions and to produce different outcomes from our research. For example, we may wish to say with some degree of certainty how many times a particular activity occurs in a given population in order to make plans for the provision of an essential service. For instance, a large city would need to know how many children between the ages of 5 and 11 years were registered within its boundaries now, and how many could be expected to be registered within its boundaries in the future, in order to fund the appropriate number of primary schools.

Alternatively we might wish to know something about the way in which the teaching of maths was approached in those schools and, therefore, some close observation of maths lessons would be called for. Although these examples are simplistic, they serve to emphasise that there is an important link between the way in which data are collected, the type of data collected and the use(s) to which they are put. To plan the number of primary schools there is a need for precise statistics in order to match the number of places to pupils, not just in the short term but also over many years. The local education authority will need to be confident that this research is accurate before committing funds to a building programme. In the case of maths teaching, there is a need for data which convey a sense of the nature or quality of the experience. Consequently, the data need to be more qualitative, providing a picture of what it would be like to be experiencing the maths lessons.

So far, the key issues raised within this introduction are:

- Research is part of our everyday lives.
- Research is about the careful collection of information to produce or enhance knowledge.
- There are different kinds of knowledge. Some may be discovered, while others may be created.
- Different approaches to research produce different kinds of knowledge.
- We use different kinds of knowledge, e.g. qualitative and quantitative, to understand different kinds of situations.

Some of these statements may seem a little confusing at first but we will return to them in other parts of the book.

Why do research?

Having started to define research in terms of the collection of information and the provision of knowledge, it may be possible to take this defin-ition a little further by considering why people conduct research. If we begin to examine what it is people hope to achieve by conducting research, then we may be able to understand more clearly what the research process entails and what research is about.

There may be many reasons for embarking on a piece of research and the reasons may be complicated by issues surrounding who the research is for, who is paying for it and to what use it will be put. However, irrespective of whether the research is being carried out for a policy maker who wants to know how to introduce changes within an organisation, for a company that wants to know what the level of demand for a new product is likely to be, for a university course or for your own curiosity, it is important to pose four questions prior to starting the research.

1 Why am I doing this research?
2 What is the need for this research?
3 Where will the research lead?
4 What are the issues that I wish to address and/ or the debates to which I wish to contribute?

Whilst these questions may in some respects appear simple, the answers to them will require considerable thought, not only in relation to why, but also to how the research should be conducted. Providing answers to the questions will help to establish a clear reason for the research and also begin the process of identifying a focus for it.

Finding a focus for research can be difficult. We may begin with big ideas about why we wish to do research and what we expect it to achieve, and whilst there may be nothing wrong with ambition, this needs to be tempered by what we might realistically achieve in research. The process of focusing, therefore, involves moving from those big ideas, which we see as an important early step in the research process, to something which is more clearly defined and achievable. Answering the four questions will help to achieve that clearly defined focus.

Whilst a text concerned with doing research must surely advocate, if not celebrate, research as a worthwhile activity, it is also fair to say that social research is often devalued by being conducted without a clear focus and a well-defined rationale. Research does have the capacity to contribute to problem solving, or to provide useful information to policy makers, or to satisfy curiosity. However, to do any of these things effectively researchers need to be sure of the problem or specific area that their research addresses and of the debates to which it is contributing. Without this it is difficult to justify research as a worthwhile activity.

There may be many questions, in addition to the four that we have identified, which need to be asked before deciding to take on or begin a piece of research. These will vary with each different piece of research and it would not be possible to list them all here. The four that we have identified represent a basic minimum. The most important message to get from this is that questions and reasons are important. Asking 'why' will be important during the conduct of the research. It is also crucial in deciding whether to do research at all.

For those of you who are doing research as part of a first degree or other similar qualification there may be little choice. Under these circumstances, conducting research is a course requirement. However, other readers of this text will be in a different situation where there is perhaps a greater policy-related or practical reason for the research. There will also be readers who are embarking on postgraduate study for a master's degree or a doctorate. Whilst research is an integral part of these degrees, there is likely to be more scope in terms of what kind of research can be done and how it might be approached. In each of these situations, however, researchers have to make decisions about the reason for their particular piece of research, its specific focus and what they hope it will achieve.

Whatever the reason for your research, the four questions outlined above remain relevant in encouraging you to think through the research, from the initial idea to what you hope it will achieve and what its likely contribution will be to the field in which it is conducted. Unless you can give a convincing answer as to why you wish to do a particular piece of research and unless you have some idea about the debates or policies/practice that you wish to engage with or contribute to, then you should perhaps think again about what you intend to do and what you hope to achieve by doing it.

In saying that researchers need to think through their research, to anticipate where it might make a contribution and to identify the debates with which it might engage, we are not suggesting that they should try to pre-empt the outcome of their work in any way. The point we wish to emphasise is quite simply that if research is to be worthwhile, that if it is to make a contribution to what we know and understand about the social world, then it needs to:

- be well thought through
- engage with debates, ideas or other research in the same area
- have clearly specified and realistic objectives
- be sufficiently interesting to sustain your attention for what may be a long period of time.

Above all, it seems to us that the research you decide to undertake needs to satisfy the most important reason for engaging in research at all, that of curiosity and wanting to know more. At the same time it needs to be underpinned by effective research design which is carefully constructed in relation both to the data-collection methods which are to be used and the kind of knowledge that you hope the research will yield. In research terminology, it needs to be both methodologically and epistemologically focused.

Methodology and epistemology

Methodology and epistemology refer to the way in which research is conducted and the way in which this relates to the knowledge which results from the research. In short, it is about what we know and how we come to know it.

In the context of social research these are important issues. Moreover, in this introduction to research we have seen that there are different methods of doing research and different kinds of knowledge which result from those different methods. An important aspect of the research process, therefore, is the choice that the researcher makes about how the research should best be conducted in order to yield the required knowledge.

Even at the preliminary stage of deciding to conduct research and identifying appropriate data-collection methods we are making a number of assumptions about methodology and epistemology which are central to the whole idea of doing research.

In the first place, as researchers, we typically assume that information exists and that by deploying the right methods it can be collected. Secondly, we may assume that there is a direct link between the information collected and the production of knowledge. We thus assume that knowledge is generated by the collection of data. If we developed this idea, then we might easily reach the conclusion that the more information we collect then the more knowledge we will have acquired.

These two assumptions are problematic. First of all they assume too simplistic a relationship between research methods and information or data. Secondly, they fail to give sufficient attention to what we mean by knowledge. For example, it may seem reasonable to assume that because we are able to identify a topic for research then, by definition, there must be data which exist about the topic, otherwise it would be impossible to identify it as a topic in the first place. However, although it may well be the case that data exist, this does not mean that they are easily or readily accessible to a researcher. Moreover, whilst we may be aware of some of the relevant data sources at the outset of the research, there may be others which come to light only as the research progresses. In this sense, not only is the scope of the research likely to change as the research process unfolds, in terms of what it focuses on, but the nature of the knowledge may also change.

To illustrate this point let us take, for example, the idea of conducting a study of the prevalence of religious belief in rural England in the early twenty-first century. A good place to start may be with the level of church attendance in rural areas. A limited amount of relevant national-level official statistics on church attendance would be available to the researcher without a great deal of difficulty (Brierley, 1988; Brierley, 1991; Winter and Short, 1993). These statistics could be examined over time and any changes in the rate of church attendance could be calculated. The researcher may also be able to home in on a number of rural parishes and gain permission to examine local records which may provide information, not just about church attendance, but also about other activities which appear to have a religious significance: for example, the number of church weddings, funerals and christenings. Financial information about the size of the weekly collection may also be publicly available to the researcher via parish records.

These methods may yield a great deal of useful data about our topic which serve as indicators of the prevalence of religious belief and we may have been able to plan these activities in advance of the research. However, as the research progresses we may become aware of a range of issues which were not obvious at the start of the research. For example, we may discover that although attendance at church in a given town is low, the number of parents seeking church schools for their children is high. On the face of it this may be taken as a further indicator of the prevalence and significance of religious belief. Alternatively, it may be an indicator of what is perceived as good education in the town and have very little to do with religious belief. To find out which, if either, is the correct explanation, it will be necessary to collect data which are quite different from those contained in official records and statistical returns. The kind of data required are those which reflect the beliefs, opinions and experiences of those parents choosing to send their children to church schools, many of whom may never step inside a church and may not recognise any link between attendance at a church school and religious belief. These data may best be collected through interviews.

As the research progresses, we may become aware of a range of factors which shed light on religious belief and behaviour. Many of these may have little to do with straightforward, readily available indicators like church attendance. Such factors are likely to illustrate the complexity of the issue being researched and to require very sensitive data-collection methods. It may also become clear that although some kinds of information exist, in practice they may not be possible to collect. Data which are highly sensitive and personal may fall into this category.

The point that we wish to make here is an important one. Research may be about gathering data, but it is not always obvious to the researcher what kinds of data he/she needs. Even when it is obvious, those data may be very difficult to collect. In terms of methodology and epistemology, the researcher will need to think very carefully about the relationship between the focus of the research or research question, the kind(s) of knowledge required to address that focus and the means by which the data will be collected in order to provide that knowledge. In our example, statistical and documentary data began to help us understand general trends in church attendance and in activities allied to the church. However, in order to understand the complexities of the research focus, we needed to get beyond general trends by gathering data which would help us to understand the importance of religion in people's everyday lives. A comprehensive answer to the research question was only possible if we collected these two different kinds of data, which in turn resulted in different but complementary types of knowledge.

Data, analysis and knowledge

Our definition of research suggests a strong link between the collection of data and the production of knowledge. However, we do not wish to suggest that data are the same as knowledge. To do this would be to focus on only a part, albeit a large and important part, of the research process.

What we wish to convey in our discussion of research is that the collection of data is not all there is to producing or enhancing knowledge. What is done to the data once they have been collected is just as important as their collection. We are referring here to a process of analysis to which data must be subjected before they can begin to contribute to the stock of knowledge. Let us return to our example of the church and family life in rural Britain.

Whilst it may be perfectly possible to gather information on church attendance in rural locations, this on its own may tell us very little. We will need to analyse that information in a number of ways before it becomes meaningful. For example, we would need to know about local and national trends over time in church attendance in order to tell whether these have changed in recent years. We may wish to compare attendances at different churches in the area over time, say the Roman Catholic and the Methodist churches, in order to examine any denominational factors which might be relevant to the research focus. We may also wish to analyse church attendance in relation to a number of social characteristics: for example, age, social class, ethnicity and gender, and marital status. In addition, we may wish to compare our rural church attendance data with data from different kinds of areas, for example urban or inner-city areas, before coming to any conclusions about the influence of the church on family life. The point to be made here is that, on their own, data do not tell us a great deal about the topic we are investigating. To make the data meaningful we need to subject them to a process of analysis. We will talk in much more detail about data analysis later in the book (see Chapters 8 and 9). Only after this can we begin to draw some conclusions that make a contribution to knowledge in the particular area of our research.

Within this general introduction and via the examples used we hope to have highlighted some of the key aspects of social research. Throughout we have focused on research as an activity, or a set of activities, directed towards the collection of data and the enhancement of knowledge about given social phenomena. Within this general definition we have drawn attention to a number of key issues which are central to the research process.

We will return to these in more detail later in the book. However, by way of summarising what we have said so far, it is worth considering these brief statements:

- Social research is about the collection of data with a view to enhancing knowledge about particular social phenomena.

- Efficient data collection is central to successful research.
- Different research methods produce different kinds of data.
- Different kinds of data yield different kinds of knowledge.
- The relationship between data and knowledge can be complex.
- Data on their own do not produce knowledge.
- The production of knowledge relies on effective data analysis.

Chapter 2 Planning and designing research: finding a framework

An integrated approach

Having established a rationale for conducting research and pursuing our theme of research as an activity, we now progress to the planning and design phase of the research project. In many ways, establishing the research rationale and designing the project are inherently linked. For example, the reason for conducting a particular piece of research may be linked to the need to examine or test specific relationships or to investigate particular issues. It may be driven by the curiosity of the researcher or be addressed towards policy questions. Whatever the rationale for the research or the desired outcomes, effective research design is crucial to any research activity.

In establishing its importance, we would argue that research design is not merely about the identification of appropriate data-collection techniques for the research but is an aspect of the research process which incorporates the following:

- literature
- theoretical framework
- type of study
- research instruments
- data analysis
- writing
- dissemination.

From the above list it is clear that we see research design not merely as something concerned with the early stages of the research process. Nor is it concerned solely with the technical aspects of research method. Rather we see research design as a form of integrated planning which takes in all the different phases of the research process, from its conception and the identification of the research question, through the selection and use of research methods, data collection and analysis, to writing and beyond.

Having described it as a comprehensive, integrated plan for the entire research process, we do not wish to suggest that research design acts as a straitjacket for the research activity. Alongside the technical aspects of the process, we see research design as an opportunity for methodological imagination to flourish, whereby the researcher can think creatively about what he/she wishes to do and how it should be done. Allied to this, we see it as a means of identifying the key conceptual questions which will focus the research. In effect we would argue that the research design phase is one in which there is scope for creativity on the part of the researcher. Moreover, given the facts that social research is concerned with people and that people are generally unpredictable, any research design needs to allow for a degree of flexibility in order to accommodate unexpected and unforeseen events.[1]

---

[1] In characterising research design in such a way we are assuming that the researcher(s) has latitude in relation to the design, focus and scope of the research. However, this is not always the case. For example, where researchers are required to investigate issues specified at the outset by a sponsor who has a specific research

Flexibility

Whilst research design seeks to plan the whole re-search process from outset to completion, we would not wish to imply that it is an activity which sets the aims and objectives of the research in stone, or one to which the researcher may not return as the research progresses. As with many aspects of research, the initial design phase needs to maintain a degree of flexibility, to accommodate changes necessitated as the research progresses.

The key issue underpinning the need for flex-ibility is the fact that social research is about the unknown. Whilst this may be a self-evident state-ment, in that if things were known and understood there would be no need for research, it is import-ant for the researcher to keep this in mind as the re-search progresses and information and knowledge are yielded. The fact that the researcher is working with the unknown may require the research design to be revised and adjusted in the light of informa-tion and knowledge as they emerge and as circum-stances change as the research progresses.

Let us illustrate this point by reference to some research into career choice and the transition to work by 16-year-old school leavers conducted as a doctoral study by Pole (1989).

The study combined some relatively large sur-veys with school-based interviews with pupils at the beginning of their final year of compulsory school-ing. The intention was that the sample would be re-interviewed towards the end of their final year, having experienced virtually a full year of careers education. The study was conducted in six different areas of England with contrasting economic and labour-market characteristics. The initial data col-lection in all schools was successfully completed and data were analysed throughout the spring and early summer of the school year. Problems arose, however, when Pole attempted to revisit the schools later in the summer term in order to carry out follow-up interviews with pupils interviewed at the start of their final year. The return visit was central to the research design and had been agreed with each of the six headteachers at the point of negotiating access. On seeking to return to the schools, Pole discovered that in one school a new headteacher had been appointed with whom access had not been negotiated, while in another a recently completed HMI visit had produced a negative report on several aspects of the school. Consequently, in both schools permission to con-duct follow-up interviews was denied on the basis that the interviews would be disruptive to pupils during the examination term. Pole was thus faced with a dilemma. Whilst he would have a full dataset for four of the schools, for two it would be incomplete. This would make regional compar-isons across the six schools, one of the key aspects of the research, impossible. Given that he was more than eighteen months into the research pro-gramme, which was scheduled to take three years, and that a large amount of data had already been collected, a total redesign was not an option. A compromise had to be found. Eventually Pole received permission from all six schools to issue a postal questionnaire to the pupils.

The changing circumstances meant that in order for the overall objective of the research, that of regional and local labour-market comparison, to be achieved, the research design was revised. In this situation, flexibility was essential. Although the nature of the research changed, with a greater emphasis being placed on quantitative data than the original design had intended, the research was able to proceed to a successful conclusion whereby its overall aims and objectives, as identified in the original research design, were achieved.

The preceding example demonstrates that a process of what Hammersley and Atkinson (1983, 1995) define as **reflexivity** underpins research design. Whilst the notion of reflexivity is fairly

---

brief, the research design may be prescribed. In such instances the role of the researcher has been characterised as that of a technician (Finch, 1986) or a messenger (Pole, 1995). Here the need for a research imagination is subsumed by a need for operational competence, as the pre-specified research design is followed. The researcher may have little latitude or opportunity for creativity as he/she follows the path identified by those who pay for the research.

complex, in this context it can be seen to relate to the way in which the progress of the research needs to be constantly evaluated in relation to the research design. If obstacles arise, as in the example above, or if the data seem unlikely to yield the kind of knowledge which was originally anticipated, then the design has to be modified accordingly. Such reflexivity, we would argue, necessitates a flexibility in approach wherein the researcher is responsive to the dynamic of the research. We would not wish to advocate, however, either a loose or an unstructured approach to research design and, clearly, change for change's sake would be unlikely to enhance the collection of data or the knowledge which they yield. Our purpose here is to introduce the idea of research design that is flexible, responsive and ongoing. In effect, a relationship is established between the research design and the research process, the result of which are the research outcomes. Pole's study also exemplifies the use of comparisons within a research design, specifically a comparison between schools and a comparison between data from the beginning and the end of the school year. We shall return to the issue of comparisons within research designs later in the chapter.

Focusing research

One of the principal objectives of research design is to identify a clear focus for the research process. Many research projects begin with vague ideas about the area to be studied and the debates to which they are to contribute. In such circumstances it is difficult to begin conducting research with any confidence that its outcomes will be worthwhile. However, the identification of vague or general questions at the outset of research is not uncommon. Moreover, such questions may be the initial step towards identifying a clear focus to the research. Indeed, at the outset there may be many questions which underpin the research and it is one of the tasks of research design to identify the relative importance and the roles of these questions in an attempt to take the research forward.

For example, there may be large contextual questions which help to identify the general field for the research. At the same time, there may be highly specific questions about particular aspects of the identified topic, which need to be linked back to the contextual questions. Malinowski (1922) referred to the large contextual questions as the 'foreshadowed questions'. He saw these as essential in locating the research in disciplinary or policy terms. Foreshadowed questions are often, therefore, the precursors of the specific questions (Mason, 1996) which form the research focus.

For example, foreshadowed or contextual questions which shaped the research we considered earlier might have included:

- What do young people do after the end of compulsory schooling?
- How do young people find jobs?
- Why do young people go on to college?
- What kinds of young people choose to stay on at school?
- Why are some young people unemployed?
- Does the area in which a young person lives affect the kind of job that they do?
- Are there gender/social class/ethnicity factors relevant to any/all of the above?

There may have been many more questions which provided a context and an initial catalyst for this research. One of the first tasks the researcher must undertake in attempting to find a focus is to think of as many of these large, contextual questions as possible. Having identified such questions, the researcher can begin a process of reviewing them and deciding on their relative importance, how they might be addressed in terms of data collection, and what their significance is in relation to the kind(s) of knowledge he/she hopes the research will yield and the debates to which he/she wishes to contribute. The intention is to break the large questions down into smaller ones which can be addressed by collecting specific data. This will require some detailed thinking by the researcher, reading around the subject (a topic we will return to in detail later in this chapter) and perhaps discussion with colleagues. The process may not seem particularly 'scientific', in so far as it is not possible to identify and apply a universal set of procedures to produce a focus, but it does mean that the researcher must explore the topic in relation not only to what the research might find, but also to whether and how it can be conducted.

The intention is, therefore, to arrive at a set of questions which are sharply focused in the sense that they require specific answers, which may only be arrived at via a process of data collection and analysis.

Returning to our example, the kinds of sharply focused questions which we might produce might include the following which could be asked of final year pupils during an interview:

- What kinds of jobs/courses are you considering?
- Why are you considering these?/What attracts you to them?
- What do you consider the most important aspects of a career/job?
- What is your opinion of the careers education programme provided by your school?
- Where do you see yourself in 5/10/15 years' time?

Again, these questions are just a few of those that could be asked of the young people. As examples, they serve to show how we have moved from the large, contextual questions concerned with school leaving in a general sense, to specific questions which are posed to individual research participants. These specific questions offer a focus to the research both in terms of its substantive content and the data-collection methods which are likely to prove most successful in seeking answers to them.

In moving from the general to the particular we engage in a process of what Glaser and Strauss (1967) refer to as **Progressive Focusing**. In doing so we are not suggesting that the large, contextual questions should be rejected as the more specific questions are identified. Rather, we feel that the different kinds of questions serve different purposes.

For example, in the context of our example, by posing the more focused questions we learn about individual experience, which in turn provides a perspective on the wider, more general questions. It is, then, a question of scope and methodology. In relation to research design, the process of progressive focusing addresses not only the substantive content of the research but also its methodological feasibility. Research may be well thought through in terms of what the researcher hopes it will produce by way of knowledge, but unless this is achievable in terms of methodology then the research design will be unsatisfactory.

Feasible research

The notion of feasibility in research relates directly to the process of progressive focusing. Whilst a researcher may successfully arrive at a series of sharply focused questions which will direct the research, these questions will be of little use unless they can be addressed through fieldwork and using the research methods that the researcher has at his/her disposal. Moreover, all research has to be conducted within the structural resources which limit it, such as time and money. For instance, to develop one of our earlier examples, it would be pointless proposing to conduct an international comparative study of the significance of religion in modern family life, unless there was sufficient funding to facilitate data collection in more than one country. Similarly, it would clearly not be feasible for a lone researcher to contemplate a study which sought to compare national trends in church attendance based on interviews. A credible study of this nature would require large-scale survey work. The point to take from these examples is that effective research design must take account of technical feasibility. If a study appears unfeasible for reasons of method, funding, time or any other structural constraint, then our advice would be to revisit the questions that have been posed in an effort to ensure a close fit between the methodology and the focus of the study.

Both the examples discussed above and the foreshadowed questions listed earlier highlight the explicit or implicit place of comparisons within research design. Such comparisons have clear implications for feasibility and will be returned to more generally later in this chapter.

Other forms of feasibility are also important to effective research design. For example, Delamont (1992) introduces questions of political and personal feasibility to her discussion of the research process. As with technical feasibility, an effective research design needs to ensure a close fit between these types of feasibility and the research focus. In many instances, political feasibility relates to issues of access. For example, how feasible would a study of the position of Prime Minister and Chancellor of the Exchequer, based on a life history approach, prove to be? Such a study would be fascinating but is unlikely to be feasible given the amount of time required to conduct life history interviews. Alternatively, to what extent would a committed Roman Catholic researcher feel able to conduct research into the incidence of abortion amongst teenage girls, without either allowing his/her moral code to affect the research process, or without becoming personally distressed in relation to the research findings?

A further area of feasibility relates to the breadth or scope of the research. As we have seen, identifying a set of sharply focused questions, which can be addressed within the constraints discussed above, is often the key to effective research design. However, our experience suggests that amongst novice researchers there can be a tendency to assume that, in order to be worthwhile, research must tackle macroscopic issues by collecting data from many locations or thousands of individuals. This assumption can often leave the researcher with a project which is not feasible on many counts. Designing a project of modest proportions that can be conducted carefully and thoroughly and that allows comprehensive analysis of the collected data seems to us to be by far preferable to research on a grand scale which promises much but delivers little.

Clearly the scope for debate about the feasibility of research is considerable. In presenting this discussion we simply wish to emphasise that in seeking to focus a research project, it is important that the feasibility of what is proposed is taken into account. When research design is unrealistic through issues either of feasibility or of scope, the eventual outcome of the research is likely to reflect a piece of work which at best has been difficult to conduct and at worst has resulted in non-completion of the task.

In short the message to be drawn here is: BE REALISTIC.

Reviewing the literature

As social research occurs in neither an intellectual nor a policy vacuum, one of the early tasks of research design is to locate the specified topic in the context of what is already known from previous research in that area. Whatever the research topic, it is likely that some relevant research has already been conducted in the area and that a literature exists. As Blaxter, Hughes and Tight (1996) point out, the existing literature is important both substantively and methodologically.

In the first instance a review of the existing literature tells the researcher what is already known or is thought to be known about his/her area. In addition, it is a way of identifying gaps in existing knowledge. In doing this it helps to provide a focus for new research by helping to identify new angles to a well-researched area, to tackle omissions from previous research, or identify a completely new area for the research. Alternatively it may alert the researcher to findings with which he/she disagrees, therefore providing scope for a critique of existing knowledge. In short, the literature allows new research to be located substantively in relation to what has gone before by identifying what is already known. It provides insight into where the new research may contribute and continues the process of progressive focusing.

Methodologically, the literature provides insight into the approaches already taken to research in the area, and allows the researcher to evaluate these in the context of the findings. On this basis the researcher may begin to make an informed choice as to the most appropriate methods for his/her research in the area. Clearly, the substantive issues are closely linked to the methodological issues and a thorough review of existing research provides insight into questions of feasibility, a theoretical framework for the research and its likely outcome.

Searching the literature

Beginning a literature search can be a daunting prospect. At one level the growth of the information society, including the Internet, CD ROMs and a host of databases, which now sit alongside traditional sources, offers much more information for the researcher. However, the number of different sources which now exist and the sheer volume of material which they hold present a problem of scale and scope. The potential exists for contemporary researchers to be far more thorough in their literature searches but, at the same time, searching has implications for time and for focus. The generation of large amounts of literature via the latest information technology is merely the start of the process. If literature is to be useful it has to be read: owning the CD ROM or making a copy of an article pulled from a database may offer a degree of security or confidence to the researcher but it is important to remember that although access to information is now great, the process by which it is made relevant to the research, namely by the researcher reading it, remains the same.

Too much literature?

Even before the impact of the new information technologies it was unlikely that a researcher would be able to read everything that had been published in his/her area. However, more than ever, the potential now exists for information over-

load. The researcher may simply not know where or how to start to access the relevant literature. Where this occurs, the foreshadowed problems or questions (Malinowski, 1922) play an important role, as it is the big questions, the broad hunches and curiosities of the researcher which give the first guide as to where to begin accessing and selecting from the literature. As the researcher delves into the literature a process of selection and focusing ensues, as its relevance is assessed in relation to the process of progressive focusing.

The process of accessing, selecting from and assessing the relevance of the literature involves a process of indexing and coding. Every researcher will develop their own methods of selecting literature but a general rule of thumb might involve the following basic taxonomy:

- **Essential literature**: that which is likely to be of central importance to the research and to which the research will make considerable reference.
- **Important literature**: that which will be referenced in the thesis or research report but may not form part of the central theme of the research.
- **Relevant literature**: that which the researcher expects to be relevant to the research and to which he/she expects to return as the research progresses.
- **Supporting literature**: that which may be relevant to an aspect of the research, to which he/she may return.
- **Irrelevant literature**: that which is unlikely to be of relevance to the research.

Whatever form of taxonomy researchers apply to the literature it is essential that full bibliographical details be kept on all sources consulted. From the outset researchers should, at the very least, record: the author(s), title, date and place of publication of each source consulted. This can be done either manually or with a word processor by using one of the several software applications that are now available. In addition researchers should make brief notes on the content of each reference and indicate its status in line with the taxonomy outlined above. As the bibliography grows, it will be possible to make cross-references within the brief notes. This will help to navigate a path through the literature as you read and reread what will usually be a wide range of material. Although this may at times seem laborious, it is certainly better than having to track down books and articles from incomplete notes at the end of the research.

Too little literature

Whilst much of the discussion above has assumed overload in the amount of available literature, researchers may also experience difficulty in identifying relevant literature, at least in the early stages of their work. For example, where the substantive research topic is particularly esoteric there may be difficulty in identifying previous research conducted directly in that area.

The claim made by some first-time researchers, that they have looked in the library and found nothing or very little on their area is not uncommon and, in many cases, is undoubtedly true. Where this occurs the researcher must look beneath the specific content of the research to the concepts and themes which underpin it. It is here that a 'hook' for relevant literature may be identified.

A specific example may help to illustrate this point. Take, for instance, a student wishing to conduct an ethnographic study of train-spotters. An initial literature search reveals little of direct relevance. However, when considering the aspects of train-spotting and train-spotters which are interesting to the researcher from a sociological perspective, he/she may identify issues of transport, leisure, gender, social class, age, stigma, collection and accumulation, and obsession. These issues thus provide a further route into the literature for the researcher, a route which is conceptually rather than substantively based. The initial observations of the researcher, that very little research has previously been conducted in the area of train-spotting, may be correct, but the identification of the conceptual framework which underpins the initial interest in train-spotters and train-spotting offers a way in to the literature by providing conceptual and theoretical insight into the topic.

In addition, researchers sometimes feel constrained by the disciplinary boundaries within which they locate their research. For example, whilst we may be conducting sociological research into a given area, it is worth remembering that sociology, like any discipline, overlaps with many others. In conducting a literature search, we may also benefit from looking at what writers in related disciplines have had to say on our particular topic. For example, as sociologists we might look towards history, politics, economics, philosophy and even towards fiction, depending on the focus of our research, as we search the existing literature.

Clearly, the identification of a conceptual framework upon which to base literature searches is not confined to situations of literature shortage. It will be equally useful where there is a literature overload in helping the researcher select and code the literature. Whatever the scope of the relevant literature and the method(s) used for selection and taxonomy, initial literature searches form an essential aspect of the research process in identifying the direction of the project, clarifying aims and objectives, identifying key concepts and questions and deciding on the methodology.

When to read

First-time researchers often assume that reading is an activity which occurs primarily at the beginning of a research project and view it as a necessary evil to be endured before getting down to the real business of research. Hopefully, our discussion of the importance that literature plays in research design will help to emphasise its importance throughout the research process. In addition to its role in identifying a substantive and methodological focus for the research we would also wish to emphasise the importance of reading and monitoring the literature throughout the research process. Clearly, if research is to contribute to a particular area, it needs to engage with the latest thinking in that area. Close monitoring of the emerging literature is, therefore, essential in this. Here, bibliographic databases, especially those which provide abstracts of the latest published material, will be essential. In addition, monitoring the topics covered and papers presented at key conferences in the area of your research will keep you alert to the latest and emerging literature in your area.

However thorough they have been, novice researchers often express a fear that they have missed something in the literature. They fear that the day on which they submit their thesis or project report a book or paper will be published which is of central importance to their work. As such, they have missed something. Such fears are easily understood. It is, however, worth bearing in mind that no one, not even the most experienced and celebrated researcher, can read everything on a given topic and there are inevitably going to be omissions in any research. However, reading for the duration of the research and adopting an integrated approach to the literature, which sees it discussed throughout the thesis or the research report rather than merely in the introduction, should ensure that most significant omissions are avoided.

Reading and the role of literature in research relate directly to the way in which others will evaluate your research. When the academic community judges research, whether for the award of a qualification or for publication, the use of literature, the ways and extent to which the research relates to previous work in the area, will form part of the basis of the judgements which are made. Effective literature work is, therefore, an integral aspect of research design and the research process, helping to establish both a substantive and methodological focus.

What counts as data?

Having begun the process of progressive focusing by identifying key issues from the literature, our next step in terms of research design is to turn those issues into research questions which may be answered by the collection of data. Here, our concern is not merely with the content of the research or any ideas we may have about eventual findings, but is also with technical questions about the kind of data required to answer the questions (Marshall and Rossman, 1989) and access to the data. Again, the researcher is involved in a process of selection. He/she may be surrounded by many potential sources of data (Plummer, 1983). However, an essential aspect of research design is the identification of what is to count as relevant data.

The question is deceptively simple. At first thought we may feel that the answer is obvious. The answer will depend on the research topic, the general theoretical perspective within which the researcher is working, the funding for the research and the time-scale within which it is to be completed. However, while we may indeed be surrounded by data, in any single study it is unlikely that we will be able to draw upon all that exists. Like identifying relevant literature, identifying the data to be used involves a process of selection.

The question 'what counts as data?' incorporates concerns about the location of data and how much we can realistically be expected to gather within the constraints of the research project. It also relates to the connection between theory and method. It is, therefore, a fundamental question which requires the researcher to evaluate the sources of information available in terms of the knowledge that they are likely to yield. In addition he/she will also need to give thought to the possibility of combining different sources of data and the pros and cons of multiple strategy research (Burgess, 1984) or triangulation (Denzin, 1970).

In some instances the existence of appropriate data may be obvious. For example, the possibility of conducting a range of interviews or a survey may be relatively straightforward. However, there may also be a range of other types of data which are not quite as obviously sources of data. For example, different types of documentary research (McDonald and Tipton, 1993) may utilise private and public documents, the media, visual representation and many other artefacts which contribute towards the construction of our everyday lives and as such constitute a relevant form of data. Similarly, there may be many sources of aural information, which, in the first instance, we may not regard as data sources. For example, conversations, jokes, stories, arguments and gossip may all yield information relevant to our research.

Posing the question 'what counts as data?' serves a number of purposes in the context of research design:

- It sensitises the researcher to the range of data which exists and encourages him/her to think beyond the usual sources by perhaps turning everyday situations and artefacts into data.
- It necessitates that attention be given to the relationship between method and substance. It requires the researcher to think not only about what data are required, but also how they can be collected.
- It assists the researcher in focusing the research by not only identifying what will count as relevant or appropriate data, but also by rejecting sources of data as inappropriate or because their use is not feasible within the constraints of the research project. For example, in an ethnographic study of a primary school it may be perfectly possible to conduct a survey of all members of staff, but the nature of the research, the theoretical framework within which it is conducted, together with the small number of people involved, would suggest that it would be an inappropriate method to use.
- It means that the researcher must think about the contribution to knowledge which his/her research will make. Without appropriate data, it will not be possible to contribute to the key debates in the area.

Data collection or data generation?

Mason (1996) draws a useful distinction between data collection and data generation. In answer to

the question 'What counts as data?' we would agree with her analysis that there is a difference between merely discovering or accessing data and actually generating or creating it. The former, involving what is often defined as secondary data, assumes a somewhat passive approach in which the researcher finds out what information exists about his/her research topic and collects it. This process has overtones of positivist approaches to social science in its assumption that data are already there, waiting to be identified and gathered. The approach implies a distancing between the researcher and the data, one in which the researcher is not involved in creating the data.

By contrast, in the case of data generation, where the data are often termed primary data, the opposite view would hold, in that the researcher is involved, through the use of particular research tools and strategies, in the actual creation of the data. This approach implies greater interaction between the researcher and the information which the tools yield. For example, in the case of documentary research (involving secondary data) the researcher may be concerned with the detailed content analysis of a range of material, but he/she will not be involved in the initial creation of those materials (Scott, 1990). Moreover, the materials will not have been created for research purposes and the data which they yield will, therefore, be a by-product of their primary function. In the case of a social survey, or a set of interviews, or a focus group (involving primary data), however, specific information is gathered in answer to specific questions designed by the researcher. In this sense, the researcher is actively involved in both the creation and collection of data.

> In posing the question 'What counts as data?' the researcher is required to evaluate the existing information which may be collected from a variety of sources and to consider what kinds of new information need to be generated and from whom.

Whilst to characterise one kind of data as passive and another as active may be illustrative of the origins of the information, it says little about the interpretation of the data and the role of the researcher in data analysis. Whether the data are primary or secondary, collected or generated, the extent to which they are useful to the research process will depend on their analysis by the researcher. Rarely do any kinds of data speak for themselves. In all research, processes of selection, classification, interpretation and analysis are what transform data into knowledge.

Making it count

Our final answer to the question 'What counts as data?' is, quite simply, that it is whatever the researcher can make count. By this we do not wish to imply that the researcher should grab or create anything and everything at his/her disposal; rather that data are only as useful as researchers can make them. In this sense, whether the data are collected or generated may be irrelevant. What is important is the way in which they are analysed and used in the context of the research process as a whole. Similarly, researchers often talk of collecting 'good' data. It is difficult to know quite what is meant by this and, by implication, if there are 'good' data there must be 'bad' data. If we accept the premise that data are only as useful as researchers make them, then the notion of 'good' or 'bad' data is meaningless. We suspect that by 'good' data researchers are referring to their potential for analysis. 'Bad' data may be those which are thought unlikely to yield anything more than is evident at the point of collection.

'What counts as data?' is, therefore, an important question in the design phase of the research process. It introduces notions of primary and secondary data, and of interpretation and analysis, together with theoretical questions about the epistemological premises of the research project and its relationship to specific research tools. It relates closely to issues of data analysis, a topic which we discuss in detail in Chapters 8 and 9 of this book.

Research constraints

All research has constraints and, to return to one of our earlier themes, being realistic about research means recognising and working within the constraints. An important aspect of research design is precisely the identification of the constraints which impinge upon the proposed research, together with a recognition of their potential impact upon it.

Some constraints are ever present in research. For example, time and resources are key technical issues (Bryman, 1988) which affect our choice of research methods, the scope of the research and ultimately what it might achieve. Not only are they ever present, but they are also known constraints. Whether research is sponsored or commissioned by an organisation to provide specific information for policy concerns, whether it is allied to the launch of a new product as with much market research, or whether it is conducted for academic reasons in partial fulfilment of the requirements for a qualification, the researcher will be aware from the outset of the time-scale and the financial budget within which he/she must work.

Time

Rather than seeing time constraints in a negative light, they may be viewed as providing an important guide for the research process. For example, having specific dates for the submission of interim or progress reports leading to a final report, as happens with much applied or policy-focused research, provides milestones for the researcher with regard to what has to be completed in what period of time. Similarly, with much academic research, university regulations specify periods of registration for particular degrees. Indeed, in the 1980s concern was expressed about completion times for doctoral research (Swinnerton-Dyer, 1982; Winfield, 1987), and the threat of blacklisting university departments with poor completion rates forced many universities to think very carefully about time constraints. Whilst many doctoral students may see the requirement to submit within four years as difficult or even impossible when they begin their research, many find that their work becomes more clearly focused and more manageable as a result of this deadline. Similarly, in our experience, undergraduates working to shorter deadlines may, at the outset of their research projects, feel that there is insufficient time in which to achieve their research aims. Usually, with efficient organisation, realistic research design and realistic expectations of what can be achieved in the time available, a successful outcome of the research is possible.

Time constraints have to be recognised and built into the research design by means of a research timetable or time plan. As an exercise conducted early in the design phase it allows the researcher to view the research process in its entirety. It allows him/her to assemble the different elements of the process along a continuum. Whilst it is important to hold on to the need for flexibility in research design, as we discussed earlier, a time plan will allow a degree of flexibility to be built into the process, whilst at the same time identifying the crucial milestones of the project. In short, a time plan allows the researcher to identify the fixed points of the research, which in many ways provide its foundations, and at the same time to take some account of the variables. A typical research project time plan might take the format illustrated in Figure 2.1.

The identification of the research question(s), key phases of preparation, data collection, analysis and writing in tandem with a time line makes clear what is to be achieved by when. In addition, the plan also details any foreseeable events in the researcher's personal and professional lives which may affect completion time. Above all, the time plan makes clear what is realistic within the time available.

The process by which the time plan is devised, bearing in mind that several may be attempted before a realistic and workable one is produced, also brings into focus the identification of appropriate research methods. For example, the time span of one year indicated in Figure 2.1 permits the use of a range of different research tools. The plan

also emphasises the need for analysis and writing throughout the research process and illustrates very clearly the end date for the research. In short, producing the time plan has helped to focus the research by revealing what is realistic in the time available, and what will produce the required data.

Where a team or more than one researcher is undertaking research it is important that all concerned agree to the time plan. Working to someone else's definition of what is achievable in the time available may make for particular strains if, or probably more realistically when, the time plan begins to slip. A form of collective responsibility may be advisable here.

Resources

All research has resource implications. These may range from the availability of library materials, through funds for travel and subsistence to secretarial support and contracts for researchers. As with the time available for research, resource issues are usually part of the known constraints which underpin a project from the outset and ultimately, whether human or material resources, they depend on the amount of money available to conduct the research.

With most research the amount of money available will exert considerable influence on the research design. For example, a project based on participant observation requiring the employment of a fieldworker for a considerable length of time is likely to cost considerably more than research which utilises a large-scale postal survey, where such intensive human resources may not be required. Similarly a small travel budget may limit the number of locations in which it is possible to conduct research based on interviews. As with time, therefore, the shape of the research project in terms of what is realistic and achievable will be influenced by the amount of money available to support the research. Whether it is the bus fare to a city centre library, the purchase of software

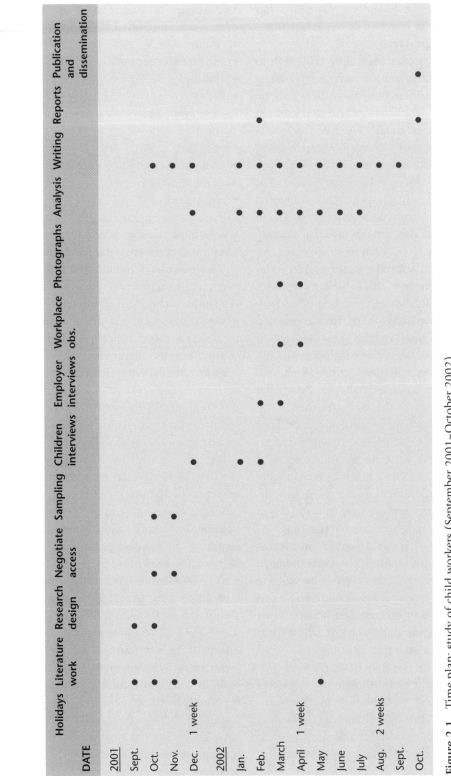

Figure 2.1 Time plan: study of child workers (September 2001–October 2002).

or the employment of fieldworkers, all research has resource implications which have to be taken into account at the design stage.

Whilst some resource issues will be evident from the outset, such as the employment of researchers or fieldworkers to collect the data, others may be less obvious. For example, although interviews are probably the most frequently used research tool and there are accounts of their use in virtually every research methods text, little is usually written about the resource implications which they bring. For example, all interviews, whether highly structured or more loosely structured, require someone to pose the questions. This usually involves a salary cost. In addition, it is often necessary for researchers to travel to a specific location(s) in order to conduct the interview. This will involve travel and subsistence costs. Whilst these two items may be obvious from the start, other factors associated with the interview may not be. For example, if interviews are to be tape-recorded a good-quality, reliable tape-recorder will need to be purchased, along with sufficient tapes and batteries. Taking the process a step further, if the tapes are then to be transcribed verbatim, significantly more expense will be incurred. As a rule of thumb, when designing research projects we estimate that one hour of tape-recorded interview takes approximately six hours for an experienced audio typist to transcribe. If the transcriptions are then to be analysed using a qualitative data analysis package such as ETHNOGRAPH or NUD*IST, further time must be spent in coding and further data-preparation tasks (Sprokkereef *et al.*, 1995). What began as a project based on a series of, say, 15 interviews can very quickly become an expensive exercise in terms of both human and financial resources, which must be found from within the project budget.

All approaches to research have resource implications and the careful design of a project means that these will be identified and their implications thought through alongside the scope, focus and research methods of the project. As a rudimentary resources checklist for all research we offer the following:

- staffing
- travel and subsistence (including insurance)
- equipment
- secretarial support
- hardware
- software
- telephone/fax
- postage
- printing
- data preparation and entry
- dissemination
- hospitality.

Whilst most research is likely to incorporate some if not most of the costs itemised above, each project will have its own requirements, some of which may become apparent only as the research progresses. For students conducting research in part fulfilment of degree requirements there is usually very little money available for their personal use and it may seem that research can and has to be conducted without great expense. However, it is worth remembering that the very fact that students are spending time conducting research involves a cost. Labour costs are by far the most significant in research. In addition, the availability of research facilities within their university also represents a significant cost. Whilst you as an independent researcher may not personally pay for computing facilities, libraries, secretarial support, office space, heating, lighting and many other things, all of which are central to the conduct of your research, they must be paid for somehow. In practice, this is usually down to the institution within which the researcher is an employee or a student. In this sense, the availability of such facilities represents a hidden cost for the individual research project. Nevertheless, the notion of the well-founded 'laboratory' in which to locate research is now high on the agenda of many organisations which fund specific research projects. It is unlikely, therefore, that organisations like the research funding councils, charities, government departments or industry would fund research in institutions where facilities such as those listed above were not available to the researcher.

The point to be made is that all research carries resource implications, which must be accounted for if the research is to be successfully designed and executed. In some cases these are obvious costs specific to the research project such as the salaries of the researchers and other project staff, or the purchase of specific hardware or software, which will be used solely by the researchers. In others, costs are less obvious to the individual research project, as they are borne by the institution in which it is located. Generally, the key message to take from this discussion so far is that all research has constraints and one of the central concerns of the research design phase of any study is to identify and work within those constraints. Again, this links directly to the need for research to be realistic and to stand up to scrutiny. Research which is designed without reference to its constraints is likely to encounter a range of both technical and substantive difficulties relating to budget, time, focus, the quantity and quality of data collected and the extent to which it is possible to analyse and write on the basis of its findings.

In addition, a further message to take from this discussion is that in order to be effective and to achieve worthwhile and interesting results, research does not necessarily need to be large-scale, generously funded or involve lots of staff. Much research is conducted within tight budgets and time-frames.

> Effective research design is about identifying realistic expectations about what can be achieved within the constraints which apply to it. It is thus about the identification of appropriate aims and objectives. Where this occurs, both large and small-scale research projects can be successfully conducted.

Ethics

Research ethics add a further set of constraints to the design and conduct of research. Whilst the literature on ethics is now considerable, and ethical codes and guidelines published by learned societies and research associations are readily available (see Appendix A for examples), questions relating to whether a piece of research is ethical continue to cause considerable concern to researchers. Moreover, the deeming of research as unethical may mean that it is not feasible from the outset. However, ethical issues are not always obvious or clear-cut at the start of a study. By their very nature, guides and codes attempt to deal with general ethical concerns, which affect the overall structure or conduct of research. However, they are rarely specific enough to deal with the detail of research projects and it is often in the detail where most ethical concerns arise. END .

Some ethical issues may be obvious from the outset. Others may only become apparent as the research progresses. For example, as part of the research design a researcher may have to decide whether the study should be conducted overtly, where those taking part in the research are aware that they are being studied, or covertly, where the researcher works undercover, collecting data without the knowledge of those from whom it is collected. Whilst decisions of this magnitude may not be easy or straightforward, they would usually be decisions which the researcher would take during the design phase of the study. Other decisions – for example, whether to regard conversations overheard in the research setting as data, or whether to inform someone in authority if instances of wrong-doing or illegal practices are discovered – may not be evident from the start. Such ethical issues will require the researcher to take decisions as the research progresses and to judge each situation on its merits and on the perceived severity of the situation. For example, it may be that researchers regularly turn a blind eye to examples of minor wrong-doing. However, in some situations it may be more difficult to do this.

For example, say that in the course of the research into working children conducted by one of the present authors (Pole, Mizen and Bolton, 1999) we had discovered evidence that one of the children was being forced to work as a prostitute by her father. Would this be a situation where we should have continued to protect the anonymity of the research participant, the child, or should we have informed 'the authorities' in an effort to remove the child from what most people would see as an unacceptable situation?

Thankfully, this was not an issue that we had to face. Had we done so, I suspect that research ethics and the personal moral codes of the researchers would have clashed and, in order to serve the best interests of the child, relevant authorities would have been informed. However, this would not have been a foregone conclusion and much debate would have ensued amongst the research team before any action was taken. In this situation one of the problems faced by the researchers would be the nature of their relationship to the research participant(s). The researchers were not in a position of authority *vis-à-vis* the children, and unlike teachers or social workers they were not acting *in loco parentis*. In addition, deciding to report the activities of the child to the authorities may have contravened part of the British Sociological Association's ethical guide which discusses the need to protect the identity of research participants. However, in this context we would perhaps feel that our basic human moral code was more important than ethical guidelines issued by a learned society.

The example serves to illustrate the significance of one of the fundamental characteristics of social research: that it is conducted by human beings into the lives of other human beings. Consequently, many of the situations which arise during the course of a research project are unpredictable. As such, it is not possible either to anticipate or control for the ethical dilemmas which such situations may present. As a result, ethical issues are often dealt with as and when a crisis occurs. Building them into the research design phase of research is difficult in anything other than general terms. Nevertheless, we would advocate that although ethical concerns may not be obvious from the start of the research and there may be a temptation to think that they will not arise, it is important at the design phase to think beyond the obvious situations where they may occur.

As part of the research design we would encourage all researchers to list the different stages of the research that have the potential for ethical concerns and to pose challenging questions about the research topic which might shed light on potential ethical dilemmas. The stages and the questions might include the following:

Stage	Ethical Questions
Gaining access	How much information should I give to potential participants about the research? (Too much may suggest excessive demands, making them less likely to participate. Too little may mean they do not fully understand the demands that will be made of them or their organisations.) Can/should the consent of *all* the participants be gained? What are the possible implications if it is not?
Data collection	Should this be overt or covert? Should the participants be able to see/comment on the data? What is to count as data? When have I collected enough data? What is my (the researcher's) effect on the data collection? What is the nature of my (the researcher's) relationship with the researched?
Data analysis	When should analysis begin? What do the data tell me? What are the gaps in my knowledge?
Leaving the field	When should this occur? What relationship should I have with the researched after the end of the study? What are the problems that my leaving may cause?
Writing	How do I protect the researched from identification? When should writing begin?

Stage	Ethical Questions
	Who should comment on draft material? Should the researched be given an opportunity to comment on or challenge the writing? Where should the research be published? When should the research be published? How should the work be attributed? How should the researched be acknowledged?
Concluding the study	Where/how should the data be stored? Who should have access to the data? What is the impact of the study? How does the study relate to the researchers' future work and careers?
General	How can the confidentiality and anonymity of the researched be ensured? What are the expectations of the sponsor/funder? What are the constraints on the research?

The above chart is designed merely to be illustrative rather than prescriptive of the kinds of ethical questions which underpin and may act to restrict the different phases of the research process. Clearly, all research projects will have their own ethical questions and concerns which are particular to the substantive field of the research and the methods deployed. The key issue to be taken from this discussion is the need to recognise the pervasive nature of ethics within research. A concern for ethics should not be left for times when things have gone wrong and remedial action needs to be taken. The above checklist shows quite clearly how ethical questions can inform all aspects of the research process. By attempting to identify potential ethical concerns at the design stage of the research process

it is hoped that some of the most difficult situations can be anticipated, if not avoided, and in some instances avoided all together. However, as ethics is a topic of central importance to research it is one to which we will return throughout this text.

Comparisons within research designs: contrasting groups and complementary data

We have seen in this chapter that research design involves balancing a set of research objectives against the constraints placed on researchers by the time and resources available to them. Where time and money are in generous supply it may be possible for a researcher to design and conduct a study which uses several different but complementary methods and which involves a number of comparisons. For example, these might be comparisons over time, comparisons between different locations or comparisons between different groups of research participants. The study by Pole (1989) discussed earlier in the chapter, involved the first two of these. For most student or novice researchers, however, resources will be at best limited, and it is likely that they will be working to a fairly tight time-scale. This will usually mean designing a study of modest proportions. Consequently, a student doing a project as one of a number of pieces of assessed work which have to be completed in a given year may find themselves restricted to a research design that involves using a single approach to data collection and which involves looking at one group of people in a single setting during one brief period of time. However, such a project may be less limited than it at first appears.

For example, the student may have chosen to look at teenage leisure activities in a rural setting in contrast with earlier research which focused on urban locations. Alternatively, the key studies in the student's topic area may have been conducted 20 years ago, leading them to wonder whether the process of pre-marital 'courtship' is the same as it used to be. Perhaps the choice of data-collection technique was a reaction to the domination of the literature relating to the student's chosen topic by a particular style of research, e.g. the student chose to carry out a qualitative, experientially oriented study of a health 'problem' which had previously been the territory of epidemiologists.

In each of the above scenarios some form of comparison is involved, whether it is a comparison of different research settings, of different time periods, or of different types of research method and data. Information from two (or more) sources is contrasted, either because the differences observed are of theoretical interest, or because the different sources provide complementary forms of information from which a more comprehensive overall picture can be put together. Hence a student can enhance the value of their research project by designing it in such a way that it complements or contrasts with earlier research. On the other hand, the more time and resources that are available to a student or researcher, the more comparisons of this sort can be an internal feature of the research design. Even a small project may provide sufficient scope for, say, an examination of gender differences based on a comparison between a group of men and a group of women, and an ethnographic study of a social club might easily benefit from a combination of observation and interviews. However, useful comparisons over time may be difficult to achieve within small projects, unless some form of relevant change is likely to occur over a period of days or weeks.

Comparisons are important features of two rather contrasting areas within the history of social research. Cross-national comparisons were central to the thinking of the 'founding fathers' of sociology (McNeill, 1990): for example, Durkheim's classic study of suicide (1951) was based on suicide patterns and trends in various European countries during the latter part of the nineteenth century. Comparisons are also central to the design and analysis of experiments. True experiments occur very infrequently in sociology and are not much more common in educational research (Cohen and Manion, 1989: 202). As a consequence, the

examples used in textbooks to illustrate social experiments are often drawn from social psychology; sometimes experiments are not explicitly discussed in social research methods texts (Gilbert, 1993b). However, the logic of comparison used in many sociological studies clearly owes something to experimental design (Bulmer, 1984), and examples of field experiments can be found in the context of policy and programme evaluations in areas such as criminology (Jupp, 1989).

Different societies

While the history of cross-national comparisons within sociological research stretches back for more than a century, this sort of comparative research has grown in frequency in recent years, perhaps as a by-product of the trend towards 'globalisation' (May, 1993), and a literature relevant to the issue has, rather belatedly, begun to develop (Oyen, 1990; Ragin, 1987; Hantrais and Mangen, 1996). Cross-national research is very often based on secondary analyses, though the data used vary from official statistics and (raw) survey data to rather more holistic, and perhaps rather speculative, assessments of different societies. There are a range of obvious problems with cross-national comparisons: the generation of primary data is costly and time-consuming, and different languages and cultures not only pose practical difficulties but may also make it inappropriate to transfer theoretical and methodological frameworks from one country to another. Furthermore, the necessity for translation places in doubt the cross-national equivalence of the data collected and their meaning. However, the differences and similarities between societies highlighted by successful cross-national research can play an important role in theory development. Erikson and Goldthorpe's study of class mobility in industrial societies (1993) demonstrated the existence cross-nationally of important underlying similarities in the distribution of life chances.

In Erikson and Goldthorpe's study, broadly equivalent data were compared for each of the different countries under consideration. In many pieces of research which are in some sense cross-nationally comparative this equivalence between countries does not exist. Primary data for one country are sometimes supplemented by more limited, secondary data for another country or countries, or are analysed within a theoretical framework developed in or with reference to a different country or countries. For example, fertility declines in less-developed countries in the latter part of the twentieth century are often contrasted with patterns and ideas relating to the fertility declines in late nineteenth-century Britain and Europe. However, care is needed to avoid twisting new data to make them consistent with existing ideas; the reverse of this is to be preferred (Szreter, 1993). The theoretical potential of cross-national research is discussed by May (1993).

Even if a student does not have the time, resources and linguistic skills to carry out primary research in two different countries, or even to make a balanced comparison of secondary data, the use of data from different countries and/or ideas relating to other countries may still be of value. In fact, many literature reviews are cross-national, as the findings cited often correspond to (implicitly) 'similar' countries. An assumption of cross-national similarity (if plausible) broadens one's sources of relevant data and findings; conversely, theories need to be consistent with observed cross-national differences.

Different groups

A more frequent type of comparison in small pieces of social research is a comparison between the behaviour or experiences of two or more categories of people. Such comparisons do not always involve explicit research design at an early stage of the research process, as post hoc examinations of differences may be possible where research has, for example, collected data corresponding to people in different social classes. However, as is discussed further in the next chapter, one aspect of good sample design is ensuring that enough research participants fall into different groups for theoretically important comparisons to be made. On the other hand, while between-group comparisons may be interesting, it may be beyond the scope of a project to incorporate them within the research design. For example, if a researcher only has the time and resources to carry out ten interviews, interviewing five women and five men may sacrifice the sharpness of focus that one would get with ten interviews with women. The crunch question here is whether the experiences of women are more central to the research objectives than an examination of gender differences. In her research on housework, Oakley chose her respondents in a way that allowed for class comparisons but restricted her sample to 'white' women of similar ages and family situations, thus allowing for one form of comparison but not others (Oakley, 1985: 36).

Not all comparisons between groups place the same emphasis on each of the groups being compared. Suppose that a researcher wished to discover whether members of minority ethnic groups were discriminated against in the context of an interview-based entry system to an educational institution. In the absence of overt and obvious examples of racism, it would almost inevitably prove necessary to compare the experiences of minority ethnic applicants with those of 'white' applicants. The 'white' applicants would constitute what is often termed a **control group**. (A rare account of a set of social experiments, focusing on racial discrimination in the housing and labour markets, is given by Smith, 1977.)

The control group is a central feature of experimental design. While few sociological researchers will ever use experiments in their research, many will make use of ideas or terminology from experimental design. It is, therefore, useful for the researcher to have a basic understanding of such ideas and terminology. In the classic experiment, an **experimental group** is subjected to a **treatment**. Some kind of outcome is then compared between the experimental group and the control group, which has not received the treatment. The aim of the experiment is to eliminate the possibility that between-group differences in outcome result from factors other than the treatment. So, in order to avoid differences in outcome which are a reflection of differences in the composition of the two groups, subjects are allocated to the groups **at random**, and/or a **matching** process is used to ensure that the two groups contain similar ranges of members.

Randomisation and matching are geared towards minimising the possibility that differences in outcome between groups are a consequence of factors confounded with the treatment, rather than of the treatment itself. Similarly, in situations where the treatment is intended to effect some before/after change, **pre-treatment** and **post-treatment** measures of the outcome variable are made, to ensure that any differences between the experimental and control groups do not pre-date the treatment. The same logic would apply in a comparison of the effectiveness of two sixth-form colleges, wherein any difference in 'A' level results would need to be qualified by the earlier achievements of students at GCSE level.

There are clearly a number of problems with implementing experiments in the context of social research. Ideally, the researcher has control over the explanatory or **independent variable** (the presence or absence of the treatment), and can thus determine group membership, eliminate the effect of confounding factors, and interpret between-group variation in the **dependent variable** (i.e. the outcome) as a response to the treatment. However, where the independent variable is something like ethnicity, membership of the 'experimental' and 'control' groups is obviously fixed. Even in situations where group membership is not fixed, the researcher may not have the power to allocate subjects to groups. For this reason, 'true' experiments are less common in social research than **quasi-experiments**, i.e. comparisons of naturally occurring groups where one group has experienced or is going to experience some form of change or treatment.

In quasi-experiments attempts are sometimes made to control for the effects of confounding factors by constructing a control group out of subjects who are 'close matches' to the members of the experimental group. For example, in an analysis of the effect of marital dissolution on unemployment, Lampard (1994) constructed a 'retrospective control group' (Rose, 1982: 63) by matching separated and divorced people with people in ongoing marriages who had similar life and work histories up until the point of separation. However, in the absence of random allocation to experimental and control groups, there is no guarantee that differences in outcome relate to the treatment rather than some uncontrolled factor correlated with the treatment. In the above example, what appeared to be the effect of separation or divorce could still be the effect, say, of anti-social behaviour which increased both the risk of marital dissolution and the risk of job loss.

Another problem with social experiments is the **experimental effect**, often referred to as the **Hawthorne effect** (Mayo, 1949). Unfortunately, an awareness that they are participating in an experiment may affect subjects' behaviour, irrespective of the presence, absence or nature of the treatment. This is similar to the well-known 'placebo effect' in medicine. The experimental effect may, perhaps, be greater under 'laboratory conditions', which contributes to social researchers' preference for **field experiments** as opposed to **laboratory experiments**. However, the absence of 'laboratory conditions' is often associated with a lower level of researcher control over the experiment. Covert experiments can eliminate the experimental effect, but pose the usual ethical questions relating to covert research. Note that ethical considerations may also restrict the researcher's control over the allocation of subjects to experimental and control groups. In general, experiments pose more than their fair share of ethical problems.

The classic text on experimental and quasi-experimental design is Campbell and Stanley (1966), though there is relevant material in many social science research methods texts, such as Frankfort-Nachmias and Nachmias (1992). While experiments fall primarily within a quantitative approach to research, the existence of 'ethnomethodological experiments' should be noted (Burgess, 1993). In such an 'experiment' an ethnomethodologist indulges in actions in a research setting which are calculated to generate some form of interesting response from people within the setting (for example, because they are bizarre or inappropriate).

Different times

Studying social change necessitates the analysis of data relating to different points in time. Since retrospectively collected data can be particularly unreliable and inaccurate, it is preferable that the data are actually collected at those different points in time. There is sometimes a temptation to use data corresponding to different age groups from a cross-sectional study as a way of looking at change. This is not a watertight strategy, since age-related differences can reflect both changes between birth cohorts and the ageing process itself.

Comparisons over time may focus on changes in the characteristics of a group or population. If this is the case, then repeated, **cross-sectional** surveys of the population can be used, with data being collected from a different sample on each occasion. For example, if a researcher is interested in trends in the proportion of unmarried people who are cohabiting, then they can compare findings from different years of the annual General Household Survey (OPCS, 1994). However, if a researcher is interested in change within individuals – for example, individuals' cohabitation histories – then some form of longitudinal or **panel** study is required. Panel studies can also help establish the causal direction of relationships: for example, a cross-sectional study might identify a relationship between marital status and depression, but only a longitudinal study could demonstrate that divorced people were more often depressed after separation than they were when married, as one would not expect retrospective data on depression to be particularly valid.

An interesting example of a longitudinal study is the National Child Development Study, which has been following a cohort of people since they were born in 1958 (Ferri, 1993). One use to which this study has been put is an examination of the effects of parental separation on their children's later experiences (Kiernan, 1992). The major advantage of a longitudinal study in this context is that it allows the researcher to look at the children's characteristics before their parents separated. Cross-sectional studies which, having taken account of socio-economic differences, still identify negative 'effects' of lone-parent families on children's life chances cannot rule out the possibility that the children's problems pre-date the separation of their parents. A more recent panel study of households, the British Household Panel Study, is now bearing fruit (Buck et al., 1994), and has led to a text on panel studies (Rose and Corti, 1998) as a by-product. A major longitudinal study has also been created by the selection of a sample of individuals and the linking of each individual's Census records for 1971, 1981 and 1991 to each other (Dale and Marsh, 1993).

All the above examples of longitudinal studies are large-scale and quantitative. However, smaller-scale, more qualitative longitudinal studies can be equally valuable: for example, a long-term study of the effects of divorce on adults and children (Wallerstein and Blakeslee, 1989), and a study of young women's changing career and family formation aspirations (Procter and Padfield, 1995). All longitudinal studies, however, potentially suffer from a range of specific limitations. Attrition, i.e. people dropping out, may distort the sample. The range of data collected at early stages may in retrospect have been less than ideal. Data corresponding to intervals between interviews can only be collected retrospectively, and longitudinal studies thus really consist of series of cross-sectional snapshots. In addition, data corresponding to the early stages of long-term studies are always somewhat 'out of date'.

Worst of all, from the point of view of the student researcher, longitudinal studies take time. However, there are some situations where potentially interesting changes can be expected to occur over relatively short periods of time. A researcher might interview people before and after they have experienced some event, e.g. attendance at an assertiveness training course, the departure of their children from home to attend university, or a change of job. Pole (1989), discussed earlier in this chapter, is a study of this sort. There may be something else to be gained from interviewing respondents on more than one occasion: for example, to see whether actual behaviour matched up with the behaviour anticipated at an earlier interview. Data collected at two points in time can also show that respondents' accounts may fluctuate in a way which is more about the absence of a clear-cut 'reality' than it is about change: for example, female respondents to the SCELI main and follow-up surveys (Gallie *et al.*, 1994), which were separated by a few months, sometimes retrospectively changed their assessment of their employment status at the time of the first survey from 'housewife' to 'unemployed', or vice versa.

Different methods or types of data

Discussions of both social experiments and longitudinal studies can be found in the text on research design by Hakim (1987), though for a briefer overview see the first chapter of Sapsford and Jupp (1996). Hakim's text also considers triangulation within research studies and programmes, i.e. the use of multiple approaches as advocated by Denzin (1978). We hope that it will be evident from this book that different research approaches and different forms of data have their own distinctive contributions to make to social research; Bryman provides an overview of different ways in which quantitative and qualitative approaches can be usefully combined (1988: 127–156), and relevant examples can be found in Brannen (1992).

On the other hand, while we advocate an open-minded approach which acknowledges the potential value of different sorts of data, effective research design is more about pragmatism than eclecticism. This chapter has already suggested that

the researcher needs to identify relevant data sources and decide whether they 'count' in the context of his or her research. However, constraints have also been noted to be crucial, and each researcher thus needs to decide what is necessary and what is feasible in relation to his or her particular research topic and objectives.

In the context of a large-scale research project such as a study focusing on the Department of Social Security's Social Fund, which provides loans in response to 'exceptional needs' as experienced on occasions by people on low incomes (Huby and Dix, 1992a, 1992b; Walker, Dix and Huby, 1992), the objectives of the research may dictate the need for the use of multiple methods:

> The quantitative component of the project was used to explore regularities and patterns and helped to elucidate some of the structural elements of respondents' needs and social fund experiences. It was clear however that, in order to understand the processes underlying respondents' interpretations of their circumstances and construction of their needs, qualitative in-depth interviews were required (Huby and Dix, 1992a: 182).

A survey and in-depth interviews thus played complementary roles by respectively providing information on **patterns** of need and **perceptions** of need. However, the two sources of data also produced contrasting, apparently contradictory findings, which indicate the way in which different research instruments can complement each other by challenging each other:

> While the [survey] . . . suggested that many respondents thought that DSS loans were a 'good idea', the in-depth interviews indicated a general dislike of loans. Rather than suggesting that one source of data was more likely than the other to be 'correct', this apparent contradiction provoked further thought and analysis (Huby and Dix, 1992a: 184).

The above research project also involved the use of secondary sources (official statistics), observation, group discussions and experiments. This eclecticism reflects in part the demands of the topic, but also reflects a well-resourced study and the complementary experience and skills of members of the research team.

Student researchers need to be wary about being seduced into multi-method research and then finding that they have bitten off more than they can chew. However, decisions to use one central type or source of data should be reflected upon and justified by the researcher. Such a justification is likely to reflect both theoretical and practical considerations. For example, in a retrospective study of female cinema spectatorship in the 1940s and 1950s, Stacey (1994) considered using existing documentary sources, but found these to be too limited, and, instead, generated a large volume of data via a questionnaire (consisting largely of open-ended questions) which she felt to be an adequate empirical basis for her thesis. Earlier research on female cinema spectatorship had focused primarily on yet another form of data, i.e. the narratives/texts of the films themselves. Stacey argues that the viewpoints of female cinema-goers had thus been neglected, giving her choice of data source added novelty and importance. However, she also compares and contrasts her findings with the psychoanalytic ideas which earlier researchers had developed by analysing the content of films, and where appropriate she additionally presents quantitative information on patterns and trends in cinema attendance.

Research which uses complementary forms of data, or which is longitudinal and thus allows the study of change, or which compares different groups, possesses an extra dimension (or dimensions) which broadens its scope. However, constraints mean that what could usefully be done in theory is rarely what can actually be achieved in practice. The important thing is for the researcher to assess what types and sources of data and what possible comparisons between groups or over time would be of value, and to design a project which includes those added dimensions whose contributions to the research objectives are greatest relative to the time and resources necessary for their incorporation.

Conclusion

Above all this chapter has attempted to emphasise the importance of careful planning in research. It has also sought to emphasise a number of things which are essential to the successful outcome of a research project. On the basis of the preceding discussion it is possible for us to say that research needs:

- a degree of flexibility in its design in order to cope with the unexpected
- a clear and unambiguous focus
- to be feasible
- to be realistic.

In addition, this chapter has sought to encourage an approach to research design which recognises the constraints under which research is conducted. It has highlighted the need to think very carefully about the sequence of the research process and to pose questions about:

- the role of literature and reading
- the nature and location of data
- the scope for and value of comparisons
- the choice of data-collection methods
- the role and place of data analysis.

The chapter has not attempted to offer a formula for research design or to suggest that it is something that can be achieved in a neat and tidy, linear fashion. As with most aspects of research, design can be messy. However, although we have stressed the need to be flexible, research design is about planning and attempting to bring a sense of order, structure and direction to the set of activities which we see as constituting research.

Without effective research design there cannot be effective research.

Chapter 3 Suitable samples: selecting, obtaining and profiting from them

Introduction

The sample of people (or other things) that you study determines the nature and validity of the findings and theory generated by your research. This chapter looks in detail at sampling from both qualitative and statistical viewpoints, and considers some related issues affecting who ends up in the sample, including access and non-response. Random sampling is the foundation of most statistical theory and analyses, so this chapter also contains introductory material relating to sampling error and statistical inference, which also helps us to establish how big samples need to be to provide accurate estimates and to allow simple hypotheses to be tested.

Two examples of samples

- A sample of teenage girls tells you that they were encouraged to study sciences by their families, friends and teachers. Should you conclude that the gendering of school subjects is a thing of the past? (Arguably the encouragement itself is evidence of the persistence of gendering.)
- A sample of divorced people stresses to you how keen they are to find new partners and remarry. Should you conclude that remarriage is an automatic goal after divorce?

Assuming that what you are being told is truthful, the above samples certainly show that some teenage girls have been encouraged to study sciences and that some divorced people wish to remarry. However, the amount that can be learned from the above information is very much dependent on which teenage girls and divorced people are in the samples, and on where the samples were obtained. If the teenage girls were sampled from a science class in a single-sex school and the divorced people were sampled from the membership list of a marriage bureau, you might well wonder whether other teenage girls and divorced people would tell you the same things.

Very often social researchers want to be able to use information gathered from a **sample** to say something about a **population**: for example, to use data obtained from a sample of teenage girls to say something about all teenage girls (or, at least, all teenage girls within a particular geographical area, say the United Kingdom). It is obviously impossible in practice to interview all teenage girls or all divorced people (i.e. to carry out a **census**); even if a researcher was interested in a much smaller category of people (e.g. Members of Parliament) there would be a trade-off between the range and depth of data that the researcher could collect and the number of people that he or she collected it from. One of the reasons that the form for the decennial (i.e. ten-yearly) Census of Population in England and Wales (Dale and Marsh, 1993) is quite short is that the cost of processing the information from one additional question is extremely high, given the millions of forms generated by the Census.

Using data from a sample to say something about a population is a process of generalisation. **Generalising** from a sample to a population is something that we often do in our day-to-day lives; for example, if you visit a number of different outlets belonging to a particular chain of pizza parlours and find again and again that you have to wait three-quarters of an hour for your main course, you may end up by generalising, i.e. assuming that all Palatial Pizza restaurants are like that. In doing this you are working on the basis that the outlets that you have visited can be taken as typical or **representative** of all Palatial Pizza restaurants. This may have less serious consequences than assuming that the teenage girls and divorced people in the samples discussed above are representative of all teenage girls and divorced people.

In many pieces of research there is no list of the members of the population of interest which can be used as a **sampling frame**, i.e. as the basis for the selection of the sample. If you needed to interview a sample of teenage girls for a research project then you might well solve the problem of locating them by finding them in a school or schools. For girls from a particular school to end up as members of the sample both access to the school and the girls' willingness to participate would be needed. Some types of school may be less likely to grant access, and teenage girls who truant may be less inclined to participate; thus issues both of **access** and of **non-response** are fundamental to the characteristics of the sample that is obtained.

A researcher looking at gender and science might be interested in schools as case studies as well as in the experiences and views of individual students. A number of schools might therefore be chosen to represent a range of types of school. The process of selecting these schools is, of course, another example of sampling. The **unit of analysis** is now the school rather than the student, but issues of representativeness and generalisability still apply. While access is often seen primarily as an issue for qualitative researchers, a quantitative survey of school students might draw samples of students from a sample of schools, in which case access to the schools would be an important issue. Whether you are carrying out qualitative research or quantitative research, or using some combination of the two approaches, the characteristics of the sample that you obtain need to be reflected upon so that you can assess the sample's coverage and representativeness and the scope for generalising from it. The two approaches frequently use different styles of sampling, in part because they often have rather different objectives, but for both approaches the findings generated by a piece of research are as broad or as limited as the sample obtained allows them to be.

Perhaps the most obvious division between different methods of sampling is between **probability sampling** (often referred to as **random sampling**) and **non-probability sampling**. Probability sampling is fundamental to much of the survey research carried out in academia and by government departments in the UK. However, while probability sampling is usually associated with quantitative research, some qualitative studies use random samples. Similarly, while most qualitative studies use some form of non-probability sampling, so do many quantitative studies carried out by market research organisations. It needs to be stressed, however, that quantitative researchers only abandon probability sampling where it is impractical or too costly; a random sample is one of the hallmarks of good-quality quantitative research, for reasons which are discussed below.

Probability or random sampling

Probability or random sampling has the profound advantage that it allows the researcher to rule out the possibility that research findings are *biased* by the way in which the sample was chosen. For example, a sample of divorced people obtained via a marriage bureau might be expected to be biased towards divorced people who favour remarriage. Establishing the magnitude of such a bias is often difficult or impossible.

The problem posed by the potential for bias in a non-random sample can be seen in the following example. Suppose that a researcher finds that, in a sample of women who are getting divorced, it was the woman herself who initiated the divorce proceedings in 70% of the cases. Assuming that wives and husbands are equally likely to initiate divorce proceedings, then the researcher would have expected the figure for the sample to have been 50%, (or, at least, close to 50%). Thus the figure is 20% higher than expected, given the assumption. This 20% differential could have come about in three ways:

- It might be the case that women are more likely to initiate divorce proceedings (i.e. that the assumption is wrong).
- It might be the case that, simply by chance (i.e. as a consequence of **sampling error**), this particular sample contains an excess of women who initiated the proceedings.
- The researcher may have selected their sample in a way which made it disproportionately likely that women who initiated divorce proceedings would be included. For example, if some of the members of the sample were recruited from a refuge for women who have experienced domestic violence, then an upwardly biased figure might not be surprising.

Random sampling eliminates the third of the possible explanations listed above. Once the possibility that the findings have been biased by the sampling method has been discounted, only two alternatives are left: either the figure of 70% reflects a greater tendency for women to initiate divorce proceedings, or the figure is 70% (rather than about 50%) simply by chance. Is it likely that a figure of 70% would have been obtained simply by chance? If there are only ten women in the sample, then it is plausible that the sample might have ended up containing seven ($70\% \times 10$) who initiated the divorce proceedings, even if women only initiate the divorce proceedings in 50% of cases ($50\% \times 10 = 5$). However, if there are

500 women in the sample, and 350 ($70\% \times 500$) of them initiated the divorce proceedings, as opposed to 150 of their husbands, it somehow seems less plausible that the 70% figure has occurred by chance.

As is implied by the above paragraph, the ability to distinguish between findings in a sample which reflect the true situation in the population and findings which have occurred by chance, i.e. which are simply idiosyncrasies of that particular sample, is dependent on sample size. On average a bigger (random) sample not only provides more accurate findings, but also gives the researcher a better chance of identifying the existence of interesting patterns and relationships. The issue of choosing an appropriate sample size will be considered later in the chapter.

It can be seen from the above that random sampling provides an appropriate context for answering a key question in quantitative research:

> Is an observed finding 'real', or could it have occurred by chance?

This question is central to the statistical analysis of data collected from a sample. To put it another way, data corresponding to a random sample reflect both underlying patterns in the population and also what is usually referred to as **sampling error**, i.e. the source of those differences between the characteristics of the sample and the characteristics of the population which occur as an inevitable consequence of the sample only being a proportion of the population.

But what is a random, or probability, sample? Many lay people would translate choosing a sample 'at random' as choosing a sample 'in any old fashion'. Interpreting the word 'random' in this fashion is an excellent way of making research methods lecturers wince. The correct definition is as follows:

> A random sample is one where every element (e.g. person) in the population of interest has a known, non-zero chance of being included.

If some people in the population have no chance of being included in the sample, then the results obtained from the sample will almost inevitably be biased because they cannot possibly reflect the characteristics of those people.

For a sample to be random the chance of inclusion has to be known for each person, but it does not have to be equal. If, for example, it is known that some people are twice as likely to be included as others then this situation can be taken into account at the analysis stage by weighting (which is discussed later in this chapter). However, in the simplest kind of random sample everybody's chance of inclusion is equal:

> A simple random sample is one where every member of the population of interest has an equal chance of being included, and where every possible combination of n members of the population is equally likely (n is the sample size).

More complex forms of random sampling (where the latter part of the above definition does not hold) are discussed later, as is sampling error within simple random samples.

Selecting a simple random sample is a superficially straightforward matter of setting up the sampling frame, or list of members of the population, and using random numbers (the equivalent of tossing a coin or throwing a die) to identify which of the members are included in the sample. The practicalities of sample selection will be returned to later; for the moment it is worth noting that random samples are usually **without replacement** (as opposed to **with replacement**), i.e. if the same random number appears twice you do not include the same member of the population in the sample for a second time.

If a researcher wishes to find out the proportion of divorces which are initiated by women, or if a researcher wishes to establish whether men are more likely than women to have been encouraged to study science subjects at school, then some form of random sampling is appropriate. These objectives are both quantitative in nature, the first being

an example of the **estimation** of a population **parameter** (i.e. the use of a sample to provide information about the magnitude of some quantified phenomenon), and the second being an example of a **hypothesis test** (i.e. the use of a sample to examine whether or not some quantitative difference or relationship exists). When the objectives of a research project are less obviously quantitative, random sampling may be less advantageous or even inappropriate.

More complex forms of probability sampling are discussed later in this chapter.

Non-probability sampling

Non-probability sampling takes a wide variety of forms and is used for a wide variety of reasons. It would be a mistake to assume that it is necessarily a less systematic approach than random sampling. At one extreme, in **convenience** or **availability** sampling the researcher exercises very little control over who is included in the sample; respondents are selected simply because they are close at hand, or easy to access. Samples obtained by such an approach are likely to be unrepresentative and as a consequence generalising from them to populations is speculative and may be inappropriate. At the other extreme, researchers using **theoretical sampling** make strategic decisions as to who should be included. Since the process of selection in this latter situation is geared towards the generation and development of theory, representativeness is less of an issue. The relevance of theoretical issues to qualitative sampling is discussed further a little later.

Another form of non-probability sampling in which the researcher exerts considerable control over who is included in the sample is **quota sampling**. This approach is particularly popular with market research companies who wish to generate samples which are reasonably representative but who also want to avoid the time and expense involved in collecting random samples. For example, if it is known (e.g. from Census data) that

10% of the population of interest to a market researcher are women aged between 30 and 39 years, then the researcher will aim to include 10 such women in a sample of 100 people. Quota sampling ensures that a sample is representative in terms of the characteristics for which quotas are set; however, it can be extremely unrepresentative in other ways. (This highlights a major advantage of random sampling; it is the only way of guaranteeing a sample which is likely to be reasonably representative of the population in relation to characteristics which a researcher decides are of relevance after the sample has been taken.) The popularity of quantitative market research using quota sampling suggests that random sampling is not necessarily essential for useful quantitative research (Tull and Hawkins, 1993: 547–548, discuss its relative merits in this context); however, academic social researchers are typically sceptical about quota sampling.

Non-probability sampling is often used for pragmatic reasons. It can be impossible in practice to generate sampling frames for some populations of interest (e.g. couples who are not married and who do not live together). A form of non-probability sampling frequently used when respondents are difficult to locate is **snowball sampling**: respondents who have already been sampled direct the researcher towards other potential respondents (or direct other potential respondents towards the researcher). The problem with snowball sampling is that it can lead to the under-representation of those types of people who are not tied into social networks. (It can also lead to ethical problems relating to anonymity: for example, it may be possible for one person in a sample to recognise quotes made by someone else that they know to be in the sample, even if the quotes have been made anonymous.)

Non-probability sampling is also often used where the aim is not to generalise from a sample to the population, and representativeness is thus of limited importance. Non-probability samples are often used at a piloting stage to develop questionnaires and other research instruments; they are also

often used in qualitative research which is broadly exploratory, or which aims to generate hypotheses or develop typologies. In the latter context **purposive sampling**, or **focused sampling**, or **judgement sampling** may be the approach used. All these terms refer to forms of sampling where the researcher makes theoretically informed decisions as to whom to include in their sample.

It may be important to include a wide range of types of people in a sample if it is thought that this will lead to as fully developed a typology as possible. This sort of **maximum variation sampling** can allow important commonalities to be established, as well as being well suited to documenting diversity (Miles and Huberman, 1994). Within the context of sampling a wide range of people, it may be useful to engage in **deviant case sampling**: theoretically useful material may be gained from individuals whose experiences are highly distinctive in relation to a research topic. Conversely, it may be thought desirable to sample a range of people who can be regarded as typical of various categories of interest, or whose experiences, behaviour or views are in some sense typical (**typical case sampling**). Arguably, the researcher should beware of focusing too much on respondents whose experiences fit in with their theoretical pre-conceptions or their current theorising and on respondents whose experiences seem central to their research focus; there is a lot to be said for sampling **negative cases** which can expose the limits of the universality of theories, and also for **peripheral sampling**, where informants who appear marginal to the research setting or the research focus may provide a distinctive and valuable perspective.

At this point it is worth noting that there are different forms of qualitative research within which somewhat different approaches to sampling may be appropriate. Carrying out qualitative interviews of a sample of single parents is different in many ways from carrying out an ethnographic study of a hospital. In the former case, while representativeness may not be vital, an emphasis on extensive coverage of the range of different types of single parent may be in order, so that any theories about single parenthood generated by the research can be felt to have reasonably wide applicability. In the latter case, the hospital itself has been selected in some way, possibly for theoretical reasons, possibly for pragmatic reasons. The process of sampling individuals within the hospital is likely to be theoretically driven; for an ethnographer the roles and activities of individuals within and in relation to the setting may determine who is sampled.

Furthermore, in ethnographic research the basic unit of analysis is likely to be something other than the individual; indeed there may be a number of types of basic unit of analysis. The ethnographer may sample activities, events, times, locations, interactions, etc. (Burgess, 1984; Miles and Huberman, 1994). For example, an ethnographer in a school might sample lessons, or interactions between schoolchildren in the playground. The type (or types) of sample units selected should reflect the objectives of the research: if the research focus is football hooligans then the researcher should sample football hooligans, but if the research focus is football hooliganism it might be appropriate to sample acts of football hooliganism, though an alternative would be to look at the acts of hooliganism carried out by a sample of hooligans. As discussed in Chapter 2, the researcher needs to decide 'what counts as data'; the sampling process necessitates a decision regarding what type(s) of item to sample as well as which specific items to sample.

Theoretical sampling and qualitative research

The term **theoretical sampling** is often used in relation to the ideas of Glaser and Strauss (1967), who developed the notion of 'Grounded Theory', in which theory is generated from empirical data, rather than tested using empirical data. (Grounded Theory thus falls within a broader approach to theorising known as **analytic induction**.) Glaser and Strauss's version of theoretical sampling assumes that the researcher's main objective is to generate

and develop theory, rather than to carry out an ethnographic study of a particular setting or to accurately document the characteristics of a group of people or to test for the existence of relationships. The relevance of their approach thus depends to an extent on the balance of these different types of objective within a research project. However, their work does in any case contain some important ideas.

Glaser and Strauss compare statistical sampling, which they see as geared towards the generation of accurate evidence about the distributions of characteristics of people, which can be used for descriptions or hypothesis testing, with theoretical sampling, which they see as geared towards the identification of concepts and their properties, with theory being generated by the examination of relationships between the concepts. In research using theoretical sampling, relationships are hypothesised rather than (at this stage) tested for existence, magnitude and direction. A researcher does not need a representative sample to hypothesise the existence of a relationship.

An ethnographer studying university students might, as their fieldwork progressed, develop the hypothesis that a student belonging to a group of friends who are by and large academically motivated will have their own level of motivation enhanced. The plausibility of this hypothesis would be enhanced by a student saying something of this sort spontaneously. The ethnographer would not need to have observed or talked with a sample of students whose range of levels of motivation mirrored that of the student population for the hypothesis to be a theoretically valuable one.

A distinctive feature of theoretical sampling is, according to Glaser and Strauss, that only limited decisions as to who should be included in the sample can be made before the fieldwork commences. A researcher using theoretical sampling selects respondents according to their perceived relevance to the developing theory. Glaser and

Strauss also discuss an idea which they term **theoretical saturation**. To achieve theoretical saturation the researcher needs to collect as wide a range of data as possible relating to his or her theories. Saturation is achieved when what the researcher sees and hears becomes familiar rather than novel, and does not lead to further development of the concepts and relationships arising from the data that they have collected. Assuming that the relevant concepts and relationships are not universal in nature and form, sampling a diverse range of respondents is an important step towards theoretical saturation. It is interesting to note that representativeness is not crucial here, but that coverage is. In fact, the term coverage used in this way is an alternative form of representativeness: a meeting involving one representative from each of the countries of Europe would constitute a sample with good coverage, but would not be representative of the populations of the countries in proportional terms. Strauss and Corbin (1990) suggest that during the early stages of a study using theoretical sampling the appropriate approach is **open sampling**, where openness implies a desire to identify the full range of relevant concepts and types of person or event.

Once the ethnographer studying university students had developed their hypothesis about motivation and friendship groups, they might arguably be expected to attempt to sample students with a wide range of levels of motivation, with different forms of motivation, and with different sorts and sizes of networks of friends. In short, they might be expected to select students whom they felt would 'flesh out' their concepts and theory.

Strauss and Corbin describe this stage within theoretical sampling as **relational and variational sampling**, the objective of which is to maximise the diversity of the people or events sampled with respect to theoretically important dimensions.

While the previous paragraph suggests that sample diversity is crucial to theoretical development, arguably there are occasions when a more constrained range of sample members may be appropriate. Patton (1990: 182) refers to this as **homogeneous sampling**. Glaser and Strauss's work also implies that minimising the differences between the members of a sample may make the early stages of theory development more streamlined by limiting the sources of variation and making it easier to identify possible causal relationships. Keeping things simple and not being over-ambitious in terms of the range of respondents sampled may also lead to more watertight hypotheses, because they have been derived from a greater number of similar respondents.

It might be better for the qualitative study looking at the level of motivation of university students in relation to their friendship groups to focus on a small number of groups containing similar types of student, rather than covering the full range of courses and types of student (various categories of students may have patterns of motivation which differ from other categories: for example, mature students; part-time students; students doing vocational courses; postgraduate students; etc.). Of course, a more focused sample produces theory which may be less convincingly general, but since, for example, the sample of students in our motivation example would quite likely be drawn from a single institution, the level of generality is going to be questionable anyway.

In fact, researchers should always be alert to the potential relevance of both the temporal and spatial locations of any sample, whether probability or non-probability. Even a nationally representative, random sample poses problems in relation to generalisation; is it reasonable to assume that what applies in the US applies in the UK, and is it reasonable to assume that what applies in 2000 also applies in 2001?

It is important to note that selecting a sample using the notion of theoretical sampling as a sole guiding light results in a sample from which the researcher may be able to generalise to a population in terms of theory but from which it would be extremely dangerous to generalise in terms of distributions of characteristics, experiences, etc. Of course, there are problems with the latter form of generalisation in relation to any form of non-probability sample, but theoretical samples are less likely than most other forms of non-probability sample to be crudely representative of the population's characteristics. Qualitative research often has theoretical objectives, but it can also have exploratory and descriptive objectives too. With a crudely representative sample, and with a critical awareness of its likely inadequacies, cautious empirical generalisations may be appropriate. There may therefore be a tension between 'pure' theoretical sampling, and sampling which is geared towards producing a sample which has some claim to being representative.

In theoretical sampling, as in quota sampling, a researcher may deliberately select respondents who differ from each other with respect to a range of underlying dimensions which are perceived to be of salience. In quota sampling, and in **stratified random sampling** (which is discussed later in this chapter), sampling takes account of a range of characteristics which may be of importance as explanatory variables in the analysis of the data collected. Such characteristics, which need to be identified before the sampling process begins, often include sex, age, occupational class and ethnicity, though characteristics more specific to the research topic may also be used. In theoretical sampling, respondents are selected if they have (combinations of) characteristics which are relevant to theory development. These characteristics may be quite specific to the theory being developed and may be identified during the course of the research; moreover they may include behaviour or views that the research is attempting to explain. Selecting respondents according to the latter kind of characteristic may make sense if the research is geared towards explaining particular outcomes, but is clearly entirely inappropriate if an aim of the research is to look at the relative frequencies of different outcomes.

In a quantitative study of the level of motivation of university students, a number of students might be selected from each department within the university, since motivation may vary inter-departmentally. However, in a qualitative study using theoretical sampling, students might also be sampled according to their level of motivation, and at some point a student might be selected specifically (as a 'negative case') because they had a low level of motivation but had a network of highly motivated student friends. In both sorts of study a certain number of mature students might be deliberately selected to complement the younger students in the sample. However, in the quantitative study the aim would be to represent mature students within the sample, because their experiences were thought likely to be different or simply worthy of specific examination, whereas in the qualitative study the aim would be to explore ways in which age might be of theoretical salience. While it would be dangerous to regard one mature student as representative of all mature students, a comparison of the experiences of one mature student with those of younger students might generate material of theoretical relevance, even if a greater number of mature students would allow the development of more detailed and better qualified theory.

In an interesting discussion of sampling, Mason (1996) stresses the importance of identifying the relationship that the researcher wishes to exist between their sample and the broader population, or as it is sometimes labelled, the **universe** of cases. Does the researcher wish their sample to be representative of the population, so empirical generalisations can be made? Or are they happy to use theoretical sampling, and to restrict themselves to theoretical generalisations? If they are content to do the latter, should they focus in considerable detail on a small number of cases, or enhance the generalisability of their theory to the wider universe by sampling a wider range of theoretically relevant cases?

What is clear is that the omission of 'important' cases can reduce the validity of both quantitative findings and grounded theory. Quantitative results from a non-random sample can be biased if a disproportionate number of people of a particular type are excluded. Theory can be limited or distorted if the researcher's theoretical sampling fails to include key cases. In addition, a typology developed from a qualitative sample can be incomplete if the range of cases included in the sample does not adequately cover sub-groups within the population containing people with distinctive types of experiences or views.

Qualitative sampling: some practical issues

Social researchers need to reflect on the decisions that they make with regard to sampling, and should be able to justify the decisions either in strategic or in pragmatic terms, so that they stand up to external scrutiny (see Chapter 1). The way in which a sample is selected sets the context for both the nature and the interpretation of the data collected. It may not always be possible for a researcher to be as systematic in their selection of cases as they would like, but there is no excuse for sampling in a haphazard way if something more measured is possible. In qualitative research, where sampling decisions are often made on an ongoing basis, documenting the reasons behind such decisions is important but may be easy to forget. Reflecting on the implications of the sampling process used is also a good way of gaining an insight into the strengths and limitations of the data collected. As discussed later in this chapter, even when representativeness is not an objective, a sound knowledge of the origins and characteristics of their sample gives the researcher an awareness of likely omissions from and idiosyncrasies within the data that have been collected.

A standard question considered by researchers which unfortunately has no straightforward answer is 'How big should my sample be?' If a researcher intends to use theoretical sampling within their research, then an obvious but deeply unsatisfying answer is 'As big as is necessary for theoretical saturation to take place.' The size needed for theoretical saturation is difficult or impossible to predict in advance, and depends on the number of theoretically important dimensions involved and the range of comparisons required. If a researcher intends to generate theory which is less than crude and which is reasonably widely generalisable, then an ideal sample size might belie the notion that qualitative studies are small in scale, and stretch well beyond what is practical for a lone student carrying out a research project to achieve. Thus, both at the start of a qualitative study, and as it progresses, qualitative researchers may have to make tough decisions as to who and what is central to their research objectives.

In fact, if the researcher is working within fixed 'budgets' of time and money the answer to the standard question is likely to be 'At least as big as it needs to be, and no bigger than I can afford it to be.' Students doing projects can get some idea of the former from their tutors; the latter needs to be estimated on the basis of the time and money it will cost to sample particular cases. Estimating the latter requires an overview of the whole research process, from selection through access to data collection, and from data collection through data analysis to report writing. In fact, the last sentence omits the 'data preparation' stage; transcribing the whole of a taped interview is a much more time-consuming exercise than the interview itself, with a day of interviewing translating into a week of transcription. (One hour of interview takes approximately seven hours to transcribe.)

The practicalities of qualitative research do not only constrain sample size. They can also throw off balance the carefully laid strategic sampling plans that a researcher develops before starting their fieldwork. Access to some of the respondents, or types of respondent, that the researcher wants to sample may be difficult or impossible. Very often there is no convenient sampling frame from which to select respondents, or there is a sampling frame, but there is insufficient accompanying information to allow respondents to be selected in a strategic way. One way of dealing with the latter situation is to collect the information needed to carry out strategic selection from a range of potential respondents, and then to sample from within this preliminary pool. This is an example of a situation where some form of random sampling may have a role to play alongside more theoretically based sampling: for example, a mail questionnaire to a random sample of adults in a locality might provide a representative backdrop from which cases with characteristics of theoretical interest might be selected. This sort of **screening** approach to sampling can also be useful when a researcher is sampling minority groups within a broader population (Hedges, 1978).

When there is no appropriate sampling frame whatsoever, a researcher's response is likely to be to assemble a range of partial sampling frames which collectively cover as much of the population as is practically possible. For example, in a study of some (unregulated) form of therapy, both the membership list of a relevant organisation and the local 'Yellow Pages' might be used. On occasions it may not be possible to develop lists of potential respondents from which to select a sample; recruiting a sample by advertising for volunteers is likely to generate a sample which is unrepresentative and which may exclude theoretically important types of case. However, it is worth remembering that all research respondents are in a sense volunteers; similar problems exist in surveys based on random sampling which have low response rates and in theoretical samples where the researcher's access has been severely constrained and they have not always been able to interview the respondents that they would have ideally chosen. In a research project on stepfamilies by Burgoyne and Clark (1984) the researchers were determined to approach stepfamilies rather than appeal for volunteers. A sample of volunteers was in a sense

avoided, but the level of response from the stepfamilies approached by the researchers was sufficiently low that the stepfamilies recruited were still very much self-selected.

In a study of formerly married people and ex-cohabitees (Lampard and Peggs, 1999), the sample was recruited in a variety of different ways including:

- snowball sampling (with both existing respondents and other contacts acting as starting points)
- advertisements and an article in the local press
- posters circulated to a variety of local organisations (in the hope that they would be displayed on noticeboards)
- a mail shot to some single-adult households selected from the Electoral Register
- face-to-face contacts established via organisations catering for formerly married people.

A US study of divorced mothers (Arendell, 1986) used a similar range of methods once an attempt at random sampling had proved only partially successful.

Other approaches were also considered by Lampard and Peggs, including:

- recruitment via local workplaces
- responding to advertisements in personal columns.

The latter was felt to pose ethical problems: in general methods of sampling and recruitment need to be reflected upon from an ethical perspective. For example, the possibility of targeting respondents who were known to have very recently separated from a partner would also have necessitated ethical reflection.

The aim of the sampling strategy in this study was to generate a large qualitative sample (the 'target' of 80 was overshot by one respondent), containing respondents with a diverse range of combinations of theoretically relevant characteristics, which would not necessarily be representative of the formerly married population, but which would provide an adequate level of coverage of various categories of respondent. The study aimed both to generate theory and to provide an account of the range of experiences and views of formerly married people (with specific reference to possible future couple relationships). The second and more descriptive of these aims ideally requires a sampling approach which is both theoretically driven and also encompasses adequate coverage of all those sub-groups of the population containing people with distinctive experiences and views: hence the need for a relatively large sample.

A number of important points arise from Lampard and Peggs' study. First of all, theoretical sampling may be constrained by situations where there is no straightforward sampling frame and recruitment is to a large extent dependent on locating volunteers. In this study, the original intention was to use a short questionnaire to collect information about potential interviewees, and to use this information to ensure that the sample contained adequate numbers of respondents with particular combinations of characteristics. However, by the latter stages of the fieldwork, when this sort of targeted sampling would have been useful, the researchers decided that turning away volunteers would have further extended a fieldwork period which had already over-run its allotted time-span. In addition, it was felt to be inappropriate to turn away individuals whose unique stories would inevitably be of some value regardless of whether they possessed the desired combination of characteristics. Had the target sample size been smaller the researchers would have had to have been more ruthless. Burgoyne and Clark also went to considerable trouble to achieve their target sample size of 40 (Burgoyne

and Clark, 1984: 34–6). In such circumstances the researcher should beware of reifying a somewhat arbitrary target and failing to reflect on the theoretical relevance and value of data from additional respondents. It may be more appropriate to devote time and effort to data analysis than to further data collection.

Lampard and Peggs' study also indicates that the absence of one, all-encompassing sampling frame may call for inventive recruitment methods to generate a sample which is not drawn from too narrow a segment of the population. However, ingenuity cannot perform miracles, and the range of sampling frames used will determine to some extent the range of respondents selected. While representativeness may not be an objective, researchers need to reflect on the potential impact on their theorising of the omission of some types of respondent from the sample. In the case of the study by Lampard and Peggs, the recruitment methods used might be expected to have generated few or no respondents who were not interested in talking about their situation as a formerly married person; such people could, for example, include some who left a partner and seldom think of their ex-partner or past relationship.

Many qualitative studies involve samples of fewer than 81 respondents. However, if a substantive topic is complex and there are a fair number of theoretically relevant factors involved in people's experiences, behaviour or views (e.g. gender, class, age, ethnicity, etc.), then 81 respondents may not be enough for theoretical saturation to have occurred, even if the sampling strategy was entirely theoretically driven. If you are a student who can only manage to interview half a dozen respondents within a small qualitative research project, this may fill you with alarm. However, it need not do so, as it is simply a case of making use of whatever scope you have. Theory derived from a sample containing half a dozen diverse respondents may be somewhat speculative; theory derived from a more focused sample containing half a dozen respondents who share many characteristics may be better developed but have less generalisability; but in neither case is the theory necessarily 'bad' theory. A more focused sample may be easier to theorise from precisely because some theoretically relevant factors cannot be considered.

Mason (1996) recommends a sampling strategy similar to quota sampling, with the main practical differences being, first, that the initial 'quotas' correspond to theoretically important categories of respondent and, second, that the quotas are subject to review. Flexibility in the quotas is important, as the ongoing development of theory may necessitate both quotas for new categories and also the modification of the original quotas as the relative theoretical importance of the characteristics defining the categories changes. Ongoing reviews of the sampling strategy need to take account of both the composition of the sample to date and also the developing theoretical agenda. The fundamental difference between this approach to sampling and conventional quota sampling is that the latter usually aims to generate an approximately representative sample, whereas the former aims to achieve adequate coverage of each of a range of theoretically important categories. In fact, some of the categories for which initial quotas are set are likely to correspond to factors which are often used in quota sampling, such as gender, age, etc. However, some of the other initial quotas are likely to apply to the experiences or behaviour which are of central interest to the researcher, and quotas developed as the research progresses are likely to correspond to characteristics which are specific to the research topic and which fall outside the standard range of classification variables (such as those discussed in Burgess, 1986). The existence of a quota for a category demonstrates that the researcher feels it necessary to recruit one or more respondents of the relevant type; however, quotas for characteristics like gender may be 'loose' rather than precise, i.e. quotas may specify a minimum for each sex but not demand an exact 50–50 split, since a recognition that gender is likely to be of theoretical importance, and that respondents of each sex are needed, does not logically imply that an exact gender balance is necessary.

In research on single women by Gordon (1994), theoretical sampling was explicitly used, with women being selected across the categories of a range of theoretically important dimensions:

> I interviewed women who lived alone and those who lived in a range of settings with other people (excluding cohabitation). I interviewed women from different social classes, in different employment. The women were from different ethnic groups and nationalities . . . I included lesbians as well as heterosexual women . . . Disabled women were also included (pp. 38–39).

Her sample also consisted of sub-samples from England, the United States and Finland. Patton (1990: 182) would label this as **stratified purposeful sampling**. Gordon located respondents in an eclectic fashion, and notes that 'Initial interviewees were easier to find, but as I had set the categories of women I wanted to interview, as the interviews progressed, particular types of interviewees were more difficult to find' (p. 39). She reflected on the composition of her sample and noted that its members, though in a range of jobs, tended to be better educated and better paid than average. Gordon was also aware that her methods of recruitment would have tended to exclude isolated, lonely women. Such reflection is important, as it can highlight the possible absence of theoretically important types of case from a sample.

The preceding discussion of sampling in qualitative research promotes a measured and systematic approach. However, a rigid idea of whom you want in your sample may be overturned by practical constraints; it is well worth having contingency plans and some flexibility in your research focus. Unfortunately (or sometimes fortunately), qualitative researchers do not always end up going in the substantive or theoretical direction that they initially intended to. You will also find that in many good pieces of research, as in the example that follows, there is as much or more evidence of pragmatic sampling decisions as there is of strategic theoretical sampling.

> In a classic longitudinal study of the adjustment of children and adults to divorce (Wallerstein and Kelly, 1980; Wallerstein and Blakeslee, 1989), the 60 families studied were (voluntary) clients of a divorce counselling service. The context in which the respondents were recruited might equally well be viewed as a research setting or as a convenient sampling frame. Families were selected if the children did not have a history of psychological difficulties, were not undergoing psychotherapeutic treatment, and did not have low levels of social or intellectual development. This reflected the study's theoretical objective of looking at the effects of divorce on families where the children were in some sense 'normal'. Beyond this restriction sampling was not carried out on theoretical grounds. While the researchers acknowledge the limitations of a sample drawn from a primarily white and middle-class locality in California, they do not appear to reflect upon the extent to which the generalisability of their theoretical and empirical findings is affected by the fact that their sample consisted of service clients.

The moral of the above example is that whether you are aiming for a representative sample or for theoretical saturation, the realities of real-world research mean that it is important to reflect on the idiosyncrasies of the sample that you actually obtain.

The forms of sampling mentioned in this section highlight the importance of:

- the range of cases sampled
- the kind(s) of cases sampled
- the way(s) in which the cases are sampled
- the links between theory and sampling.

While Patton (1990: 182) lists an impressive range of sampling strategies, it is the ideas behind the strategies which are important. As noted by Patton, combining different strategies may be appropriate, as, for example, in **random purposeful sampling**, in which cases are sampled at random from within theoretically determined categories.

Selecting and gaining access to a research setting and the people within it

In some qualitative studies the process of gaining access to respondents may be very similar to the way in which quantitative researchers usually get respondents to participate in a survey, i.e. entirely on an individual-by-individual basis. In surveys attention is typically paid to non-response, i.e. the failure to 'gain access to' some respondents; there is thus material of potential value to qualitative researchers in the literature on avoiding non-response.

However, in ethnographic research (and in some pieces of survey-based research) the researcher has to select a research setting (or settings), and to gain access to it (them). Where surveys take place within specific research settings, issues of access are of considerable relevance to quantitative researchers. As issues of access and non-response overlap in many ways, this section should be read in conjunction with the later section on non-response.

The process of selecting a research setting, or settings, should be theoretically driven, but will often also reflect practical issues, including access. In fact, convenience and quality of access are frequently cited in empirical studies as key reasons for the choices of research setting that were made. Furthermore, the identification of a 'fertile' research setting is sometimes the stimulus for research on a particular topic. Making a theoretically informed choice may be easier if more than one setting is being selected; the use of two or more settings immediately gives the researcher scope to make comparisons between settings which differ in theoretically important ways. Different theoretical objectives may result in radically different choices of a single setting: an educational researcher with an interest in discipline might view a school with a particularly problematic history of pupil misbehaviour as likely to be particularly informative, but conversely might wish to carry out research in a more 'typical' school. The generalisability of theory generated from research in the second school might be greater, but the validity and value of the theory developed would not necessarily depend on which of the schools was chosen. A single setting cannot be 'representative'; however, if it is particularly distinctive in some theoretically relevant way then the theory developed may be particularly context-specific.

Some important themes within the broad issue of access are power, ethics and the researcher's interpersonal and negotiating skills. Key individuals within settings may have the power to act as **gatekeepers**, i.e. they may be in a position to facilitate access or to deny it. A gatekeeper may occupy a powerful position within the setting, which may have potential implications for the researcher's relationships with less powerful people within the setting. Gatekeepers may also have the power to place constraints on the researcher's activities within the setting and on the research output. The researcher may occupy a less powerful and lower-status position within society than those within the research setting (e.g. a student researching in an elite setting such as the City, or a firm of city lawyers: see Flood, 1983), or may occupy a less vulnerable and higher-status position (e.g. an academic doing research focusing on homeless people on the streets: see Paige, 1973). The approach needed to gain access is likely to vary according to differences of this sort; the researcher needs to create a favourable impression on gatekeepers and respondents without appearing deceitful or to be acting a part. The status and visible characteristics of the researcher will inevitably facilitate access to some contexts and deny them access to others. Note that gatekeepers may be able to grant physical access to a setting and may have the power to deny the researcher access to potential respondents within the setting, but they may not be able

to guarantee the participation of other people. In addition, ethnographers are likely to want access to specific locations, events, documents, etc., as well as a range of people. Negotiating access is therefore an ongoing process which may only be partially successful.

The source of financial sponsorship for a research project may facilitate access or may arouse the suspicion of gatekeepers. Another form of **sponsor**, i.e. someone who can underwrite the researcher's good intentions, may be very useful where the researcher is new to the setting. However, it is often advantageous if the researcher has an existing connection with or role within the research setting, as this may by-pass the need for establishing trust that an outsider would have. In general, access is likely to depend on the level of trust that the researcher can generate and maintain. Assurances of anonymity and confidentiality may help; informed consent is not only necessary in ethical terms but may also reassure wary respondents. Both gatekeepers and respondents more generally are likely to show an interest in the researcher's motives for doing the research and will be more likely to help if they see the research as worthwhile. While the researcher may hope that potential respondents will be inclined to be public spirited and participate without gain to themselves, there are also obvious advantages to 'scratching respondents' backs' by making the research attractive or beneficial to them if at all possible.

The above discussion assumes that the research is **overt**; access to some research settings may only be possible if research is **covert**. Perhaps this distinction between overt and covert research is too clear-cut; arguably fully informed consent and a researcher whose motives and intentions are totally transparent are something of a rarity. Arguably, the crunch question is whether whatever needs to be revealed about the research to satisfy ethical considerations can be presented in such a way that it does not deny the researcher access to the setting or dissuade people in the setting from participating in the research. Not only may covert research be ethically questionable, but it is also likely to require that the researcher has the necessary attributes and interpersonal skills to play a role in the setting.

When negotiating access, researchers need to be able to distinguish between a situation where patience and persistence may pay off and a situation where they are banging their head against a brick wall. Sometimes access may be contingent on the deliberations of a formal Ethics Committee working to strict guidelines (this is often the case in medical sociological research; see also Delamont, 1992). A researcher can present an excellent justification for their research, appear professional and competent, be sensitive to the concerns of gatekeepers and potential respondents, guarantee confidentiality and anonymity, and still not gain access to a particular setting.

Gaining access to a particular setting is likely to pose similar problems to those experienced by researchers who have studied similar settings in the past. A literature review in the substantive area of your research can therefore give you advance warning of methodological pitfalls as well as strengthening your substantive and theoretical knowledge.

In her research on law, marriage and the reproduction of patriarchal relations, Smart (1984) interviewed people in various legal occupations. Before approaching solicitors, she gained the approval of the secretary of the local Law Society. To gain access to magistrates, she had to undergo a formal interview by the Magistrates' Courts' committee. Finally, to obtain permission to interview registrars she had to apply to the Lord Chancellor's Department, who granted permission but vetted and placed restrictions on her interview schedule. Not all the magistrates that she approached agreed to participate, highlighting the point that access to a group of people does not guarantee access to individuals. Smart notes that conveying the legitimacy and value of her research may have been crucial to her initial access, but that obtaining the time and cooperation of individuals seemed to depend on her ability to put herself across as a bona fide, high-status researcher. She recognises the not inconsiderable importance of dress in this context: 'It was also difficult to gauge whether to try to look like a probation officer, a solicitor or a stereotyped woman academic' (Smart, 1984: 153).

In their research on the process of seeking help for marital problems, Brannen and Collard (1982) recruited respondents in two ways: via a hospital marital service with which they already had links, and via practitioners working under the auspices of Marriage Guidance Councils. Recruiting respondents from the second source proved to be problematic: while the national and local Marriage Guidance Councils were relatively supportive and helpful, individual counsellors were (understandably) cautious about facilitating the researchers' access to their clients. The counsellors appeared to act as defensive gatekeepers, presumably for ethical and professional reasons. Brannen and Collard note that 'Operating through a chain of intermediaries, however cooperative and sympathetic to the research, deprives the researchers of the control necessary in meeting the requirements of systematic investigation' (p. 19). Obtaining a representative sample of clients was impossible, and the theoretically important objective of interviewing clients as early as possible in the counselling process was frustrated.

Sampling distributions

As stated earlier in the chapter, random sampling rules out the possibility that patterns in the data collected from a sample are a reflection of biases generated by the sampling method. However, such patterns could still be a reflection of sampling error rather than of underlying patterns in the population. It was suggested earlier that a larger sample size should lead to greater confidence that a finding is 'genuine' rather than due to sampling error, but how large a sample is needed before the researcher is satisfied that the observed pattern also exists in the population?

Returning to the example used earlier of a sample of women in the process of getting divorced, let us consider what we would have expected to have found in the sample if women and men were equally likely to have initiated the divorce proceedings.

- If there was no gender difference, and we selected one woman at random from the population of women getting divorced, then there would be a 50% chance that she had initiated the proceedings, and a 50% chance that her husband had.
- If we selected two women at random, the chance that both had initiated the proceedings would be 50% of 50%, i.e. 25%. The chance that neither had initiated the proceedings would also be 25% (again, 50% of 50%). The chance that one had and one had not done so would therefore be 100% − 25% − 25% = 50%.
- If we selected three women at random, the chance that all three had initiated the divorce proceedings would be 50% of 50% of 50%, or 12.5%. The chance that two had and one had not done so would be three times as big (37.5%). This is because the one who had not done so could be the first woman selected, or the second woman selected, or the third woman selected. The chances that one had done so and that none had done so would be 37.5% and 12.5% respectively.

Suppose that we took a series of samples of women in the process of getting divorced. Table 3.1 is based on the figures calculated in the above bullet points and shows graphically how frequently each possible number of 'women initiators' would occur, according to whether we took a sample of one, two or three women. A similar table corresponding to samples of four women is shown in Table 3.2. You can see that a pattern is beginning to emerge, whereby the most likely numbers of

Table 3.1 Number of women initiating the divorce proceedings

Percentage of samples	Sample size = 1		Sample size = 2			Sample size = 3			
50	*	*		*					
37.5	*	*		*			*	*	
25	*	*	*	*	*		*	*	
12.5	*	*	*	*	*	*	*	*	*
	0	1	0	1	2	0	1	2	3

Table 3.2 Number of women initiating the divorce proceedings

Percentage of samples	Sample size = 4				
37.5			*		
31.75			*		
25		*	*	*	
18.75		*	*	*	
12.5		*	*	*	
6.25	*	*	*	*	*
	0	1	2	3	4

women initiators that you would get in a sample would be numbers close to 50% of the sample size (i.e. in the case of a sample of four women, 50% × 4 = 2). Conversely, the least likely numbers of women initiators that you would get are the extreme values (all of the sample, or none of the sample).

If there was no underlying gender difference, and your sample was of 100 divorcing women, how many women initiators would you expect to find in your sample? The obvious answer is 'about 50'. You would certainly have been surprised if it had been 0 or 100 (indeed, you might have then queried whether there really was no gender difference, or whether the sample really was a random one). You might still have been surprised by 25 or 75 women initiators, but would probably have been less sceptical. In fact, Figure 3.1 shows how likely different numbers of women initiators would be to occur in a sample of 100 women, given no gender difference

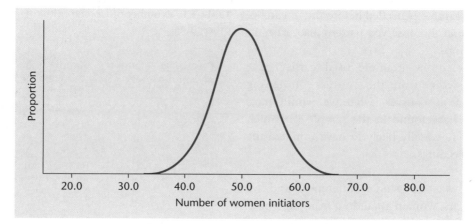

Figure 3.1 Proportion of random samples (of 100 women) which contain a given number of women initiators.

in the likelihood of initiating proceedings in the population. In effect, the figure shows what would happen if a very large number of samples of 100 women were taken, with the proportion of these samples containing a specified number of women initiators determining the height of the curve above that specified number. Figure 3.1 is an example of a frequency **distribution**; more specifically, it shows the **sampling distribution** for the number of women initiators in the sample, given that half of the women in the population initiated the divorce proceedings.

In any random sample the percentage of people with a characteristic may differ from the population percentage because of the 'noise' resulting from the chance element in the sampling process. Figure 3.1 shows the extent to which this **sampling error** is likely to result in a sample percentage which differs to a given degree from the population percentage (which is 50% in this example). Note that the distribution has a distinctive bell shape. It is similar to the distribution that would occur if the sample size was infinity rather than 100 (were such a sample size possible). The distribution in question is known as the **normal distribution** (or, less frequently, as the **Gaussian distribution**).

The curve in Figure 3.1 indicates that figures of 70 or more would occur relatively infrequently if

the percentage of women initiators in the population was 50%. Thus, for a sample size of 100, the figure of 70% given when this example was first introduced would have been unlikely to have occurred simply as a consequence of sampling error. In fact, the probability of getting a figure of 70% or more by chance depends on the height of the curve above the values from 70 upwards compared with the height of the curve above the values below 70. Hence this probability is approximately equal to the area under the curve to the right of the figure 70 as a proportion of the whole area under the curve. You can see that this probability is minuscule. In other words, there is very little chance of the figure of 70% having occurred by chance, i.e. simply as a consequence of sampling error. For a random sample, the figure of 70% could not reflect a biased sampling method either. It would therefore make sense to conclude that the figure of 70% reflected a situation in the population where women initiated divorce proceedings in more than 50% of cases.

The above echoes the logic underlying all statistical (hypothesis) testing. If you want to know whether a pattern in the data that you have collected using random sampling is of significance, you ask yourself the question 'Could it have occurred by chance?', and you then establish how likely the pattern is to have appeared (by chance) in your sample if the same pattern does not exist in the population. If the probability of the pattern having occurred by chance is low, then you conclude that it did not occur by chance, i.e. that it reflects a pattern in the population.

You might well ask how unlikely it needs to be that a pattern has occurred by chance before you conclude that it reflects something real in the population. The conventional answer is 5%, or one occasion in 20. However, this figure is arbitrary, and is simply a rule of thumb which has become reified over a long period of time. When researchers feel the need to be particularly confident that an observed pattern is not a coincidence, they sometimes adopt figures of 1%, or even 0.1% (one in a thousand). What really matters is that the more unlikely a pattern in a sample is to have occurred by chance, the more confident you can be that it genuinely reflects a pattern in the population. Certainly, patterns which happen more than 10% of the time by chance can scarcely be regarded as unusual, so using a measure of rarity greater than the standard figure of 5% is not to be recommended.

You will also, no doubt, have realised that on some occasions the unusual patterns which occur in samples are simply coincidences, i.e. a consequence of sampling error. It is by no means impossible that 70 out of 100 women in a random sample of divorcing women would have initiated the divorce proceedings, even if only half the women in the population had done so. It is, however, extremely unlikely. Despite this, it is still important to remember that statistical testing involves a small but unavoidable risk of drawing the wrong conclusion.

The above example will be considered in a more formal statistical way later in this chapter.

Beyond simple random sampling

This section considers forms of probability sampling geared towards increasing representativeness and accuracy, and towards reducing costs.

Suppose that you were carrying out a study of the satisfaction of residents in a geographical area with the local recreational facilities. In order to select a simple random sample you would need a sampling frame, e.g. a list of the people living in the area. If the locality was in the UK and you were happy to restrict attention to adults, you might use the Electoral Register, though this has some known inadequacies as a sampling frame (since it is always at least slightly out of date and a small but relatively distinctive minority of adults are missing from it).

If there were 12 000 adults in the locality and you intended to use a **sampling fraction** of 1% (i.e. to sample 1% × 12 000 = 120 adults), then you would need to obtain 120 (different) random numbers between 1 and 12 000 and to locate the corresponding 120 names, having assigned to each of the names on the Electoral Register for the locality a number between 1 and 12 000. Tables of random numbers used to be included at the back of many statistics textbooks; nowadays calculators and statistical packages on computers can often be used to generate random values between 0 and 1, which can be converted to random numbers between, say, 1 and 12 000 by multiplying them by 12 000 and rounding each of them up to the next integer (whole number).

However, generating 120 random numbers, sorting them into ascending order, and laboriously going through the list of adults looking for the 3476th person, etc., would not be much fun. An alternative approach would be to use **systematic random sampling**. In systematic random sampling a case (person) is randomly selected from the first few cases on the list and further cases are selected at equal intervals as you go down the list. In our example, a random number between 1 and 100 would be used to select the first person, and every 100th person thereafter on the list would be selected (e.g. the 34th person, the 134th person, the 234th person, etc.). Note that the **sampling interval** is the reciprocal of (i.e. 1 divided by) the sampling fraction.

Systematic random sampling can be seen to be consistent with the definition of random sampling given earlier, because the probability of each member of the population being included in the sample is known and non-zero. It often generates a lower level of sampling error and a more representative sample by ensuring that a spread of cases is selected. In our example, systematic random sampling would ensure that a few people were selected from each large street and one person was selected from each of a sub-set of smaller streets (i.e. those with less than 100 residents on the Electoral Register). However, problems can arise with systematic random sampling if the sampling interval coincides with **periodicity** in the list: for example, sampling every twelfth house along a terraced street might result in a sample containing too many (larger) end-of-terrace houses if the terrace is arranged in blocks of six houses. Fortunately, this sort of problem does not often arise.

A more sophisticated way of increasing the representativeness of a sample and reducing sampling error is **stratification**. In stratified random sampling the population is divided into a series of strata, which are known to be or thought to be relevant to the topic of the research. Random samples are then taken from within each of the strata. In relation to our example, the types of people and households living in different streets will vary in terms of age, social class, ethnicity and family structure, and hence might be expected to be interested in different forms of recreational facility. Thus we might wish to categorise the streets in the research locality into different types, and to take separate random samples from each group of streets. In practice it would make sense to list all the people in the first group of streets, followed by all the people in the second group of streets, and so on, and to select the sample using systematic random sampling applied to the reordered list of names.

The sample obtained would by definition have the right balance of people from each sort of street. Furthermore, since the likelihood of some sources of sampling error (e.g. a sample containing a disproportionately large number of retired people) would have been reduced, the findings would be more precise. This, however, assumes that people in different types of street do feel differently about recreational facilities, and that the categorisation of streets distinguishes adequately between these types of street. Clearly, in order to use **stratified random sampling,** a researcher needs to have enough information about the population to divide it into strata, and the variables used to divide the population into strata must relate to the topic of interest for this form of sampling to improve the precision of the results. The researcher thus needs prior knowledge both about the population and about the topic. Stratification has the additional benefit that it ensures the correct balance of cases across the strata; this is important if the researcher wishes to carry out more focused analyses of one or more of the strata. (See the later section on adjusting for non-response for a description of post-stratification.)

Suppose that the recreational facilities study involved short interviews with the respondents. There would certainly be time and financial costs involved in visiting them all. However, the costs would be much greater if the study focused on the whole of a large city rather than on a small locality, even if the sample size was the same, since the sample would then be spread over a greater geographical area. One solution would be to restrict attention to a random sample of areas within the city. So, rather than five or so people being interviewed in each of a couple of dozen areas, 20 people would be interviewed in each of six, randomly selected areas. This kind of approach is known as **multi-stage sampling,** because it involves selecting **primary sampling units,** and then selecting sub-samples from within each of those units. It is also known as **cluster sampling,** as the sample consists of a series of clusters of cases, one cluster within each primary sampling unit.

A common form of multi-stage sampling is the selection of one individual from within each of a sample of households. In this form of sampling, a sampling frame consisting of a list of addresses can be used and a list of individuals' names is thus not needed; the selection of an individual from each household is achieved by the interviewer listing the individuals in the household and selecting one via a pre-determined approach: for example, via a Kish grid (see Hoinville *et al.*, 1977: 82).

Cluster sampling has the further advantage that a full sampling frame is only needed for those primary sampling units which are included in the sample. This is very helpful where a sampling frame has to be constructed by the researcher, or where access to the sampling frame has to be negotiated separately within each primary sampling unit. However, cluster sampling usually increases sampling error and reduces precision. This is because the sample is not representative of people in those primary sampling units which are not included in the sample. For example, in the recreational facilities study, by deliberately restricting the spread of areas in the city from which we drew our sample, we would inevitably have a sample that was less representative of the city as a whole, and our results would probably be less precise. However, the results would not be biased, so long as the areas covered in the sample had been chosen at random. It is also worth noting that cluster sampling reduces the precision of findings for a given sample size, but that savings in time and costs could be funnelled into a larger sample size, which would increase precision. The similarity between individuals within each cluster also has implications for the statistical modelling of data from cluster samples, with more complex techniques being needed to take account of this (e.g. multi-level modelling: see Chapter 9).

You may have already realised that it would be sensible to use stratified random sampling to select the areas of the city to be studied, as it would make sense, for example, to have a balance of more and less fashionable areas, and possibly also to have a geographical spread of areas to take account of their proximity to centralised recreational facilities. Stratified random sampling could also be used to make sure that respondents were selected from different types of street within each of the areas. Stratifying at each level within multi-stage sampling is likely to increase the precision of the findings. By maximising the number of clusters and

hence minimising the number of respondents in each cluster the researcher can reduce the negative effect of cluster sampling on the precision of the findings, given that this effect occurs because of the tendency of individuals within a cluster to be similar to each other, with bigger clusters therefore containing a greater number of relatively homogeneous individuals (Moser and Kalton, 1971: 105).

Multi-stage sampling when primary sampling units vary in size

We now move on to a larger-scale example. Suppose that a researcher was carrying out a study of experiences of urban life in big cities. The researcher might decide to sample one person in 10 000 from the cities within a simple random sample of five out of the 20 biggest cities (judged in terms of population) in Great Britain. The only problem would be that, since about 40% of the people living in the 20 biggest cities in Britain live in London, either more than three-quarters of the people in the sample would be from London, or none of them would be from London. Neither of these samples would be very representative. This problem reflects the fact that primary sampling units, as in this example, often vary in size. The solution is to definitely include London as one of the primary sampling units selected, but to compensate for this by reducing the sampling fraction for people living within London. Since the probability of London being included in the sample would have risen from 5/20 = 0.25 to 1, i.e. by a factor of 4, the sampling fraction would have to drop from one in 10 000 to one in 40 000. Since the probabilities of inclusion for the other 19 cities would decrease, the sampling fractions for the other cities selected would have to slightly increase, with the overall aim being to ensure that people in each city had the same chance of being included in the sample, i.e. one in 40 000.

More generally, the usual approach to dealing with primary sampling units which vary in size is to sample them with **probability proportional to**

size (**PPS sampling**). For example, as Birmingham is more than three times as big as Coventry, its probability of inclusion would be more than three times as big as well. The average probability of inclusion is the sampling fraction, which in our example is 5/20 = 0.25. Since London would definitely be included, the average probability of inclusion for other cities would be 4/19 = 0.21. Birmingham, which is larger than the average for the 19 cities outside London, would have a probability of inclusion of 0.33, whereas Coventry, which is smaller than average, would have a probability of inclusion of 0.10. Note that PPS sampling can be used in combination with stratified random sampling and systematic random sampling. In this case the cities might be stratified according to geographical region, and listed stratum by stratum, with the sample being selected using systematic random sampling starting with a random number between 0 and 1, using a sampling interval of 1, and taking into account the probability of inclusion of each city.

Note that the use of different sampling fractions within each primary sampling unit means that the size of the sub-sample within each primary sampling unit is the same for all those primary sampling units which did not have a probability of inclusion of 1. In our example, 200 people would be selected from London, and 75 from each of the other four cities selected. The possibility that the sample would be distorted by being dominated by Londoners has thus been avoided. PPS sampling is likely to improve the precision of results because it removes the possibility that the sample will be distorted by the inclusion of an excessive number of people from a large primary sampling unit.

In most situations none of the primary sampling units will have a probability of inclusion of 1, i.e. none will be guaranteed inclusion in the sample. If this is the case, then the same number of people will be chosen from within each of the primary sampling units selected. This can have practical advantages: for example, if one interviewer is assigned to each primary sampling unit selected, the interviewers will have the same number of inter-

views to carry out. Perhaps more importantly, a standardised number of people enhances the potential to usefully examine each primary sampling unit separately. In our example, the sub-sample size for Coventry, if Coventry was included, would be 75 using PPS sampling but only 30 otherwise.

Unequal inclusion probabilities and weighting

In the various forms of random sampling discussed so far all the members of the population have an equal chance of inclusion in the sample. However, an equal chance of selection is not a necessary condition for unbiased results. Consider the last example, where a sample of 500 people would contain 200 from London and 75 from each of four other cities. It might be preferable from a researcher's point of view to have 100 people from each of the five cities, if the findings for each city are going to be examined separately, as well as being combined to give an overall picture. However, only sampling 100 people from London would give Londoners a markedly smaller probability of inclusion in the sample than people from the other cities, and this would mean that the views of Londoners were under-represented.

The solution to this problem is to **weight** the findings at the analysis stage, in order to take account of the unequal chances of inclusion in the sample of people from different cities.

- Suppose that 60% of Londoners enjoy city life, as opposed to 40% of the population in other cities. This would mean that, across all the cities (60% × 40%) + (40% × 60%) = 48% of people enjoy urban life.
- If the findings in the sample mirrored the underlying pattern in each of the cities exactly, and 100 people were sampled from each of the five cities chosen, the percentage of people who would be found to enjoy urban life would be {(100 × 60%) + (400 × 40%)}/500 = 44%, i.e. 4% too low.

- However, we know that in such a sample Londoners are under-represented by a factor of 2 (200/100), whereas people from other cities are over-represented by a factor of 1.333 (100/75). You may be able to see that it makes intuitive sense to multiply the results for Londoners by 2, and to divide the results for people from other cities by 1.333 (or, equivalently, to multiply them by 0.75).
- If we do this, our formula for the percentage of people enjoying urban life becomes $\{(2 \times 100 \times 60\%) + (0.75 \times 400 \times 40\%)\}/500 = 48\%$.

The values of 2 and 0.75 are weights, and the process of using them to correct for unequal chances of inclusion in the sample is known as **weighting**.

Quite frequently there is a sub-group of the population (e.g. unemployed people, disabled people, etc.) in which a researcher is particularly interested, but which only forms a small proportion of the population. Over-sampling that sub-group (i.e. giving its members a greater chance of inclusion in the sample) can be counterbalanced by weighting at the analysis stage. There are also situations in which allowing the chance of inclusion in the sample to vary between members of different sub-groups of the population may increase the precision of research findings. Such situations arise when some of the sub-groups are more homogeneous in composition than others. For example, if a researcher wished to estimate the average level of alcohol consumption per week among British adults, it would make sense to over-sample men and under-sample women, since not only is the average level of alcohol consumption higher for men than for women but levels of alcohol consumption are also more varied among men. (It also makes sense to under-sample sub-groups of the population if they are more expensive to interview than average, as the loss of precision through under-representing these sub-groups will be more than compensated for by the increase in sample size that can be achieved by spending the money saved on interviewing more people in the other sub-groups.)

Using PPS sampling and varying the probabilities of inclusion of members of different sub-groups according to how homogeneous the sub-groups are both require information about the characteristics of sub-groups of the population (how large they are; how homogeneous they are). This information may not be available to the researcher, but, if the researcher is able to make reasonable estimates of these pieces of information, then precision will probably still be improved by integrating the information into the sample design.

As you will realise by now, once a researcher goes beyond simple random sampling to more sophisticated forms of random sampling, the precision of the research findings is very much dependent on the sample design, with, for example, cluster sampling reducing precision and stratification increasing precision. The effect of the sample design on sampling error is often quantified in the form of **design effects**, or **Deffs**. Design effects are simply multiplicative factors which indicate the extent to which the sample design has increased or decreased the precision of the research findings.

A Deff compares the variance of a quantity estimated using a sample of a given design with the variance of the same quantity estimated using a simple random sample of the same size. The precision of estimates is usually assessed in terms of standard deviations, where the standard deviation is the square root of the variance. Hence, it is the square root of a Deff which is of primary interest. For example, an estimated percentage, which if derived from a simple random sample could be assumed to be within 1% of the population percentage, could only be assumed to be within 1.5% of the population percentage if it was derived instead from a sample with a more complex design which had a Deff of 2.25 (since the square root of 2.25 is 1.5). Alternatively, a Deff can be viewed as the negative effect of the sample design on the effective sample size; a Deff of 2.25 would thus indicate that for a particular finding the effective sample size was less than half of the actual sample size.

An example of a survey which used a relatively complex sample design is the National Survey of Sexual Attitudes and Lifestyles, henceforth referred to as NATSAL (Wadsworth *et al.*, 1993; Johnson *et al.*, 1994). This survey, famous as 'the survey that Mrs Thatcher tried to ban', aimed to collect data on sexual behaviour from a representative sample of British adults aged 16–59, which could be used to improve researchers' understanding of the spread of HIV in the population and to inform health education strategies. The sampling frame used was the small users' Postcode Address File (PAF), because its coverage is better than that of the Electoral Register and it is less likely to systematically under-represent particular types of people (Lynn and Lievesley, 1992).

The sample design reflected work carried out in a pilot/feasibility study. NATSAL used multi-stage, stratified sampling; the primary sampling units (PSUs) were wards, which were stratified by region, population density, age structure and male unemployment level (using Census data). Wards were selected using PPS sampling, with probability proportional to the number of PAF delivery points. In total 750 wards were selected, and a cluster of either 50 or 100 addresses was chosen from each ward using a variant of systematic random sampling (which sampled addresses at intervals of 14 addresses). An eligible individual was selected from each address using a variant of the Kish grid (Hoinville *et al.*, 1977: 82). Since sampling addresses meant that individuals in small households were more likely to be included in the sample, to take account of this the data were weighted at the analysis stage by the size of the household. Design effects corresponding to the various findings relating to sexual behaviour were largely in the range 1.10 to 1.30 (with the negative effects of the clustering within the sample and of the over-sampling of individuals within small households outweighing the gains achieved through stratification).

Measures of location, measures of spread and the sample mean

This section continues our consideration of sampling distributions, and looks at the situation where we want to use a sample to estimate the average value in the population of some characteristic or other. To illustrate this, let us consider some data relating to the ages at marriage (in months) of a simple random sample of 105 female graduates marrying for the first time in the 1980s (in Britain). Note that age at marriage is an interval-level characteristic (see the discussion of levels of measurement in Chapter 9). Figure 3.2 is a bar chart showing the frequencies of various ages at marriage in the sample (the ages mainly being aggregated into two-year bands). Note that very few of the sample married at an age of less than 21, that the bulk of the sample married at ages between 21 and 28 inclusive, and that a small and diminishing number of the female graduates married at ages of 29 or above. The sample suggests that the distribution of ages at marriage in the population is **skewed**, i.e. that the frequency of marriage rises steeply with increasing age until it peaks at around age 23 or 24, and then falls more gradually thereafter, leading to a 'tail' of marriages at higher ages (as in Figure 3.3). A skewed distribution where the tail is to the right is said to be **positively skewed**, and one where the tail is to the left is said to be **negatively skewed**. (Note that it makes theoretical sense for the distribution in the population to be positively skewed; graduates who were university students between the ages of 18 and 21 are unlikely to have married at an age of less than 21, whereas there is no obvious upper bound for age at marriage.)

If we are interested in what the sample can tell us about the 'average' age at marriage of female graduates, then we need a summary **measure of location** for the ages in the sample. Perhaps the most straightforward choice for the 'typical' age at marriage is obtained by putting the 105 ages into ascending order of magnitude and selecting the value of the middle, or 53rd, case. This measure is

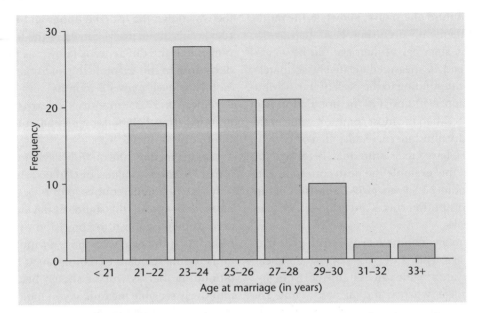

Figure 3.2 Ages at marriage of female graduates marrying for the first time in the 1980s ($N = 105$).

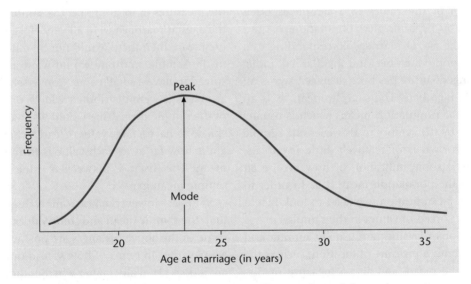

Figure 3.3 Possible frequency distribution (in the population) for age at marriage of female graduates marrying for the first time in the 1980s.

known as the **median**, and in this example is 303 months (25 years and 3 months). An almost equally obvious approach is to average the ages by summing them and dividing the total by the number of female graduates. This measure is known as the (arithmetic) **mean**, and is the measure most frequently use in statistical analyses. In this example the mean is 308.18 months (just over 25 years and

8 months). A third alternative, known as the **mode**, is the most frequently occurring age at marriage. In this example, since age at marriage can be viewed as a scale, and is measured relatively accurately, the value corresponding to the peak of the distribution which appears to exist in the population is of more relevance than the most common value in the sample. A distribution curve like that shown in Figure 3.3 is referred to as **unimodal**, because it has one peak. In this example the peak corresponds to a value of about 23.5 years (282 months). On rare occasions distribution curves are **bimodal**, i.e. they have two peaks.

You will notice that the mean age is higher than the median age. This is the case because the mean is pulled upwards by the values in the tail of higher ages at marriage, whereas the median is not. The mean uses information from all the sample members, which is a good thing, but is susceptible to distortion by extreme values (often referred to as **outliers**), which is not such a good thing.

The mean of the values in a sample is often represented by a specific piece of notation, $\bar{x}$. The x represents the age at marriage corresponding to a particular sample member, and the 'flat hat' indicates that this quantity has been averaged across all the sample members. The **sample mean**, $\bar{x}$, is an *estimate* of the **population mean**, which is usually represented by the symbol μ. However, the sample mean on its own is of relatively little use to us; we also need some indication of how precise an estimate of the population mean it is. In order to obtain such an indication, we need to look first at the range or spread of values in the sample.

Distributions of values are usually summarised in terms of both a measure of location, such as the median or the mean, and also a **measure of dispersion**, i.e. a measure of spread. The most obvious measure of spread is the **range**, which in this case is 245 months (or 20 years 5 months). However, this range clearly says very little about the values corresponding to the bulk of the cases. A better measure is obtained by listing the values in descending order of magnitude, and looking at the difference between the values a quarter and three-quarters of

the way down the list (the **upper** and **lower quartiles**). This difference is known as the **interquartile range**; half the difference is known as the **quartile deviation**. In this example the interquartile range is 54.5 (just over 4 years 6 months) and the quartile deviation is 27.25 months (just over 2 years 3 months). Thus half of the values fall into a range of values of less than 5 years.

Like the median, the quartile deviation is not distorted by extreme values, or outliers. However, it is only useful for descriptive purposes. A different measure of spread, the **standard deviation**, can be used to help establish the precision of the sample mean. As is the case with many formulae, the formula for the standard deviation can at first sight be off-putting, but as will be shown below, it is an intuitively sensible measure if you look at the steps represented by the formula.

STEP 1: The first step is to consider the ages at marriage in a sample as being spread around one of the measures of location, i.e. the sample mean $\bar{x}$. If the ages at marriage were all very close to the sample mean, then there would not be much variation in the sample, and one would want a measure of spread to have a small value. Conversely, if the ages at marriage were distributed widely on either side of the sample mean, one would want a measure of spread to have a large value. Clearly what is important is how far away each value is from the sample mean. The distance between a value, x, and the sample mean is $x - \bar{x}$.

STEP 2: However, since some values are bigger than the sample mean and some values are smaller, some of the above distances are positive and some are negative. In terms of how spread out the values are it does not really matter whether they are bigger than the sample mean or smaller than the sample mean, so what we are really interested in is the difference between a value and the sample mean, rather than whether this is positive or negative. The distance between each value and the sample mean, $x - \bar{x}$, can be either negative or positive, but we can convert the distance into a positive value for each case simply by ignoring the minus sign if $x - \bar{x}$ is negative. For example, 320 − 308.18 would stay as 1.82, but 302 − 308.18 would become 6.18 instead of −6.18.

Unfortunately, making all the distances positive in this way turns out to be a mathematical dead end. However, various other statistical techniques are based on the calculation of (sums of) squared differences; hence it is better to make all the distances positive by squaring them, i.e. by multiplying each distance by itself (bearing in mind that a negative number multiplied by a negative number gives a positive number). Each squared difference can now be represented by $(x − \bar{x})^2$.

STEP 3: In order to summarise the amount of spread for all the values in the sample you simply sum this quantity across all the sample members. This summation process is represented by the symbol Σ, meaning 'sum of'. So the overall amount of spread in the sample is equal to $\Sigma(x − \bar{x})^2$.

STEP 4: If we want our measure of spread to show how far away from the mean a typical value is, we need to divide the amount of spread by the number of people in the sample, n. This gives us $\Sigma(x − \bar{x})^2/n$. This quantity is known as the **variance**.

STEP 5: However, we squared the distances to make negative distances positive, so the variance is based on squared distances. In order to get back to something akin to straightforward distance, we take the square root of the variance (you may wish to think of this as 'unsquaring'). This process is represented by the symbol $\sqrt{\ }$. The quantity obtained by taking the square root of the variance is $\sqrt{\Sigma(x − \bar{x})^2/n}$.

In fact, for technical reasons, the formula for the **sample standard deviation** (usually given the label s) is marginally different from the formula given above, with the sample size n being replaced by $(n − 1)$. This is to ensure that the sample standard deviation is an **unbiased estimate** of the **population standard deviation**, since using n would on average result in an estimate of the standard deviation in the population which was somewhat too small. The population standard deviation,

usually represented by the symbol σ, has the formula $\sqrt{\Sigma(x − \mu)^2/n}$, since it summarises the spread of values in the population around the population mean, μ.

In our example, the sample standard deviation is 38.09 months, or just over 3 years and 2 months. Like the mean, the standard deviation can be distorted by outliers. In this case, the highest value of 477 months (39 years 9 months) is markedly higher than the next highest value (though arguably not enough to make it a true outlier). If this value was excluded, the sample standard deviation would drop to 34.43, or just over 2 years and 10 months. Two useful rules of thumb are that about two-thirds of values are within a standard deviation of the mean (in either direction), but that only about one in 20 cases are more than two standard deviations away from the mean. In this example 75 (71%) of cases are within a standard deviation of the sample mean, and 3 (3%) of cases are more than two standard deviations away from the sample mean.

Calculating the standard deviation of three ages at marriage

Values (x) = 246, 288 and 372
Mean (μ) = (246 + 288 + 372)/3 = 302

STEP 1: $(x − \mu)$	
	246 − 302 = −56
	288 − 302 = −14
	372 − 302 = 70

STEP 2: $(x − \mu)^2$	
	$(−56)^2 = 3136$
	$(−14)^2 = 196$
	$(70)^2 = 4900$

STEP 3: $\Sigma(x − \mu)^2$ 3136 + 196 + 4900 = 8232

STEP 4: $\Sigma(x − \mu)^2/n$ 8232/3 = 2744

STEP 5: $\sqrt{\Sigma(x − \mu)^2/n}$ $\sqrt{2744}$ = 52.4

The standard deviation of the three values is therefore 52.4.

Distributions of sample means

We know that, as a consequence of sampling error, the sample mean of 308.18 in our main age at marriage example is almost certainly different from the mean in the population. The difficulty is that we do not know by how much the sample mean differs from the population mean. We can, however, establish a range of values into which the difference between the two means is very likely to fall, and thus can use the sample mean together with this range of values corresponding to its imprecision to establish a range of values within which we can have some confidence that the population mean lies.

So, how accurate can a sample mean be expected to be? It is fairly easy to show that the level of precision must be dependent on the sample size. Consider a (relatively easy) examination where 10% of the candidates score full marks (100%), and the population mean score is, say, 85. A sample mean based on a sample containing a single candidate is quite likely to be 100; in fact there is a 10% chance that it will be so. However, a sample mean based on a sample containing two candidates is much less likely to be 100, since both candidates in the sample would need to have scored 100 (the chance of which is 10% × 10% = 1%). If we had a sample size of 6, the chance of the sample mean being 100 would be one in a million. In general, as sample size increases, the chance of getting a sample mean which is a long way from the population mean decreases, and the chance of getting one which is close to the population mean correspondingly increases.

Note that it is sample size that matters in the context of the precision of survey findings, rather than the proportion of the population which is sampled. This is an unfortunate fact for small countries conducting national surveys; in order to produce findings of a given accuracy Luxembourg needs national surveys of the same size that France needs. Note also that the precision of findings from surveys where a large proportion of the population is sampled is dependent on a correcting factor called the **finite population correction (fpc)**. So long as the sampling fraction is no more than 10% this correction can be safely ignored (Moser and Kalton, 1971). The fpc takes account of the fact that as the sample size approaches the size of the population, sampling error must logically diminish to zero.

It is even simpler to show that the precision of the sample mean depends on the spread of values in the sample. Consider a population in which everyone married at 25 years of age, i.e. in which the spread of values was minimal (zero). The mean age at marriage in a sample from this population would necessarily be 25 years. Consider a second population in which everyone married at an age of between 24 and 26 years. The mean for a sample from this population would necessarily be somewhere in the range 24 to 26 years. However, in a sample drawn from the British population, in which people marry at any age from 16 years upwards, the mean could take on a much wider range of values. More generally, the greater the spread of values in the population, the less accurate a sample mean is likely to be.

Consider now a situation where samples are repeatedly taken from a population and the sample mean is calculated for each sample. Just as we can look at the distribution of values in a sample, we can similarly look at the distribution of sample means obtained from this succession of samples. What is the most likely value for a sample mean to take? Given a large enough sample size, you will not be surprised to hear that the answer is the population mean. What sort of distribution do the sample means have? This is more surprising. Again, given a big enough sample size, the sample means would be more or less **normally distributed**, i.e. they would have an approximately **normal distribution**, as illustrated in Figure 3.4. (For completeness, note that for a small sample size the sample means would have a slightly different distribution, a *t*-distribution.)

The normal distribution, which was mentioned earlier in the chapter, is one of the great natural phenomena within statistics. It does not matter

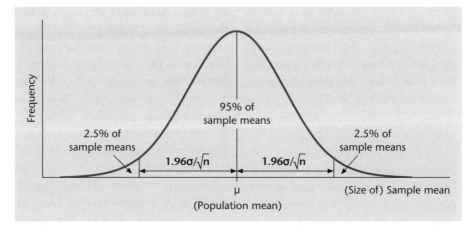

Figure 3.4   Frequency distribution for sample means (given a large enough sample size).

whether we consider sample means for samples taken from a population with a distribution of values like that in Figure 3.3, or from a population with an even more skewed distribution, or even from a population with a bimodal distribution, the distribution of sample means will almost certainly be close to being a unimodal and symmetric normal distribution as long as the sample size is large enough (say over 50, or perhaps even over 30).

The **central limit theorem**, of which the above result is a part, also relates the spread of values in the distribution of sample means to the spread of values in the population. Specifically, the theorem says that the **standard deviation** of the sample means, often referred to as the **standard error**, is equal to $\sigma/\sqrt{n}$, where σ is the population standard deviation and n is the sample size. This formalises the relationship between the precision of the sample mean, the spread of values in the population and the sample size, the existence of which was predicted by the earlier discussion.

Confidence intervals

One of the properties of a normal distribution is that 95% of the values lie within 1.96 standard deviations of the mean. Thus, in the distribution of

sample means shown in Figure 3.4, 95% of the sample means are within 1.96 standard errors ($\sigma/\sqrt{n}$) of the population mean μ. Conversely, 5% of the sample means (those in the 'tails' at either end of the curve) are more than 1.96 standard errors away from the population mean μ.

The above can be written as a formula as follows. Given a large enough sample size, in 95% of samples the following is true:

$$\mu - 1.96\left(\frac{\sigma}{\sqrt{n}}\right) < \bar{x} < \mu + 1.96\left(\frac{\sigma}{\sqrt{n}}\right) \quad \text{(Equation 1)}$$

This equation can be rearranged to focus on the difference between the sample mean and the population mean. Thus, in 95% of cases:

$$-1.96\left(\frac{\sigma}{\sqrt{n}}\right) < \bar{x} - \mu < 1.96\left(\frac{\sigma}{\sqrt{n}}\right)$$

Thus, from the above, we have a level of precision for the sample mean, i.e. $1.96(\sigma/\sqrt{n})$, which applies 95% of the time. The equation can also be rearranged to focus on the population mean, μ. In 95% of cases:

$$\bar{x} - 1.96\left(\frac{\sigma}{\sqrt{n}}\right) < \mu < \bar{x} + 1.96\left(\frac{\sigma}{\sqrt{n}}\right)$$

Thus we can specify an interval that we can be 95% confident includes the population mean, i.e. a **95%**

confidence interval. The only problem is that in practice we do not usually know what the population standard deviation, σ, is. The solution is to use the sample standard deviation, s, as an estimate of σ. Thus the 95% confidence interval for the population mean that is used in practice is

$$\bar{x} - 1.96\left(\frac{s}{\sqrt{n}}\right) < \mu < \bar{x} + 1.96\left(\frac{s}{\sqrt{n}}\right)$$

In our age at marriage example, $\bar{x}$ is equal to 308.18, s is equal to 38.09 and n is equal to 105, so $(s/\sqrt{n})$ is equal to 3.72 and the relevant interval is thus 300.89 to 315.47, sometimes written as (300.89, 315.47). Thus, on the basis of our sample, we can be 95% confident that the population mean age at marriage for female graduates marrying for the first time in the 1980s is between just under 25 years 1 month (301 months) and just over 26 years 3 months (315 months).

The choice of 95% as a level of confidence is arbitrary, and reflects the conventional pre-eminence of 5% as a quantification of rareness. There is no reason why another figure should not be used; all that happens to the above equations is that the figure of 1.96 is replaced by a different value. So, for example, if a researcher wanted a 99% confidence interval, i.e. wanted to be even more confident that the population mean lay in the stated interval, 1.96 would need to be replaced by 2.58. This reflects the fact that in a normal distribution 99% of the values lie within 2.58 standard deviations of the mean.

Null hypotheses and significance testing

Suppose that we have a theory that the mean age at marriage of female graduates marrying for the first time in the 1980s is different from the mean age at marriage for all women marrying for the first time in the 1980s, which is known to be 280.82 months (just under 23 years and 5 months). We can attempt to show that this theory may be the case by testing the hypothesis that the two means

are the same, i.e. by testing the **null hypothesis** that the mean age at marriage of female graduates is the same as that for all women. Null hypotheses are hypotheses that allow us to confirm our **research hypotheses** by rejecting the alternative possibility, which is typically that there is no difference between groups, no relationship, etc. This makes the assumption that our research hypotheses are usually going to be that there *is* a difference, *is* a relationship, etc.

The way in which the null hypothesis can be tested is by calculating how likely it is that our sample mean would have differed from the suggested population mean (henceforth labelled k) by as much as it does or more, given that the suggested population mean was correct. In other words, we consider whether the difference between $\bar{x}$ and k (the suggested value for μ), is too big to have plausibly occurred by chance. In our example the difference $\bar{x} - k$ is 308.18 − 280.82, i.e. 27.36. As was shown earlier, the precision of the sample mean, i.e. the amount that it varies because of sampling error, is dependent on the standard error, $\sigma/\sqrt{n}$, so we adjust the difference between the sample mean and the suggested population mean to take account of this. This gives us a **z-statistic**, which thus has the following formula:

$$z = \frac{\bar{x} - k}{\sigma/\sqrt{n}}$$

It can be shown by rearranging Equation 1 that if the suggested population mean, k, is equal to the actual population mean, μ, then in 95% of samples z will lie in the interval −1.96 to +1.96. Hence, if z lies outside this range of values, either an unusual event has occurred, i.e. the difference between the sample mean and the suggested population mean is quite large, by chance, because of sampling error, or the assumption that k is equal to μ must be wrong. Given a choice between concluding that an event which would occur less than 5% of the time by chance has occurred and concluding that the null hypothesis is incorrect, the convention is to reject the null hypothesis and accordingly draw the conclusion that $\mu \neq k$. Conversely, if z lies within the specified range of values, then the observed difference between $\bar{x}$ and k is quite likely to have occurred by chance, and the convention is therefore to accept the null hypothesis that $\mu = k$, i.e. that, in our example, the population mean for female graduates is the same as the population mean for all women.

Once again, in practice the researcher does not know the value of the population standard deviation, σ, so the sample standard deviation, s, has to be used as an estimate of it. Thus, for our example:

$$z = \frac{308.18 - 280.82}{38.09/\sqrt{105}} = \frac{27.36}{3.72} = 7.35.$$

Since the above value of z is much greater than 1.96, we reject the (null) hypothesis that the mean age at marriage of female graduates was the same as the mean age at marriage for all women marrying for the first time in the 1980s. Note that this z-test produces the same result as can be obtained by checking whether the suggested population mean of 280.82 lies within the 95% confidence interval. (This reflects the fact that the z-test and the confidence interval are based on the same equation; hence it is not surprising that when z is greater than 1.96 or less than -1.96 the suggested population mean lies outside the confidence interval, and vice versa.) Both the above z-test and the confidence interval have the same objective, i.e. establishing whether a given value could plausibly be the population mean.

The above z-test is an example of a **significance test**. The sample mean can be said to be **significantly different** from the suggested population mean, with the measure of rareness used, 5%, being the **significance level**. The term 'significance' here refers to statistical significance; a statistically significant finding is one which is unlikely to have occurred by chance, given the null hypothesis.

Statistical significance is not necessarily the same as sociological or **substantive significance**. The difference of over two years between the sample mean for female graduates and the mean for all women suggests that there is a sociologically interesting difference between graduates and other

women. However, while a difference of one month would have been much less interesting in sociological terms, such a difference could have been found to have been statistically significant if the sample size had been large enough. Very large samples can identify the existence of patterns in data which are of negligible substantive importance, i.e. statistically significant findings may be of negligible substantive significance.

It is important to note that a statistically significant result does not **prove** that the null hypothesis is wrong and that the research hypothesis is correct. If the significance level is 5%, then, by definition, there is a 5% chance that even if the null hypothesis is, in fact, correct, we will reject it anyway. This is known as a **Type I error**. Conversely, if the null hypothesis is, in fact, wrong and the research hypothesis is correct, we may not reject the null hypothesis since the data from the sample, while consistent with the research hypothesis, may also be consistent with the null hypothesis. This situation, which is known as a **Type II error**, often arises as the result of the sample size being too small to confirm the existence of a weak pattern or relationship in the population. The **power** of a statistical test is the probability that it will correctly identify that the null hypothesis is incorrect, which is equivalent to the probability that a Type II error is avoided. A bigger sample is more likely to allow the existence of patterns in the population to be verified, i.e. significance tests performed on bigger samples have greater power.

Note also that the above significance test is an example of a **two-tailed** test. This is because the research hypothesis was that the mean age at marriage of female graduates differed from the mean age at marriage for all women. Clearly, 'differed' could mean either 'was greater than' or 'was less than'. However, we might instead have hypothesised that the mean age at marriage of female graduates was greater than that for all women. This would have been a sensible hypothesis given how easy it is to come up with an explanation for that sort of difference, i.e. it seems reasonable to assume that post-compulsory education used to get in the way of marriage for quite a long time in the case of female graduates. Testing this **one-tailed** hypothesis differs from the earlier z-test only in as much as the z-statistic would need to be compared with a single value of 1.65 rather than with both −1.96 and 1.96. You will notice that it is easier to get a statistically significant result in a one-tailed test of the significance of a given value, since the z-statistic only has to exceed 1.65 rather than 1.96. Two-tailed tests are more cautious, as they correspond to a research hypothesis that does not rely on the researcher's assumptions about the direction of the difference that is being tested for significance. (Two-tailed tests and one-tailed tests owe their names to the 'tails' of the (normal) distribution; the former take account of the extreme values at both ends of a distribution, whereas the latter only take account of the extreme values at one end.)

Returning to the z-test in our example, the z-statistic produced is much bigger than 1.96, and indicates that the sample mean is 7.35 standard errors greater than the suggested population mean. We know from the above that the probability of getting a z-statistic of 7.35 by chance, i.e. if the null hypothesis is true, is less than 5%. But precisely how likely is it that as big a value as 7.35 would have been obtained if the suggested population mean was correct? The answer is provided by identifying the **P-value** (short for probability value) corresponding to values which are 7.35 standard deviations or more away from the mean of a normal distribution. In fact, the relevant P-value is 0.000000. There is thus less than a one in a million chance that a sample mean of 308.18 would have been obtained if the null hypothesis was correct and the population mean for female graduates was 280.82.

A z-test of a proportion

At this point we can return to the example discussed earlier in the chapter involving a sample of women in the process of getting divorced. The null hypothesis in this example is that divorce pro-

ceedings were initiated by women half of the time (i.e. in 50% of cases). If cases where the woman initiated the divorce proceedings are assigned a score of 1, and those where the husband initiated the divorce proceedings are assigned a score of 0, then the suggested population mean, k (given the null hypothesis), is 0.5. In the sample, 70% of the women had initiated the divorce proceedings, so the sample mean ($\bar{x}$) is 0.7. The sample size (n) is 100, and the sample standard deviation can be calculated using the formula $s = \sqrt{k(1 - k)}$, and is therefore $\sqrt{0.25} = 0.5$. The z-statistic for this example is therefore as follows:

$$z = \frac{0.7 - 0.5}{0.5/\sqrt{100}} = \frac{0.2}{0.05} = 4.0.$$

A z-statistic as big as this is not only bigger than 1.96 but also has a P-value of 0.00006. In other words, there is less than a one in 15 000 chance that a sample mean of 0.7 would have occurred by chance if the suggested population mean of 0.5 was correct. The sample mean of 0.7 is thus significantly bigger than the suggested figure of 0.5, i.e. the difference between the sample proportion and the suggested population proportion is statistically significant.

How big can the P-value become before a finding is not statistically significant? The answer is 0.05, the ubiquitous 5%. If a z-statistic is bigger than 1.96 (or less than −1.96), its P-value is less than 0.05. If a z-statistic is between −1.96 and 1.96, its P-value is greater than 0.05. If z is equal to 1.96 or to −1.96, its P-value is exactly 0.05. P-values are a much more general phenomenon than the z-statistic; we will discover later in this book that the value of any statistic used in significance testing has a corresponding P-value. Basically, the P-value is the probability that a finding or pattern as distinctive as the one observed would have occurred by chance given some null hypothesis. Since researchers are forever asking the question 'Could this interesting finding in my sample have occurred by chance, or is it a genuine reflection of a pattern in the population?', the P-value is a key phenomenon in quantitative social research.

Note that the normal distribution is applicable in this last example because the sample size is fairly large; the relevant distribution for tests of proportions based on smaller sample sizes would be the **binomial distribution**. The diagrams in Tables 3.1 and 3.2 corresponding to samples of between one and four divorced women show binomial distributions; as sample size increases, the shape of the binomial distribution converges with that of the normal distribution.

Sample size in random or probability samples

Earlier in the chapter it was shown that the sample size needed for a qualitative study is one that is big enough to allow the researcher to achieve their theoretical and descriptive aims. In a quantitative study based on random sampling, the typical objectives are to estimate certain quantities and to test for the existence of certain relationships. Thus, the sample size needed depends on how accurately the researcher wishes to estimate those quantities, and how certain the researcher wishes to be that their study will verify the existence of relationships of a given magnitude. For example, a researcher might wish to estimate the level of support for a political party, the Pragmatic Party, to within 2.5% of their actual level of support, and might also wish to be able to verify the existence of a difference (of, say, 10% or greater) between the levels of support for the Pragmatic Party among middle-class people and among working-class people.

By rearranging Equation 1, a formula can be obtained for the minimum sample size needed for a researcher to be 95% confident that estimates are within a given level of accuracy. If the level of accuracy, δ, is defined as the maximum acceptable difference between the sample mean (or proportion) $\bar{x}$, and the population mean (or proportion) μ, then the formula in question, which relates to a simple random sample, is:

$$n = \frac{(1.96)^2 \sigma^2}{\delta^2}.$$

The value of δ for our Pragmatic Party example is 2.5%, or 0.025. However, σ, the population standard deviation, is unknown. It is therefore necessary to make an 'educated guess' as to its value. If the proportion of people supporting the Pragmatic Party is q, then the population standard deviation (σ) is $\sqrt{q(1-q)}$. Therefore, if we 'guess' that q is 0.4 (40%), then the appropriate estimate for σ^2 is 0.4 multiplied by $(1-0.4)$, i.e. 0.24. Therefore, in this case:

$$n = \frac{(1.96)^2 0.24}{(0.025)^2} = 1475.$$

Political opinion polls in Great Britain often have sample sizes of between 1000 and 1500. This is because, as in our example, the aim is to estimate the support of major parties to within 2% to 3% of the true figure. Once again, the level of precision depends on the sample size rather than on the proportion of the population which is sampled.

A similar formula applies if we need to know the sample size required to obtain an estimate for the population mean μ of a scale-like (i.e. interval-level) variable that we can be 95% confident is within a given distance of the actual mean. The formula is as follows:

$$n = \frac{(1.96)^2 \sigma^2}{\gamma^2 \mu^2} = \frac{(1.96)^2}{\gamma^2} \times \left[\frac{\sigma}{\mu}\right]^2.$$

In this case γ, the level of accuracy required, takes the form of the ratio of the maximum permissible inaccuracy to the population mean. So, if we want an estimate of the mean age at marriage of women which is within one year of the actual value, and we guess that the mean is about 25 years, then $\gamma = 1/25 = 0.04$ (4%).

If we specify the required level of accuracy in percentage terms, then γ is simply that percentage expressed as a proportion. For example, requiring an estimate to be within 10% of the truth would lead to a value of γ of 0.1. Note that in order to calculate n using the above formula, we need to estimate both the population standard deviation and the population mean, or at least to estimate the ratio of these two figures, i.e. σ/μ, which is sometimes referred to as the **coefficient of variation**.

Where a greater level of confidence than 95% is required that the estimate is within the distance specified of the actual value, this can be obtained by replacing 1.96 in the above formula with a larger value. (You may recall that 95% of cases lie within 1.96 standard deviations of the mean of a normal distribution, whereas 99% of cases lie within 2.58 standard deviations of the mean. Thus, for a 99% level of confidence, the value required would be 2.58.)

Surveys often have multiple objectives: if the aim is to estimate a number of different quantities to specified levels of accuracy then the minimum sample size necessary for each of these objectives can be calculated and the highest of these sample sizes selected for use (resources permitting). If accurate estimates are required for sub-groups within a sample, then the minimum sub-sample sizes needed can be calculated; the overall sample size may consequently need to be increased, or unequal sampling fractions used within the different sub-groups. The objectives of the NATSAL survey included the estimation of the prevalence of rare forms of sexual behaviour in small sub-groups of the population, and, since there was insufficient information for strategic over-sampling to take place, the sample size needed was estimated to be 20 000 (Johnson *et al.*, 1994).

When a complex sample design is used, the sample size needs to take account of this: the sample size should be multiplied by the largest of the various design effects corresponding to the key quantities to be estimated. In addition, to achieve the sample size required, account needs to be taken of the likely level of non-response; for example, in a mail survey with an expected response rate of 50%, twice as many questionnaires as the desired sample size would need to be sent out. In the NATSAL survey 50 000 addresses were issued to interviewers, of which 30 000 contained eligible respondents, leading to under 19 000 interviews.

Calculating the sample size needed to verify the existence of a relationship is a complex exercise.

Furthermore, the sample size needed to give a researcher a good chance of identifying the existence of a moderately strong relationship may seem disconcertingly large. In the example that follows approximate formulae are given for the sample size needed to verify the existence of a difference in proportions between two equal-sized groups.

Consider the researcher's comparison between the proportions of middle-class and working-class people supporting the Pragmatic Party. Estimating this class difference involves comparing two proportions, each of which is based on a sub-sample of approximately half the size of the overall sample. It is therefore not surprising that to verify the existence of a class difference, given an underlying difference of $D\%$ in the population, a sample size is needed which is four times as big as that needed to estimate the overall level of Pragmatic Party support within an accuracy of $D\%$. (In the following formula, δ is $D\%$ expressed as a proportion.)

$$n = \frac{4(1.96)^2\sigma^2}{\delta^2} \qquad \text{(Equation 2)}$$

However, such a sample size would only give the researcher a 50–50 chance of verifying the existence of a class difference. This is because there is a 50% chance that the difference between the two sample proportions will be less than the difference between the two population proportions. In other words, the difference between the sample proportions may be smaller than the difference between the population proportions, and, as an unfortunate consequence, be more difficult to show to be significant.

To increase from 50% to 97.5% the researcher's confidence that the sample will verify the existence of a difference in proportions (this figure being the power of the test for a difference) necessitates a further four-fold increase in sample size, giving:

$$n = \frac{16(1.96)^2\sigma^2}{\delta^2}. \qquad \text{(Equation 3)}$$

As shown earlier, the appropriate estimate for σ^2 is 0.24 (given an estimated level of overall support for the Pragmatic Party of 40%). The researcher is interested in differences of 10% or greater, so $\delta = 0.1$. Thus, entering these values into the above formula, the sample size needed is, once again, 1475. The researcher is thus in the fortunate position that both his or her objectives can be achieved with a sample of this size.

It may seem disturbing that a sample of this size is needed to achieve objectives which do not seem particularly demanding. However, much can be learned from smaller samples. For example, consider a population where half the people regularly cook meals, but where there is a gender difference and the figures for men and for women are one-third and two-thirds respectively. σ^2 in this case is $0.5 \times 0.5 = 0.25$, and $\delta = 1/3 = 0.33$. Entering these values into Equation 3 indicates that a minimum sample size of 141 is needed for a researcher to be 97.5% confident of verifying a relationship of this sort. However, using Equation 2, a sample size of 35 (i.e. 17 or 18 people of each sex) would still give the researcher a 50–50 chance of identifying a relationship of this sort of magnitude. Furthermore, testing for differences relating to interval-level variables such as age at marriage may require rather smaller sample sizes.

Non-response

In theory, random sampling eliminates the possibility of biased findings by ensuring that the only source of inaccuracy is sampling error. In practice, however, problematic sampling frames and non-response mean that very few studies using random sampling generate samples which are truly random. In interviewer-based surveys, non-respondents can usefully be divided into those whom the interviewer sees, but who either refuse to participate or are otherwise unable to be interviewed (e.g. because of communication difficulties or poor health), and those whom the interviewer fails to contact (either because they are no longer to be found at

that location or because they are not present when the interviewer visits the location).

While non-respondents may not always conform to stereotypes, non-response is a problem primarily because of the collective distinctiveness of non-respondents. Research has been carried out on patterns of non-response (e.g. Goyder, 1987), which among other things suggests that people who occupy 'marginal' positions within society are less likely to end up as respondents, but it would be dangerous not to consider non-response within a specific study on its own merits.

The negative effects of non-response depend both on its magnitude and on the extent to which non-respondents are distinctive. Thus the response rate for a survey is only a crude guide to the likely level of bias in its findings. However, response rates of 70–80% are fairly standard for high-quality, large-scale interview surveys, whereas response rates of less than 50% are not unusual for postal surveys, with non-response being a major problem in the context of the latter. Keeping the level of non-response in a postal survey to a minimum requires the materials sent to respondents to be eye-catching, to hold the respondent's attention, and to interest them enough to stimulate a response; it is clear, given the volume of junk mail that many people receive, that this is a difficult task.

Minimising non-response in face-to-face research is to a large extent a question of maximising the proportion of respondents that interviewers manage to contact and minimising the frequency of refusals. The likelihood of non-contact can be reduced by repeated attempts to contact a respondent at different times of day (such tactics are discussed in more detail in the section on survey fieldwork in Chapter 5). Refusals are minimised when the research is presented in as positive a light as possible, which necessitates pre-planning and good interpersonal skills on the part of the interviewer(s), and when potential respondents are approached at a time when and in a context where they feel able to devote time to participating in the research.

The response rate for the NATSAL survey was 63.3%, less than that for many government surveys, but comparing favourably with response rates to other surveys relating to sexual behaviour. The vast majority of the non-response was due to various forms of refusal, as repeated calls resulted in a low frequency of non-contact. As is often the case, the response rate for Greater London was lower than response rates elsewhere. The refusal rate increased with age, and the response rate for men was lower than that for women, primarily as a consequence of a lack of contact or a 'proxy' refusal by a third party. Clearly a high level of non-response through refusals in a study of a sensitive topic may potentially lead to significant biases in the findings. However, the non-respondents in this case could well be heterogeneous and may include disproportionate numbers both of people who indulge in 'unusual' sexual activities and also of people whose sexual behaviour is tied to convention and hamstrung by taboo.

Documentation showing that a piece of research is 'official' and giving reasons why it is of value may be useful, and interviewers should be prepared to respond to specific questions along the lines of the following:

- Who is doing the research?
- Why is the research being done?
- What happens to the answers I give?
- What is in it for me?

While respondents are rarely paid, it may be appropriate to promise them a summary of the research findings. However, while making the research interesting or beneficial to potential respondents can be valuable, stressing the value of their participation may also have a positive effect. Making a potential respondent feel that they have something useful and interesting to contribute costs nothing.

Putting pressure on a respondent to participate in research at a particular point in time may be counterproductive. 'Backing off' and suggesting that you come back at some other time may avoid a refusal, though it is obviously better to choose an appropriate time to approach the respondent in the first place. Arguably this problem can be avoided by contacting a potential respondent in advance to suggest or negotiate a time at which to interview them. However, sending letters to potential respondents in advance of contacting them face to face may encourage them to avoid you; telephoning them may make it easier for them to refuse to participate than if you are face to face with them.

While avoiding refusals increases the sample size, it does not necessarily decrease the level of bias in the sample, as the avoided refusals may correspond to respondents who are more similar to other respondents in the sample than they are to non-respondents. Note also that using substitutes as replacements for non-respondents increases the sample size but almost certainly does not reduce the degree of bias in the findings. This last point has important echoes for failed access and non-response in qualitative studies; qualitative researchers need to remember that refusals to participate may be a reflection of theoretically important characteristics, and that a desire for adequate theoretical coverage should provide as strong a motivation to avoid non-response (or at least to reflect on it) as a desire for unbiased quantitative findings does.

In addition to non-response at the level of the individual respondent, **item non-response**, i.e. the failure of respondents to answer specific questions, may be a problem: for example, where sensitive questions are embedded in a survey which is not in general on a sensitive topic.

Evaluating the representativeness and coverage of samples

It is universally acknowledged to be good practice for survey researchers to carry out checks to establish how representative their samples are. However, it is also good practice for a qualitative researcher to establish the extent to which their sample mirrors the broader population. While representativeness may not be a central issue in some pieces of qualitative research, the range of characteristics of the people in a qualitative sample still determines the nature and generalisability of the theories and typologies which are developed from the data collected. A qualitative sample which has partial coverage or no coverage of theoretically important sub-groups in the population generates theory which is correspondingly limited in terms of its generalisability. All researchers need to reflect on the extent to which their findings and conclusions would have been different if the composition of their sample had been different.

There are two different approaches to establishing the characteristics of people who are not included in a sample relative to the characteristics of people who are in a sample. The direct approach focuses on what the researcher knows about non-respondents or people to whom access has not been gained. Some useful information may be derived from the sampling frame: for example, if the sample has been selected from the Electoral Register the researcher would have information about the geographical location of non-respondents and the composition of the households that they lived in. Information may also be forthcoming from the fieldwork process; if the interviewer has seen a non-respondent or even just where they live then at least the researcher has some knowledge about them. The researcher also usually has some potentially useful information about why people were not included in the sample; refusals to participate and barred access may be particularly informative. Researchers sometimes specifically attempt to collect data from at least some of the non-respondents about the reasons for their non-response.

The indirect approach involves a comparison between the characteristics of members of the sample and the characteristics of members of the population, based on data obtained from some external source. Comparisons with Census data are fairly often used to assess the representativeness of samples in terms of standard demographic variables; when the representativeness of a sample in relation to a relatively specific characteristic needs to be established, a more specific external data source may be needed: for example, the health-related characteristics of a sample might be compared with data from the annual Health Survey for England (Colhoun and Prescott-Clarke, 1996). Clearly, comparisons of this sort are only as valid and relevant as the nature and quality of the external source allow them to be. It may be necessary to carry out secondary analyses of external sources, since published data may not be specific enough to provide the necessary basis for a comparison. Indirect assessments of representativeness usually look at the demographic or behavioural characteristics of samples, but there is no reason why other forms of comparison should not be made. For example, the British Social Attitudes Survey (BSAS: Jowell *et al.*, 1996) can be used as an external source of attitudinal data.

An undergraduate supervised by one of the authors doing a project on attitudes towards welfare spending relating to lone parenthood compared the attitudes of her qualitative sample with the attitudes of BSAS respondents, and found that her respondents were more positive than average (the BSAS sample is nationally representative) about that form of welfare spending. She hypothesised that the reason for this was that her sample was drawn from within a relatively small geographical area in close proximity to relatively large numbers of lone parents receiving benefits, and that as a consequence her sample contained very few respondents who were remote from the realities of the lives of such lone parents. She correctly concluded that the generalisability of her findings, whether theoretical or empirical, was correspondingly limited.

In the case of the NATSAL survey there was direct evidence from the fieldwork of the effects of gender and age on non-response, and comparisons of the sample with Census data reaffirmed the existence of these effects. Comparisons of the sample's marital and socio-economic characteristics with General Household Survey data (OPCS, 1991a) showed little in the way of systematic differences, and neither did a comparison of the ethnic composition of the sample with Labour Force Survey data (OPCS, 1990a). Data from the sample corresponding to heights and weights were similar to results from the Health and Lifestyle Survey (HALS; Blaxter, 1990), and data on therapeutic abortions among sample members paralleled official statistics (OPCS, 1990b). However, these checks on the representativeness of the NATSAL sample do not include checks on its representativeness with respect to its main focus of interest, sexual behaviour. A major stumbling block to assessing representativeness is where there is no convincing source of comparable data.

In the study of formerly married people and ex-cohabitees by Lampard and Peggs (1999), comparisons of the sample with Census data suggested that the sample contained a markedly higher proportion of middle-class people (and a consequently lower proportion of working-class people) than the formerly married population. Thus the **representativeness** of the sample in this respect was found to be questionable, though the **coverage** of people with working-class occupations was felt to provide an adequate basis for the examination of this sub-group. The criteria for assessing the adequacy of a qualitative sample will usually relate more to the coverage needed to generate theory and to develop typologies than to the representativeness needed for quantification.

Census data also indicated that the sample should have contained a handful of people from minority ethnic groups; in fact there were very few such people in the sample, limiting the generalisability of the findings. It seems likely that formerly married people from some minority ethnic groups were disinclined to volunteer to participate. These comparisons highlight a major limitation of samples of volunteers; they are arguably likely to over-represent better-educated people, and they are certainly likely to under-represent sub-groups of the population who are reluctant to talk about the research topic.

Adjusting for non-response and sampling error

In quantitative research, one way of compensating for the over-representation of some sub-groups in a sample and the under-representation of others is to use weighting. As outlined earlier in the discussion of disproportionate sampling, a weight is generated for each of the various sub-groups of sample member. This weight is equal to the number of people from that sub-group that there should have been in the sample, divided by the actual number of people from that sub-group in the sample. For example, if data from an external source indicate that there should have been 20 people with no qualifications in a sample and there were actually 10, then the weight is $20/10 = 2$ and each of the 10 respondents is in effect counted twice. Within this weighting process is an implicit process of **stratification after selection**, or **post-stratification**. If the difference between the distribution of the sample across sub-groups and the corresponding distribution in the population is solely due to sampling error, then post-stratification is likely to improve the precision of the study's findings.

However, there is a major problem with weighting to compensate for over- and under-representation if this is instead due to non-response; this makes the implicit assumption that the non-respondents from a sub-group are similar to the respondents within that sub-group. In the example given above, the people with no qualifications who participated in the research might be disproportionately people who had been occupationally successful without qualifications. Double-weighting the data corresponding to those people would not in that case solve the problem of a bias against the educationally disadvantaged. Weighting to compensate for non-response can, in fact, increase the level of bias; there is certainly no guarantee that it will reduce it.

However, the potential benefits of weighting to compensate for non-response may outweigh the risks involved in making assumptions about the relative distinctiveness of non-respondents. In the NATSAL survey, weighting was used to compensate for regional differences in the level of non-response. A failure to have done this would have led to an under-estimation of the national prevalence of homosexual experiences, as the frequency of such experiences was found to vary markedly across regions, with much higher levels in Greater London than elsewhere (Johnson *et al.*, 1994).

Moser and Kalton (1971) discuss an ingenious method of compensating for the component of non-response which reflects lack of contact; it assumes that non-respondents of this sort are similar to respondents whom the researcher was 'lucky to catch in'. However, a researcher does not have to be ingenious to place bounds on the effect of non-response on their findings. For example, suppose a survey with a response rate of 80% found that 40% of people support the Pragmatic Party. This means that at least 40% of 80%, i.e. 32%, of the intended sample, including non-respondents, support the Pragmatic Party. If all the non-respondents support the Pragmatic Party, then this would mean that 32% + 20% = 52% of the intended sample do so. Thus if there had been no non-response the percentage support for the Pragmatic Party in the sample would have been between 32% and 52%. However, if the researcher is prepared to assume that the level of support for the Pragmatic Party among non-respondents is not too different from the level among respondents, i.e. that it is between 30% and 50%, then this range shrinks dramatically to 38% to 42%.

Further reading

Not all accounts of research studies adequately document the sampling process and the characteristics of the sample collected. However, examining methodological chapters or appendices in research studies that interest you can give you a good idea of the strengths and weaknesses of the sampling approaches used. Remember that you need to make a critical assessment of these approaches; there are few studies where the sampling process and the sample generated are ideal.

You may be able to acquire a cheap second-hand copy of Moser and Kalton (1971), which is still an excellent source of material on survey sampling. Hoinville *et al.* (1977) contains somewhat more practically orientated material on sampling, and both books discuss non-response. Interesting discussions of qualitative sampling can be found in Mason (1996), Patton (1990) and Strauss and Corbin (1990). Discussions of access can be found in Burgess (1984) and Hammersley and Atkinson (1995).

Introductory material on sampling error, distributions, etc. can be found in a wide range of introductory statistics texts published over the last 30 years: Rowntree (1981) and Reid (1987) are more accessible than most texts in this context. A couple of personal favourites are Hays (1973), which contains very detailed coverage of basic statistical material, and Kalton (1966), which is extremely brief and to the point.

Chapter 4   Observation: looking to learn

Introduction

In many respects, observation is something which we all constantly experience as part and parcel of our daily lives. In all of our everyday interactions with people at home, in work, at university or college, in social settings and in formal situations, we observe and make judgements which inform our opinions and our actions, both in relation to and beyond those interactions. We may be part of what we observe, actively contributing to the social action as it is created and evolves around us, or we may be more distanced from it, looking in from the margins or from a greater distance on events upon which we can have no influence.

From the outset, therefore, we may assert that observation is something with which we are all familiar; we do it all the time in order to go about our ordinary and not so ordinary lives. However, in the context of social research, to speak of observation merely in terms of what can been seen, is to neglect many of the different facets of observation, which frequently involves a comprehensive and multi-faceted approach to data collection. Rather than merely watching we would prefer to define observation in terms of experiencing social phenomena at first hand. In this sense, observation is about being there. It can be as much about hearing, feeling, enjoying, fearing, interpreting, talking and sharing as it is about watching. In this wider definition, therefore, observation is for all those researchers who have the capacity and the opportunity to be there, and to experience events, institutions, people and places at first hand as they happen.

Types of observation

Traditionally, research methods texts have drawn distinctions between different kinds of observation based on the degree to which the researcher participates in the activities being observed. The most frequently cited of these texts is that by Gold (1958) who identifies four different kinds of observation ranging from situations where the researcher is primarily a participant and the data collection is covert (Complete Participant) to situations of surveillance (Complete Observer) where interaction with those being observed is kept to a minimum and may involve the use of cameras and other devices. Between these ends of the spectrum the researcher may adopt approaches where participation is emphasised more than observation (Participant as Observer) or vice versa (Observer as Participant). Such distinctions are useful in analysing and reflecting on the research process, but in practice can convey little of the complexity of the experience of observation, whatever the degree of participation involved.

Our perception of observation as a method of gathering data is one which fits closely with our characterisation of research as active and processual. Regardless of the degree of interaction with those being researched, observation is about the first-hand involvement of the researcher(s) with the social action as it occurs. Whether the researcher is participating or watching, he/she is present as activities and events occur and is, therefore, involved in immediate and ongoing analysis and interpretation of those events and activities.

For us, observation is a highly complex set of activities which involves the researcher interfacing with the research setting and the emerging data at a number of levels. Of all the many definitions of observation that are to be found in the research methods literature, the one closest to our understanding is one offered by Foster (1996) in the introduction to his book on observing schools. He states:

> Observation is a matter of collecting information about the nature of the physical and social world as it unfolds before us directly via the senses, rather than indirectly via the accounts of others. But observation is more than just this. Our minds must make sense of the data they receive. To do this we order, interpret and give meaning to incoming information. Physical objects are recognized and categorized, their category labels symbolizing their key features and qualities. Similarly by employing our existing knowledge, conceptual schemata and theories, we recognize and give meaning to the human behaviour we witness (p. vii).

Foster's definition leaves us in no doubt that observation is demanding and complex. By implication, however, it is also very rewarding in allowing the researcher direct access to a social world different from his/her own. By emphasising the role of the researcher in attributing meaning to what is observed, Foster implies that observation may be as much about the construction of data as it is about its collection.

Why observe?

The short answer to this question is that we choose to observe in order to learn with a view to understanding social behaviour. However, this is a reply which could just as validly be applied to virtually every research method and to research itself. The critical issue here is the perspective from which the researcher seeks to learn and understand. By observing, the researcher is attempting to gain entry to the world of the researched, to witness the activities which constitute their world, either by actively taking part or merely by being there or watching. In this sense, the observer is part of what is going on and is attempting to understand from the inside. The perspective is one, therefore, which stresses the importance of context and direct experience.

Observation is a research method which perhaps more than any other relies on the capacity of the researcher to interpret a situation as it unfolds around him/her. The researcher, whether observer or participant observer, is, therefore, the principal instrument (Wolcott, 1981) of the method. He/she is able to gather data as they emerge from the social setting. Moreover, where participation is emphasised, the researcher may also be directly responsible for some of the social action which he/she is observing. Taking all of this into account, observation is perhaps the most demanding of research methods, necessitating a great deal of thought and practice. The problem here, of course, is that practice can only effectively occur in real research situations.

Observation is about collecting data in natural settings. Unlike the interview or the survey, it is not an artificial situation which relies on the willingness of the researched to do things which they would not normally do. It seeks access to the everyday worlds of social actors and may be just as interested in the mundane and regular occurrences as it is in the spectacular or the untoward.

Planning observation

Researching in natural settings where the researcher seeks to witness and become a part of what is happening without exerting any undue influence requires flexibility. Unlike many other methods it is difficult to plan observational research in any great detail, as we can never be absolutely sure of what will happen. And it is precisely that unpredictability of social life that observation wishes to capture. A simple example from our own research will illustrate this point.

Pole (1993) conducted a study of the use and development of records of achievement in a rural secondary school. The research utilised a range of data-collection methods including some sustained periods of observation wherein the emphasis rested more on observation than on participation. On one particular morning the plan was to observe a discussion between a teacher and a pupil who had been disruptive throughout his time in the school and had so far refused to take part in the record of achievement process. The discussion was to feed into the preparation of a joint statement by the pupil and his form tutor about the pupil's time at the school and would, therefore, make an important contribution to the record of achievement. Consent had been gained independently from both the pupil and the teacher for the discussion to be observed. The observation was to be unstructured and amounted to Pole sitting with the teacher and the pupil, but not, however, contributing to the conversation unless invited to do so, and making a written record of the meeting and the discussion as it occurred. At the same time, the conversation between teacher and pupil was to be tape-recorded. The observation would, therefore, yield two sources of data: that provided by the audio tape-recording and that yielded by Pole's observations of the interaction between teacher and pupil. The approach would allow content analysis of the conversation in terms of substance: for example, the topics covered and the ways in which they were pursued. It would also provide some basic quantitative information about the amount of time each of the

participants was talking and the length of time particular topics were discussed. In addition, the visual observation would provide information on body language and gesture and the use of space in the interview room, alongside an interpretation of the ways in which each of the participants presented themselves during the interview. The visual data would, therefore, provide a commentary which would contextualise the audio tape-recording of the interview. The plans for the observation were agreed in advance with each of the participants, who were also assured that the data collected would be treated sensitively and that they would not be identified in anything written based on the observation.

The written account of the meeting shows that, to the surprise of the teacher, the pupil arrived at the designated time at the interview room. The discussion began fruitfully with the pupil answering the teacher's questions and talking about a range of issues relating to his history of poor behaviour in the school. However, approximately seven minutes after the start of the discussion another, more senior, member of staff entered the room claiming that he had booked the room for a similar discussion with one of his tutees. He duly produced the revered room booking record and insisted that we vacate the interview room. At that point there was no other suitable room available in which to continue the discussion. The pupil was told to return to the interview room at the next available opportunity, which was after lunch. The teacher and I arrived at the agreed time but the pupil did not. I subsequently learnt that the boy had not returned for afternoon school.

The above example raises a number of issues central to observation. The events of that morning and the following afternoon were not planned and required flexibility on the part of the researcher as they did on the part of the teacher and the pupil. Initially, the premature termination of the discussion could have been seen as a negative aspect of the observation session where an opportunity was lost. In relation to gathering information about this specific pupil this was true. However, the events leading to and following the termination of the discussion revealed a great deal about a range of issues relevant to the focus of the study. The incident raises issues about:

- the role of the interview room
- the availability of space in the school for discussions with pupils
- staff relations and hierarchies
- the procedures for room allocation
- the timing of teacher–pupil discussions
- the importance of records of achievement to disaffected pupils.

Arguably, the early termination of the discussion revealed more about the organisation of the record of achievement process than the planned observation of the discussion could ever have done. Clearly, where the purpose of the research method is to observe the natural behaviour of the participants it would have been inappropriate for the researcher to have attempted to influence the course of events. Meanwhile the focus of the observation shifted accordingly from issues of content and the record of achievement to those of process.

The research design needed to be sufficiently flexible to accommodate such a shift which could not have been planned or anticipated at the start of the study. Whilst there was indeed a considerable degree of planning, which involved obtaining the agreement of the participants and deciding on a strategy of audio and visual observation, there was, of course, no way in which the unforeseen termination of the discussion could have been planned for. The opportunity to observe what the researcher expected to be an interesting interview was lost with its early termination and the failure of the pupil to return for the afternoon session. However, the fact that the interviewer was able to observe, at first hand, the events surrounding the interview meant that data of a different kind were able to be collected, which, in themselves, were revealing of the organisation of interviews for record of achievement purposes in that school.

In observation studies where the emphasis is firmly on observation rather than participation, however, there may be a more systematic attempt at planning observation. Again, an example from our own work will illustrate the point whilst at the same time demonstrating the wide range of approaches which the term 'observation' covers. This example is also drawn from school-based research. However, in this instance the research was centred on the classroom, focusing on the teaching of English in the National Curriculum. The study, which focused on the teaching of English at Key Stage Two, involved the close observation of primary children in the classroom. Amongst the specific concerns of the study was the extent of interaction between teachers and pupils, and also between pupils themselves, both in relation to, and beyond, the English tasks which they had been set. Other concerns were the frequency with which pupils used books and other reference material at their disposal and their capacity for concentration, indicated by the time they spent at their desks concentrating on a given task. Principally the study was concerned with measuring the amount of time in minutes and seconds, or the number of occasions, which the pupils spent engaged in particular activities.

In this instance observation was more structured than in the previous example, as those funding the study had requested that specific quantitative data be collected. However, the emphasis was still on the lived experience, in this case that of primary school children. The classroom and the usual activities which took place there as part of the teaching of National Curriculum English still constituted a natural setting. However, the emphasis on quantification and structure meant that data were to be recorded on observation schedules, prepared prior to the beginning of the designated period of observation. Moreover, they were prepared in such a way as to facilitate the capture of the specific data required by the sponsors. To ensure comparability between lessons, and between schools in different parts of the country, the same observation schedule was to be used for every lesson observed in every school in the study. Here, the intention was to achieve uniformity of data collected across the research sites, which would enable general trends to be identified in the behaviour of pupils during National Curriculum English lessons. The data gathered by this more structured approach to observation, although in some respects more limited than that collected in the previous example of school-based observation, relied nevertheless on the presence of the researcher in the natural setting, recording events, or at least particular aspects of events, as they happened.

The operationalisation of the observation schedule required the researcher to identify two pupils (one boy, one girl) at the start of each lesson that was to be observed and to record their activities in accordance with the schedule. Every time one of the pupils talked to a friend, or sought the assistance of the teacher, this would be noted on the schedule. Similarly the pupils' movements throughout the lesson would be recorded on a plan of the classroom, drawn by the researcher at the start of the session. Titles of all books and materials used by the pupils during the lesson would be noted and the amount of time spent on particular tasks would be recorded using a watch which recorded seconds as well as minutes. The researcher was to take a seat in a position which would allow a clear view of the nominated children.

The observation schedule required the observer to pay close attention to the children throughout the lesson, listening to them and making brief notes on their conversations in addition to their actions in the classroom. Recording the activities of two children simultaneously proved difficult, especially when one or both decided to move around the room or became involved in group activities where it was difficult to determine individual contributions to the interaction. In most cases, however, the observations were conducted successfully in so far as a record of the children's activities during the lesson was made, or at least as much as possible of their activities and conversations was recorded within the constraints of the observation task. In turn these observations could be compared

with those made of other lessons in other schools and would be analysed collectively in order to produce a national picture of the experience of English lessons at Key Stage Two in the National Curriculum.

Although in this instance the observation was more highly structured than in the first example, as the required information was specified before the lesson began and there was a requirement to collect and compare data from different locations, it too necessitated a degree of flexibility on the part of the observer. As the observation was to focus on two children, the observation schedule and the observer had to be sufficiently flexible to accommodate all their activities, some of which were not anticipated in advance of the lesson. For example, in one instance the boy being observed got a nosebleed during the lesson and left the classroom accompanied by the teacher. Not only did this remove one of the key subjects of the observation exercise but it also impacted on the class, who were left without a teacher for 12 minutes, and on the English lesson being taught. The unfortunate occurrence of the nosebleed had a number of consequences for the observation and hence the data collected. First of all, the researcher had to decide whether to be faithful to the social action and to record what had happened to the subject of the observation or whether, in his absence, to choose another boy. If the focus of the study was on the teaching of English, how could a nosebleed be relevant? The answer to this question needed to be considered in the context of the study as a whole, in relation to the incidence of nosebleeds and other occurrences which took pupils out of the classroom and the impact this had on the experience of English lessons. On this occasion, the researcher decided to be true to his data and record the boy as missing. He did not, however, follow the boy from the classroom but chose instead to concentrate on the activities of the girl.

The absence of the teacher also raised an issue about the role of the researcher. Her absence from the room for 12 minutes meant that the pupils were unsupervised. The level of noise and the scale of activities unrelated to the tasks which they had been set both increased considerably as her absence progressed. As the only other adult in the room the researcher was faced with the dilemma of whether he should assume the role of teacher and quieten the class down, thereby directly influencing the progress of the English lesson, or whether to abandon the observation as an atypical lesson. Again, in this instance, the researcher chose to continue the observation and to record what he saw. However, the absence of the teacher meant that what he saw was most probably very different from what he would have seen had the teacher been present throughout the lesson.

These two examples of school-based observation highlight a number of issues which demonstrate how the act of observation differs according to the structure imposed on it, the substance of what is being observed and the eventual use to which the data will be put. In the first example an audio tape-recording of the discussion was made alongside the visual observations. Given the number of people involved (two) and the location of the discussion this was easily accomplished. The second setting, that of a noisy classroom in which the pupils under observation were not necessarily sitting close to each other, did not lend itself to tape-recording. Moreover, the need for detailed data about discrete activities, in such a way as to facilitate quantitative comparisons across a national sample, necessitated a highly structured observation schedule. Where a detailed picture of the totality of the social action was required, as with the first example, then a more holistic approach to observation was selected with the intention that this would provide insight into the social and educational processes surrounding the record of achievement. In both cases, however, the observation required careful planning. Whilst the second example was chosen to illustrate a more structured approach to observation, it also, nevertheless, shows the need for flexibility in observation techniques.

Whatever the degree of structure in the observation, flexibility is essential. Observation is concerned with the witnessing, experiencing and recording of human behaviour and it is the unpredictability of human behaviour which necessitates flexibility. Having said this, we do not wish to imply that research which utilises observation should not be carefully planned. However, this can only, in the main, be limited to technical issues of where and when the observation is to be scheduled, what its intended focus is and how the data are to be recorded. The substance of the observation will inevitably remain as unpredictable as human life.

What to look at

In the two examples cited above the focus of the observation was clearly identified at the outset. In the first the record of achievement discussion provided the focus and in the second it was the English lesson. However, identifying such a focus is not always so easy. Our experience, both as researchers and as supervisors, of those doing research has meant that we have often faced the question 'What am I supposed to be looking at?' Depending on the research setting this is by no means obvious.

Many of those who conducted now celebrated observation studies (e.g. Whyte, 1943; Burgess, 1983; Hockey, 1986; Hobbs, 1988; Holdaway, 1983) spent a period of time during which, although they were clear about the general parameters of their studies, they were not entirely sure of their exact focus. The initial phases of these observation-based studies involved, therefore, a period of time in which the researchers became familiar with and acculturated to the research setting. This allowed them to identify a range of issues of interest which could gradually be refined to constitute a focus. As these and many other studies demonstrate, the identification of a focus for observation requires, of itself, a period of observation during which the researcher will select from a range of interests, processes and issues which have the potential to provide a focus.

However, finding a focus for observation also involves reflecting upon the reason for adopting observation as a data-collection method. As with any research method, there needs to be a clear rationale for the use of observation and a belief that it is the most appropriate technique for the research setting and the substance of the research. The researcher also needs to be sure that it will yield the kind of data which are ontologically and epistemologically appropriate for the study. This will involve deciding on the particular type of observation which is to be used. For example, if the intention is to collect data from a large number of sites with a view to producing generalisations and explanations which are valid across populations, then a highly structured and systematic approach to observation will be the most appropriate method. If, on the other hand, we are concerned with capturing the detail and uniqueness of social interaction within a particular setting, then a more loosely structured approach which yields a more holistic view may be appropriate.

Similarly, in attempting to find a focus for the observation, researchers will also need to consider their own role in the observation and the extent to which they are able, or it is appropriate for them, to participate in what they are observing. However, the relationship between role and focus is complicated and it is not merely a question of choice on the part of the researcher. Indeed, the focus of the observation and the role adopted by the observer have a mutual dependency on each other, in so far as the capacity for participation in a research setting will influence the focus of the research and, equally, the focus of the research will influence the level of participation in the observation.

Prior to any observation study, therefore, it is essential that researchers engage in preliminary investigations and observations of the research site(s) which will aid the identification of a focus and of an appropriate role. Moreover, in the case of highly structured observation, such pilot work is essential to the construction of an appropriate observation schedule which will enable the observer to record quickly, comprehensively and accurately what he/she sees.

The question of what to look at and the location of a focus for observation may, therefore, be difficult to address at the start of a research project and perhaps it is only when the research has progressed a little that these questions can be answered. However, some comfort can be taken from Wolcott (1981) who, although concerned specifically with loosely structured ethnographic studies, draws attention to the degree of uncertainty which underpins all research. In our view Wolcott's point is relevant to the many studies where observation is a principal method of data collection. He sees the identification of a focus as a central aspect of the observation process. He says:

> Thus the problem of 'what to look at,' . . . is a particularly vexing but also a totally intriguing one for ethnographers of a traditional bent. In my opinion if a researcher knows in advance what information is wanted (i.e., knows precisely what to look for), then following a broad ethnographic approach seems a most inefficient way to go about gathering the information (p. 254).

Wolcott is one of the few researchers to offer some practical advice about what to look at and how to look. He proposes four strategies for identifying a focus for observational research which in our view are an interesting and useful starting point for the observer. Merely considering the four strategies will be instructive in the early stages of observation. The four strategies are as follows.

Observing and recording everything

Here, the intention is to observe and record as much as possible of whatever is happening and also what is not happening. However, because the researcher cannot possibly record everything, he/she starts to intuitively select from what is available. Consequently, a large mass of data is generated from which, through various stages of analysis (see Chapter 8), a focus for further observation and to the research in general will emerge. The strategy also helps the observer to develop his/her own role in relation to recording what is observed and to participation. What Wolcott terms 'the broad look around' provides contextual material for later more focused observations and for subsequent writing from the data.

Observing and looking for nothing in particular
Here the intention is to treat the research setting as a flat landscape in which nothing warrants any greater attention than anything else. By doing this, the observer is able to identify quite clearly anything which stands out from the flat landscape. Wolcott believes this approach to be equally applicable to situations which are familiar to the observer, in which he/she is looking for occurrences which differ from 'business as usual', and to unfamiliar settings, where 'looking at nothing in particular offers a way of coping with so much to look at occurring so quickly'.

Looking for paradoxes
Here, Wolcott suggests that in giving attention to actual behaviour and comparing this to anticipated behaviour, the observer learns more from the ensuing social action. An example of this technique is given by Delamont (1992) who says:

> During the ORACLE project we found that children drew more in ordinary lessons than they did in art, and moved more in ordinary classes than they did in PE. Paradoxically, art is the last place where drawing is done, and much of the PE lesson is spent standing still (p. 115).

In this instance, the observed paradoxes not only provide insight into the lessons which were observed but also give rise to a range of questions about why the paradox exists. For example, in the case of Delamont's observations, one would wish to ask why children were spending much of their time in PE lessons standing still and why pupils did not draw during art lessons. The paradoxes provide an additional avenue of enquiry for the observer to pursue as the research progresses.

Looking for the key problem confronting the group
Wolcott attributes this strategy to Becker et al. (1961, 1968) who advocate concentrating on a problem, or the problem, which the group at the centre of the observation study must solve. Whatever that problem may be, Wolcott says 'How they deal with that problem provides an effective way to observe them at work by looking at something rather than at everything.'

Underpinning Wolcott's strategies is the need for a focus to the observation. His concern is that the researcher should look at something rather than at nothing. To this end, the researcher may use any or all of the four strategies simultaneously. The point is to add some kind of structure to the observation and to make the most of the time available for it. Few researchers have the luxury of unrestricted time and access to a research population or location. It is important, therefore, to make the most of what time is available by having a strategy for the observation and a rationale for the approach taken.

Finding a focus

Much of what we have discussed in the preceding pages may be seen in terms of strategies to find a focus for observation. The issue of focus is pursued explicitly by Delamont (1992), who places greater emphasis on the extent to which the observer is reflexive in his/her observations and is able to record them than she does on the substantive focus of the observation. She says that the focus of the observation will depend on the observers' personal and academic interests. In our view, such a separation of substance and technique is unhelpful. We would argue that observers need to be both reflexive and focused and, if necessary, to observe in this way in areas which extend beyond their personal interests. Whilst the researcher's curiosity about a topic may be the initial motivation for a particular study, we would argue that it should be the interests and actions of those being observed which provide the focus. In this sense, the focus of the observation, at least that kind of observation which is not highly structured, may change as it progresses and more is learnt about those who are the principal object of the research. In situations where a highly structured observation schedule is used, such reflexivity on the part of the observer may not be possible.

What we are advocating, therefore, may be seen as a kind of multi-stage focusing of observation. We would agree with Delamont (1992) that researcher interest is what drives the study initially and identifies the general area for observation. However, as the research progresses we would argue that it is the emerging data and their ongoing analysis which provide the ever sharper focus to the work. Our approach is, therefore, broadly in line with that espoused by Glaser and Strauss (1967) within their discussion of progressive focusing.

How to look

As we noted above, the separation of what to look at from how to look is in many ways an artificial separation, as the act of looking or observing is closely associated with, and will vary in accordance with, what is being looked at or observed. Nevertheless, providing guidance for the novice researcher about how to look, or indeed addressing the issue oneself, remains very difficult. Thinking about how to look raises many issues, not only about observational technique but also about the role of the observer, methods of recording what is observed, and the ethics of observation.

The role of the observer

Whilst many methods texts draw a distinction between participant and non-participant observation, our characterisation of the act of observation in terms of a continuum, in line with Gold's (1958) classification stretching from complete participant to complete observer, allows us to eschew any notion that there can be observation without participation. Whether the researcher participates in the social action as it occurs or participates in terms of reflexive analysis of the collected data, we would argue that it is important to see the researcher as a participant in the construction of the social action which is the focus of the study.

In some observation studies, where the researcher participated in the social action as it unfolded (e.g. Fine, 1987; Hey, 1997; Hockey, 1986; Mac an Ghaill, 1994; Thorne, 1993), the role which the observer was to play was not immediately obvious from the outset of the research. In most cases a period of negotiation occurred between the researcher and the researched during which both parties assessed their roles in relation to each other. Where the research was conducted covertly such negotiation occurred seemingly as part of the normal course of events when a new person joined an established group or institution. The presence of another person meant that the behaviour of those who were already part of the group or institution inevitably changed, as they now had to take account of the newcomer. Even where the person conducting the observation may not have been new to the organisation (e.g. Mac an Ghaill, 1994), their very presence as a member of the group or the institution had an effect on all the other participants.

When addressing the question of how to look, therefore, the observer has to develop a sense of the management of the self (Goffman, 1959) in the interaction which is being observed. In this sense, the researcher needs to be attuned not only to the activities of the observed but also to his/her own presence in the setting and the effect that this might have on what is being observed. Whilst in most observation studies it is not possible to control for the presence of the researcher without having further impact on the situation being observed, the development of an awareness of self is an attempt to take account of the role of the researcher in the social action. In looking, therefore, the researcher must be aware of his/her actions in addition to those which are the focus of the observation.

The management and awareness of self is relevant to all studies where observation is employed. As part of this Hammersley and Atkinson (1995) introduce the notion of audience and its role in the creation of data. In all observation studies, but in particular those which are overt, there is the possibility that what happens has to some degree been staged or conducted with the idea that the researcher is an audience for what is occurring. Whilst this may be an aspect of 'best behaviour syndrome' akin to that displayed by a school during the week when it is visited by government inspectors or a university department during inspection by the Quality Assurance Agency, it may have important consequences for the data. For example, in a study concerned with the use of communications technology in schools, where loosely structured observation of classroom activities was a principal method of data collection, Pole (1994) was constantly aware, not least from the comments made by some of the pupils, that particular pieces of equipment or a certain amount of lesson content had been included principally for his benefit, on the day of a pre-arranged visit to the school. In this study, he was clearly identified as an important audience by the participants who wanted to show that they were making innovative use of the resources with which they had been provided.

In learning how to look, therefore, the observer, like the school inspector, needs to find ways of getting behind the facade or the best behaviour which is presented for his/her benefit. For example, the observer may be able to visit the research site at a range of different times which makes it more difficult for 'the show' to be arranged. In addition he/she may be able to arrive unannounced, which would also preclude planning on the part of the researched. Adding this degree of unpredictability to the research can, perhaps, be achieved most effectively where observation is to be conducted over a prolonged period of time. In the case of the records of achievement research cited earlier in this chapter, where Pole (1993) had open access to the school over a period of a full term, it was extremely difficult for the school to constantly be on its 'best behaviour'.

Other strategies geared towards avoiding false impressions include the triangulation of research methods where, for example, observation data are cross-referenced with those collected by interviews or documentary analysis. In addition, findings from observations made at a research site should, where possible, be compared with those from other studies in the same substantive field. This is not to suggest that observations and findings that are different from those in published sources should be rejected, rather that just as at any other stage of the research process, the literature will provide a means of contextualising the collected data and suggest further questions which might be posed by them.

In learning how to look, therefore, the observer needs to engage constantly in a process of what might be described as reactivity checks. This involves adopting an approach to data collection where nothing is taken for granted or at face value. As part of this the researcher seeks to cast off the role of audience, and experience at first hand the mundane, the ordinary and the everyday occurrences, as well as the spectacular and the untoward.

In advocating an approach based on a process of constant questioning, however, we do not wish to suggest that it is always the intention of those being observed to deceive. The desire to present a positive picture to an outsider, which is often the way in which the observer is inevitably characterised, seems only to be expected and is not, in our view, likely to result in the collection of data which are either unduly biased or invalid. This issue is addressed by Hammersley and Atkinson (1983) who question whether invalid data actually exist. Their point is that whatever data are collected are valuable. If it appears that the data are a reflection of best rather than everyday behaviour, then what is interesting is why and how the best behaviour has been presented. The researcher should not reject the data as being of little use or value. Hammersley and Atkinson explain that 'data in themselves cannot be valid or invalid; what is at issue are the inferences drawn from them' (p. 191).

Learning how to look is about adopting an appropriate role which allows the researcher to get behind the 'best behaviour' and become part of what is happening. This involves a careful management of self and others as the researcher seeks to establish a rapport with the participants and to develop their trust. However, as we shall show below in our discussion of observation and ethics, maintaining the right balance in such relationships can be fraught with difficulty.

Achieving an appropriate balance in the field role involves establishing a rapport with those being observed but it also involves maintaining a critical distance which enables the observer to stand back from what is observed, to ask questions and to analyse the data as they emerge and are recorded. This may mean that, in studies where the emphasis is on participation, the researcher has to remind him/herself that the purpose of participation is research and that the researcher role always has to take precedence over that of participant. Much of the early literature on participant observation (e.g. Junker, 1960; Gans, 1968; Jarvie, 1969) draws on an analogy derived from earlier anthropology wherein it is thought that the researcher needs to be both stranger and friend if he/she is simultaneously to obtain rich data and to engage with it as a social scientist. Gans (1968) cites Hughes (1960) who, recognising the inherent difficulties of the observer/observed relationship, characterises it in terms of a dialectic, which distinguishes it from the relationship which underpins other methods of data collection, including interviewing and documentary work. Hughes states:

> The unending dialectic between the role of member (participant) and stranger (observer and reporter) is essential to the very concept of field work, and this all participant-observers have in common: they must develop a dialectic relationship between being researchers and being participants (p. xi).

Managing this dialectic is central to a successful role as observer. Avoiding any temptation to abandon the research role and 'go native', but at the same time maintaining an effective rapport with those who are the focus of the study is the key.

Methods of recording the data

The quality of the data gathered via observation can only be as good as the method(s) used to record what is seen and what is experienced. When planning any kind of observation, therefore, and attempting to devise appropriate strategies for how to look, it is imperative that careful thought is given to the means by which the data are to be recorded.

Where a structured approach is to be used and those being observed are aware of the fact, then it is usual for an observation schedule to be produced which reflects the level of detail sought. For example, in the case of systematic and highly structured classroom observation (cf. Croll, 1986; Galton, 1988), an observation schedule might require the observer to record the number and the nature of verbal exchanges between teacher and pupils, the position of the teacher in the classroom at pre-specified time intervals, the use of resources and the layout of the classroom. Alternatively, if a similarly structured observation of a meeting were to be conducted, the observation schedule may need to accommodate data on the positions of the participants, the number and the content of their contributions to the meeting defined in terms of pre-specified categories and details of any documents tabled before or during the meeting. Clearly, the nature of the required data will vary in accordance with the substantive focus of the study, the level of detail required and any alternative sources of data. Whatever the variations, however, the principle remains constant. With highly structured observation the schedule needs to be easy and quick to use, with as many pre-specified categories as possible requiring just a tick or a number to be entered as the researcher keeps abreast of the activities he/she is observing. Figure 4.1 provides an illustration of a structured observation schedule which might be used in the kind of study cited above.

As with all such schedules, the intention is to gather detailed factual information as the action continues. The observer acts as a conduit for the data and at this stage is not concerned with interpreting or analysing the data but merely with recording what he/she sees and hears. The data are to be collected in as 'pure' a form as possible for analysis when the observer leaves the field.

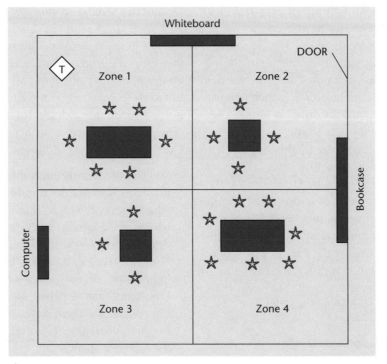

★ = Pupil

Lesson of 35 minutes	Teacher–pupil Interaction	Teacher position
0–5	Talks to whole class	Zone 1 (At whiteboard)
5–10	Silent work	Zones 1, 2, 3 and 4
10–15	Talks to pupils in Zones 1 and 4	Zones 1 and 4 (Takes book from bookcase)
15–20	Demonstrates on whiteboard	Zones 4 and 1
20–25	Talks to pupils in all zones	Zone 4
25–30	Silent work	Zones 1, 2, 3 and 4
30–35	Talks to pupils in all zones	Zone 1

Figure 4.1 Classroom observation (diagram and table).

Where the observation is not as structured, data collection may not be as clear-cut as in the example given above. In particular, where the observer is also a participant, there may be a problem of not only what to record but how and when to record it. For example, recording an account of a series of activities raises issues of technique, selection, interpretation and the observer's relationship with those whom he/she observes.

In our experience, notes made during observation where there is no pre-specified observation schedule are usually particular to the observer, in so far as they are written in a form of personal short-hand which, whilst capturing the essence of the situation being observed, is unlikely to make a great deal of sense to anyone other than the observer. In this context, the notes taken in the field are the first stage in data recording, which will usually require further work in order to render them intelligible and useful to the study.

One of the best examples of this approach to data recording which uses this note taking and elaboration process is given by Delamont (1992). The way in which she develops the original 'real-time' version of events in a cookery lesson in to a more detailed and accessible account, while remaining entirely true to the data is worth quoting at length. Delamont is observing pupils in an inner city comprehensive school. She records her observations during the lesson as follows.

Real-Time Version

10.10
Groups them in one kitchen - show them something.

They are very slow to obey-

She stops everything - reminds them,

Why did she say when told to stop/come round - they must
Vol. Inaud

Mrs B - Not the reason I gave

V. Danger

Mrs B - Yes - Might be an accident about to happen

Pupils not all clear re teasp
tablesp

Like word for 'spatula'
'spatula boys'

Boy coughs all over dem. Of how to put mixt. In tin

sent away - 'If didn't so many cigs wouldn't have such a bad chest - no sympathy (pp. 52–53).

Delamont's style is economical and to her, having witnessed the lesson, is clear, unambiguous and realistic in its scope. As she herself says, although in this form the notes mean nothing to anyone but their author, they are about all an observer is able to record in real time as the situation unfolds. Her notes provide the skeleton for a much fuller field-note which also draws on her memory of events. The fuller version is as follows.

Mrs Bamff goes through the recipe so far, and discovers some of the pupils are not clear about which spoon is which. That is they do not know which of the spoons is the teaspoon, which the dessertspoon and which the tablespoon.

As the recipe calls for teaspoons of some ingredients and tablespoons of others (although Mrs Bamff had weighed and measured all the ingredients for them before school), she stops her demonstration to explain and demonstrate the different spoons.

Mrs Bamff wants to demonstrate 'dropping consistency' with a wooden spoon, and cleaning the mixing bowl with a spatula. She tells them the word for 'spatula', saying 'spatula, boys'.

Bernard has an attack of coughing, and coughs all over the demonstration of how to use the spoon and spatula to put the loaf mixture into the loaf tin.

Mrs Bamff sends him away from the table, saying: 'If you didn't smoke so many ciggies you wouldn't have such a bad chest. I've no sympathy with you (p. 54).

Whilst the substance of the note is exactly the same, the elaboration has changed its status from an observation note to a fieldnote (Lofland and Lofland, 1995). We do not learn anything additional from the fieldnote but its elaboration now means that it is accessible to people other than the researcher and whilst at this stage it remains a descriptive note, it is now possible to see how the record of the observation can be analysed and links can be made with other observations and other data. For example, the fieldnote invites questions about gender, teaching styles and health issues.

These may be themes which are pursued through other forms of data collection such as interviews, and may be identifiable in other observations.

The elaboration is important, therefore, in providing detail, context and links with other data. For it to be successful by remaining true to what actually happened and to avoid the observer's memory working overtime, it is clearly necessary for the elaborated version to be produced as close to the real-time version as possible, to produce what Kleinman and Copp (1993) describe as notes on notes. In addition, the observer needs to develop his/her own comprehensive form of shorthand which is quick and easy to use and is used consistently throughout the study. The real-time notes also need to be taken unobtrusively and in such a way as to avoid suspicion from those being observed. Being conscious that their every move and utterance is being noted may lead some participants to modify their behaviour. In relation to this the observer will need to decide whether it is appropriate to share the notes with those he/she has observed.

In a study of new recruits to the British army, Hockey (1986) decided to leave his observation diary open on his bed for the squaddies to read if they chose to do so. He did not, however, give them access to more analytical fieldnotes written as a field diary and posted home. Due to the frequently arduous and physical nature of the activities in which Hockey participated he was often unable to take real-time notes. For much of the time, therefore, he relied on fieldnotes written as soon as possible after the activities had ended. Despite this constraint, the result is a highly detailed, analytical account of events.

In Delamont's study, as with most school-based research, it was possible to take notes openly as the lesson proceeded. The culture of the classroom is such that note taking by adults is an accepted practice. Pupils and teachers are likely to be comfortable with this, having from time to time witnessed school inspectors, colleagues, teacher trainers and probably other researchers doing the same. Whilst this may be the case, we should not, however, assume that the researcher and the act of note taking have no effect on what happens in the classroom.

We have already discussed the way in which the very presence of another person has an impact on what takes place and consequently what is recorded. Moreover, there have been some ingenious attempts by researchers to overcome such effects. For example King's (1978) study of a primary classroom entailed him hiding away at the back of the room in the Wendy house to avoid contact with the children! Equally ingenious was Llewellyn's (1980) attempt to pass herself off as a pupil in her study of female sub-cultures in a comprehensive school. Others, for example Hey (1997), Nieuwenhuys (1996), relied on their rapport and capacity to get on with and relate to the young people they were working with to overcome any observer effect. However, perhaps the most bizarre attempt to overcome researcher effect was that taken by Griffin (1977), a white researcher who in order to blend in with the black population of New Orleans, which was the focus of his study, changed the colour of his skin with the aid of medication and make-up. Critics argue that Griffin was not a convincing black man and that identity is much more than skin deep. In a similar vein Sullivan et al. (1958) decided to undergo plastic surgery for his study of recruits to the US airforce. Clearly, not all researchers would be prepared to take such steps for the sake of their work and, moreover, the evidence would suggest that those who do so are not successful in achieving the full integration which they seek.

Despite the use of a variety of measures to facilitate 'blending in', in many observation studies it has simply been impossible to record what is happening as it happens. Most obviously the studies where the researchers act covertly preclude open note taking, as to do so would be to reveal the identity of the researcher and the existence of the study. Covert studies have traditionally relied on researchers writing detailed notes of their encounters soon after leaving the field. Whilst there is anecdotal evidence that covert researchers have taken notes secretly by leaving the research site for a short while, the present authors cannot claim to have ever taken a fieldnote in a toilet! Moreover Parry (1987) provides an interesting and amusing discussion of the practical difficulties associated with covert note taking in her study of a naturists' club.

The main message from the examples cited above must be that note taking:

- is an essential part of observational research
- needs to be undertaken as close in time to the observed activities as possible
- has to be meaningful to the observer and capable of being elaborated for colleagues
- should be clear and unambiguous
- should be undertaken with discretion and in such a way as to minimise its impact on participants.

Confidentiality and anonymity

In addition, in all cases, researchers' decisions about data recording need to give careful attention to preserving confidentiality with respect to the research participants and the data which are collected. Whilst this may be clearly understood by researchers when it comes to preparing material for publication, where the use of pseudonyms and other techniques to conceal the true identity of individuals, locations and institutions is common practice, it is less common for researchers to adopt the same practice with observation and fieldnotes. From the outset it is good practice for researchers to use pseudonyms or abbreviations which effectively conceal the identity of their sources of data. They would do well to remember that information does not have to be published to be harmful in the wrong hands. The use of pseudonyms and other anonymising techniques can go some way to protecting research participants from the outset.

The ethics of observation

All research methods have the potential for ethical dilemmas. However, observation is perhaps the one most likely to bring them to the fore. When considering what to look at and how to look, the researcher should always try to be aware of the ethical implications of his/her work. What a researcher looks at and the way in which observation is conducted may have serious implications for the research participants, which at the beginning of the research are not fully appreciated either by the researched or the researcher. In deciding how to look, however, the researcher needs to pause and attempt to see the possible consequences of what he/she proposes from the perspective of those who are to be the focus of the research. This may not eradicate all possible ethical difficulties but it may go some way towards avoiding some of the most obvious ones.

Whilst for many years there has been a growing literature on research ethics (e.g. Barnes, 1979; Bell and Newby, 1977; Bulmer, 1982; Hobbs and May, 1993; Homan, 1991), and many learned societies and research associations go to considerable trouble to produce ethical codes and guidelines (e.g. BERA, 1992; BSA, 1996; BPS, 2000; see Appendix A), it is our view that none of these can fully prepare the researcher for every potential ethical dilemma he/she meets. As with many aspects of research, the only way to appreciate fully the scope for ethical dilemmas is to experience them at first hand. Having said this, however, we do not wish to suggest that the literature concerning ethics or the ethical codes and guides which exist are worthless. On the contrary, we would encourage all researchers to familiarise themselves with these at the start of their work. What we are suggesting, quite simply, is that all research situations are unique and as such present unique ethical challenges. In this context, when an unforeseen ethical dilemma arises, researchers need to think on their feet and to act quickly in order to protect their work, the research participants and themselves. However, the protection of all three of these may not be mutually compatible. Researchers, therefore, need to be aware of the possibility of ethical problems throughout their research. They cannot adopt an ostrich perspective or assume that 'everything will be all right'. By being aware at the outset of some of the possibilities for ethical difficulties the researcher may be able to avert the worst of them.

Openness vs. deception

Within observation, ethical dilemmas relate principally to the extent to which the researcher is open and honest about his/her role and to what use the research will be put. Extreme cases of deception can be found in several of the covert studies cited earlier where the research was conducted without the knowledge or consent of those being researched. In particular, Humphreys' (1970) study of homosexual practices in public toilets violates any notion of informed consent and had the potential to cause considerable damage to the men whom Humphreys observed engaging in a variety of (illegal) homosexual acts. In this case it was highly unlikely that Humphreys would have received permission from the research participants to conduct such a study. Consequently he conducted the research covertly.

Whilst Humphreys' study presents what might be considered an extreme and rare example of ethically challenging observation, there are numerous studies where the consent of those being observed has not been obtained. Many studies of public or relatively open places fall into this category. For example, studies of football stadia and football hooliganism (Buford, 1992; Williams, Dunning and Murphy, 1984) have involved close observation of group behaviour before, during and after football matches. However, in none of these studies was the consent of the great majority of those attending the matches and therefore potentially the focus of the research, obtained. The sheer number of people involved and the fact that the great majority of them would not be included in any specific observations, have been offered as justification for failing to acquire consent. Equally the technical difficulties involved in excluding those who withheld consent, but at the same time including those who gave it, would have been extremely difficult to surmount in this context.

In the case of both Humphreys and Williams *et al.* a clear breach of ethical protocol exists. However the severity of the breach seems qualitatively different and far greater in Humphreys' study of homosexual behaviour than in Williams *et al.*'s study of football hooliganism. Both studies were conducted in public places (public toilets and football stadia, respectively), they were both concerned principally with male activity and involved the researchers in a participant observation role. However, whilst one (Humphreys) generated great concern amongst the academic and gay communities about violation of privacy, together with charges of academic voyeurism, the other (Williams *et al.*) has been greeted favourably and accepted as an important contribution to our understanding of hooliganism and is frequently referred to by the football authorities, government representatives and other policymakers charged with tackling problems of violence in and around football stadia. The different ways in which these studies were received can be attributed to a number of issues which are central to debates about ethics and observation.

In the first instance the number of people involved in the football studies was far greater than in the study of homosexual activity. The potential for 'damage' to be done to individuals was, therefore, far greater in the latter than in the former. In the football studies there was a dilution effect where the focus was upon the behaviour of the crowd in which individuals were difficult to identify. As a consequence, the failure to secure consent from the football supporters is not seen in the same way as failing to secure it from the men in the public toilets. The likelihood of being singled out by the researchers was far greater in the latter situation than in the former. With these studies, as with many others, issues of scope and impact appear to have been significant in relation to whether or not the research is perceived to be ethical.

In addition, there are also issues surrounding the nature and substance of the focus of the studies which were both concerned with socially unacceptable and, in some cases, illegal behaviour conducted in public places. However, whilst one was frequently characterised as a scourge on society which needed to be stopped and the perpetrators punished (football hooliganism), responses to the other were more complicated, involving issues of individual choice and liberty, discrimination against particular social groups and concerns about morality. Football hooliganism was, therefore, seen as something which needed to be dealt with and eradicated. Research which helped to do this was welcomed even if it did violate notions of informed consent. Homosexuality, on the other hand, was (in the USA during the 1970s) slowly becoming if not accepted, then at least more tolerated. It was no longer seen as a problem or a threat to society in the same way as football hooliganism was in Britain during the 1970s/80s. In simplistic terms there appeared to be more of a reason for Williams *et al.*'s work which it was felt would give tangible results. In the case of Humphreys' research, the issues were not so clear-cut. The rationale for the research was not clearly defined and although the research, or at least most of it, was conducted in a public place, the perception remained that there was something essentially private and personal about its content.

The debates about the merits or otherwise of Humphreys' work have been considerable and it is not our task to evaluate them here. The study, when compared with Williams *et al.*'s, is a useful heuristic device for a discussion of ethics and observational research. From the foregoing discussion we can identify a number of factors which structure observational studies and which influence the extent to which a study is regarded as ethical or unethical. The factors to arise from our discussion so far are:

- the extent to which the research is founded on deceit
- the substantive focus of the research
- the capacity of the research to have a detrimental impact on the participants
- societal views regarding the activity/institutions/individuals which are being observed.

What is clear from this list of key points is that deciding what is ethical and what is unethical observation is by no means easy and that the decision is always a matter of judgement on the part of the researcher. What for some will appear ethical, will for others seem unethical, and vice versa. Ethical guides and codes like the examples included in Appendix A act as a useful reference point but do not provide all the answers.

While acknowledging the many constraints under which observation studies are conducted, it is our view that the researcher should always seek to preserve the confidentiality of those who participate in the research and should be as open as possible about the research, its focus and how and why it is being conducted, together with details of the anticipated outcome. Having made such a statement, however, one can immediately think of a number of circumstances where even these basic ground rules could not be followed, as to do so would preclude effective research.

The conclusion to draw from this discussion is, perhaps, that the notion of ethical research is a relative notion where ultimately nothing is ruled out providing an effective rationale can be offered for it. In providing that rationale and deciding on the research design, however, we believe that researchers should always pose themselves the simple question, 'Do the ends justify the means?' In itself the question does not overcome the difficulty of ethical research being relative, but it does force the researcher to examine very carefully the methods used and the reasons for their use. Our view would be that if the ends do not justify the means, then the research should not be conducted in the way initially proposed or possibly at all.

Relationships with research participants

With the exception of studies based on covert means of surveillance, such as hidden cameras or two-way mirrors, research based on observation inevitably brings the researcher and the researched into face-to-face contact. Although we discussed some issues relating to this topic earlier in the chapter, there are others which we feel relate specifically to issues of ethics and are, therefore, worthy of discussion here.

In cases where an observation study involves a prolonged period of participation by the researcher, there is a need for careful management of this contact. We have already seen that, whether the observation is covert or overt, the relationship between observer and observed can be central to the success or otherwise of the research. The management of relationships in the field is, however, a further area in which the researcher potentially faces a range of ethical dilemmas.

Successful observation, particularly where there is an element of active participation, depends to a large extent on the creation of a rapport between the observer and those who are being observed. This will usually involve a degree of role playing on the part of the researcher, whose work relies on the cooperation of the research participants and with whom he/she, therefore, needs to maintain good relations. Also relevant to the notion of role playing is the fact that the observer and the observed have different reasons for taking part in whatever is being observed. From the outset, therefore, the relationship between observer and observed is an unequal one and, furthermore, can be very complex.

For example, although the observer designs the study and may have clear ideas about what is to be the focus of the observation, he/she does not control the research site or the participants. In many ways, therefore, the role of the observer is both powerful and powerless, in that he/she controls the research design but not the research site or the activities which will constitute the focus of the study. Similarly, in many observation studies, the observer is only granted access to a specific research setting by the participants, who also have the capacity to either stop or seriously limit the observation if they so wish. Participants could, for example, exclude the researcher from certain kinds of action by blatantly refusing requests for access to particular events. Alternatively, more subtle kinds of exclusion can be deployed which see the observer invited only to particular events, or recommended

to visit on certain days or at times which would be most convenient for the participants. In this respect control appears to rest with the observed rather than the observer.

To avoid the tactics of exclusion which result in the observer being marginalised, he/she needs to portray a friendly, non-threatening self in an effort to gain the trust of the participants. Frequently, the observer may develop or seek to establish a particular rapport with one person. This person may then become central to the research, providing an introduction and means of entry for the researcher to other participants and aspects of the research site. Such people are usually known as gatekeepers or key informants. Many of the observation studies already cited in this chapter have made effective use of gatekeepers and key informants. For example, Foster (1990) in her study of petty crime in South London relied on Chris, a regular in the Grafton Arms, for her introduction to the ladies' darts team and subsequently to many of the characters who provided the focus of her observations. Pryce (1979), in his study of West Indian culture in Bristol, came to rely on Sigi for entry and introductions to many places and people within the St Pauls area of the city. However, perhaps the most celebrated gatekeeper is Doc, who facilitated much of Whyte's (1943) study of street-corner gangs in Boston.

In all these cases the relationship between the researcher and the gatekeeper was central to the success of the study. A rapport and in some cases a friendship was established upon which much of the research came to rely. It is here, within the nature of this relationship, that the potential for ethical difficulties exists. To describe the relationship between researcher and gatekeeper as a friendship may be accurate in some cases. However, its basis would, in most cases, be the researcher's intention to use the gatekeeper in order to gain access to and information from a particular research setting. An ethical issue is, therefore, present from the outset, as the underlying reason for the relationship is the researcher's need for access and information. In this context, the researcher is prepared to use the friendship, which may be characterised as exploitative, to obtain these. Whilst the researcher may be fully aware of this, the gatekeeper may not be.

The relationship/friendship is unlikely, therefore, to be one based primarily on mutuality and reciprocity. The gatekeeper may be able to do a great deal for the researcher, who in turn merely accepts what is provided. Ethical dilemmas exist, therefore, in the extent to which the researcher is prepared to continue to use the relationship to facilitate the research. As part of this the researcher may place the gatekeeper in a difficult position *vis-à-vis* other participants, a situation that Doc faced as a result of Whyte's (1943) work. In addition, the observer must keep in mind that the gatekeeper or key informant is also a participant and, therefore, is also a subject of the study. This, then, imbues the relationship with further ambiguity, which, if the gatekeeper fails to appreciate this, could result in feelings of betrayal and exploitation by the researcher when material from the study is published and the gatekeeper finds him/herself discussed therein – something which Doc was to claim after the publication of *Street Corner Society* (Boelen, 1992).

This brief consideration of ethics and observation demonstrates that the whole area of research ethics is highly complex. It is, however, central to the conduct of social research and its complexity should not be used as a reason for failing to address the potential for ethical dilemmas and difficulties. It is our view that researchers have a number of responsibilities which they must honour as the process of their work unfolds. Their responsibilities are to: their informants, their data, themselves and their own careers, their discipline, their colleagues and their institutions, to future research and researchers and, in some cases, the funders/sponsors of the research. That so many responsibilities exist is in itself a dilemma, as they may not always be compatible. The researcher will, therefore, be faced with choices, and depending on which one(s) he/she takes, will be seen as ethical by some and unethical by others. Whilst in absolute terms all research may be seen as exploitative and unethical, our view is that in some cases it is more ethical to be unethical than not. But please do not expect us to say which ones.

Conclusion

Our discussion of observation has highlighted some of the complexities of the method. It has provided insight into some of its strengths and weaknesses and offered some practical support for the novice observer. Above all, we hope it has given some idea of the way in which it can help provide interpretations and understandings of social action. Like many of the methods and techniques discussed in this text, it is an approach which has to be experienced to be fully appreciated. Even then it can be frustrating, exhausting, infuriating, lonely and difficult. Observation takes practice, self-confidence, time, resources and belief in its capacity to uncover data that are unavailable in any other way. It is our view, however, that the fact that observation can give rise to so many contrasting experiences is testimony to its versatility and strength, not just as a method of collecting data, but as a key to unlocking institutions and individual and collective behaviour. For this reason alone we would urge you to have a go.

Chapter 5   Survey research: practicalities and potential

Introduction

Surveys constitute one of the most important tools used in contemporary social research. It would be difficult to over-estimate the value of large government surveys such as the General Household Survey, both to policy makers and to academic researchers with interests in areas such as poverty and inequality. Surveys carried out by academics and by doctoral students have made important contributions to our knowledge and understanding of social phenomena and processes in areas such as work, education and health. More generally, small-scale surveys can be of value wherever and whenever a researcher has a quantitative objective, i.e. wishes to answer some form of 'How many?' question.

However, in common with other forms of quantitative research, the survey method can generate a diverse range of responses from the 'person in the street', varying from uncritical acceptance and respect to irrational distaste, and from fascination to boredom. This range of reactions has also long been evident among students and academics, with the prestige of survey research varying markedly both between and within academic disciplines and institutions. In the early 1980s Cathie Marsh felt that there was a need for a vigorous defence of the survey method against its critics (Marsh, 1982). However, at the beginning of the twenty-first century, the trend towards a near-universal recognition within British social research of the contributions that both quantitative and qualitative methods can make reduces the necessity of taking such a stance. On the other hand, much can be learnt from the critics of survey research; reflecting upon criticisms is a good way of ensuring that surveys are constructed and implemented in a fashion calculated to generate valid and useful data, and that they are used for research tasks to which they are well suited. Reflexivity is as important for the survey researcher as it is for the qualitative researcher.

Marsh provides us with a very general but also very useful definition of the (social) survey. In her view a survey takes place when:

1   systematic measurements are made of the same set of properties, or **variables**, for each of a number of cases;
2   the resulting data can be laid out in the form of a rectangle, or **matrix**, in which the rows correspond to the cases and the columns correspond to the properties or variables (see Figure 5.1 later in the chapter);
3   the intention is to look at patterns in the variables by aggregating information from the different cases (Marsh, 1982: 7).

Key features of this definition are the collection of a standardised range of information corresponding to each member of a set of cases and the counting process implicit in the aggregation of information across cases. (For example, a researcher may count how many members of a survey sample identify with the Labour Party.) The validity of this counting process depends on the equivalence of the information collected from the various cases, i.e. standardisation is a foundation of quantification.

Clearly a matrix consisting of cases and variables can be generated in a variety of different ways, not just by administering a questionnaire or interview schedule to a sample of individuals. For example, the observation of a class of school pupils in a number of different hourly lessons might generate a matrix where the cases (rows) were the various pupils and each variable (column) indicated whether a pupil had asked a question in a specific lesson. Furthermore, additional variables (columns) might contain information about each pupil (e.g. their gender, ethnicity, etc.). Alternatively, the units of analysis may be something other than people. For example, the rows of a data matrix might correspond to different countries and the columns to various aspects of the countries' populations (e.g. population size, death rates, fertility rates, etc.) obtained from official statistics. Thus the source of the data in a data matrix may be questionnaires, documents, observation, etc., and the units of analysis may be individuals, parliamentary constituencies, nations, etc.

Furthermore, it is worth noting that data from unstructured interviews can be quantified and laid out in the form of a data matrix. Thus the very broad definition of a 'survey' given above covers a multitude of different forms of data collection. However, the process of standardisation needed to convert qualitative data into this form may result in a matrix of data which have little meaning or value. In addition, the type of counting process inherent in the analysis of the data in the matrix may be of little value in the absence of random sampling (see Chapter 3) or some near equivalent, except, perhaps, where the object of the counting process is simply to establish whether the cases are broadly representative of a wider population. (For an example of the use of counting in qualitative research, see Silverman, 1993: 162.)

Having acknowledged that rectangles of data comparable to those produced by the administration of a standardised questionnaire or interview schedule to a sample of individuals can be produced in many different ways, the rest of this chapter concentrates on this 'conventional' form of survey. Chapter 3 demonstrated the importance of sample design to the researcher's ability to generalise from survey data; in interview-based survey research good-quality fieldwork is also needed to ensure that the data are adequately representative. The interpersonal nature of the survey interview highlights the fact that survey research is not a mechanical process; the data collected are contingent on the dynamics of the interviewer–respondent encounter. Even in the case of postal surveys, a form of communication between researcher and respondent takes place via the questionnaire. The extent to which the validity of survey findings is affected negatively by reactive effects and the lack of standardisation generated by the specificity of human interactions is something upon which researchers need to reflect.

A central topic covered by this chapter is questionnaire design. While its practicalities are considered, questionnaire design is not just a technical exercise, since the construction of a data-collection instrument cannot be separated from the processes of theorising and data analysis. The choice of concepts to be covered within a research instrument inevitably reflects the researcher's substantive and theoretical agenda, as does the way in which the questions designed to measure those concepts are constructed. The process of **operationalisation**, i.e. the generation of measurable 'indicators' of concepts, is fundamental both to the form of research findings and to their validity. The contents of the research instrument and the operationalisation process are also determined to some extent by the researcher's plans for coding and analysing the data collected.

The above highlights a significant difference between survey research and qualitative forms of research such as ethnography. In survey research the important concepts to a very large extent need to be pre-determined, and the concepts deemed to be important dictate which data are collected. In ethnographic research, especially where a Grounded Theory approach is being used, there is much more scope for the data to dictate which concepts are important. The fact that the survey researcher has to decide in advance what is important would inevitably seem to prioritise the researcher's perspective on the research topic over the respondent's perspective. There is certainly a major danger that a survey researcher who adopts a narrow theoretical perspective or who has a limited understanding of their chosen research topic will omit to collect crucial data. However, a survey researcher's theoretical ideas about and substantive knowledge of a particular research topic is often rooted in an extensive literature which in part reflects lay perspectives on the topic, and which is sometimes rooted in earlier, qualitative research. Conversely, ethnographic researchers do not work with the data that they collect in a theoretical vacuum; hence even the concepts which emerge from 'Grounded Theorising' may reflect the researcher's perspective as much or more than they reflect that of the respondent.

Perversely, survey research is sometimes portrayed as a limited and mechanical tool for hypothesis testing, but is also sometimes portrayed as generating findings which are (inappropriately) presented as 'speaking for themselves'. So, on one hand, it is portrayed as a narrow tool for the verification of theory, and on the other hand as dangerously presenting itself as a source of findings whose meaning can be understood without theoretical interpretation. In practice, surveys often collect a range of data which can be used to generate and elaborate upon hypotheses, and competent researchers who present or analyse survey data are often either very cautious in their theoretical interpretations or present a (sometimes theoretically eclectic) range of competing explanations of their findings. The theme common to the latter alternatives is an acknowledgement that there

may be more than one plausible explanation of an observed pattern or relationship.

Learning from criticisms of survey research

Quantitative research has for many years been dogged by accusations of **positivism**. Halfpenny discusses a dozen different usages of the word positivism (Halfpenny, 1992), and Bryman's discussion acknowledges the 'fuzziness' of the term (Bryman, 1988). Central to the term, however, are the notions that the appropriate tools for social research are those of the natural sciences and that phenomena which can be perceived with one's senses and measured constitute the only legitimate and valid source of knowledge.

Accusations of positivism have often been accompanied by a range of other epistemological and political criticisms. Some feminists have expressed a profound scepticism about the validity of quantitative research. Other academics have noted the 'capitalistic roots' of survey research, or even portrayed it as a mechanism by which the ruling group within a society is able to abuse its power and carry out the ideological manipulation of the rest of society. Other critics (i.e. some ethnomethodologists) have suggested that a different form of knowledge has a monopoly on validity and meaning. (For relevant discussions see Stanley and Wise, 1993; Graham, 1982; Marsh, 1982; Bryman, 1988.)

We reject the argument that quantitative methods are a wholly invalid way of generating knowledge about society and social processes. However, some survey researchers, and hence some pieces of survey research, are positivistic, sexist or manipulative. Survey research can also be 'scientistic' and ignore the consciousness and agency of its subjects, etc. However, what is most important is for a social researcher to be able to recognise these failings in other people's research, and to be aware of and learn from issues raised by the above criticisms which are of relevance to their own research.

Theoretical perspectives, political agendas and survey research

Professional survey research organisations (such as the National Centre for Social Research) often document the technical aspects of their surveys in an impressively meticulous fashion, but may be less inclined to contextualise their research theoretically. Survey findings can thus become divorced from the process that created them and take on 'a life of their own'. Politicians and journalists sometimes reify survey results, treating them as neutral, scientific truths, and interpreting them (often superficially) in a way that suggests that the interpretation that they give is the only possible explanation of the patterns in the data. Survey researchers are much less often guilty of this kind of positivistic, empiricist behaviour.

Historically, a high proportion of survey research has been carried out by the 'powerful' (e.g. men) on behalf of the 'powerful' (e.g. government bodies or commercial organisations). However, the roots of survey research lay in studies of poverty, and in contemporary Britain survey research has often been used to demonstrate the continued existence of various forms of social inequality, and to examine aspects of the lives of 'disadvantaged' groups such as women (e.g. Roberts, 1990). On the other hand, official survey research is often stimulated by and consequently prioritises administrative needs; hence official surveys of disability have been criticised for conceptualising disability in a fashion that reflects their purpose as a resource allocation tool rather than reflecting the perspectives of the disabled themselves (Martin *et al.*, 1988; Abberley, 1996). Note that secondary analyses of official survey data can be markedly more 'radical' than the origins of those data. (The pros and cons of official statistics and data are discussed in more detail in Chapter 7.)

A researcher making use of existing survey data should evaluate the extent to which the survey's research instrument and the range of data collected reflect the theoretical perspectives and political agenda of those who have designed and imple-

mented the survey. A researcher carrying out their own survey should reflect upon the suitability of the survey method as a way of attaining their research objectives, and should also try to make explicit the way in which their theoretical ideas and research objectives are embedded in the research instrument. This kind of reflexive approach does not guarantee unproblematic research, but is likely to result in appropriate qualifications to findings.

The 1972 Oxford Mobility Study is a classic academic survey which led to the finding that the relative social mobility of different social classes in post-war Britain had remained more or less constant, suggesting that society had not become more 'open' in this respect (Goldthorpe *et al.*, 1987). However, the survey focused exclusively on the social mobility of men, reflecting the underlying theoretical assumption that women were only of marginal significance to the class structure, an assumption that Goldthorpe made explicit at the beginning of a long-running debate on women and social class (Goldthorpe, 1983; Roberts, 1993). Note that the survey's findings do not in themselves prove the existence of ongoing and unfair discrimination on the basis of social class; additional theorising and empirical evidence is needed to support or refute this conclusion (Saunders, 1989, 1995; Marshall and Swift, 1996; Lampard, 1996). Thus it can be seen that both the nature and the interpretation of survey findings are contingent on a researcher's theoretical perspective. This is, however, arguably true of findings generated by other research methods.

The social dimension of social survey research and the actor's perspective

It is very important to recognise the potential for differences between research in the natural sciences and social survey research. Social survey respondents are conscious social actors, and such surveys involve interpersonal communication via language which is assumed to have a meaning which is common to the researcher and all the respondents. For researchers who wish to collect data which are consistent with the viewpoint of the social actor (e.g. those who adhere to a phenomenological perspective; see Bryman, 1988: 50), it is important that a survey collects data which reflect the meanings attached to events and processes by the respondents, rather than the data simply being the product of the researcher's understanding of these events and processes. This is a key point in Abberley's critique of the OPCS Disability Surveys (Abberley, 1996). While it is an issue in all social research, there is a particular risk that survey research will collect data which reflect the researcher's interpretation of some form of behaviour or social process rather than the actor's perspective. (Arguably, in research whose objectives centre around the effects of social structure rather than the consequences of social action, neglecting the actor's perspective may be relatively unproblematic.) However, if a researcher is confident that he or she shares with respondents a common understanding of the meaning of the survey questions, and also that the questions tap adequately the actor's perspective on the issue under investigation, then the survey may be relatively consistent with a phenomenological perspective.

In order for the counting process inherent within survey research to be a valid one, the various respondents to a survey must have a near enough identical understanding of what the questions mean. This might be seen merely as a technical problem, where the solution lies in a suitable choice of vocabulary and phrasing for each question. However, a question such as 'How many friends do you have?' illustrates a major difficulty: how can the researcher amend such a question in such a way as to provide comparable answers from different respondents without implicitly imposing some definition of friendship on respondents which does not correspond with their subjective and varied understandings of the concept?

It is quite likely that a researcher will feel that some form of qualitative research is needed if their research is properly to reflect the actor's perspective. This might constitute an alternative to survey research; to suggest that surveys are suitable for all social research tasks is to lay oneself open to justifiable accusations of positivism. On the other hand, qualitative research can be used as a preliminary stage to enhance the validity of survey research (Morton-Williams, 1978). Alternatively, qualitative research can be used to complement survey research (or vice versa). Finally, in situations where the actor's perspective is of considerable interest but where survey data embodying the researcher's perspective appear in themselves to have some theoretical or substantive value, the survey results can be presented with appropriate qualifications.

A critique of a survey

Stanley has carried out a detailed evaluation of the merits and limitations of various sex surveys (Stanley, 1995). Her discussion of the National Survey of Sexual Attitudes and Lifestyles (NATSAL) highlights a number of the issues discussed above (Johnson *et al.*, 1994; see also Chapter 3, and Devine and Heath, 1999: Chapter 6). She suggests that the failure of NATSAL to research the meanings of sexual behaviour to the social actors involved has negative consequences for the researchers' understanding of sexual behaviour, and makes an adverse comparison between NATSAL and 'Little Kinsey', a sex survey carried out in 1949, which also collected qualitative data more in tune with a phenomenological perspective (Stanley, 1995: 4). Stanley notes the epidemiological flavour of the survey (a central objective of which was the generation of data relevant to the spread of HIV), and comments that it lacks a discernible interpretational stance and that its approach appears to be one which is at the same time 'scientific' and based on 'common sense'.

She also points out that NATSAL emphasises certain 'high-risk' forms of sexual activity, including some forms of male homosexual behaviour, but that it seems to use heterosexual activity as its point of reference. Furthermore, Stanley suggests that the survey under-estimates the extent of both male and female homosexuality in contemporary Britain, because the potentially sensitive nature of homosexuality can be expected to have resulted in a significant amount of non-disclosure and selective non-response.

From Stanley's point of view the researchers who were involved in NATSAL do not appear to have adequately reflected upon the way in which the survey embodies implicit theoretical assumptions. Undoubtedly the findings from NATSAL do not prioritise the actor's perspective. The key question which needs to be answered if we wish to assess the extent to which this limitation is a problem is whether the actor's perspective is fundamental to the survey's research objectives. If the information needed for effective epidemiological models of the spread of HIV consists simply of patterns of behaviour, then the actor's perspective may not be crucial. However, if the models are based on assumptions about the choices and decisions made and risks taken by social actors, then there is, perhaps, more of a problem. There is certainly a problem if the survey's assessment of the frequency of particular forms of 'high-risk' sexual behaviour is inaccurate, given that such information is likely to be central to the epidemiological models. However, the problem here is not that the wrong 'sort' of data was collected, but that the survey may have been less effective than it might have been in carrying out what was bound to be a difficult 'counting' task. Overall, Stanley's critique demonstrates clearly that the data collected by the NATSAL survey reflect both the research objectives and the theoretical assumptions of the researchers. Even if NATSAL had been more orientated towards its respondents' own understandings of their sexual behaviour, it

seems reasonable to conclude that qualitative data would be needed to provide a broader understanding of sexual behaviour as a form of social activity.

Surveys, causality and context

Adverse comparisons are often made between surveys on the one hand and both experiments and ethnography on the other hand, in terms of the ability of research to say something useful about causality. However, it is rare in social research for it to be practical and ethical to carry out some form of social experimentation, in which the ability to intervene and careful research design can rule out alternative explanations of an observed relationship between 'cause' and 'effect' (see Chapter 2).

In cross-sectional survey research there is always the possibility that an observed relationship between two variables is 'spurious', i.e. that it reflects relationships between both variables and a third variable. In addition, it is the researcher who has to assume which variable is the 'cause' and which is the 'effect'. The second of these problems can sometimes be resolved by longitudinal survey research, since causality can only operate in one direction if the two variables are clearly 'temporally ordered'.

Survey research is actually quite good at rejecting alternative causal explanations of observed phenomena, since multivariate statistical analysis can demonstrate whether a given third variable explains the observed relationship between two variables. However, it is arguably the case that a qualitative researcher carrying out longitudinal participant observation has a better chance of observing social processes in a sufficiently intensive and holistic way to give them direct evidence of linkages between 'causes' and 'effects'. In addition, the actor's perspective on causal processes reflecting decisions and choices may be an important tool for the development of causal narratives. While survey research may be capable of collecting data relating to the actor's perspective, qualitative research may do this more effectively.

Whatever the form of research, causality is usually inferred rather than clearly demonstrated, and statements relating to causality reflect a process of theorising as much as they reflect data. The important lesson to be learned here is the old chestnut that 'correlation is not causation', i.e. assuming that an observed relationship between two variables shows that one causes the other is both positivistic and lazy. Some form of plausible narrative linking the two variables is needed: a narrative generated by theoretical reflection, possibly with the aid of additional data, whether quantitative or qualitative. (In addition to discussions relating to causality in Bryman, 1988, and Marsh, 1982, an extended discussion is given by Hage and Meeker, 1988).

A more pertinent criticism of the survey method is the accusation of **atomism**, i.e. the tendency to collect data from survey respondents in a way which divorces them from their social context and severs their connections to other individuals. However, this is a more pertinent criticism of what surveys usually do than of what they can do. Most surveys collect some 'contextual' data: for example, about other household members, workplaces, or even respondents' social networks. In recent years sophisticated statistical techniques which simultaneously take into account different levels of analysis (e.g. pupils, schools, local education authorities) have become more widely used (Goldstein, 1995; see Chapter 9). On the other hand, it is much more straightforward and much more usual to use survey data to describe the aggregated characteristics of a group of people than it is to use them to describe the dynamics of the interpersonal encounters within such a group. Techniques for the analysis of 'relational' data are less widely known and used than those used for the analysis of more conventional forms of quantitative data. (A discussion of tools for the analysis of social networks can be found in Scott, 1991.)

To avoid an unnecessarily atomistic approach, it is therefore important for the researcher to remember at the design stage of a survey that each respondent does not live in a social vacuum, and for them to gear their research instrument to the collection of any contextual information which is likely to be of value (and which can in practice

be collected). At the analysis stage, the theoretical importance of contextual effects needs to be borne in mind, even if recognising this only serves to highlight the limitations of the data collected. Of course, in some circumstances alternative research methods may be better suited to looking at social behaviour and processes 'in context'. As is often the case, a combination of the survey method and other approaches may be most productive.

Making constructive use of scepticism about surveys

Many students and some researchers are sceptical about the value of social surveys. However, such scepticism can in itself be of value, since it stimulates a range of questions which need to be in the mind of an appropriately reflexive researcher using the survey method or evaluating existing survey data.

- Can the phenomenon of interest be quantified in such a way as to produce values which are valid measures of respondents' characteristics?
- Are these values comparable and hence the aggregation inherent in 'counting' them legitimate?
- Are the variables generated by a survey theoretically meaningful and relevant, and are their assumed meanings consistent with the respondent's perspective on the phenomenon?
- Can the data collected by a survey be used to answer theoretically interesting questions, or do they pose interesting substantive questions which require further theorising or data collection?

Setting the scene for questionnaire design

One of the frustrating aspects of analysing existing survey data is that there are invariably questions that the secondary analyst would have liked the original researcher to have included in their research instrument which they in fact did not include. However, it is even more frustrating for a researcher to find that he or she has not asked all the necessary questions in their own survey. The difficulty for survey researchers is that they need to identify in advance all the concepts which will be important to their analyses. The early part of the process of conceptual development, of which 'questionnaire design' is an aspect, pre-dates even the research design stage of a project; the gradual accumulation of information and ideas about the research topic, through lived experience, digestion of the existing academic literature and theorising, generates a substantive and theoretical pool of concepts from which those operationalised in the research instrument are drawn. Halfpenny and his co-authors carried out a study of the process of questionnaire design (Halfpenny *et al.*, 1992) and refer to the first stage of this process as 'mapping the semantic domain', by which they mean the identification of the range of relevant concepts (and the theoretical relationships between them) and the selection of the concepts to be operationalised within a questionnaire.

From a practical point of view, the researcher ideally needs to identify:

1 the concepts which are used in theoretical discussions of the research topic, and in any broader theoretical literature which it is felt applies to the research topic;
2 the concepts which have been derived from or operationalised within past empirical research on the research topic;
3 the concepts which are embedded within lay viewpoints on the research topic.

In other words, the researcher needs to read up on their research topic, capitalise on other people's research, and (if it is practical and seems necessary) do some preliminary qualitative research. Carrying out a 'brainstorming' exercise with some colleagues, or organising a small focus group, may help in relation to point 3 above. Of course, a researcher's own theoretical insight may also suggest additional relevant concepts.

Suppose that the core of a researcher's topic is the relationship between social class and voting behaviour. Social class is not a unidimensional, clearly defined concept: for example, is the researcher interested in subjective social class or some 'objective' version based on occupation? Is the researcher interested in class in an 'economic' sense, or are they more concerned with social status and prestige? Is it someone's current class that matters, or their class of origin? Turning to voting behaviour, is it actual voting behaviour that the researcher is interested in, or party political identification, or both? What might seem at first sight to be a single relationship between two concepts may fragment into a number of possible relationships between a range of related concepts, or sub-concepts, or facets of concepts. Once the researcher starts trying to elaborate upon the relationship between class and vote a range of other factors become potentially relevant: material circumstances (such as income, wealth and housing), political and social values, education, past voting behaviour, public/private sector occupations, etc. Data relating to respondents' feelings about the high-profile political issues of the day may be needed to put the class/vote relationship into context. Furthermore, variations in the class/vote relationship according to gender, age differences, geographical location, etc., are likely to be of interest.

It can be seen from the above that the range of relevant concepts expands with the breadth of the research objectives and the depth of theoretical elaboration planned. As noted by De Vaus (1996), the questions asked in survey questionnaires can be categorised into four groups:

1 measures of the dependent variables;
2 measures of the independent (explanatory) variables;
3 measures of variables which contribute to the explanation of the relationships between the independent and dependent variables;

4   measures of 'background' variables (for example, the sort of 'key variables in social investigation' described in Burgess, 1986).

The above categorisation should act as a reminder that the researcher has to cast a wide net to identify the full range of concepts which need to be operationalised in a survey questionnaire. The need to include questions relating to a wide range of concepts is even more pressing in multi-purpose surveys (such as the General Household Survey and the British Social Attitudes Survey) which are, at least in part, geared towards future, unspecified secondary analyses. Surveys are costly in terms of both time and money, and anticipating possible future research objectives may result in a survey which generates a reservoir of data to which the researcher can come back again and again.

The operationalisation of concepts

It is rather unlikely that a researcher will be able to operationalise the concepts of interest to them adequately simply by sitting down and having a session thinking up indicators for the concepts and writing down specific questions for the indicators. For a start, it may make sense to make use of the ways in which previous researchers have operationalised concepts, both to avoid re-inventing the wheel and also to make the survey findings more comparable with the results of previous research. In the mid-1990s various government departments in the UK agreed to harmonise the concepts and questions that they use in social surveys to increase comparability, and details of the standardised questions have been published (ONS, 1996b). In addition, the Economic and Social Research Council has funded a resource on the World Wide Web known as the 'Question Bank', which allows Internet users to access questionnaires and other survey-related material corresponding to a growing number of significant British surveys (for more details see Chapter 7).

While starting from scratch may result in a square wheel, borrowing an existing way of operationalising a concept can result in a wheel which does not fit on the axle of a specific research project. If a researcher is using questions inherited from earlier surveys, then it is important for them to assess what theoretical assumptions are embedded in the questions, and hence to evaluate whether the concepts of interest are operationalised in ways which appear consistent with their own research objectives and understanding of the concepts.

In practice, 'tried and trusted' ways of operationalising concepts are likely to work at least tolerably well. Indicators which researchers dream up themselves may be ideal in theory but less than ideal in practice. An important function of the piloting of questionnaires, i.e. trying preliminary versions out on a smallish sample of potential respondents, is the evaluation of how effective indicators are in practice. At an earlier stage, preliminary qualitative fieldwork can also contribute to the development of indicators which tap underlying concepts in ways which are consistent with the respondents' understandings of the concepts. The process of operationalisation can also extend beyond the fieldwork stage of the research process into the data preparation and analysis stage, since the same set of questions can sometimes be used to operationalise a concept in a number of different ways. Secondary analysts are often inventive in their use of the questions available to them as indicators of the concepts which interest them, though the relationship between indicator and concept is not always as convincing as those found in primary research.

An example: operationalising social class

The operationalisation of social class can serve as a useful illustrative example, but is also of importance in itself. While there is an ongoing debate about the degree of relevance of the concept of social class to an understanding of contemporary societies (Lee and Turner, 1996; Pakulski and Waters, 1996), questions from which social class can be derived have been and will continue to be a standard feature of social survey questionnaires (Marsh, 1986). As noted earlier, class is a complex, multi-dimensional concept which can be and has been operationalised in a variety of different ways. The most common indicator of social class is, of course, occupation, but the range of occupational information collected by a survey, and the way in which that information is converted into a value within a class-related column (variable) in a data matrix, are very much dependent on the researcher's theoretical understanding of the concept of class.

Suppose that a researcher views a respondent's own occupation as an important factor in determining their class position. A fairly obvious starting point is the respondent's job title. However, this starting point assumes that the respondent currently has an occupation. The decision as to whether a past occupation (or a future occupation, if the respondent is waiting to start a job) is an adequate substitute depends on the purpose for which the researcher wants a measure of class. There is also the question of what to do with respondents with more than one job.

Occupational titles can be incredibly uninformative (e.g. 'civil servant', 'engineer'), so surveys often ask what kind of work respondents do most of the time, and what qualifications and training are needed for their jobs. Implicit in the latter is the notion that skills or a need for 'professional' qualifications help locate an occupation in the class structure. Similarly, further questions are often asked relating to the existence and magnitude of supervisory responsibilities and to employment status (i.e. employee, self-employed, employer; if the respondent is an employer then the number of their employees may be requested). This reflects the assumed theoretical relevance of authority and of whether the respondent is an exploiter of wage labour or has their labour exploited!

An example of a series of questions of the above sort is given below; similar series of questions in the format that they take within interview schedules can also be found in Johnson *et al.* (1994: 417), and in Heath *et al.* (1985: 213). Many of the questionnaires included in the ESRC's Question Bank on the Internet contain such questions (see Chapter 7). Questions are also often asked in relation to other aspects of the respondent's occupation: for example, what their employer makes or does at their workplace, whether they work full-time or part-time (or their specific working hours), and whether their occupation is in the public sector or the private sector.

Questions about occupations (which can be used to operationalise social class)

- What is your job?
- What is the name or title of the job?
- What kind of work do you do most of the time? (What materials/machinery do you use?)
- What training or qualifications do you have that are needed for that job?
- Do you supervise or are you responsible for the work of any other people? (How many?)
- Are you an employee or self-employed?
- What does your employer (do you) make or do at the place where you usually work?
- Including yourself, how many people are employed at the place you usually work at (from)? (Do you have any employees? How many?)

The information gathered via a series of occupation-related questions is used to assign the respondent's occupation to one of a large number of occupational categories, often using the Standard Occupational Classification used in official statistics (OPCS, 1991b), or an international equivalent (ILO, 1990). These categories are sufficiently detailed that it is primarily the way in which they are aggregated into 'classes' which highlights the specific theoretical perspective being adopted. (Note that there is a broad consensus that ownership, authority and expertise are important aspects of social class.) The most familiar set of 'classes' to British social scientists is probably Registrar General's Social Class (RGSC), which has been used up to now in official statistics. Unfortunately, RGSC is rather atheoretical, being based on vague notions of skill and standing within the community, and having been updated in an ad-hoc fashion as the twentieth century progressed. Among other weaknesses, RGSC emphasises the difference between 'non-manual' and 'manual' occupations in a way which is not necessarily theoretically desirable: for example, routine non-manual occupations in sales can be similar to many manual occupations in terms of employment relations and conditions, and are not necessarily any better rewarded economically. Perhaps not surprisingly, a review of the social classifications used by government has now been completed and a new set of categories is being introduced (Rose and O'Reilly, 1997). More overtly theoretically based class groupings than RGSC have been produced by Goldthorpe (Goldthorpe *et al.*, 1987) and Wright (1985). A discussion of the theoretical bases of these sets of classes is given by Crompton (1993): the former is broadly neo-Weberian, and focuses on the 'market situation' of occupations, whereas the latter is broadly neo-Marxist, and is elegantly defined in terms of employment status, authority and expertise. Unfortunately, the elegance of Wright's class schema does not translate into effectiveness as a tool for empirical research (Marshall *et al.*, 1988).

Theoretical considerations and the objectives of the research are also relevant to whether respondent's current (or last) occupation on its own is deemed to be an adequate indicator of the concept of class. Class consciousness may be thought to relate to class of origin as well as to current occupation, and medical sociologists increasingly view the effects of class position throughout the life course as being cumulative. The latter suggests a need for the collection of occupational histories; the former requires the collection of data on parental occupations (information in relation to which is often requested for the time when the respondent was 14). More obviously, occupational data relating to respondents' spouses will be needed if it is felt that the household is the (theoretically) appropriate unit of analysis. The assignment to social classes of households and of married women is a topic which has generated fierce debate (Roberts, 1993); evidence exists that class of origin needs to be operationalised in terms of mothers' occupations as well as fathers' (Lampard, 1995).

The use of a 'standard' way of operationalising social class is clearly advantageous in terms of comparability with existing research. However, while adopting an existing class schema also saves the researcher time and effort, there is always the risk that the inherited operationalisation is flawed or unsuitable, given the research objectives and theoretical considerations. Using existing ways of operationalising concepts does not mean that researchers can avoid reflecting on the validity of the operationalisation process in the context of their own research projects. It may also be the case that a researcher cannot include the full range of questions that they would ideally like to; hence there may be a need to simplify or truncate an inherited approach. Note also that the ways of operationalising class discussed above do not pay explicit attention to the actor's perspective on social class: this reflects an emphasis on class structure rather than class consciousness or class action.

A good example of the way in which theoretical ideas are embedded in particular ways of operationalising concepts is the fact that, in the above discussion, the class structure is implicitly viewed as consisting of a set of discrete classes based on categories of occupations. However, in US research, the class-related concept of Socio-Economic Status (SES) is typically operationalised as a scale (i.e. as a hierarchical range of scores). Furthermore, Goldthorpe classes were preceded by the Hope–Goldthorpe scale (Goldthorpe and Hope, 1974), and researchers at Cambridge have developed a scale of occupational scores (Prandy, 1990). Many concepts can be operationalised in a common-sense way either as categories or as a scale; while the choice of categories or scale is sometimes made for technical reasons, there are often implicit theoretical nuances attached to such a decision.

The construction of scales

One approach to the operationalisation of concepts which involves the use of more than one question and results in an indicator in the form of a scale is the construction of an index or attitude scale from a series of related questions, or **items**. The logic behind this approach is based on the recognition that for many concepts it is difficult or impossible to identify a single question which is on its own an adequate and comprehensive indicator of the concept in question. However, there may be a number of different questions which can act collectively as an adequate indicator. An overall indicator is usually constructed by assigning values to the answers to each question, and then summing the values across all the questions. Scales of this sort are often used in the measurement of attitudes (Procter, 1993; Oppenheim, 1992). Indeed, many texts (e.g. Sudman and Bradburn, 1982) make a distinction between attempts to tap 'knowledge' or 'facts' and attempts to tap 'attitudes' or 'subjective views' and view scaling as an appropriate way of addressing the latter objective.

One example of the use of a set of related items to produce a scale is the use of the Bem Sex Role Inventory to generate 'masculinity' and 'femininity' scores. Respondents are asked to indicate (on a scale of 1 to 7) the extent to which each of a list of (60) personality characteristics is true for them: for example, to what extent do they feel that they are 'friendly', 'aggressive', 'loyal', etc.? Of the 60 items, 20 are deemed to be 'masculine' traits, 20 'feminine', and 20 'neutral'; hence by adding the values for the 20 'feminine' items the researcher can produce a 'femininity' score with a value of between 20 and 140 inclusive. These scores have been used in research examining the extent to which gender differences in health can be attributed to between-sex differences in masculinity and femininity, and also the extent to which within-sex variation in health reflects within-sex variation in masculinity and femininity (Annandale and Hunt, 1990).

Note that the respondent is not informed of the purpose of the inventory, so they are not consciously reporting their degree of self-perceived 'masculinity' or 'femininity'. The actor's perspective is thus not prioritised here. On the other hand, neither (one would hope) is the researcher's perspective, since masculinity and femininity are social constructs, and the validity of the interpretation of the scores as measures of masculinity and femininity depends on the extent to which the items tap a society's understanding of these concepts. There are clearly some assumptions being made here: for example, that masculinity and femininity are one-dimensional concepts with consistent meanings across the whole of a society, and that an indicator can be transferred between times and places without loss of validity. Indeed, since the scales described above were originally developed some time ago in the United States, their use in contemporary Britain certainly merits the usual consideration of the validity of an 'inherited' indicator.

Turning briefly to the issue of reliability, i.e. the extent to which respondents consistently respond to a measure in the same way, multi-item indicators are arguably more reliable than single-item indicators, since fluctuations in a respondent's answers to the various items are likely, to some extent, to cancel each other out (De Vaus, 1996). Reliability also has a slightly different (and more specific) meaning in the context of scales based on a number of items, i.e. the extent to which a respondent's answers to the various items tend to be consistent with each other. Clearly, if the answer to each item was a perfect measure of the underlying concept, the items would all vary in an entirely consistent way. However, individual items inevitably reflect not just one but a variety of underlying factors, and they may also be unreliable in the sense that they are prone to (meaningless) fluctuation. Thus a reliable scale is achieved by the use of a set of items which are strongly correlated with each other, and in a reliable scale each of the individual items is strongly correlated with the rest of the scale. When a scale is being developed, the range of items included is often chosen because they collectively maximise a measure of reliability such as Cronbach's alpha (Cronbach, 1951). This particular measure varies between 0 and 1, with a higher value corresponding to greater reliability, and scores of about 0.7 or greater indicating a scale with a satisfactory degree of reliability. (An example is given a little later.)

The reliability of a scale, as, for example, judged by Cronbach's alpha, is rather easier to assess than its validity. The assessment of validity can involve an examination of the following forms of validity:

- the scale's **construct validity**, i.e. the extent to which it relates in practice to other variables to which theory predicts it should relate
- the scale's **criterion validity**, i.e. the extent to which it is related in practice to other indicators of the same concept
- the scale's **predictive validity**, i.e. the strength of its relationship with relevant later events or behaviour
- the scale's **content validity**, i.e. the extent to which the items cover the full breadth of the concept
- the scale's **face validity**, i.e. the extent to which the items 'appear' to tap the concept.

Assessing any of the above forms of validity, but especially the last two, involves a degree of subjectivity; unfortunately, at the end of the day the validity of a scale cannot be established with any certainty. A very reliable scale is measuring something reliably, but there is no guarantee that it is measuring the concept of interest to the researcher.

An interesting example of a 'tried and trusted' scale is the score produced using one of the variants of the General Health Questionnaire (GHQ). This is a measure of 'psychological well-being' that has been included in many health-related surveys, including the Health and Lifestyle Survey (HALS: Cox, 1987; Blaxter, 1990). Respondents are asked (up to) 30 questions, an example being the following:

'Have you recently been finding life a struggle all the time?'

The range of answers permitted for this question is:

More so than usual; same as usual; less so than usual; much less than usual.

The answer for each question is assigned a value of between 1 and 4 inclusive, giving an overall score of between 30 and 120.

How many indicators?

It is interesting to note that the GHQ was originally developed as a method for identifying psychiatrically ill people (Goldberg and Blackwell, 1970); arguably the concepts of (general) 'psychological well-being' and 'psychiatric illness' are not one and the same. Indeed, the concepts of 'health' and 'illness' more broadly are arguably too complex and multi-dimensional for single indicators to do more than tap one aspect of one sub-concept, and Macintyre (in Burgess, 1986) notes that: 'there would be great difficulties in devising a simple composite measure [of health] that could be elicited easily by an interviewer in the way that age or gender are'.

In a classic piece of research on class-related health inequalities, the main indicator of 'health' is mortality and class is operationalised in the form of Registrar General's Social Class (Townsend *et al.*, 1988). Clearly, mortality is a sensible indicator of some aspects of health, but not of mental health or, perhaps, of disability.

In a large survey orientated towards health such as HALS, there is scope to include a range of indicators covering the many dimensions of health. However, in surveys where health is of interest but the central focus is on other concepts, and where space is at a premium, only a small number of indicators can be included. An extreme example of this is the 1991 Census, which included a single health-related question. After much reflection and some preliminary testing (Dale and Marsh, 1993), the question included was:

'Does the person have any long-term illness, health problem or handicap which limits his/her daily activities or the work he/she can do?'

Thus research on health using the Census is really research on limiting long-term illness. Space considerations can also lead to the use of fewer items in multi-item indicators: for example, a four-item version of the GHQ was used in the Social Change and Economic Life Initiative (SCELI) survey and still permitted interesting analyses to be carried out (Burchell, 1994). In this case, however, it was the reliability and validity of the indicator which were potentially affected rather than the coverage of the concept. As can be seen below, however, the Cronbach's alpha for the four-item version of the GHQ suggests that it is more than adequately reliable.

Cronbach's alpha for a four-item version of the GHQ scale

(SCELI data; n = 6077; see Burchell, 1994).
  Overall value of alpha = 0.785

Item

Have you recently . . .	*Alpha if item removed*
. . . been feeling reasonably happy, all things considered?	0.723
. . . been able to enjoy your usual day-to-day activities?	0.755
. . . been feeling unhappy and depressed?	0.688
. . . been losing confidence in yourself?	0.755

Possible answers (shown to respondents on card):

First two items: More so than usual, same as usual, less so than usual, much less than usual.

Last two items: Not at all, no more than usual, rather more than usual, much more than usual.

Note that the correlations (see Chapter 9) between (pairs of) items are all 0.345 or greater; removing any of the items can be seen to result in a noticeably smaller value of alpha.

While there may be scope for the inclusion in a survey of a number of indicators of a concept, it is important for the researcher to get clear in their mind what the various dimensions of a concept are, and whether some dimensions are crucial and others less vital. It may be preferable to include a number of indicators relating to a key dimension rather than a single indicator for each of a range of dimensions. Such decisions can only be properly made on a theoretical basis with reference to the objectives of the research, though the decisions may also reflect the degree of confidence that the researcher has in their indicators, since there is clearly a risk attached to using a single, newly developed indicator for a key dimension.

Questionnaires and questions

Both self-completion questionnaires and the interview schedules utilised in 'face-to-face' surveys involve the use of questions to generate data which can be quantified in the form of a case-by-variable data matrix. The label 'questionnaire' is applied to both forms of research instrument in the discussion that follows.

Good questionnaire design takes the form of a process, rather than an event. It flows out of a period of theoretical reflection and concept operationalisation, and flows into the early stages of survey fieldwork. Getting a superficially satisfactory wording of a question down on paper gives the researcher something 'concrete' to work on, but the question needs to be piloted before the actual survey takes place. Furthermore, a questionnaire needs to be considered as a whole rather than simply as a list of questions; hence both questions and questionnaire need to be piloted, quite possibly more than once. The form as well as the wording of questions may change as the piloting process takes place; questions often start off as **open**, i.e. the respondent is free to give a spontaneous answer in their own words, and end up as **closed**, i.e. the respondent is directed to select an answer from a given range of alternatives.

When designing a questionnaire, the researcher also needs to recognise that the administration of a questionnaire is a social process, involving communication between the researcher and respondent, possibly with an interviewer as an intermediary, and requiring that the respondent provides the researcher with information. As noted by Bateson (1984), the respondent needs to understand what information is being requested of them, and to be able and willing to give it; reflecting on these three concepts of **understanding**, **ability** and **willingness** can give the researcher an insight into whether questions will generate valid and useful data.

The concept of 'understanding' can be broken down further into two overlapping but subtly different sub-dimensions: the extent to which respondents grasp the broad thrust of a question, and the extent to which the issues raised by the question and the words used in the question have a common meaning for the researcher and for the various respondents. Interpersonal communication between humans usually 'works' despite minor variations in the perceived meanings of words; the process of collecting data via questionnaires is for this reason never completely standardised across a sample of respondents. The key question is whether the degree of variation in the meanings attached to a particular question by respondents is too great for their answers to be aggregated validly.

Data collected by open questions within questionnaires are clearly qualitative in a way that data collected by closed questions are not, since open questions allow respondents to control the range and nature of the answers that they give. On occasions the inclusion of open questions in survey questionnaires may help counteract some of the limitations of quantitative research. However, it is unusual for such questions to be anything other than subordinate to the survey's quantitative objectives. Oppenheim sees data from open questions as playing a largely illustrative role, since 'statistical tabulations are important and must remain our first aim' (1992: 112). Oppenheim also suggests that all closed questions with fixed sets of answers should start their lives as open-ended questions, with the piloting process allowing a range of answers to a question to be identified and also establishing that the respondent's understanding of the question matches the researcher's understanding. In this situation, open questions are seen as a transitional form, to be replaced with closed questions as the piloting process proceeds.

Where did you meet your present partner?

This question could be asked either as an open question or as a closed question. An open question might generate data which were more informative about the process of couple formation, but a closed question could provide useful information about the distribution of first meetings across a range of geographical and social settings.

A piloting process involving an open version of the question might reveal that most people met their partners in the following range of settings:

- workplaces
- discos/dances
- pubs and bars
- friends' and relatives' houses
- schools, colleges and universities.

However, a significant minority of people will have met their partners in a diverse range of other locations: for example, at a sports club or at a wedding. Thus it may be difficult to fully 'close' an open question.

Open-ended questions are often viewed as a luxury to be used sparingly. A major reason for this is the cost in time and money of such questions, both during the interview and afterwards when the data are processed. If the answers are to be coded into a set of categories, the crunch question is how much would be lost by classifying the respondent at the point of data collection via a question with a fixed range of answers rather than allowing the respondent freedom to answer in their own way. In either case the researcher ultimately has control over the classification of the respondent's answer, so the use of a closed question which has been piloted in an open form may well produce data which reflect the respondents' perspectives as adequately as data from an open question which have been post-coded. Indeed, a graduate who met their partner at a bar in a Student Union building might respond to a closed question by indicating that they met their partner at university, whereas their response to an open question might not mention the location of the bar and hence might be post-coded to the (less appropriate) 'pubs and bars' category.

It is worth noting that open questions can be quite demanding for respondents, and the answers given may reflect the first thing(s) that come into respondents' heads, which may or may not fit in with the purpose of the question. While the range of answers provided in the case of a closed question may serve to 'construct' the responses obtained, this may on occasions be useful as it avoids a situation where a respondent fails to give a particular answer because it did not occur to them. There is a balance between a researcher finding out what he or she wants to know, and the researcher hearing what a respondent wishes to tell him or her; if the researcher asks respondents the following:

'Which party political leader would you prefer to be Prime Minister?'

then the answers 'None of them' and 'John Smith' (i.e. the leader of the Labour Party whose death resulted in Tony Blair becoming party leader) may be extremely informative viewed from some perspectives but are not much help if the researcher wishes to establish the respondent's preference out of the leaders of the three 'main', nationwide parties in Britain in early 2001.

In a situation where a closed question has been inherited from earlier research, which was carried out in a different social or geographical context, or which can be regarded as having taken place in a markedly different historical period, piloting may reveal that the range of answers provided is inappropriate or inadequate. In a situation where a new closed question has been designed by a researcher, but time constraints have not allowed it to be piloted in open form, the range of answers may once again fail to be all-embracing. Indeed, even closed questions which have been piloted in open form will not necessarily include rare but important categories of answer. It is therefore often important to include an answer category along the lines of 'Other [Please specify]'. This, for example, would allow a (small) category of people who met their partners while on holiday to be identified.

Including an 'Other' category has the additional benefit of avoiding irritating respondents by omitting the category to which they belong; one of the authors remembers being sent a questionnaire as a student which assumed that all students were either studying 'Science' degrees or 'Arts' degrees. (There is also often a case for including 'Don't know' and 'Not applicable' as distinct categories of answer; these may be an important way of avoiding a spurious answer or no answer at all.)

Asking an interview respondent to choose between a number of possible answers may be facilitated by showing them a card with the possible responses listed on it. Attaching labels (e.g. letters) to the answers listed on a 'show card' of this sort may make respondents more inclined to answer sensitive questions (e.g. about income).

Question order and questionnaire layout

The same question is sometimes asked within a questionnaire in both open and closed forms. The open version is asked first to minimise the extent to which the answer to the second version is influenced by the answer to the first version. For example, an open question about where a respondent met their partner could be followed by a closed version with a pre-specified range of answers. The rationale for the ordering of the two versions highlights an important and more general issue: since at a given point in a questionnaire respondents are aware of the questions that have already been asked and the answers that they have already given, the answers to questions should not be viewed as being given in a 'vacuum'. While the spontaneity of answers to open questions may be reduced if they are placed towards the end of a questionnaire, it is interesting to note that one form of conventional wisdom suggests that open questions should be placed at the end of questionnaires to avoid a situation where respondents get 'bogged down' with them earlier on. (There is certainly a strong case for the final question to be open-ended, and to request feedback from the respondent on the questionnaire or interview.)

Question order has a potentially significant effect on the willingness of respondents to continue answering the questionnaire in a careful and thoughtful fashion, or even at all. The conventional wisdom is that personal, demographic and classificatory questions should be left to the end of a questionnaire, since respondents may find them boring, irritating or intrusive, and that the questionnaire should start with questions which are 'interesting', easy to answer, and relate to the topic of the research as presented to the respondent. However, since respondents may, consciously or unconsciously, be playing a guessing game called 'What is this questionnaire driving at?', starting a questionnaire with, say, a question about party political identification may encourage some respondents to answer further questions in a way which they perceive to be consistent with their given identification and which shows them to be thoughtful and politically aware individuals.

The interpersonal nature of the respondent–interviewer encounter may push respondents into answering questions in a 'socially desirable' fashion, i.e. one which they expect to make the interviewer think well of them. This clearly has implications for the interviewing process, but it is also important to reflect on the way in which questionnaire design may encourage responses which are distorted by the respondent's desire to impress. Gallup (1947) has suggested that a cluster of questions on a particular issue should be ordered as follows:

- questions establishing the respondent's awareness of the issue
- questions on general feelings about the issue
- questions on specific feelings about the issue
- questions tapping the respondent's reasons for their feelings
- questions relating to the strength of their feelings.

The above schema indicates the value of a systematic approach to question order, but perhaps the most important message is that the researcher should establish that a respondent has knowledge of a topic before asking them detailed questions about it. Since people on the whole do not like to appear ignorant, asking them about things that they do not know about is a very good way of constructing spurious survey data.

The Gallup schema is consistent with the notion that related questions should move from the general and broad to the particular and specific, both for the benefit of the flow of the questionnaire (and hence the ease with which respondents give answers) and also to avoid the 'contamination' of answers to broad questions with ideas put into the respondent's head by specific questions. Asking open questions before moving on to more structured questions on a topic fits in with this. One particularly useful category of 'broad' question consists of questions which establish whether it is relevant to ask a respondent some of the questions which appear later in the questionnaire. An example of a **filter** question of this sort is one which establishes whether the respondent lives with a partner, since if they do not there is little point in asking questions about their partner's occupation, where they met them, etc. Very often the 'route' through a questionnaire followed by a respondent is determined by a number of filter questions, such as the following (from the British Social Attitudes Survey; see Brook *et al.*, 1992):

'May I just check, are you married or, not married?' 'Can I just check, are you over (MEN:) sixty-five (WOMEN:) sixty?'

However, the researcher needs to take care that, for example, a filter question on marriage does not result in a failure to collect data about cohabiting partners.

It may only be after a researcher starts trying to structure their 'comprehensive' list of variables and associated questions into a set of sections within a questionnaire that the need for some filtering questions becomes evident. Arguably, such questions can be viewed as part of a broader set of instructions to interviewers and/or respondents which also includes the following:

- introductions to sections
- pre-specified interviewer probes and prompts
- any other material and text which allow the questionnaire to function in a smooth, effective and standardised fashion.

This is a context in which being a pedantic and nit-picking person may be unusually advantageous: for example, if you want a respondent to tick one box in answer to a particular question then you should tell them to do precisely that.

Filtering questions, prompts, etc. can make life much easier for the respondent and/or interviewer, as can a clear and well-designed questionnaire layout. It is also worth remembering that someone usually has to transfer data from the paper questionnaires into electronic form (this being the explanation of the otherwise mysterious 'column numbers' on some interview schedules; these indicate the location in the case-by-variable data matrix of the variables derived from questions). Layout may also affect the nature of the data collected: for example, the amount of space left in self-completion questionnaires for answers to open questions, and for 'Other [please specify]' answers to closed questions, is likely to affect the amount of detail given by the respondent. There may be something to be gained (for example, in terms of response rate) by making a questionnaire visually attractive in terms of, say, its colour scheme and design. It is not easy to say where the boundary lies between a professional appearance and an over-official one; perhaps the assessment of 'user-friendliness' is yet another task for the piloting process. Finally, just as it is sensible to include a cover sheet providing information on the research and what will happen to the respondents' answers, it is also polite and appropriate at the end of a questionnaire or interview schedule to thank the respondent for their participation (and it may be pragmatic to do so as well, if the researcher is also asking the respondent whether they are willing to be interviewed again at a later date).

Asking questions the 'right' way: vocabulary and wording

What 'choice of words' maximises the chance that a question will be understood by the respondent and that they will be able and willing to answer it in a valid fashion? Again, the piloting process is extremely important, but there is a range of 'rules of thumb' which are worth bearing in mind. Perhaps the most obvious of these is to keep questions short and simple. It is dangerous to assume that respondents will be familiar with unusual words or technical terms, and equally dangerous to assume that respondents can take in and grasp long, complex sentences. There is an obvious risk of appearing to be patronising, but a questionnaire that is to be administered to respondents of a range of ages and educational backgrounds can only benefit from the use of standardised questions if it asks them in a way which is comprehensible to all the respondents. Using appropriate vocabulary is particularly important if a researcher is surveying children, people who do not share the same first language, etc.

Unfortunately, even the most superficially simple and common-place of words may be open to interpretation in a variety of different ways by different respondents: for example, the famously ambiguous meals 'tea' and 'dinner'. The same word may have different meanings according to context: for example, one of the authors used to live in Coventry (city) but sometimes went into Coventry (city centre) to do some shopping. Ensuring that a question is interpreted in the same way by all respondents necessitates the omission, where possible, of ambiguous words and the clarification, via the question's context or the rest of the question, of other words which can clearly be interpreted in different ways. For example, if a researcher wishes to use the term 'family' in a question, then he or she probably needs to specify who counts as a family member. The Oxford Mobility Study (Goldthorpe *et al.*, 1987) collected data relating to people that its respondents spent their spare time with, which is arguably safer than using the term 'friend'. The following question from the 1995 British Social Attitudes Survey (see Jowell *et al.*, 1996) highlights a number of the above issues:

'Thinking now of *close friends* – not your husband or wife or partner or family members – but people you feel fairly close to, how many close friends would you say you have?'

Difficulties are likely to arise with words (like the word 'friend') which apply to a category of people, or a category of activities, or a category of objects, but where the boundaries of that category are not clearly defined. For example, the following question:

'Have you bought a new car recently?'

generates a number of possible problems:

- If the respondent's wife or husband has purchased a car for communal usage, does this count? (i.e. how specifically does the 'you' apply to the respondent?)
- Does 'bought' mean 'bought for your own use'? It is not impossible, for example, that an affluent respondent has bought a car as an eighteenth birthday present for their child, or buys cars as part of their occupation.

- Does the word 'car' include or exclude a small van? A respondent may use a van for both personal and work purposes.

The words 'new' and 'recently' are also problematic, as they are relative rather than absolute terms. In addition, for some respondents, buying a second-hand car may constitute buying a 'new' car, because it is 'new' to them. For other respondents, 'new' may imply never owned by anyone other than the manufacturer and the garage who sold the car to them.

The word 'recently' in the above question raises the broader issue of questions where time is a relevant factor. There are obvious advantages to being more specific, i.e. 'Have you bought a new car within the last year?' However, the researcher needs to reflect carefully on their choice of time period, since the most appropriate choice is likely to depend on both the 'normal' frequency of the behaviour in question and the extent to which the researcher can safely rely on the respondent's memory of events. Questions which include frequency-related phrases like 'how often' and frequency-related answers such as 'usually' or 'rarely' pose problems both in relation to the respondent's ability to answer accurately and also in relation to their interpretation of the meaning of terms such as 'rarely'.

Questions are, of course, more than the sum of the words of which they are composed. While individual words may have negative connotations, the overall way in which a question is asked may also strike the respondent as rude, inconsiderate, patronising, etc. As in other interpersonal encounters, there are benefits to be gained by asking questions in a polite, fluent and grammatical fashion. An appearance of even-handedness is also often appropriate; questions which appear to imply that an attitude or particular form of behaviour is appropriate or inappropriate may push the respondent towards an answer biased towards what appears to be 'normal' and acceptable. For example, the 1991 British Social Attitudes Survey (see Brook *et al.*, 1992) asked the following:

'Do you think that churches and religious organisations in this country have too much power or too little power?'

However, there are potential benefits to be gained by the deliberate use of 'leading questions' in the context of sensitive issues; Oppenheim gives the example of masturbation, where asking a question in a way which emphasises the 'normality' of such behaviour may make respondents less disinclined to answer questions on the topic (Oppenheim, 1992: 140).

If a researcher wished to discover whether respondents had used (or considered using) personal advertisements to meet potential partners, then it might be useful to precede the crunch question with a preliminary sentence such as 'Many people these days who are looking for a partner use advertisements in personal columns.' This example springs to mind because the use of personal advertisements to find a partner is a classic example of a form of behaviour which many people apparently view as acceptable for other people, but say in relation to themselves 'but I wouldn't do it, because I'm not that desperate'. De Vaus notes that the use of questions asking about other people's behaviour or attitudes can sometimes be an appropriate preliminary or alternative to more direct and personal questions (De Vaus, 1996).

An alternative approach is to establish a respondent's views on an issue by ascertaining their reaction to one or more **vignettes** (Lee, 1993). The following is an example of a vignette used in research on family responsibilities:

John Highfield is a married man in his early thirties. He has a wife and two young children. John is unemployed but has a chance to start his own business. He can get various grants to help him get started, and the bank will lend most of the money he needs. But he still needs about £1500.

a. If he thought his parents could afford to help, should he ask them for the money?

b. (If yes) Should he ask for a gift or a loan?

c. He does not like to ask his parents for the money, but should they *offer* it?

(Finch and Mason, 1993: 132)

Various other approaches to asking sensitive questions in surveys are also illustrated by Lee. He notes that both the context of sensitive questions and the language used in them may be important; 'leading in gently' to sensitive questions and using the preferred vocabulary of the respondent (which they may find less stigmatising) may be advantageous.

Two classic types of problem question are 'double-negative' questions and 'double-barrelled' questions. If a question asks whether a respondent agrees or disagrees with a statement that contains the word 'not', such as the biblical commandment 'Thou shalt not commit adultery', then choosing the answer 'disagree' creates a double-negative. This can be sufficiently confusing that some respondents will choose the answer which conveys a meaning directly opposite to the one that they intend. A double-barrelled question is two or more questions spliced into one: for example, 'Do you like drinking tea and coffee?' It is not clear exactly what an answer of 'No' to this question means. More subtly, questions like 'How often do you visit your parents?' and 'Would you marry someone from a different ethnic group?' may superficially appear unproblematic, but in fact respectively assume that the respondent's parents (if both, or all, alive) are 'welded together' and that all people in ethnic groups different from the respondent's can be treated as equivalent.

Oppenheim (1992) and De Vaus (1996) provide summaries of some of the standard problems of question wording and questionnaire design. However, good questionnaire design is as much an experimental process as a theoretical process; any new questionnaire will have its own idiosyncratic set of problems and flaws, will need to be reflected upon in the light of its specific purposes and, above all, will need to be piloted.

Scale items and other common forms of question

In the earlier section focusing on scale construction the Bem Sex Role Inventory and the General Health Questionnaire were discussed. The first of these requires respondents to rate the extent to which various characteristics apply to them; the second requires respondents to report the extent to which they are currently experiencing various sorts of feelings about themselves and their lives. These two sets of questions are similar to two classic types of scale item. The items used in **Likert scaling** are a set of statements, in response to each of which respondents are required to give one of the following set of answers: 'Strongly agree'; 'Agree'; 'Neither agree nor disagree'; 'Disagree'; 'Strongly disagree'. On some occasions seven possible answers are listed rather than five; sometimes the answer 'Can't choose' is also permitted. Items in **semantic differential** format consist of pairs of polar opposites (e.g. 'Tense' and 'Relaxed'; 'Quiet' and 'Talkative'), with respondents rating themselves on a seven-point scale between the two poles. There are many examples of these types of question in the annual British Social Attitudes Surveys; the following examples come from the 1991 survey (Brook *et al.*, 1992):

Extract from Question 2.38 (Version A: Self-completion questionnaire)

Please tick one box for each statement to show how much you agree or disagree with it:

b. People receiving social security are made to feel like second-class citizens.
c. The welfare state encourages people to stop helping each other.
d. The government should spend more money on welfare benefits for the poor, even if it leads to higher taxes.

(Boxes are labelled as follows:
Agree strongly; Agree; Neither agree nor disagree; Disagree; Disagree strongly.)

When a series of Likert or semantic differential items is used, the standard practice is to vary the orientation of the items (as in the above example) to avoid a situation where the respondent's responses become mechanical. There may even be a case for mixing up items (with the same format) from a number of different scales. Oppenheim (1992) provides an extensive discussion of more complex and unusual forms of scale and scale items.

Generating good attitude scale items is a rather different sort of activity to producing good 'factual' questions, since the attitude in question is arguably as much constructed by the scaling process as measured by it. Items for scales are sometimes generated using material from qualitative fieldwork, and it may be the case that items which appear rather vague or unfocused work well in practice. As noted earlier, assessing the validity of scales is a rather less clear-cut exercise than assessing the validity of 'factual' questions. The validity of the data from the latter can on occasions be checked by comparisons with external sources (e.g. voting turnout; see Swaddle and Heath, 1989).

Questionnaires also sometimes contain one or more of the following:

*   checklists (e.g. 'Which of the following household items do you own?')
*   lists of items to be ranked by the respondent (e.g. 'Place the following attributes of a potential marriage partner in order of their importance to you')
*   questions which ask respondents to select one of a set of alternatives (e.g. 'Which of the following statements is closest to your own view?').

There is also occasionally a good reason to include a 'quiz' or test of knowledge in a questionnaire: for example, to test a respondent's knowledge of current affairs (as in the 1992 British Election Survey; see Heath *et al.*, 1994) or to test the respondent's knowledge of the law, as in the following example from the NATSAL survey. However, care must be taken not to irritate the respondent or make them feel belittled.

Example question from the National Survey of Sexual Attitudes and Lifestyles (see Johnson *et al.*, 1994)

'Would you tell me whether you think each of these things is legal or illegal under the law:

For a woman aged *under* 16 to have sex?
For a man aged *under* 16 to have sex?
For a man to have sex with a woman of *under* 16?
For a woman to have sex with a man of *under* 16?
For two men aged over 16 but under 21 to have sex together?
For two women aged over 16 but under 21 to have sex together?'

(Answers coded as: Legal, Illegal, or Don't Know.)

Specific research objectives often demand specific ways of collecting data. The collection of information on a series of past events – for example, jobs within work histories or changes of residence (as in the SCELI survey) – is often achieved using some form of chronologically defined grid. Respondents are sometimes asked to keep diaries, so that information relating to the amount of time spent on different activities, or relating to day-to-day patterns of expenditure (as in the annual Family Expenditure Survey; see Down, 1999), can be collected. The research instruments used in past social surveys can act as a source of ideas for appropriate ways of collecting data, as well as supplying individual questions.

Developing and piloting questionnaires

It is difficult to over-emphasise the importance of getting feedback on questions and questionnaires

from other people. The researcher can meticulously examine their questions on a word-by-word basis, and they can read the questions in their interview schedule aloud to get an impression of whether the questions sound fluent, but they cannot assess how the questions will come across to other people, and they are unlikely to be able to distance themselves from their own questions sufficiently to be able to identify all the potential problems. Academics with some expertise in survey research are often asked to look at questionnaires; it is usually easy for them to come up with some pertinent comments, since first-draft questionnaires invariably contain at least a few potential ambiguities, omissions, etc.

Feedback from a researcher's colleagues or fellow students is likely to be of some value, but if the target population is, say, 12-year-old schoolchildren from a diverse range of class backgrounds and ethnic groups, the relevance of feedback from adults in the higher education system may be of limited relevance. The real 'experts' on whom a researcher should try out a questionnaire are potential respondents (though if other people are going to act as interviewers or code the data from completed questionnaires, then their views may be of value). Feedback regarding the pilot respondents' understandings of and reactions to the questions and questionnaire should be actively sought during the piloting process, as inferring how respondents feel about a survey is infinitely less satisfactory than collecting empirical material about their experiences of the process.

To the extent that it is possible, a pilot sample of respondents should mirror the diversity of the target population. The size of pilot sample required may thus partly reflect the diversity of the target population, but is more likely to be determined by the most important objectives of the piloting process; if scales are being developed or answers to open questions are being collected in order to 'close' those questions, then a substantial sample size will be needed. A substantial sample size will also be needed if the pilot study aims to provide estimates of population characteristics which can be used to ensure that the main survey has a sample design that is as efficient as possible, or if the pilot study involves the experimental evaluation of alternative question wordings. The size of a pilot sample may also be dictated by time, by resources, by the availability of respondents (or near-equivalents) whose participation will not prejudice the main survey, and by the intended sample size of the main survey. For this reason it is difficult to give a helpful 'rule of thumb' for the appropriate sample size for a pilot study; a sample of at least 50 respondents will often be needed to achieve some of the quantitative objectives of a pilot study, but a pilot study with a markedly smaller sample size than this may still make invaluable contributions to the quality of the main survey.

Ideally, every aspect of a research instrument and its implementation should be piloted as a whole. However, since two of the objectives of a pilot study are the development of some questions and the exclusion of others which prove ineffective, it is unlikely that the last pilot version of the questionnaire will be identical to the version used in the main survey. The piloting of a questionnaire often takes place in a series of stages, building towards the final research instrument; as noted by Oppenheim (1992), a questionnaire may need to be 'boiled down' during this process. If all of this seems slightly alarming to a reader planning to do a small-scale survey as a project or dissertation, it should be borne in mind that what can and should be done in advance of a professionally organised survey of several thousand respondents is inevitably more elaborate than what can be done by a sole researcher with minimal resources and time. Some form of pilot study, however, is good insurance against useless and invalid data. (A pilot study can also help establish how time-consuming and costly the main survey is likely to be, and hence can facilitate the choice of an appropriate sample size.)

The distribution of answers given to each question in a pilot questionnaire can be helpful to the researcher in a variety of ways:

- In the case of a set of items which are meant to form a scale, a systematic assessment of the scale's reliability, unidimensionality, etc., can be carried out using the pilot data.
- Questions which do not discriminate between respondents, i.e. where all the answers are near-identical, may be of negligible value.
- Questions which produce surprising distributions of answers may have been misinterpreted by some or all respondents.
- Closed questions where many answers are in the 'Other [Please Specify]' category may not be adequately closed.
- If the answers to two questions are close to being perfectly correlated, there may be a case for omitting one on the grounds of redundancy.
- An examination of the answers to a question may make the researcher realise that their motivation for asking the question is unclear.

A pilot study can be viewed as a piece of research in its own right; moreover, in many ways it is likely to be a qualitative piece of research. The range of answers given to a question may suggest that respondents are having difficulties in answering it, but this may in any case be self-evident to the interviewer(s) carrying out the pilot interviews. The interviewer's experience of the pilot interviews is also likely to be instrumental in identifying flaws in relation to the way in which the questionnaire is administered. It is important to remember that the way in which a survey is introduced may be as crucial a determinant of its success as the merits of the questionnaire; a pilot study can help iron out some of the wrinkles in the fieldwork process, as well as dealing with snags in the questionnaire. Note in this context that the interviewer is part of the research instrument; hence a struggling interviewer may pose a greater threat to the research than a few flawed questions. Piloting can contribute to the development of interviewer instructions, which may grow from simple beginnings into a sophisticated piece of documentation. Well-prepared interviewers and a streamlined fieldwork process are an important goal in survey research.

Survey fieldwork

Having designed their survey and fully developed their questionnaire or interview schedule, the researcher moves on to the survey fieldwork and the actual collection of the data. This stage of the research process shares something with those that precede it; i.e. it should be systematic and well documented. By the end of the data-collection process the researcher should have a written record of the sample design and of the way in which the fieldwork was organised and carried out, as well as accounts of the design of the research instrument and of the piloting process. The data collected by a survey are only as good as the survey itself, and they cannot be evaluated properly if the survey is not adequately documented.

Survey research aims to collect data which support generalisations to a wider population, and which can be aggregated across cases in a meaningful fashion; hence the ideal survey achieves a high response rate and collects valid data via fieldwork which achieves an adequate degree of standardisation. Poorly organised fieldwork can jeopardise the response rate, the level of standardisation and the validity of the data collected. Forethought is also required in relation to fieldwork costs (in money and in time). An adequate number of appropriately paid interviewers is required to complete the fieldwork within the allotted time period without 'interviewer exhaustion' prejudicing data quality. Someone will also have to be available to liaise with the interviewers (e.g. in relation to payments and expenses claims), to process the questionnaires/interview schedules as they come in, and to answer queries about the survey; personnel will also be needed to code the questionnaires and process the data. Questionnaires (paper and printing), envelopes and (importantly) both outgoing and return postage need to be budgeted for, with an apparent over-supply being needed to take account of reminders, lost questionnaires, etc. Realistic planning and timetabling are also important, especially if all the above-mentioned tasks are to be carried out by the researcher him/herself, since a lone researcher may be more acutely aware of financial constraints at the design stage than they are of time constraints.

A lone researcher may have little choice but to carry out their survey by post. Mail questionnaires have the advantage of constituting a low-cost approach which can be used to collect data from a sample spread over a wide geographical area; self-completion questionnaires are also sometimes used to collect data on sensitive issues within an otherwise face-to-face interview (e.g. in the NATSAL survey). However, boring questions in mail questionnaires may discourage respondents from completing and returning the questionnaires, and complex questions and open questions (requiring the respondent to write an 'essay-style' answer) may prove difficult for respondents to deal with and hence generate data of poor quality. Long mail questionnaires may encourage non-response, though short ones which can be interpreted as 'trite' may also suffer from this problem. Response rates to mail surveys are contingent on the points in time when the questionnaires drop through respondents' letter-boxes, so the timing of sending the questionnaires out also needs to be considered carefully.

Face-to-face survey interviews have potential advantages both in terms of response rates and in terms of the quality of the data collected; an interviewer can both control and facilitate the collection of data, helping the respondent where necessary and collecting supplementary information about the context and dynamics of the interview. Social survey research is a social process, not a mechanical one, and interviewers' interpersonal skills are thus an important component of successful survey research. Interviewing itself is discussed in detail in Chapter 6, but this section considers other aspects of the interviewer's role within survey fieldwork.

Some approaches to data collection combine some of the pros and cons of both interviewer-administered and mail questionnaires. For example, the researcher may be able to deliver self-completion questionnaires to respondents, so that some level of face-to-face contact is achieved.

Alternatively, the researcher may be able to supervise the simultaneous completion of questionnaires by a group of respondents, such as a class of schoolchildren, hence reducing costs and allowing an additional degree of control over the data-collection process, but increasing the risk of cross-fertilisation between the different respondents' answers. Telephone interviewing is an approach used frequently by market researchers and in research focusing on businesses, where it is viewed as preferable to mail questionnaires. Like mail questionnaires, telephone interviews are relatively cheap, allow access to a sample of respondents spread over a wide geographical area, and remove the necessity for cluster sampling. It is also easier to supervise and monitor telephone interviewers than face-to-face interviewers. However, it may be more difficult to obtain the respondent's cooperation with a telephone interview, especially if the telephone call is made without warning, and achieving a rapport with the respondent and 'getting them involved' with the survey may also be more difficult. The use of telephone interviewing may reduce the quality of the data obtained, and it is certainly not safe to assume that face-to-face and telephone interviews are interchangeable (Sykes and Collins, 1988). In the United States, telephone surveys often generate their samples using random digit dialling, though this can potentially cause problems in terms of the coverage of the target population. Of course, not everyone in the target population may have a telephone.

Securing respondent participation: ethics and practicalities

Another consequence of the interpersonal nature of social survey research is that survey researchers are no less obliged than qualitative researchers to reflect upon the ethical issues raised by their research (Fowler, 1993; Sieber, 1982), and it would be dangerous to assume that survey research does not generate ethical dilemmas. Social researchers have obligations to society, to their sponsors, to colleagues (including employees), and, perhaps most importantly, to their respondents (SRA, 1996). The researcher needs to assess whether their research is unduly intrusive or constitutes an invasion of privacy (Bulmer, 1979), and whether it will have harmful effects on the respondents. Informed consent should be obtained from respondents, and their identities should not be disclosed, or be discernible from other information disclosed. In some instances, such as health surveys, a survey may not be able to proceed without being judged as acceptable by an ethics committee (e.g. Cartwright and Seale, 1990). The ethical guidelines of the British Sociological Association can be found in Appendix A and at: http://www.britsoc.org.uk.

One positive aspect of surveys in this context is that the aggregation and counting of cases inherent in survey research usually (though not always) means that respondents are assured of a de facto anonymity in published output. However, the frequent use of survey data in secondary analyses poses problems both in terms of informed consent and in terms of the anonymity of respondents. The form of informed consent obtained needs to take account of possible future secondary analyses, and the researcher may thus be constrained in what he or she can guarantee about data usage (Homan, 1991). The release of the Samples of Anonymised Records from the 1991 Census was preceded by a lengthy consideration of the likelihood that individuals would or could be identified on the basis of the data released, and while efforts were made to make such identifications even less likely, users of the SARs data have to agree to refrain from even trying to identify individuals from the data (Marsh et al., 1991).

In the case of the NATSAL survey, the supposed 'intrusiveness' of the survey led to the withdrawal of government support and sponsorship, despite the success of a feasibility study and contrary to advice from official bodies (Johnson et al., 1994). Funding was therefore obtained elsewhere instead. The example of the NATSAL survey highlights a number of important points:

- The survey had relatively clear-cut public health objectives, and indicates that the evaluation of a survey in ethical terms may necessitate the weighing up of costs and benefits.
- The survey illustrates how preliminary field-work can be used to provide evidence of the feasibility of research on a sensitive topic.
- The survey suggests that assessments of an acceptable level of intrusiveness are subjective.

In general, research ethics is not an area where there is a nice, well-defined set of black-and-white rules which can be adhered to. There is, perhaps, something to be said for erring on the side of caution, but the argument that the best way to do ethical research is to do no research ignores the possibility that there is a need for the research, which thus provides it with a moral and ethical impetus.

Sincere assurances of confidentiality are an important way of keeping down levels of non-participation. The use of self-completion booklets for some of the more sensitive questions in the NATSAL survey reassured the respondents that their answers to these questions were anonymous; this degree of anonymity at the level of data collection is considerably rarer than anonymity at the level of published output. However, it is the way in which a survey is introduced which is most likely to have an effect on the likelihood of the respondent agreeing to participate. Introductory letters and pamphlets outlining the survey's credentials and explaining its purpose are important; issuing identity cards to interviewers and setting up other ways for respondents to reassure themselves that the survey is a bona fide piece of research (e.g. a contact telephone number; notifying the local police of the interviewer's activities) are also of value. The appearance of both documents and interviewers ideally achieves a balance between being professional and being pleasant; it may be counterproductive for an interviewer to resemble either a salesperson or a stereotypically scruffy student.

Respondents are likely to ask how and why they were chosen as participants and how long the interview will take, and the interviewer should be ready to field such questions, assuming that they are not covered by the survey's introduction. The interviewer should also be alert to warning signs that a refusal is imminent and be prepared to negotiate a different time for the interview; backing off under these circumstances may be desirable in ethical terms, and it may also eventually result in an interview when pressing for an immediate interview might not do so. Even attempting to make an appointment may be risky; the best refusal-avoidance technique in some cases may be to back off quickly and come back unannounced. It may be preferable for further attempts at securing an interview to be made by a different interviewer: for example, where the respondent seems wary of the first interviewer.

Respondents are most likely to participate if they judge that doing so will be interesting and will not bore, irritate or upset them. Survey interviews are no less exchange relationships than other forms of interview (Groves, 1989), and anything that gives the respondent an incentive to participate is potentially useful. Incentives are occasionally financial: for example, payment for participation in a survey interview, or entry into some kind of draw in the case of a postal survey. It is more or less essential to include a stamped return envelope for the return of a mail questionnaire. However, emphasising the importance of the survey and the value of the respondent's contribution to it may help obtain their cooperation, and promising to make the results of the research available to them can be an appropriate (if potentially costly) incentive. Ideally, the researcher should create the impression that he or she expects the respondent to participate without seeming to imply that they should participate or appearing to put undue pressure on them to do so.

Notifying a respondent in advance that the researcher wishes to interview them may facilitate the fieldwork process but it may also encourage a certain amount of evasive non-response. Advance letters may reassure respondents that a survey is bona fide, and preliminary calls in person or by telephone may enable interviews to be scheduled in an effective fashion, but approaching respondents by telephone in the first instance may increase the likelihood of a refusal or that the respondent is not there at the time at which the interview was arranged to take place. On the other hand, preliminary contact can increase the response rate of mail surveys.

Clearly, arriving unannounced on a respondent's doorstep means that there is a fair chance that they will not be in; hence professional surveys achieve reasonable response rates by calling back at addresses four or more times, varying the times at which the calls are made and including calls in the evening and at the weekend. It may be possible for interviewers to obtain information about the whereabouts of the respondent from neighbours; information gathered during unsuccessful calls may also be of value in terms of documenting the characteristics of non-respondents. If, as is often the case, the desired respondent is not at home but another member of their household is, or the respondent is at home but someone else answers the door, the interviewer should try to avoid a 'proxy refusal' and make every effort to make face-to-face contact with the respondent. Interviewers should also make diplomatic attempts to avoid the presence of third parties during interviews, or, failing that, to minimise the degree of third-party intrusion.

In the case of mail surveys, the researcher should specify a return date on the questionnaire or covering letter, allow an appropriate period of time beyond this to elapse – for example, a week – and then begin to follow up non-respondents. The initial follow-up is likely to be a simple reminder, such as a postcard, indicating how the respondent can obtain another copy of the questionnaire if they have mislaid it. After a further interval – for example, a fortnight – a replacement questionnaire should be sent. Further follow-ups might be carried out by telephone or via personal visits. In order to target follow-up communications on non-respondents, a record needs to be kept of who has and who has not responded. This has implications for anonymity, but linking each questionnaire to its intended recipient via a unique identification num-

ber at least means that the respondent's name and address need not be recorded on the questionnaire.

In longitudinal and panel studies non-response has a longitudinal aspect, i.e. sample attrition. Keeping in contact with respondents is of central importance. In addition to asking whether respondents would be willing to participate in further interviews at a later date, it may be useful at the end of the first interview for the interviewer to request an address via which the respondent would expect to be contactable in the event of their moving. Respondents can be encouraged in various ways to inform the researcher of changes of address; Christmas cards and newsletters about the progress of the research may serve to keep respondents interested in the research and prompt them to keep the researcher aware of their movements. Some other approaches to minimising attrition are discussed in the chapters by Farrington et al. and by Murphy in Magnusson and Bergman (1990).

Computers and interviewing

In most cases interview-based surveys involve the interviewer using a paper-and-pencil approach to noting down the responses to questions made by the respondent. The interviewer ticks boxes, circles pre-coded answers, or writes down the respondent's answer in full or in a condensed form. A certain amount of interviewer coding may take place, whereby the interviewer uses his or her judgement to allocate the respondent's answer to one of a range of pre-determined categories, or to convert it into a form which can be easily recorded. In survey interviews where open questions result in a de facto qualitative component within the interview, it may be appropriate to tape responses, or the whole session, since writing down verbatim responses may be impractical.

However, large surveys increasingly make use of microcomputers within their interviews (Saris, 1991). Computer-assisted telephone interviewing (CATI) has existed for some time, but the development of easily portable lap-top computers has allowed the introduction of computer-assisted personal interviewing (CAPI). Since the late 1980s, large surveys have increasingly made use of CAPI (Martin and Manners, 1995); for example, it is used in the government's Family Resources Survey (DSS, 1996). Computer-assisted interviewing can have a positive effect on data quality (DeLeuuw *et al.*, 1995). The direct entry of answers into the computer reduces transcription errors and allows some interviewer errors to be identified as they are made, and hence immediately corrected. The software used reduces the likelihood that questions will be erroneously omitted or that the wrong route will be followed through the interview schedule.

Both interviewers and respondents respond well to CAPI, and it can result in more fluent interviews. However, the programming (which uses specialised software) is time-consuming, and the costs of acquiring the lap-top computers and training interviewers to use them are not negligible. Thus CAPI is for the moment restricted to large surveys carried out by organisations with the requisite technical expertise and resources. For most people reading this book, paper-and-pencil interviewing (PAPI!) will be the only available option, but an awareness of the benefits of CAPI can act as a reminder that survey research is a social process and that errors can occur in survey research using PAPI both at the time that data are entered onto the interview schedule and at the time that they are transferred from it into a computer.

Survey interviewers: recruitment, training and supervision

Survey interviewers are human, and hence can be both wilful and fallible. It is well known that the social characteristics of interviewers, such as gender and 'race', can affect the data collected by interviews; survey research has confirmed this empirically (e.g. Anderson *et al.*, 1988; Catania *et al.*, 1996). However, interviewers also frequently 'misbehave' by failing to follow the instructions that they have been given (Kiecker and Nelson, 1996), and hence need to be recruited carefully and trained effectively. Training can both improve data

quality and increase response rates, since interviewers who have been thoroughly briefed, and who are familiar with the survey materials, are more likely to behave in a consistent and error-free fashion, and interviewers who have been trained in refusal-avoidance techniques (see Groves, 1989) will end up interviewing a higher proportion of their quota of respondents. Obtaining field staff who are capable of the degree of 'standardised flexibility' required may not, however, be easy or even possible. Fluent, articulate people who can respond to one-off queries or situations in an appropriate fashion are a valuable resource; survey organisations where possible retain the services of competent, trained interviewers. Interviewers may be required to carry out the coding of answers to some of the questions in the field; this is only to be recommended if they have the skills and training to do so in a reliable fashion.

Specific briefing sessions should be used to familiarise interviewers with the idiosyncrasies of the questions on the interview schedule, and interviewers should have the opportunity to 'practise' administering the schedule, especially if a CAPI approach is being used. Role-playing exercises may be helpful. Interviewers should also be provided with project instructions and/or a manual that they can refer to; the project instructions for the 1992 British Election Survey (Heath *et al.*, 1994) stretched to nearly 20 pages. (This survey was carried out by SCPR, now the National Centre for Social Research.) Novice interviewers can be accompanied at their first interview(s) by a supervisor who then provides feedback. A certain amount of supervision of interviewers is also needed to ensure that interviews have actually been carried out, and that the interview schedules which they return are not problematic. More generally, debriefing interviewers can also help identify problems with a survey.

In their death-related study, Cartwright and Seale (1990) found that the interviews had a marked emotional impact on the interviewers, resulting, in a few cases, in reduced data quality and interviewer drop-out. The subject matter of the NATSAL survey also resulted in some interviewers, who had anticipated being able to cope, dropping out (Johnson et al., 1994). This emphasises how important it is that a researcher who is employing or supervising others is alert to their feelings; apart from having an ethical responsibility towards them, the researcher should also monitor their well-being for pragmatic reasons. The researcher can make life easier for interviewers in various ways: for example, by organising their workload in a way that minimises unnecessary travel (which also saves money) and in a way which allows the interviewer flexibility in scheduling their quota of interviews. The researcher should also be aware of, and respond appropriately to, safety issues: for example, where the interviewers are going to private homes.

Data preparation and coding

This section concentrates on the processing and coding of data from questionnaires or structured interview schedules. However, as noted by Jane Fielding in Gilbert (1993b), there are marked similarities between quantitative and qualitative research in relation to coding, not least because the inclusion of open-ended questions in many questionnaires and structured interviews generates data which are essentially qualitative in form.

Before considering the coding of quantitative data, it is worth (briefly) considering the quantitative coding of qualitative data. Qualitative data from a sample of cases can always be quantified and counted, even when the data have been collected via unstructured interviews (though the reliability of quantified data from unstructured interviews may be questionable). However, as noted by Swift in Sapsford and Jupp (1996), the quantification and counting of qualitative data is only one, potentially rather limited, way that a researcher can make use of such material. Fielding points out that the major distinction between qualitative and quantitative approaches in the context of coding lies in what is done with the coded material: is it counted, or is it used in some other way? Other approaches

to coding and processing qualitative data are discussed in Chapter 8.

Before the data collected by a survey can be analysed, the questionnaires or interview schedules need to be edited and fully coded, and the data need to be converted into electronic form (**data entry**). Coding and data entry sometimes occur simultaneously; however, the former shapes the data, whereas the latter is a more mechanical process. Data are often entered twice to minimise transcription and typing errors, and the codes used for answers are almost always numerical (rather than, say, letters), since numerical data are easier to manipulate. In some cases data from some questions are also coded twice to increase the reliability of the coding process. In general, a process of **data cleaning** needs to take place (both during the editing stage described below and once the data have been entered); checks for inconsistencies, typing errors, etc., need to be carried out and any necessary corrections made.

There are a number of good reasons for carrying out a detailed examination of at least some of the questionnaires before coding and data entry commence. While pre-coding and the results of pilot work may have made the task of coding easier, the development of an adequately comprehensive **codebook** may necessitate the examination of a sizeable number of questionnaires. Clear instructions are particularly important where someone other than the researcher does the coding and data entry, especially where a team of coders is being used, but the nailing down of a framework for coding and 'punching' will in any case lead to more consistent and systematic processing of the survey data. The systematic documentation within a codebook of the basis used for coding decisions is also vital if the survey data are to be used for secondary analyses at a later stage.

The codebook and the data matrix

The codebook for a survey sometimes consists of an annotated questionnaire together with additional pages containing coding information relating to the open-ended questions and any other questions which were not pre-coded, and also containing information relating to data corresponding to the fieldwork process (such as identity codes for the interviewee and interviewer, the time and duration of the interview, etc.). Very often the documentation corresponding to a survey dataset also contains information relating to the construction of **derived variables**, i.e. 'second generation' variables which have been generated by the manipulation of one or more other variables, and which are thus often based on more than one of the survey questions. (As will be discussed in Chapters 7 and 9, survey analysis often involves the derivation of new variables by the manipulation and recoding of old ones.)

The information provided within the **coding frame** for each question includes the following:

* the question number and wording
* the numerical codes for each category of answer and a description of what each category covers
* the location(s) of the data generated by the question in the data matrix produced by the data entry process.

Bateson (1984) notes that for coding to be reliable it is necessary that the 'meaning' of each category is sufficiently clear to the coder that they can in practice make appropriate decisions as to the category membership of respondents. He suggests that, in addition to having a title and explanation, each answer category needs to be illustrated by an appropriate range of examples, and to have its boundaries illustrated using 'borderline' cases. This kind of information is as important to the survey analyst as it is to the coder. An example from the British Social Attitudes Survey is included below:

Example from the 1991 British Social Attitudes Survey (see Brook *et al.*, 1992)

Documentation regarding the coding of Question 101 (Version A questionnaire)

'Do you regard yourself as belonging to any particular religion?'

The documentation includes:

* Interviewer instructions for the question (e.g. CODE ONE ONLY; DO NOT PROMPT), and routing to the next question(s)
* Categories and codes, including:

  01   No religion
  03   Roman Catholic
  06   Methodist
  12   Sikh
  14   Other non-Christian (WRITE IN:)
  27   Other Protestant (WRITE IN:)
  97   Refused / unwilling to say
  98   Don't know
  99   N/A (not answered)

* The location in the data matrix of the variable corresponding to the question i.e. Card 13 Columns 1333–1334.
* Coding instructions, including the following: 'Other Protestant (27) should include members of any church that separated from the Roman Catholic Church in the sixteenth century, or of any church, chapel or group that separated from a church that itself separated from the Catholic Church in the sixteenth century. In practice, this means any *Western* Christian church that is not Roman Catholic'.

[Further text follows, including a list of churches.]

'The final category, Other non-Christian (Code 14) can include other clearly non-Christian religions. Examples might be:

Baha'i
Believer in God, but not Christian
Church of God of Prophecy
Hare Krishna
Humanist
Satanist
Spirit worship
Wicca, or white witchcraft.'

- A description of a derived variable (labelled RELIGSUM), specifying how the categories of answer from the above question are aggregated into the six categories of the derived variable, and identifying its column location (Column 2519).

The categories of the derived variable are:

1 Church of England / Anglican / Church of Ireland
2 Roman Catholic
3 Other Christian
4 Non-Christian
5 No religion
8 Don't know / Not answered.

Row Numbers ⇓	Column Numbers ⇒	00000000011111111112222222 12345678901234567890123456
1		00113722699999999912112211111
2		00214123099999999912112111121
3		00312319999999999912221211211
4		00525522239439944121222111122
5		00725241826299999912182821211
6		00816032299995799121192111111
7		01025622799999999912112212223
8		01122169999999999911222222221
9		01312952528999999912122121211
10		01423822599999999912111211211

Note: Columns 1–3 contain a 3-digit ID number. Column 4 relates to sex, Columns 5–6 to age in years, and Column 7 to marital status. Columns 8–17 (in pairs) correspond to age in years at various marital events. Columns 18–27 relate to ten 'Yes/No' attitudinal questions.

The above rectangle of data has been generated artificially for illustrative purposes. For other examples of data matrices containing real 'raw' data see Frude (1993), Reid (1987), or the example data sets in Marsh (1988).

Figure 5.1 An example of a data matrix generated within a text editor or word processor.

The information in the coding frame relating to the location of the data may include a variable name (which is often an abbreviation of some sort: for example, age at first marriage in years might be called AAFMYRS), and is also likely to include **column numbers** (indicating which columns in the data matrix are occupied by the data from the question). Note that the range of column numbers is determined by the maximum number of digits required for a given variable: for example, age at first marriage in years would require two columns, though an extremely cautious researcher might allocate three columns. In the above example, respondent's religion requires two columns (1333–1334), but the derived variable RELIGSUM has sufficiently few categories that it only requires one column (2519).

Column numbers frequently appear towards the right-hand edge of the pages of questionnaires. In the past data were often converted into electronic form by punching holes in cards, with each case having its own card or cards and the locations of the holes indicating the values of variables (each variable being represented by a column or columns on the card and each value by the row in which the hole was punched). This is why data entry is sometimes referred to as data 'punching'. (The data were read into the computer using a card-reading device.)

More recently, data matrices have often been created by typing the data into a text editor or word processor, generating a rectangle of numbers such as the one shown in Figure 5.1. Again, the columns correspond to variables, but each row corresponds to a particular case. If the number of columns required is more than 80 (which is often the case), then a number of rows (referred to as **records** or **cards**) in the data matrix correspond to each case. In this situation the coding frame for a question will also include the record or card number (as in the above British Social Attitudes Survey example). The maximum of 80 columns is simply a reflection of the fact that computer monitors are not infinitely wide (and that punched cards had 80 columns). Data entry using statistical software such as SPSS for Windows, or using a spreadsheet, avoids the need for more than one record per case. Some forms of specialist data entry software mimic the appearance of the questionnaire, or have other helpful features, such as allowing the data puncher to enter in one keystroke an appropriate (missing value) code for each of the variables corresponding to a series of questions that a particular respondent was not required to answer.

On occasions, in order to facilitate rapid data punching, data are transcribed from questionnaires onto coding sheets with grids printed on them. The rows and columns of the grid are numbered (and there are often 80 columns). Sometimes sheets are used which can be scanned optically; in fact, in some surveys the questionnaires are designed with optical scanning in mind, and the layout and the way in which answers are recorded are set up so that scanning is possible. However, scanning remains the exception rather than the rule (and definitely needs to be discussed with the scanning service at the questionnaire design stage). The impact of technological advances can be seen in the changing research methods literature; many of the classic quantitative methods texts (e.g. Moser and Kalton, 1971) date from the era of punched cards; Babbie (1990) looks back at the developing role of technology in data entry and analysis. The rectangular data matrix, however, remains at the heart of survey data processing, and while modern software may render this matrix partially invisible, the transfer of data between different software packages may involve a return to what is sometimes referred to as ASCII format, which in effect means a rectangular block of numbers like that shown in Figure 5.1 (ASCII stands for American Standard Code for Information Interchange). Note that on occasions some columns within a data matrix are deliberately left blank, to make visual examinations of the data less daunting. Data entry using SPSS for Windows is described and illustrated on the website corresponding to this book, and is also discussed in detail in Bryman and Cramer (1997) and in SPSS publications such as Norusis (1993).

More about editing, coding and data processing

In most surveys the coding stage is preceded by an editing stage. The dual aims of the editing stage are, first, to identify any problems with questionnaires, such as a lack of completeness, apparent inaccuracies or inconsistencies, and interviewer errors, and, second, to get the questionnaires into a fit state for quick and efficient data entry to take place. Editing may allow problems to be solved that cannot be dealt with at a later stage: for example, problems which necessitate contacting the respondent again to collect information which is currently missing or unclear, or problems which necessitate discussing an interview schedule with an interviewer while the interview is still reasonably fresh in their mind.

Reading through whole questionnaires may also be a more effective way of identifying some forms of problem than looking at the data on a question-by-question basis at a later stage (though the opposite may be true for other forms of problem). On the other hand, while a respondent's 'real' intended answer to a question may seem 'obvious', or evident from information elsewhere in the questionnaire, correcting an apparent error at the editing stage may on occasions be less advisable than postponing a response to the problem to a later stage. Note that 'corrections' made during editing are best made using a distinctive colour of ink, to distinguish them from the original information.

Questions with a pre-coded range of answer categories are likely to be easy to process, especially if standardised coding schemes are used for clusters of questions with the same answer categories. However, it may become evident at the editing stage that the range of codes allocated to a pre-coded question may need extending: for example, if data collected via the 'Other (Please specify)' safety net are theoretically or empirically important. Poorly worded and other problematic questions may also generate responses to pre-coded questions which lie outside the anticipated range of answers. For example, a researcher might not anticipate that the question 'Did you vote in the last General Election?' will receive the answer 'I was not eligible to do so' from some respondents. This kind of problem emphasises the importance of piloting the questionnaire, though this will not rule out situations such as the one in which a respondent indicates that they both agree and disagree with a statement. Should this be interpreted as 'It depends'? Or is it simply an inappropriate answer to the question, or perhaps an interviewer error? In interviewer-based surveys, interviewers should be encouraged to annotate answers which would otherwise be mysterious.

Some forms of pre-coded question are slightly more difficult to handle because they generate more than one answer. In a situation where respondents are asked which of a specified range of leisure activities they regularly take part in, the question will simply generate one variable for each leisure activity specified. However, if respondents are asked to identify the three activities that they take part in most often, and to rank them from one to three, then three variables will be required, corresponding to the first-, second- and third-ranked activities. Variables for each leisure activity, identifying whether they were one of the 'top three', can either be entered separately or can be derived at a later stage. Fielding, in Gilbert (1993b), gives an example of different approaches to handling multiple-answer open-ended questions. Many questionnaires contain a significant number of multiple-answer questions, which can lead to an alarming proliferation of variables at the data processing stage. The converse of a multiple-answer question is a set of questions which (eventually) feed into a single variable. However, while it may be a 'composite' variable which is of interest to the researcher, coding and entering its components as individual variables keeps alive the possibility of tinkering with the 'composite' variable and examining its separate components.

On occasions a certain amount of field coding is carried out by the survey interviewer. This requires sound judgement on the part of the interviewer, but may allow better coding decisions to be made because the interviewer can take account of contextual information which is unavailable at a later stage. The interviewer needs to be provided with a coding frame for each of the relevant questions, and field coding is therefore impractical if, for example, the researcher wishes occupations to be coded using a very detailed and extensive coding frame. Office coding also has the advantages of taking place under more appropriate conditions than the hurly-burly of fieldwork and of being more easy to supervise. Computers have on occasions been used for post-coding but, as noted by Bateson (1984), machines are not easily programmed to understand language in the way that people do, and they can also lack the flexibility and contextual awareness of human coders.

Just as pre-coded questions are often inherited from earlier research, post-coding often makes use of pre-existing coding schemes such as the Standard Occupational Classification (OPCS, 1991b) to ensure comparability with other pieces of research. These coding schemes can be very elaborate and detailed, and they can only be used sensibly if enough information is collected to make the assignment of cases to categories a relatively clear-cut and straightforward process. The use of a scheme with too many categories can make it difficult to assign responses to categories accurately. On the other hand, it is sensible to code questions into variables which retain as much detail as possible, since less-detailed versions of variables can always be created at the analysis stage, whereas lost detail cannot be reclaimed. Whatever the level of detail of the categorisation which is adopted, there will be some cases for which the information provided in answer to a question is insufficiently detailed to allow precise classification. In this situation it may be preferable to adopt a rule of thumb for the classification of such cases: for example, to assign those whose occupations are simply given as 'engineer' to a particular sub-category of engineers, rather than treating the information given as totally uninformative. Alternatively, the researcher might make use of a category such as 'Engineers (not elsewhere classified)'.

Inadequately informative (or indecipherable) answers are one source of missing values in survey datasets. Numerical codes are often assigned to missing values, and the variety of ways in which missing data can arise often results in the use of a number of different missing value codes. The most important rule of thumb in allocating missing value codes is that they should not have values which are meaningful, and could thus be mistakenly interpreted as 'genuine' values. The kinds of missing value code that one comes across frequently in survey datasets are negative numbers such as −1 and −2, 0 (zero), and strings of 9s. In Figure 5.1, 99 has been used as a missing value for variables corresponding to respondent's age at various marital events. This is not an entirely watertight strategy, since, for example, a respondent might have been widowed at the age of 99, but in this case the value 98 could be used to represent ages of 98 or more. On the other hand, values ending in 8 are fairly often used to indicate answers of 'Don't know'. (Should 'Don't know' be regarded as a missing value or a valid response?) Different codes should probably be used to distinguish between the following:

- questions that the respondent was not required to answer
- questions that the respondent refused to answer
- questions to which the respondent answered 'Don't know'
- questions that the respondent answered incomprehensibly
- questions that the respondent just did not answer.

One of the standard features of the data cleaning process is checking the variables in a computerised dataset for inappropriate codes. You can imagine that failing to enter one of the digits in the data matrix shown in Figure 5.1 (or entering an extra, spurious digit) could produce some rather unusual values for variables: for example, a respondent separating from their first marriage partner at 9 years of age! Error checks often include the following:

- checks that values lie within valid ranges;
- checks that variables do not mysteriously have values when the respondent should not have answered the question: for example, in the case of a never-married respondent who married for the first time at the age of 69;

- 'logical checks', for example, that respondents have not divorced before they got married!

Such checks can require a lot of thought, and are likely to be in part survey-specific, but these kinds of data error occur quite frequently in surveys, and a checking process of this sort is thus advisable.

Coding in large surveys is often carried out by teams of coders working on batches of questionnaires on a question-by-question basis. Unlike editing, in which the examination of whole questionnaires can be important, coding is most efficiently carried out in a piecemeal fashion. Questionnaires containing answers which are difficult to code can be 'tagged' as such and brought to the attention of a supervisor or the researcher. Even if the coder is the researcher him/herself, putting aside awkward cases and returning to them at a later stage minimises interruptions to the flow of the coding process.

Similarly, data entry does not need to be carried out on a whole-questionnaire-by-whole-questionnaire basis; different sections of a questionnaire can be processed separately as long as the data from each section for a particular case are accompanied by a unique ID number which can be used to match up the data from the different sections at a later stage. Breaking down the survey data into a series of self-contained sub-sets may also make the management of the overall dataset less awkward. In addition, it is not unusual for supplementary information (e.g. about the respondent's residential locality, based on their postcode) to be spliced into the dataset at a later stage.

Even if coders are well trained, properly supervised and have decent conditions of employment, there is almost certain to be a degree of coder variability (Kalton and Stowell, 1979). Systematic checking of the results of the coding may help, but Moser and Kalton present the findings of an experiment which provided clear evidence that the reliability of individual coders can be low, and that between-coder discrepancies are not uncommon, especially where open-ended questions are being coded (1971: 423–428).

Open-ended questions: developing coding frames and coding

The degree of coder variability that can occur in the context of open-ended questions is indicative of the extent to which coding involves the structuring and interpretation of data by both the researcher and the coder. When the researcher develops a coding frame for an open-ended question, they may have to decide how many variables to derive from the answers, as well as deciding what the categorisation of responses within each variable should be.

The following quote from Moser and Kalton illustrates the way in which the development of a coding frame reflects both the researcher's pre-existing theoretical ideas and the data generated by an open-ended question:

> The researcher may begin by setting up the code categories according to his [sic] own ideas and aims, but he [sic] must be prepared to modify them in the light of an analysis of a sample of replies (1971: 416).

When developing categories, the researcher needs to get a feel for the raw data, but also needs to bear in mind the uses to which the coded data will be put. Swift, in her discussion of coding in Sapsford and Jupp (1996), highlights the roles of theory and data in the coding process. While the categories generated should be consistent with the types of responses made by respondents, it would be dangerous to assume that the coding frame will be unconnected to the researcher's theoretical perspective and to the purposes of their research. In practice, the researcher will often have in their mind a range of categories based on the types of answer that they expect to arise, before they examine the actual range of responses to a question. Some of these expected categories may not correspond to any actual cases; conversely, the data may necessitate the development of new categories.

A standard starting point for coding an open-ended question is to take a sample of 50 to 100 questionnaires (or a number of questionnaires that will generate that many actual responses to the question), and to use these to establish the kinds of answer and their approximate frequencies of occurrence. The sample may be selected randomly, or may be chosen in such a way as to achieve a diverse spread of respondents and hence, perhaps, the widest possible range of answers. The next stage is to sort the answers into a set of mutually exclusive categories which:

- are reasonably internally homogeneous
- differ from each other in theoretically relevant ways
- exclude very few answers as 'unclassifiable'.

Rose and Sullivan (1996) point out that, overall, 30 or more cases will be needed in each category of a variable for multivariate statistical analyses to be carried out on the data, but small categories may be theoretically significant, so the value of retaining categories needs to be assessed in terms of analytic importance as well as frequency of occurrence.

The categories derived from the sample of 50 to 100 questionnaires form the basis of a trial coding frame which can then be applied to a further sample of questionnaires. If virtually all of the answers in the second sample of questionnaires can be classified using the trial coding frame without much difficulty, with only a few cases necessitating the creation of new categories, then the coding frame (with any minor adjustments having been made) can be applied to the rest of the questionnaires. If, however, some cases seem to fit into two categories or otherwise suggest that the categories of the trial coding frame are inadequate, then the coding frame will need to be revamped.

The categories generated by the procedure described above may appear to fall into clusters, and individual categories may appear to contain a number of distinct sub-categories. This highlights the possibility that the answers to the question may well belong to a hierarchical structure. For example, it might be possible to classify people's answers to an open-ended question focusing on the most important quality of a prospective partner into 'personality attributes', 'physical attributes' and 'economic attributes', but it would probably also be possible to sub-divide these categories into more detailed ones: for example, the last category might be sub-divided into 'employment attributes' and 'material circumstances attributes'. It would certainly be possible to reduce the number of categories to two by treating 'personality and physical attributes' as a single category. If you picture the various responses to the question as leaves on a tree, the appropriate level of detail for the categorisation might be twigs, small branches or large branches. The one thing which is certain is that neither the leaves nor the tree trunk would be much use for making comparisons between categories!

Coding open-ended questions can be time-consuming; hence the extent to which open-ended questions are coded, and the level of detail of the categorisations generated, are likely to be constrained by the time and resources available. In addition, the purposes to which the data generated will be put may only justify a relatively crude and quick coding process. Indeed, in some cases it may be appropriate to put aside the coding of open questions, and to merge them with the data from the other questions at a later stage. In addition, the answers to open-ended questions may contain qualitative data of sufficient importance that the answers need to be transcribed in full and examined in that form before they are quantified (or even instead of being quantified).

A note on imputation

In some surveys, missing values for some variables are estimated using other data and included in the dataset (Kalton, 1983; Little and Rubin, 1987). This process of **imputation** at first sight seems rather like making up the survey's results. However, if the value of a variable is calculated using the responses to a number of questions – for example, the items making up a scale – then relatively low levels of item non-response can cumulate and result in missing values for many cases. Some key variables such as income suffer from high rates of non-response

and cause the exclusion of many cases from multivariate analyses, if the missing values are not imputed. The codebook entry corresponding to a variable whose values are imputed for some cases should indicate this; ideally a variable of this sort should be complemented by another version where the values for the problematic cases are treated as missing rather than imputed, to allow analyses both with and without imputation to be carried out. Imputation has been used in the British Household Panel Study with respect to a range of income and housing cost variables (see the BHPS website: http://www.iser.essex.ac.uk/bhps/doc).

Further reading

In addition to the general survey texts by Moser and Kalton (1971), Hoinville *et al.* (1977) and De Vaus (1996), the reader might benefit from looking at a collection of linked texts edited by Fink (1995), and including texts discussing the different ways of administering surveys (Frey and Oishi, 1995; Bourque and Fielder, 1995). Alternatives to the standard text on questionnaire design by Oppenheim (1992) include Sudman and Bradburn (1982), Converse and Presser (1986) and Fowler (1995). Readers wishing to look at the methodological context of surveys should refer to Bryman (1988) and Marsh (1982).

Probably the best way to learn about survey research as an activity is to look at material relating to the design and implementation of actual surveys, and to look at methodological material produced by relevant organisations. Cartwright and Seale (1990) is a good account of the technical and methodological issues inherent in a specific survey, and the reports from many academic and government social surveys contain a certain amount of information about the survey research process. Government social survey researchers also produce a *Survey Methodology Bulletin* and researchers at SCPR (now called the National Centre for Social Research) produce a *Survey Methods Newsletter*; the text by Hoinville *et al.* (1977) is one of a number of publications generated by SCPR, and government survey researchers have published a guide to weighting for non-response (Elliott, 1991) and a handbook for survey interviewers (McCrossan, 1991). Journals such as the *Journal of the Market Research Society* and *Public Opinion Quarterly* also contain up-to-date articles relating to survey techniques. Finally, the Question Bank website contains an extensive range of examples of survey research instruments (http://qb.soc.surrey.ac.uk/).

Chapter 6　Interviewing: listening and talking

Definitions

Interviewing is perhaps the most common of all research methods. We have already seen in Chapter 5 how survey interviewing is frequently used to generate standardised quantitative data which may be subjected to statistical analysis, and in this chapter we will consider a range of approaches to interviewing which yield different kinds of data and require different kinds of analysis. Whilst interviewing is a well-established and tested research tool which many methods books discuss in detail (e.g. Bogdan and Biklen, 1982; Burgess, 1984; Denzin, 1989; Hammersley and Atkinson, 1995; Hollway and Jefferson, 2000; Keats, 2000; Lincoln and Guba, 1985; Mason, 1996; Morton-Williams, 1993; Mishler, 1986; Scheurich, 1997 – to cite only a few of the many), few make the point that interviewing performs many roles in our society. Whilst these roles may be slightly different and the interviews may be conducted for different purposes, they share many similar characteristics.

For example, market researchers conducting their work in the high street, seeking views on new products or services, or testing political opinion, commonly use interviews. They are also used by a range of official and quasi-official agencies with whom we might come into contact from time to time, such as the Department of Social Security, the police, the careers services and the Inland Revenue, and are often used as the principal method of selec-

tion for jobs and places at colleges and universities. In addition, interviews can also be a popular form of entertainment. The large audiences throughout the world for television chat shows, in all their various forms, provide testimony to the capacity of interviews to inform, entertain and amuse. They also frequently provide the basis for newsgathering and the dissemination of opinion and comment from those making the news.

Given the range of different kinds of interviews which contribute to our everyday lives there can be few of us who have not experienced some kind of interview, both as an interviewee and as a consumer of interviews as entertainment or news. This familiarity of experience is indicative of common principles which unite the different kinds of interview activity and help us in formulating a definition of an interview. In essence, an interview may be described as:

A verbal exchange of information between two or more people for the principal purpose of one gathering information from the other(s).

Bogdan and Biklen (1982), Lincoln and Guba (1985) and Burgess (1988) amongst others provide a caveat which we might add to this basic definition of an interview. They stress that interviews take place for a specific purpose, usually defined by the interviewer, who would usually be responsible for initiating the interview.

We go along with the notion of purpose in so far as it provides a basic rationale for the interview, but we would also like to keep our definition fairly loose in order to accommodate the range of different kinds of interviews which exist. Moreover, the definition does convey the essential purpose of all interviews, which is the collection of information by one party from another. Or, as Patton (1990) asserts, the interview enables the interviewer to find out what is on someone else's mind.

However, this notion of a one-way collection of information is, for some, problematic in itself. For example, long-established feminist critiques of interviewing (Cook and Fonow, 1990; Finch, 1984; Fonow and Cook, 1991; Oakley, 1981; Skeggs, 1994; Woolf, 1996) have stressed the need to see interviews as an opportunity for the exchange of information between the two parties involved, to the extent that the definitions of interviewer and interviewee become almost interchangeable. We would agree with many of the feminist writers about the need to develop an effective rapport with an interviewee and for the interview to be seen as an exchange of information rather than a unidirectional collection of information by the interviewer. At the same time, however, we would also argue that even where such a rapport occurs, there remains a significant difference between the parties in their reasons for engaging in an interview. This generally places one party primarily in the position of gathering information and the other primarily in the position of providing it. In this sense, an unequal power dimension is inevitable.

More recently, writers from a postmodernist perspective (for example Lather, 1991; Stronach and MacLure, 1997; Scheurich, 1997) have called into question the entire process of interviewing, not only in terms of the relationship between interviewer and interviewee but also in terms of the relationship between language and meaning. They pose fundamental questions about the methods of analysis applied to interview data, which usually take the form of transcripts. Their concern, as Scheurich (1997) points out, relates to the 'complexity, uniqueness and indeterminateness of each

one-to-one human interaction' (p. 64). As s they believe that the analysis of any interview will tell us very little beyond the particular circumstances in which it was conducted.

We would not disagree with the importance of recognising the complexity or uniqueness of information gathered by an interview but we would, however, wish to stress the need to recognise that an interview, of whatever kind, is an artificial act. It relies on two or more people coming together at a particular time, usually in a particular location to discuss particular things. The planning and premeditation which are the pre-requisites of any interview make it a 'special' occurrence. In this respect, the act and the process of the interview can never be entirely natural. Consequently, we can conclude that interviews are usually unique and artificial situations.

Developing our definition of an interview further, we can say that it is a socially constructed event which results in a collection of information about particular social phenomena involving particular people at a particular time and in a particular place. Consequently, we believe that the knowledge which any kind of interview yields is inevitably constrained and shaped by the particular circumstances in which the interview is conducted. It is the job of the researcher, therefore, to recognise these constraints and to take account of the extent to which they have influenced the nature of the interview. To expect any kind of interview to uncover the truth or the essence of individual belief, experience or opinion is to fail to recognise the basis upon which interviews are conducted. In our view, based on the experience of conducting many different kinds of interviews over the years, they are unique, socially constructed and context-specific events which may be asymmetric. However, their specificity and asymmetry are simply aspects of the interview which the researcher needs to reflect upon and account for in their analysis. Whatever approach is taken to interviewing, the data yielded are a reflection of the circumstances under which the interview is conducted.

To re-cap then, our definition of an interview is:

> A verbal exchange of information between two or more people for the principal purpose of one gathering information from the other(s).

In addition, to begin to understand the process of interviewing, we need to recognise that interviews are artificial situations and are conducted for a purpose (Burgess, 1988).

Types of interviews

Though we may encounter a range of different kinds of interviews from time to time, it is essentially the social science interview with which we are concerned here. That is, we are concerned with the interview as a tool for social scientific research, rather than for marketing or entertainment purposes. Having said this, there are of course many different kinds of social science interviews and there have been many attempts to categorise these different types.

Interviews and structure

Interviews are frequently categorised in relation to their structure. Many methods texts (for example Burgess, 1984; Moser and Kalton, 1971) talk of **structured** and **unstructured** interviews. Here reference is made to the extent to which questions are fixed prior to the interview in terms of both their wording and their order, to the way in which questions are posed by the interviewer(s) and to the type of questions asked: for example, whether they are open-ended, requiring an opinion or detailed factual information, or whether they are closed and can be answered by reference to a pre-determined attitude scale.

Other authors, for example, Hammersley and Atkinson (1995), argue that all interviews have a degree of structure and that a more useful way of categorising them is to think in terms of a distinction between standardised or reflexive inter-

views. Whilst we would agree that all interviews, even those that are commonly referred to as unstructured, do have a structure, we see this as an essentially semantic argument. Hammersley and Atkinson's labels of standardised and reflexive are in many respects synonyms for the more commonly used labels of structured and unstructured.

We would argue that it is more important to consider the type of interview in relation to the kind of data that it will yield than to get overly concerned about whether it is best described as structured or unstructured, reflexive or standardised. Furthermore, we would argue that many researchers deploy a combination of structured and unstructured approaches during the same interview. For example, there may be some factual questions which require a short, standardised or numerical response and others which require an expansive response from the interviewee. The researcher may be required to stick to the same interview schedule with all interviewees as far as possible, but may also need to 'probe' and seek clarification on some issues.

In our view, the issue of structure is most important in relation to the kind of data required by the researcher and the purpose that the interview will serve (Mason, 1996) in the context of the study as a whole. This takes us back to Chapter 2 on research design, where we stressed the need to ensure that the methods chosen fit the topic being researched.

Whether a researcher decides to take a highly structured or a loosely structured approach to interviewing will depend on a number of technical factors, including:

- the topic being researched
- the number and kinds of people to be interviewed
- the type of access possible and the location(s) of the interviewees
- the size of the research budget
- the time and human resources available.

Other theoretical factors which link the type of information required to the forms of analysis which will be conducted on the collected data include the following:

- the extent to which generalised findings are required from the research
- the range of data and analyses generated by earlier research on the topic
- the relationship of the interviews to other data-collection methods used
- the type(s) of data analysis to be conducted
- the importance attached to the experiences and opinions of individual interviewees
- the importance attached to the actual words or 'voice' of the interviewee
- the importance of understanding the topic from the perspective of an insider
- the importance of understanding the topic from the perspective of an outsider.

By considering these factors at the research design stage, it should be possible to identify the most suitable kind of interview for the needs of the research. By this we mean that the researcher considers the various technical and theoretical factors, as outlined above, alongside what he/she hopes to achieve by using interviews as a data-collection method. Having done this, he/she will then be able to decide on what kind of interview to use and to draw up an interview guide or discussion document accordingly.

For example, the decision to carry out interviews which use a highly specific, pre-determined schedule of questions, which requires the interviewer to ask all interviewees exactly the same questions, using exactly the same words, intonation and expression, and in exactly the same order, is generally founded upon a desire to collect data from which it is possible to produce generalisable knowledge. The intention is to collect a type of data which, when analysed will identify trends across a population. The approach is one which is based upon the reduction of individual responses to specific questions to numerical codes which can then be entered into a software package for statistical analysis.

This highly structured approach is one which depends upon a high degree of uniformity in the questions asked, the way in which they are asked and the way in which responses are recorded and coded. The need for uniformity is often extended to the type of people engaged to conduct the interview. For example, there may be an attempt to match physical characteristics like the sex, age and ethnicity of the interviewer with those of the interviewee. As such, the interviewer is, as far as possible, a neutral tool of the research, acting as a conduit for information and as such has the same, little, influence on the data collected from any/all of the interviewees. In addition, uniformity may also be sought in relation to the locations and the time at which interviews are conducted. The approach is one which seeks to reduce, as far as possible, the effect of extraneous interference on the research process and hence on the data which are collected. It is, therefore, an approach which tries to mirror that of the natural or experimental scientist as he/she attempts to control the research environment, to prevent contamination of the data. In doing so, the researcher is attempting to achieve consistency and reliability in the data. In many cases, the researcher will wish to test this reliability by applying a test of significance to the data.

Examples of some of the most highly structured approaches to interviewing are the opinion polls conducted by research organisations during the campaign preceding the time of a general election. Here the number of questions is quite small, they are clearly focused around a limited number of related topics, the language in which they are expressed and which is read out by the interviewer is clear and unambiguous and the means of recording the responses is equally clear-cut and easy to put into practice. More detailed information on voting behaviour is collected by the post-election British election study (Heath *et al.*, 1994), similar, but in some senses more limited, data being collected by the annual British Social Attitudes Survey (Jowell *et al.*, 1992). An example of an interview schedule used by the British Social Attitudes Survey is provided in Figure 6.1. The questions, which

B89a. In general would you say that people should obey the law without exception, or are there exceptional occasions on which people should follow their consciences even if it means breaking the law?

Obey law without exception	1
Follow conscience on occasions	2

b. Are there any circumstances in which *you* might break a law to which you were very strongly opposed?

Yes	1
No	2
(Don't know)	8

B90. How likely do you think you are to vote in the next General Election . . . READ OUT . . .

. . . very likely,	1
quite likely,	2
not very likely,	3
or, not at all likely?	4

B91. Which do you think is generally better for Britain . . . READ OUT . . .

. . . to have a government formed by one political party,	1
or, for two or more parties to get together to form a government?	2

B92. Some people say that we should change the voting system to allow smaller political parties to get a fairer share of MPs. Others say that we should keep the voting system as it is, to produce more effective government. Which view comes closest to your own . . . READ OUT . . .

IF ASKED, REFERS TO	. . . that we should change the voting system,	1
'PROPORTIONAL	or, keep it as it is?	2
REPRESENTATION'	(Don't know)	8

CARD S

B93. Please choose a phrase from this card to say how you feel about . . . READ OUT . . .

	Very strongly in favour	Strongly in favour	In favour	Neither in favour nor against	Against	Strongly against	Very strongly against	(Don't know/ can't say)
a. . . . the Conservative Party?	1	2	3	4	5	6	7	8
b. . . . the Labour Party?	1	2	3	4	5	6	7	8
c. . . . the Liberal Democrat Party?	1	2	3	4	5	6	7	8
SCOTLAND								
d. . . . the Scottish Nationalist Party?	1	2	3	4	5	6	7	8
WALES								
e. . . . Plaid Cymru?	1	2	3	4	5	6	7	8

Figure 6.1 Extract from interview schedule (1991 British Social Attitudes Survey; see Jowell *et al.*, 1992). Courtesy The National Centre for Social Research, www.scpr.ac.uk

are clearly specified, are asked of all respondents in the same order using the same words and phrasing. Similarly, the answers to the questions are pre-specified and presented to the respondents as a series of alternatives, either on cards or by being read out by the interviewer. The intention is to produce findings which are comparable, reliable and can be generalised across the British population as a whole. Such highly structured approaches also seek to minimise the interviewer's impact on the findings and to provide an objective and hence valid analysis of public opinion.

By way of contrast, interviews which do not make use of a rigid schedule of questions and in which there is the capacity for the interviewer to explore issues as they arise, are often seen as providing insider accounts of social phenomena with the interviewer and the interviewee having a much closer relationship based on a conversation rather than an interrogation. Rather than being oriented towards generalisation with respect to a population via statistical analyses, such an approach seeks a depth of understanding wherein the researcher is interested in the detail of the specific case. Such interviews are often described as unstructured or loosely structured. However, we take a similar view here to that espoused by Hammersley and Atkinson (1995), who believe that to see such an approach to interviewing as unstructured is erroneous.

The conversation which forms the basis of the interview is in general structured in a number of ways. In the first instance it is structured by its content, in that it will usually focus on a range of issues identified as important by the researcher. However, the conversation will also give full consideration to issues introduced by the interviewee. Moreover, although there may be no rigid interview guide, there will, nevertheless, be certain topics which the researcher wishes to cover during the course of the conversation. It is likely, therefore, that he/she will steer the conversation towards these to ensure that this objective is achieved. At a more fundamental level, the conversation will also be structured in its use of language, and its meaning will depend on the extent to which the participants share an understanding of the language. Such an understanding relates not only to the words and phrases used but also to the social and cultural conventions which structure the use of language, to expression and dialectic and also to non-verbal communication (Neill, 1991) which accompanies the conversation and may reveal much about emotions, experiences and beliefs.

If we accept that all interviews are structured, then the description of an interview in relation to structure is a relative description. However, we would not wish to imply by this that there are no significant variations in type of interview or in the data and knowledge which they yield. Where an interview is based on specific questions, posed with specific words and asked in a specific order, and where the answers to those questions are expressed in statistical terms, the knowledge yielded is likely to be very different from that yielded by more loosely structured interviews. Here the interview is based on an exchange between the participants around a number of loosely identified issues, and data capture is usually by means of tape-recording and subsequent verbatim transcription of the interview.

Where the so-called structured interview typically seeks generalisable, statistically reliable data, the so-called unstructured or loosely structured interview seeks depth and detail which are specific to a much smaller number of cases. With a life history interview, the depth and detail may relate to one individual. The unstructured interviewer sees value in individual experience and does not necessarily seek to extrapolate from that experience to a wider population. Rather than an interest in general patterns and trends or in objective, factual information, the unstructured, or what is often referred to as the qualitative interview, aims to tap into the subjective experiences of the interviewee. It is a means of exploring social phenomena from the perspective of individual social actors, though as Mason (1996) reminds us, not at first hand, but via their personal recollections.

Mason suggests that it is the ontological and epistemological position of the researcher which is influential in determining the approach taken to the interview. By this she refers to the way in which the researcher sees the world: their view of what is the most appropriate kind of knowledge for explaining social phenomena. With regard to unstructured or loosely structured approaches she states:

> Your *ontological* position suggests that people's knowledge, views, understandings, interpretations, experiences, and interactions are meaningful properties of the social reality which your research questions are designed to explore.
>
> Your *epistemological* position suggests that a legitimate way to generate data on these ontological properties is to interact with people, to talk to them, to listen to them, and to gain access to their accounts and speculations (pp. 39–40).

O'Connell Davidson and Layder (1994) also identify a researcher's ontological and epistemological position as influential in their choice of methods. In their discussion of what they describe as the 'orthodox approach to asking questions', they offer a useful comparison to Mason's position as outlined above when they state:

> We do not want to rely on the individual interviewer's subjective perceptions of how sexist or racist an interviewee is, for example, since the interviewer's subjective judgements are unreliable. The social sciences need a method which can strip away the subjective meanings that people attach to behaviours, ideas and events, and discover objective truths about the social world. It is therefore necessary to apply, as closely as possible, the methods of the natural sciences to the study of the social world (p. 117).

The different positions outlined in these competing views of social research suggest that the degree of structure which underpins the interview may be more a reflection of the beliefs and theoretical disposition of the researcher than it is a reflection of the research itself. Whilst we would acknowledge the importance of theoretical influences on the researcher, we would also suggest that to see epistemo-

logy as the determining factor in the choice of research tool, be it an interview or something else, is to remove the researcher's capacity for individual agency and choice of approach. It fails to recognise the importance of the content of the research to the approach taken. In short, it would seem erroneous to conduct research in a particular way merely because of our own preferred theoretical or epistemological position. It is our view that the approach needs to fit the substance. Moreover, in taking such a pragmatic view, we also challenge the division between structured and unstructured methods, often represented in an over-emphasis of the differences between qualitative and quantitative methods. In our view, real research projects rarely involve a stark choice between structured and unstructured or between qualitative and quantitative approaches. Like Bryman (1988) and Morrison (1998), we see the choice of method as the key research issue which has to be decided in the context of the particular study. Indeed, the decision may be to use a combination of methods, incorporating both structured and unstructured or both qualitative and quantitative approaches.

Group interviews and focus groups

An approach to interviewing which has grown in popularity in recent years, although originating at least as early as the 1940s (Merton and Kendall, 1946), is the focus group interview. In some respects focus groups and group interviews offer a degree of synthesis between structured and unstructured or qualitative and quantitative approaches.

In particular, focus groups have been used in market research (Dibb *et al.*, 1997; Kotler, 1997), mass communications research (Morrison, 1998) and, most recently, in the area of political opinion testing (Kitzinger and Barbour, 1999). As with all interview techniques, they rely on speaking and listening. However, rather than being a solitary one-to-one experience involving an interviewer and an interviewee, group interviews and focus groups bring a number of people (ideally between six and

10) together with a facilitator in order to discuss a particular issue or set of issues. Whilst the discussion is guided by the researcher or what is sometimes referred to as the facilitator, the interaction between the participants is central to the generation of data. It is this combination of a fairly specific discussion guide or interview schedule with what will always be an unpredictable encounter between the group members, which gives the focus group its unique character. As Morgan and Spanish (1984) argue, focus groups bring together a number of different methods. For example, they combine the strengths of semi-structured interviews with the opportunity to observe human interaction in the form of the group dynamics. A skilful researcher will be able to take account of the impact of the group interaction on the data generated during the discussion.

Benefits of the focus group interview are identified (Krueger, 1994) in terms of its capacity to relax participants, to allow them to lose their inhibitions and hence reveal their opinions, feelings and emotions. In addition, observation of the group dynamics or interaction may yield important contextual data to accompany those gathered from the verbal exchanges. On the other hand, the limitations of focus groups are seen by Krueger to include less control by the interviewer when compared to structured one-to-one encounters, the possibility that some group members may dominate the encounter and hence discourage others from expressing their own views, and the fact that data are more difficult to record and to analyse as it is not always clear, unless the session is video-taped, who is speaking. Finally there may be problems with the composition of the group. For example, as Krueger (1994) says, 'One group may be lethargic boring and dull; the next selected in an identical manner might be exciting, energetic and invigorating' (p. 36).

Like all data-collection methods, focus groups and group interviews have their strengths and weaknesses and, as we have seen, what one person sees as a weakness another may see as a strength. The decision whether to use a focus group should be made based on the substantive content of the research. Again, we return to the importance of the correct fit between method and subject.

Interviewing in practice

Having advocated what is an essentially pragmatic approach to the question of structure in interviews it will now be useful to consider the more practical aspects of interview design and conduct. This is best done using examples of different kinds of interviews conducted in actual research projects.

As we have already considered an example of a highly structured interview schedule from the British Social Attitudes Survey (Figure 6.1), our next example will be of an interview conducted for a study of young women, family and work in the 1990s, conducted by Procter and Padfield (1998). Here the researchers' intention was to collect information from approximately 70 women, who at the time of the interview were aged between 18 and 27. The different sections of the interview schedule (see Figure 6.2 for an example section) focused on issues of education, family, work and future intentions. The research sought to identify patterns across the sample group and to make comparisons between individual women on the basis of a common set of questions posed, whilst at the same time preserving the individuality and uniqueness of the individual interviewee. The interviews were based on a structured interview schedule which, whilst it did not act as a straitjacket for the research, did provide a clear structure for the interview. For example, the questions reproduced in Figure 6.2 are clearly stated and relate to specific issues, there is a linear progression to the order in which they are to be posed and all interviewees were to be asked the same questions.

There are a number of practical pointers to be drawn from this example of a successful structured interview schedule:

- Questions need to be clearly specified and unambiguous.

3. If employment

i) Factual information
Can I ask you a few factual questions about this job?
When started and finished?
Occupation
Industry
Employer IF SELF-EMPLOYED MOVE TO SELF-EMPLOYED SECTION
Full-time or part-time
Was this linked to a training scheme? SHIFT TO TRAINING SCHEDULE
Did she have a second job at all? IF YES: NOTE AND ASK THE QUESTIONS ON
MOONLIGHTING AT END OF THIS SECTION.
IF THIS JOB WAS ONE OF A SERIES OF SHORT-TERM FIXED-CONTRACT JOBS,
SHIFT TO THE TEMPORARY JOBS SECTION.

> DEFINITION: TEMPORARY JOBS ARE
> A) A MULTIPLE SERIES OF
> B) FIXED-TERM CONTRACTS.
> SO IF WOMAN HAD
>   EITHER JUST ONE TEMPORARY JOB
>   OR   A JOB WHICH WAS PERMANENT BUT BRIEF
> THEN ASK EMPLOYMENT QUESTIONS FOR THAT JOB

> If this is the present job change tense!

ii) Job choice
How did you go about getting this job?
Prompt:
    Difficulty in getting a job
    Job of her choice or did she settle for a job because of availability rather than choice?
    Assistance in obtaining a job, from whom?
Let's suppose that you had been a young man, would you have taken this job?

iii) Structural characteristics of job

A) COMPOSITION OF WORKFORCE
Thinking back to the people doing *the same kind of work* as you, what sort of age were they?
Were they men or women?
In that workplace, what sort of jobs did men do and women do?
Did you think that was fair?
Prompt:
    Why do you say that?
Were there WHITE/BLACK people working in your workplace?
Did white people and black people do the same sort of jobs or different jobs?
Did you think that was fair?
Prompt:
    Why do you say that?

B) UNIONISM
Was there a union amongst people doing the work you did?
If yes:
Prompt:
    Was she a member?
    Did the union have an active equal opportunities policy as she perceived it?
    Did she feel the union was of benefit to women workers?
If no:
Prompt:
    Did that matter to her at that time?

C) TRAINING AND QUALIFICATIONS
Can I turn to matters of training in this job? Were you provided with any training?

Figure 6.2 Extract from Procter and Padfield's interview schedule (see Procter and Padfield, 1998).

Prompt:
    Picking things up as you went along?
    Structured training – describe.
Did it lead to qualifications?   DETAILS.
At this time did you undertake any education/training in your own time?   DETAILS

D) PROMOTION
In this job were there opportunities for promotion?

NOTE: WE COUNT MOVE FROM PART-TIME TO FULL-TIME AS PROMOTION

If yes:
Prompt:
    Was she interested in promotion at that time?
    Did she ever apply for promotion?
    Was she promoted?
If no:
Prompt:
    Did the lack of promotion possibilities matter to her at that time?

iv) Significant others in work

A) SUPERVISORS
Can you think back to people who supervised you in this job? Were they men or women?
Do you think your supervisor(s) brought you on or was s/he just concerned with getting the job done?
If yes:
Prompt:
    How did s/he do this?
If no:
Prompt:
    How did you feel about that?

B) OTHER WORKERS
What about other people doing this kind of job. Were there any of your colleagues who showed an interest in your future at work?
If yes:
Prompt:
    Who?
    How?
If no:
Prompt:
    How did you feel about that?

C) UNION OFFICIAL
IF A UNION PRESENT
Did you receive any encouragement from your shop steward/union representative?
If yes:
Prompt:
    How?
If no:
Prompt:
    Do you think s/he should have done?

D) SEXUAL HARASSMENT
There is much more talk today about sexual harassment at work. In this job did you experience what you regarded as sexual harassment?
If yes:
Prompt:
    Tell more and give examples
If no:
Prompt:
    Do you think your experience was typical or unusual?

Figure 6.2   *(cont'd)*

- Questions should be posed in language which will be fully understood by the interviewees.
- The interview should follow a linear and incremental route in order that questions follow in a logical order.
- The interview should begin with relatively straightforward questions which can be answered easily and so contribute to a feeling of confidence on the part of the interviewee.
- Questions should not pre-judge answers but provide latitude for a range of different views, including those which may be contradictory in relation to answers to previous questions.
- The interview schedule should include clear instructions on when to probe or seek clarification and when not to. It should also provide examples of probes.
- The interview should come to a conclusion allowing any loose ends to be tied up (although with a structured interview schedule such as the one in Figure 6.2, there should be very few loose ends).
- There should be an effective and unobtrusive way of recording responses either in written format or by tape-recording.
- Where responses require the use of an attitudinal or numerical scale, this needs to be clearly specified and unambiguous. In some structured interviews the use of 'showcards' containing scales or ranges of pre-determined responses may be appropriate, and in others with perhaps a greater qualitative focus, cards with particular vignettes for the interviewee to comment on may be used.
- The number of questions needs to reflect the amount of time which has been requested from the interviewee.

Procter and Padfield's work provides an example of an interview with a reasonably tight structure, which would permit the aggregation of data across the sample, lending itself to the kind of analysis underpinned by an epistemology similar to that outlined by O'Connell Davidson and Layder (1994) as quoted above.

By way of contrast, a series of interviews conducted as part of a study of postgraduate education and training, in which one of the present authors was a member of the research team (Burgess, Hockey and Pole, 1992), provides an example of a more loosely structured approach which can be described as semi-structured. Here the objective was to interview first-year postgraduates in three social science disciplines across nine universities. The intention was to collect detailed data which related to individual experiences of socialisation and supervision which could be analysed in line with the basic principles of Grounded Theory (Glaser and Strauss, 1967; Strauss and Corbin, 1990, 1997). To this end it was our intention that interviewees would be given latitude to talk about issues which were relevant to themselves and which related to their own, often unique, experiences. Having identified this as our primary intention, our preliminary literature work identified a number of specific issues which we wished to pursue with each interviewee, as these were central to current educational and sociological debates about postgraduate education and training. In addition, our work was part of an ESRC initiative (Bulmer, 1992) and had been funded on the basis of a proposal in which we identified specific issues which would be addressed. In this respect, the research had a degree of structure from its inception and the approach to the interviews, which were the prime method of data collection, reflected this.

Given a general theoretical orientation which was shared by the three researchers who were to conduct the interviews, a loosely structured interview guide was devised. The intention was to provide a basis for discussion in the interviews, which would cover the topics in the guide, but not to constrain the conversation or to ignore or neglect the importance of issues raised by the interviewee during the course of the discussion, or indeed by the interviewer.

The topics could be introduced and discussed in any order with the expectation that they would emerge naturally in the course of the discussion. Given that the research was team-based, with each of the three researchers taking responsibility for different research sites, we felt that it was important to have some baseline information collected from all interviewees which would serve as a point of comparison between the cases. The intention was not to constrain the conversations or to neglect the uniqueness of the individual experiences of the interviewees; rather it was to facilitate analysis across key educational and sociological themes which would be relevant to all interviewees. The approach also afforded a reasonable degree of reflexivity of the kind identified by Mason (1996), which meant that key themes were not set in stone but open to revision as the research progressed.

An approach like this, when used by a team of researchers, relies on effective communication between team members based on an ongoing analysis and discussion of the emerging data. It is only possible to identify themes and issues to pursue across various research sites with individual interviewees if each researcher has access to the interview transcripts of his/her colleagues and there is collective discussion and analysis of the transcripts. In terms of our discussion of structure, therefore, this example is one where some structure is given to the content of the interview by the identification of specific areas for discussion which must be covered in all interviews, but provides latitude for the individuality of the interviewee to emerge. This approach is perhaps best described as semi-structured and variants of the format are perhaps those most commonly employed in social science interviews.

For our third example of a different interview format we draw on a life history study conducted by one of the authors. Here, the focus of the research was on the lives and careers of a group of black teachers. The study (Pole, 1999) sought to examine, in detail, the paths that took 20 black teachers of different ages and different lengths of service in England into the teaching profession and to examine their experiences as teachers. As with life history approaches in general (Hatch and Wisniewski, 1995; Goodson, 1992; Klockars, 1975;

Sikes, Measor and Woods, 1985; Shaw, 1930; Wolcott, 1983), the interviews which yield the data are detailed, highly personal and individualistic and take a long time to conduct. The data collected depend largely on the rapport which is developed between the interviewer and interviewee.

Burgess's (1988) description of the research interview as 'a conversation with a purpose' is perhaps most apt in relation to the life history interview, particularly in the study being discussed here. The purpose of the interview is to explore the experiences of the interviewee by engaging with his/her memory (Schratz and Walker, 1995) of particular events and of life more generally both within and beyond his/her job as a teacher. To facilitate this exploration, the interview is open and wide-ranging. Whilst it would be inaccurate to describe the interview as unstructured, since the purpose inevitably provides a degree of structure, it is, nevertheless, unencumbered by pre-determined questions or, to a large extent, the kinds of key issues which shape semi-structured interviews. Each life history interview, therefore, is an attempt to discover the uniqueness of the subject. A holistic approach sees merit in studying the single case and may be seen as a celebration of the life in question. Whilst it may be the intention of the researcher to draw comparisons between the different lives, as in this study, this does not detract from the centrality of the complete picture which the life history seeks.

Having described the life history approach in such a way, it is clear that there is something of the notion of the Ideal Type (Weber, 1949) about it, in which its characteristics, although desirable, remain largely unattainable in practice. For example, although it may be an exploration of the experiences, beliefs and opinions of the individual, which is guided and shaped by the interaction of the interviewee and interviewer as the conversation proceeds, the interviewer will, nevertheless, encourage the interviewee to pursue certain themes, will place less emphasis on others and will seek to orient the conversation in accordance with the general objectives of their research. In addition, the purpose of the interview is also likely to have been outlined and discussed with the interviewee, which, as a consequence, may result in the interviewee shifting the conversation in directions which he/she perceives to be desired or required by the researcher.

To return to the example of the life histories of black teachers, here a loose structure is provided since, as with many life histories, a basic chronology is followed. We start by talking about the interviewee's childhood and family background before progressing through their experiences of schooling and education, career choice, training and employment as a teacher. However, the degree of detail in the conversation means that the path taken is rarely as linear as this account may imply. For example, talking about childhood and early experiences of education may mean the interviewee discusses the education of his/her parents or grandparents as a means of contextualising his/her own experiences. Similarly, he/she may wish to compare his/her own career route with those of siblings or school friends. As a consequence, the life history of the individual black teacher inevitably incorporates information, which may also be detailed, about the lives of significant others. Similarly, when recalling particular courses of action, interviewees have frequently explained decisions with reference to wider political and economic issues, perhaps in their country of origin, which accounted for or influenced their career paths. In one case, the civil war in Nigeria led a black teacher to seek employment in the UK via contacts with a Church of England missionary organisation. This fascinating account of how a young Nigerian teacher came to be teaching art and design in the south of England in the 1990s involved an explanation of the origins of the civil war in Nigeria, the role of the Church of England missionaries and of his future hopes for Nigeria. Clearly, the story is unique and the wealth of information yielded by the conversation over a period of approximately 10 hours, conducted over three months, could not have been achieved with the use of a pre-determined interview schedule or by identifying only a few key issues or by sticking closely to a chronology of events.

The discussion and recounting of significant events by the teacher is, of course, only one aspect of the life history. The detail and the duration of the interview, plus the fact that it was essentially the teacher who was directing the conversation, allowed us to explore his feelings, to recall emotions and to stand back from past events and analyse their consequences. In many respects, it is the capacity for this personal reappraisal and evaluation which is the strength of the life history interview. The subjective interpretation of events by the interviewee him/herself is at least as important as the recounting of particular events and processes.

Although not all loosely structured interviews or conversations with a purpose are life history interviews, we believe that it is in the life history that the 'purest' form of this method of data collection is found.

By using the life history interview, the structured and semi-structured qualitative interviews and the social attitudes survey as examples, our intention has been to demonstrate the breadth of practice which the term interview incorporates. Whilst there are many differences between the various types of interview, we believe there are also many similarities. Above all, their enduring common feature remains the imparting of verbal information via a form of conversation or questioning.

Asking the questions and conducting the interview

From the various types of interview that we have identified, it is clear that there will be considerable diversity in the types and styles of questions by which they are constituted. For example, the life history interview described above does not operate via questions in a strict sense, but proceeds by engaging the interviewee in conversation around a set of events. The semi-structured example, meanwhile, relies on the introduction of key topics into the conversation in a way which is unobtrusive but ensures that they are adequately discussed. The highly structured example relies upon the posing of specific questions, using pre-determined language and in a set order. Despite these variations, there are a number of issues common to all types of interview, which relate to asking questions or, in the case of unstructured interviews, establishing and maintaining the conversation. In any interview situation it is important to consider the following points.

The time available All interviews are constrained by time. Even the life history approach has to acknowledge that individuals cannot devote unlimited amounts of time to discussion. In all interviews it is good practice to give the interviewee some idea of how much time you expect the interview will take. However, this is often a chicken and egg situation, as the amount of time for which an interviewee is available to you, the interviewer, usually determines the scope of the interview, or at least determines how many times you request to see the same person. For example, we estimated that the discussions with postgraduate students in the semi-structured study used as an example above, would take approximately one hour. This estimate was based on a number of pilot interviews that we conducted with postgraduates known to us, who agreed to stay for as long as the interview took, and on the range of topics that we thought it was important to include. In addition, we felt that to ask for more than an hour would be asking for too much and would be likely to result in a refusal.

With the life history approach it is more difficult to specify or even to give an indication of the time required. Whilst the overall purpose of the interview is known, the nature of the process and the required level of detail makes it far more difficult to estimate the time required. Many of the classic life histories took many hours to complete. For example Shaw (1930) collected Stanley the Jack-Roller's life history over a period of six years, using interview and conversation techniques alongside a written autobiography which Stanley produced. Bogdan (1974) spent more than 100 hours interviewing the transsexual Jane Fry, and Klockars (1975) tended to spend between four and five hours

per interview with Vincent the professional fence. In each of these cases, the resulting life history is rich in detail and covers a wide range of issues and events which shaped the life of their subject. To put a time limit on such interviews may, therefore, seriously limit not only the amount of data collected but also their quality and scope. Having said this, however, it would be unrealistic to think that life history interviewees have unlimited time to devote to curious social researchers. Much will depend on the personal characteristics and circumstances of those being interviewed. For example, the amount of time an old or retired person has to offer a researcher (cf. Fairhurst, 1981) may be considerably more than, say, that of a young, busy doctor (cf. Gathorne-Hardy, 1984). Similarly, the location of the interview may preclude, facilitate or even encourage long sessions. For example, Klockars' (1975) interviews with Vincent tended to start over dinner in a restaurant before continuing back at Vincent's home. The relaxed and intimate nature of the setting added considerably to the story which Vincent was to tell. However, not all life history researchers benefit from similar situations where lengthy and uninterrupted conversations may be conducted. Many interviews take place in more formal institutional settings such as hospitals (Atkinson, 1981), factories (Cavendish, 1982; Pollert, 1981; Westwood, 1984), schools (Ball, 1981) and on manoeuvres with the army (Hockey, 1986). Here the demands of the institution can place restrictions on the amount of time available for an interview. For example, Pole's (1993) experience of conducting research in schools was that interviews with staff and pupils frequently had to be fitted into the school timetable. Typically, teachers would agree to be interviewed during a free period. This meant that the interview needed to be completed within 50 minutes.

Pace Given that we have already identified all interviews as artificial situations which inevitably have some form of structure, and have noted that interviewees do not have unlimited time to give to researchers, it is important for all interviewers to

n to managing the pace of the inter-
day conversations there is a pattern to
e. In basic terms, this usually involves
in.......ry remarks or exchanges in which the
participants either introduce themselves or reaffirm
their acquaintance. This is followed by fairly complex exchanges in which the 'business' of the conversation is conducted. This will vary in its content
and style according to the nature of the relationship
between the participants. After a time the conversation will either come to a 'natural' end or be
brought to an end by one or more of the contributors. At this stage the contributors make closing
remarks, which may include details of their next
planned meeting, and go on their way.

For example, if two acquaintances who had not
met for some time were to meet up for a drink or a
meal, one might assume that the conversation
would be likely to follow a pattern where the two
greet each other, enquire after each other's health
and that of their families. At this stage of essential
updating, they may each be talking and listening
as much as the other, through a series of short
exchanges. They may continue to exchange news,
say about common acquaintances, in a similar
way, and then perhaps move on to more serious or
fundamental issues: for example, about changes in
their roles at work, a recent bereavement, opinions
of recent political or current affairs issues or their
future plans. Here there may be longer periods of
uninterrupted talk and listening as each participant provides a detailed account of their views and
experiences. Before parting, the acquaintances may
reminisce about past shared experiences before saying how much they have enjoyed the evening and
pledging to do it again sometime.

In many respects an interview, of any kind, follows a similar pattern and pace: the gentle start
before tackling the big or central issues and then
easing out of the conversation by stressing its value
and perhaps keeping open the option of a further meeting is a sequence of events common to
everyday conversations and to many interviews.
Clearly, the amount of time and attention devoted
to each of the three periods of the interview will

vary according to the individuals involved, the focus
or purpose of the interview and the total amount of
time available. The general pattern, however, is one
which is applicable to any interview and requires
some careful consideration by the researcher.
Thinking in this way about a possible pattern for an
interview will help in the efficient use of the time
available. It will usually be the responsibility of the
researcher to move the conversation on, deciding
how long to spend on a particular topic and in
what direction the conversation should be steered.
There will, of course, be exceptions, where the
researcher is happy to let the conversation emerge
and follow its own 'natural' course or, indeed, the
course that the interviewee prefers. Even in these
situations, however, the researcher takes an active
decision to allow the interview to progress in
such a way. He/she may decide that the pace and
direction of the interview should not be determined by the interviewer or that it should be determined by the interaction between interviewer and
interviewee.

Types of question Managing the pace or pattern of the interview means that the interviewer
needs to give attention to the types of questions
posed. It is clear from our own experiences of interviews, either as researcher, interviewee or consumer
of interviews as entertainment, that it is possible
for the skilful interviewer to ask different kinds
of questions which yield different kinds of data.
Various writers have attempted to categorise the
different kinds of questions at the interviewer's disposal. For example, Spradley (1979) draws a distinction between 'descriptive' questions requiring
descriptive answers, which merely recount a set of
events and describe an occasion or a social setting,
'structural' questions, which invite the interviewee
to explain how things happen, and 'contrast'
questions, which encourage introspection and discussion of the meanings of social action, perhaps
through comparisons of a set of events. Burgess
(1984) develops Spradley's typology in his detailed
example of an interview with a 16 year-old less-able
school student, and identifies an interview path,

which uses 'simple', 'complex structural' and 'contrast questions'. He explains his approach thus:

> In the interview several approaches are used. First, in different sequences I start with simple questions that require description, move on to more complex structural questions before posing contrast questions where comparisons are required (p. 117).

Hammersley and Atkinson (1995) talk about 'directive' and 'nondirective' questions where the former usually require short factual answers and the latter more detailed replies based on experience or opinion. In many ways the labels attributed to the different questions posed are not important. What is important is that they yield different kinds of data which shape the pattern and pace of the interview.

Clearly, the mixture of different kinds of questions will vary in accordance with the degree to which the interview is structured. In a highly structured interview, which seeks to collect quantitative data, the majority of questions are likely to be descriptive, directive or simple, depending on which typology one wishes to adopt. The intention is to elicit accurate, well-defined answers to a series of questions which can be posed quickly and in a standardised way. Where opinion is sought, this is often structured by the use of scales or indices, which enable the opinion to be converted into a numerical or simpler verbal format.

With our example of semi-structured interviews with postgraduate students, a greater combination of directive/non-directive, simple/complex questions was used. All interviews required the collection of some baseline factual data such as age, previous universities attended, degrees held, source of funding for the Ph.D., focus of their research and their expected time of submission. This enabled us to construct an overall profile of the population of students with whom we were working. Given that the research related to processes of socialisation and supervision in the early stages of the doctorate, there was a limit to the amount of data that we could collect from such questions. Consequently, as each interview progressed, more non-directive,

descriptive and complex questions were asked which provided an opportunity for interviewees to be more discursive, to give greater detail on practices and processes, to reflect on their experiences and to offer opinions. Within the boundaries of the interview's structure, the style of questioning gave greater latitude to the interviewee to pursue issues which were important to his/her circumstances.

In the case of the life history interviews with black teachers, the questions posed were, in the main, non-directive/complex and were asked within the context of a wide-ranging conversation. There was need for some factual information: for example, age, qualifications, length of teaching service and previous teaching posts held, but this tended to be collected as part of the more general conversational style rather than through specific directive questions.

As we have already stated, in all interviews there is a need to manage the conversation by progressing through initial ice-breaking questions to more complex and/or sensitive issues before winding the conversation down and ending the encounter. We would recommend, therefore, the careful use of the different types of questions that we have discussed to facilitate this process.

Whilst only highly structured interviews can adhere to a pre-determined format we would suggest, nevertheless, that interviews in general benefit from a series of opening questions which are easy to answer and allow a relaxed exchange of conversation between interviewer and interviewee. It is at this stage, hopefully, that a rapport will begin to be established and it is important that neither of the participants dominates the conversation. In the semi-structured and life history interviews, as the interview or conversation progresses, more use should be made of the non-directive and complex questions, which facilitate an exploration of complex issues. Finally, a series of questions that invites the interviewee to summarise their thoughts or to reflect on the overall content of the conversation is often a useful way of winding down the interview before thanking the interviewee and bringing it to an end.

As a general rule, interviewers should remember that whatever and however questions are posed the interview is not a test and interviewees should not be made to feel uncomfortable or inadequate if they do not know an answer to a question or have no opinion on a particular issue. Similarly, King (1996) recommends that interviewees be made aware of an opt-out clause which means that they do not have to answer every question. She believes this gives the interviewee a degree of control over the interview and some protection from over-inquisitive researchers. King's recommendation is useful in reminding us that researchers can only work at the discretion of those they are studying. If an interviewee chooses not to answer a question or to terminate the interview there is little we can do about it.

Location

Although we have already drawn attention to the effect that location may have on the length of the interview, there are more general points to consider. In our experience, it is important to choose a location for the interview in which the interviewee feels comfortable and cannot be overheard. This may mean that the interview is conducted in a formal or semi-formal setting: for example, in the interviewee's office, if they have one, or even in the interviewer's office. Whilst the situation may not ostensibly lend itself to a relaxed ambience, it may give the interviewee a feeling of confidence, encouraging him/her to speak freely and from a position of knowledge. If the interviewee and the interviewer feel at ease in the location it is likely that they will be able to give greater attention to the interview, confident that they will not be overheard or interrupted.

However, establishing general rules for the location of interviews is not easy. For example, Pole (1993) in his study of a secondary school had assumed that 14-year-old pupils would be more at ease talking to him away from the formal classroom situation and went to some trouble to secure the use of what he considered to be a more informal and relaxed room in which to conduct individual interviews. The room was generally reserved for individual pupil–teacher discussions about records of achievement and was equipped with soft chairs and pot plants and posters on the walls. However, it soon became apparent that pupils were more reticent in interviews conducted in that room than they were in those conducted in an empty classroom or even a corner of the school hall. It became clear that pupils associated the record of achievement room with work and assessment and even with disciplinary issues, not a location where they were usually made to feel at ease, despite the soft furnishings. It seems likely, therefore, that these associations may have contributed to their reluctance to talk openly in the interviews with Pole.

On a similar theme, Lampard and Peggs (1999) in their study of marriage and remarriage gave their participants a choice of whether to be interviewed in their own homes or in the researchers' offices at the university. Most of the participants chose the latter, suggesting that talking to a 'stranger' about personal issues may be something that seems to be most appropriately and comfortably done away from the interviewee's home territory. The example demonstrates further the difficulty of establishing general rules in this context.

Another issue, which has particular significance in the context of interviews with children, but which also has a more general resonance, concerns the protection of the researcher from allegations of misconduct and inappropriate behaviour towards the interviewee. We would urge researchers to consider very carefully the place made available to them in which to conduct interviews. In schools, for example, where space is often at a premium, researchers may be offered the medical room, a stock room or a similar small room in which to interview pupils. Where such rooms are without windows and are away from general and easy access by other members of the school, our advice would be to look for an alternative location, which is more open and accessible. Turning the situation around, researchers need also to be aware of potential threats to their own safety. Here common sense must prevail – for example, in relation to travelling to unknown locations to meet largely unknown interviewees. The offer of conducting an interview in the interviewee's home (Hughes, 1991) may seem a good one, but it is important not to let the desire to gather good data override personal safety. To this end we would suggest that interviewers always inform colleagues, secretaries, friends or family members, whichever is most appropriate, of their interview location, providing the address, telephone number and name of the interviewee or contact person. It is important, however, that those informed of the location of the interview agree to abide by the conventions of confidentiality which govern all social research.

Listening

As the title of this chapter suggests, interviewing is not just about talking and asking questions, it is also very much about listening. In fact, much of the foregoing discussion could be seen in terms of an attempt at alerting researchers to the importance of creating the best conditions for effective listening. By asking the right questions in the most appropriate way, in suitable locations, we are encouraging the interviewee to talk in order that we, the researcher, might listen to and record what is being said.

It may seem blatantly obvious to say that interviewing is about listening, and pointing this out is not an attempt to problematise something that we do all the time merely for the sake of it. Indeed Blaxter et al. (1996), in their chapter on what they describe as 'everyday life skills for research' (p. 55), make the following point:

> We spend much of our time, consciously or subconsciously, listening: to friends and members of our families, to our colleagues and associates, to the people we meet in the street or in the shops, to radio and television programmes, to music, to the 'background' sounds of our environment. Through this constant listening you will have developed skills in identifying different people's voices, their attitudes and emotions, their openness and honesty. You will have learned how to relate this information to that coming to you from other sources (p. 56).

Whilst we would agree with much of this statement, we would also argue that although listening is undoubtedly an everyday life skill for most people, to go on to suggest that listening in everyday life and in research are the same thing would be to overlook many of the nuances of the process of listening in a research context and much of what the researcher seeks to achieve from it. For example, King (1996) widens the scope of listening to include body posture and non-verbal communication and refers to this as 'effective attending'. Her point is that effective, 'active' listening can enhance the data-collection process by showing the interviewer is engaging with the interviewee. She says:

> Effective attending (for instance, conscious use of physical position, posture and eye contact) places the interviewer in a position to listen carefully to the other person's verbal and non-verbal messages. Part of a researcher's critical awareness includes becoming conscious of how mannerisms and responses can affect the participant (and vice versa), and aware that, in this sense, the story that results is a joint production (Mishler, 1986). The power of suggestion through an 'approving' nod or a 'disapproving' shake of the head can lead to a change in the interviewee's response, so that it no longer represents what the individual originally intended to convey (p. 185).

The characterisation of listening in this active way relates especially to interviews which are not highly structured, where the interviewer effect needs to be monitored. In less structured situations of this sort it reinforces the notion of the researcher as an active rather than a passive participant in the data-collection process. Moreover, by citing Mishler, King makes it clear that she sees the knowledge yielded by the interview as, at least in part, constructed by the interaction between interviewer and interviewee and, consequently, views the way in which one listens as an important part of this process of construction.

Rather than relying on everyday life skills, we would urge researchers to give special attention to techniques of active listening in the following ways:

- by ensuring that they are attentive to the interviewee throughout the interview
- by looking at the interviewee
- by making encouraging comments and appropriate noises (for instance, 'uh huh, I see') as the interviewee talks
- by being aware of body posture which shows you are listening and interested in what is being said.

In relation to the issue of posture, Mason (1996) reminds us that it is not only our own body language and non-verbal communication that we need to be aware of but also that of our interviewees. She says:

> This means making sure you are tuned in to body language and to demeanour so that you are recognizing when people become bored, tired, angry, upset, embarrassed (p. 46).

The need for effective non-verbal communication on the part of the interviewer and the capacity to recognise it in the interviewee emphasises the complexity of the interview as a data-collection tool and the need for effective ongoing monitoring of the process as it occurs.

We might conclude from the preceding discussion that interviewers, like many counsellors, medical doctors, psychiatrists and others whose work relies on effective verbal communication, are often cast in the role of 'preferential listener'. In all of these situations we would expect the listener to be self-aware and reflexive in his/her approach. As such, the interviewer must be able to listen in such a way as to encourage the interviewee to talk. This will require the ability to judge when to probe, when to keep quiet and when to encourage the interviewee by contributing to an exchange of information and, very importantly, when to bring the interview to a close.

Recording the data

An integral part of any interview procedure is the method by which the data are recorded. Although the interview may be conducted effectively, resulting in a relevant, interesting and detailed conversation, its principal value will be lost if there is no efficient way of recording it. It is imperative, therefore, that the planning of an interview includes a consideration of the means by which it will be recorded. Returning to our previous examples of interviews gives us an opportunity to consider the most common means of recording interview data.

In the highly structured social attitudes interview the data for each separate interview are recorded on a prepared pro-forma usually by ringing codes, by writing down a numerical value or ticking boxes which indicate the selection of a particular option offered to the interviewee, or which might indicate a frequency, a quantity or a specific place on a scale. The pro-forma is designed to record a relatively large amount of data quickly and uniformly without 'contamination' from the interviewer. Moreover, interviewers making use of such pro-formas increasingly have them available for use during the course of an interview on the screen of their lap-top computer. The pro-forma should also facilitate the transfer of data in a similarly efficient and speedy manner into electronic form, for subsequent examination via a data analysis software package. The approach is one, therefore, which records only what is deemed, before the interview takes place, to be essential information. Like the interview itself it is highly focused and aims to be precise and replicable across the interview population.

The great majority of the interviews with postgraduate students and all the life history interviews were tape-recorded, with the knowledge and permission of the interviewees. A verbatim transcription was then produced. Like the interviews themselves, the method of recording was geared towards detail. In particular, the life history approach, which encourages wide-ranging conversation, needs to be complemented by a method of recording data which can capture the detail and retain an accurate and complete record of the interview for analysis, whilst allowing the researcher to be free to interact with the interviewee and to be reflexive.

In a minority of cases, postgraduate students would not agree to their interviews being tape-recorded. Consequently notes were taken throughout the interview. Although we must admit to some disappointment when permission to tape-record is refused, the detail and quality of data which can be collected by note taking should not be underestimated. Unlike tape-recorded interviews, those recorded in note form will involve a process of selection by the researcher which will reflect not only his/her proficiency and speed in taking notes but also what he/she interprets as the most important pieces of information which arise as the interview proceeds. Researchers would do well to develop their own form of shorthand which would allow them to record information quickly and accurately, but they should not expect to get verbatim quotations of any great length via this method. At best, where notes are taken, researchers should aim to paraphrase rather than quote directly from their interviews.

Other tricks of the trade to facilitate good note taking include very basic but often forgotten things, like ensuring you have a good supply of note paper which you can access as the interview progresses, plenty of pens and somewhere or something to rest on when taking notes. Ensure that the notes that you write down can be attributed to a specific question on the interview guide by using a number system which corresponds to the guide. This also avoids the need to write down every question posed, although those not on the interview guide will need to be written down. Numbering pages of your notebook in advance of the interview is essential to ensure you have the correct sequence of the conversation. After the interview it will often be necessary to rewrite or at least annotate the interview notes while information is still fresh in your mind. This annotation might usefully include notes about the interview process. At the time of summative analysis, this broader contextual information may become very useful in helping to understand not just what was said but also why it was said. Depending on how legible your handwriting is, and whether the notes are to be used by other people, it may be necessary to type them after each interview. Where the researcher has access to a laptop computer and is a quick and competent typist, many of these paper-based note-taking suggestions become obsolete. Nevertheless, the need for effective note taking and accurate and full labelling, numbering and the like remain.

Whether a transcript or handwritten notes are generated, it is important to remember that the record of the interview is the raw material of the research. It is important, therefore, to make copies of the data – either photocopies, copies on disk or both – and to make sure that the transcript or the notes are set out in a way which will facilitate data analysis.

All methods of recording data have their drawbacks: a pre-coded pro-forma records very little of the detail of an interview and, like note taking, relies on the researcher to extract what is deemed to be most relevant or important from what is said. Note taking similarly means that a complete record of the interview is impossible. In addition, the act of writing down what an interviewee says can be off-putting and prevents the interviewer from engaging in eye contact with the interviewee and from observing non-verbal communication. Blaxter *et al.* (1996) also note that:

> Putting pen to paper may lead interviewees to think that they have said something significant. Conversely, when you don't make a note, they may think that you find their comments unimportant (p. 155).

Coping with writing, asking the questions and establishing a rapport with the interviewee is very demanding. It can, however, be done and valuable data are frequently collected via the note-taking method. Like many aspects of social research it takes practice.

Tape-recording, whilst offering the most comprehensive method of recording dialogue, also has a number of inherent difficulties. Some interviewees may refuse to be tape-recorded, fearing that the tape may be played to people who they may not wish to hear their opinions. Such a reticence may lead to a reluctance to talk freely. In addition, other basic problems that can hinder effective use of the tape-recorder include excessive background noise, quietly spoken interviewees, exhausted batteries, faulty tapes and a problem of recording over a previous interview before it has been transcribed. Whilst all these things may seem very straightforward and obvious, our own (sometimes bitter) experience leads us to encourage all researchers to take them into account at the start of every tape-recorded interview.

Potential difficulties do not end with the taped interview. The reason for tape-recording is to obtain a complete record of the conversation; this usually means that tapes need to be transcribed for the purpose of analysis. Our experience has shown that not only can tape transcription be a tedious and laborious task but it is also extremely time-consuming. When calculating costs for research projects we usually work on the basis that one hour of talk takes six hours to transcribe by an experienced audio typist working with a good transcription machine. The implications for time and cost are obvious. Depending on the research budget and the time available, this may mean that it is not possible to transcribe all the tapes or that only certain sections of tapes can be transcribed. Where this occurs it is imperative that the researcher(s) listen to the tapes and make notes on their content before deciding which bits or which tapes to transcribe. However, whatever the method of data recording it is essential that researchers become very familiar with their data. In addition, listening to taped interviews is, among other things, an opportunity for the researcher to evaluate his/her own performance.

When is an interview not an interview?

So far our discussion of interviews and their structure and of the examples used has characterised interviews as events or a series of linked events which are carefully planned and premeditated and have readily identifiable roles for the participants. However, as we have already seen, some feminist commentators (e.g. Finch, 1984; Oakley, 1981; O'Connell Davidson and Layder, 1994) have questioned the attribution of clear-cut roles of interviewer and interviewee, believing that successful and more ethical interviews are about an exchange of information rather than a unidirectional transfer of data. In addition, Scheurich (1997), from a postmodernist perspective, has cast further doubt on the categorisation of interview participants into interviewer and interviewee. His concern is with the construction of the conversation, which constitutes the interview, and with the ambiguity of the whole process. He states:

> Some of what occurs in an interview is verbal. Some is non-verbal. Some occurs only within the mind of each participant (interviewer or interviewee), but it may affect the entire interview. Sometimes the participants are jointly constructing meaning, but at other times one of them may be resisting joint constructions. Sometimes the interviewee cannot find the right words to express him/herself and, therefore will compromise his/her meaning for the sake of expediency. There may be incidences of dominance and resistance over large or small issues. There may be monologues. There may be times when one participant is talking about one thing but thinking about something else. A participant may be saying what she thinks she ought to say (p. 67).

Seeing the interview as a more equal and ethical exchange between the participants, in which the conversation and the meanings it conveys are constructed from the interaction of the participants, challenges the whole idea of identifying interviews as discrete, premeditated events, whatever their degree of structure. Moreover, Scheurich's comments challenge the very idea that interviews can be planned. He continues:

> Indeed, the 'wild profusion' that occurs moment to moment in an interview, is I would argue,

ultimately indeterminable and indescribable (p. 67).

If we accept Scheurich's argument either in total or in part, we must surely open a range of possibilities for data collection, which have the common features of being based on a verbal exchange between two or more parties. For example, if interviews are characterised by 'wild profusion' and are 'indeterminable', then conversations in the street, arguments, debates, verbal exchanges in a shop or restaurant may all be seen to convey information which is as reliable as that conveyed in an interview. They may all, therefore, offer the possibility of data collection.

Conclusion

In conclusion, the simple point that we wish to make here is that interviews, in the way that we have characterised them so far, present only one possibility for research using the medium of speech. Just as Plummer (1983) stated that the world is constructed of documents, we would argue that the world is constructed of verbal interactions. It is the job of the social scientist, therefore, to maximise his/her opportunity to gain access to such interactions, to record them and subject them to the same kinds of rigorous analysis as we apply to what we rightly or wrongly identify as interviews.

Chapter 7

Documents, official statistics and secondary analysis: mining existing data sources

Using existing data: themes and issues

One of the main aims of this chapter is to make readers aware of ways in which they might make appropriate use of various sources of data which some other texts either neglect or view with undue scepticism. These are, on the whole, sources of existing material, i.e. material which is not generated by the researcher's own, primary research. Day-to-day life in contemporary advanced industrial societies is suffused with bits of paper (Plummer, 1983) and other forms of written information (including vast numbers of web pages on the Internet). University libraries are stuffed with official statistics (if you know where to look for them and are inclined to do so), and all the data generated by a huge survey can be sent to you on a single CD ROM. With all this information readily available, who needs their own interviewees, survey respondents, etc.? While this is a tongue-in-cheek question, and primary research has distinctive qualities, the value of the roles that can be played by existing data should not be under-estimated.

Clearly, primary research is only really necessary when suitable existing data are not available, and there would thus seem to be a strong case for carrying out a 'data review' alongside the literature review that a researcher typically carries out. How-

ever, the 'suitability' of apparently relevant existing data should certainly not be taken for granted. As with other second-hand items such as cars, existing data need to be treated cautiously, and it is advisable for the researcher to carry out an evaluation of the source of the data and to build up something akin to a 'full service history'. On the other hand, the use of existing data does have the benefit of constituting a non-reactive, unobtrusive approach to research (Webb *et al.*, 1966), and of being more naturalistic than other, interactive approaches (though this is contingent on the way in which the data were generated in the first instance).

The various forms of existing data are used more frequently than a novice researcher might expect, given their lack of prominence in methods texts and teaching. However, that very lack of prominence may in part explain why researchers often fail to exploit fully, and are sometimes unaware of, what is available. The relative invisibility of the use of existing data sources may also reflect the kinds of preliminary, complementary or supplementary roles that such sources often play in research projects.

Existing data may be used in a variety of ways during the early stages of a research project; they may provide a starting point or a benchmark, or they may alternatively contribute to aspects of the research such as:

- planning and research design (e.g. sample design)
- the development of concepts and the formulation of research questions
- the construction of research instruments.

Later in a research project, once any primary data have been collected, existing data may serve to contextualise these new data or help in the assessment of their representativeness.

While existing data from a single source will on occasions provide the empirical core of a research project, very often existing data are used in combination with primary data, or existing data from different sources (or of different kinds) are pooled together. Comparisons of data from different sources may reveal reassuring similarities or highlight interesting inconsistencies; the aggregation of data from different sources may help the researcher build up a fuller or more balanced picture of the social phenomenon of interest to them.

Of course, the value to a researcher of data from a particular source mirrors the source's credibility and relevance. The synthesis of information from different sources is thus a creative and challenging activity, which not only involves the mechanical integration of findings but also necessitates an assessment of the nature and quality of the information to be synthesised. When reviewing or utilising existing data the researcher needs to do something akin to what they would probably do when reviewing an item of literature: that is, both summarise the content of the item and form an assessment of the author's viewpoint, conceptual framework, agenda and technical competence. The need to assess existing information with reference to the process which produced it is one of the key themes of this chapter.

On occasions existing data from different sources may be sufficiently comparable to justify a **meta-analysis**, i.e. an analysis which aggregates the findings of a number of studies, with the aim of achieving greater generalisability or precision on the basis of the studies collectively than can be obtained from the individual studies. Formal, quantitative meta-analyses often involve the splicing together of statistics (e.g. means or P-values) from different studies to give overall figures, as well as typically involving checks for significant between-study differences in findings (Rosenthal, 1984; Wolf, 1986). When the raw data from the studies are available (as opposed to summary statistics such as means), more sophisticated meta-analyses are possible.

This chapter considers both quantitative and qualitative forms of existing data. Thus many of the issues which arise echo or pre-empt material in earlier and later chapters. There are other ways in which the boundary between the use of existing data and the collection of primary data can become blurred: for example, both pre-existing diaries and diaries written at the request of researchers have been used in social research. In this text, as is frequently the case elsewhere, breaking social research down into a set of separate, self-contained activities can introduce artificial distinctions between forms or aspects of research which share many common features. Research using existing data raises issues which in many instances echo parallel issues relating to the use of other research methods:

- As in primary research, the researcher using existing data needs to evaluate the validity and reliability of this 'secondary information' (the label attached by Stewart, 1984, to data collected by other people).
- Existing data need to be located and accessed, and the selection of the data to be used by the researcher is a form of sampling.
- The researcher needs to be reflexive about their role in this selection process, and to be aware more generally of the ways in which their usage of existing data is shaped by their theoretical perspective and intellectual agenda.
- A more practical similarity with other approaches to research is that the best way of learning to use existing data is by doing it.

There are, however, some issues which are specific to the use of existing data. The researcher is obviously constrained by the historical nature and pre-determined range of existing sources. The range of data available is as much socially determined as the nature of the data available is, and can reflect various dimensions of power and dominance within society: e.g. data which have been generated by 'malestream' social research (such as the Oxford Mobility Study; see Goldthorpe *et al.*, 1987) may be of limited value to researchers focusing on women's lives. There is a risk that the constraints of data availability may divert the researcher away from some topics and towards others.

Furthermore, existing data, like social research data more generally, have been socially constructed, and are thus in part a reflection of the person or people involved in their construction. In order to properly assess their meaning and relevance, the researcher needs to consider the purpose for which the existing data were originally intended:

* Were they generated for research purposes, or for some other purpose?
* If they were generated for research purposes, how close a match is there with the researcher's own agenda?
* If the data were not generated for research purposes, were they generated as an incidental by-product of some administrative process, or were they constructed as a source of information aimed at a specific audience?

The General Household Survey (GHS; ONS, 1997) is a source of existing data which were generated for research purposes. However, a researcher whose agenda focuses on the link between contraceptive usage and religion will find that the GHS collected data on the former but not on the latter.

A researcher who is interested in the economic history of a particular geographical area may find valuable data within the commercial directories generated as a by-product of the development of trade and industry in the eighteenth and nineteenth centuries, which list merchants, manufacturers, etc. (Scott, 1990: 158).

All existing data, whether generated 'wittingly' or 'unwittingly' (Finnegan, 1996: 150) need to be interpreted with reference to the context of their production. If the only existing data are of questionable value, the researcher may have to choose between modifying their research agenda and making optimistic assumptions about the validity of the data for their research purposes.

Thus far we may have given the impression that existing data are of interest to the researcher primarily because they are records or measures of something that the researcher wishes to know about. However, as noted above, existing data are as much social constructions as they are measurements. For some researchers, it is the process of construction of the data, together with the data themselves, which are of central interest. In other words, while for some researchers existing data may constitute **resources**, providing information about social phenomena, for others existing data may constitute **topics**, which are of interest in their own right. In the first case it is the 'content' of the data which is of primary interest, whereas in the second case it is the 'nature' of the data which is of central significance (Scott, 1990: 36). However, as noted by Scott (1990: 38), this distinction may in practice be an artificial one. For example, to a researcher who is interested in health inequalities, a recent volume on cancer survival trends in relation to deprivation (ONS, 1999) may not only be an information resource but also an indicator of a new government's attitude to documenting health inequalities compared with that of its predecessor.

As we shall see in this chapter, the forms taken by existing data are diverse, but in recent years advances in information technology have meant that the relative importance of electronic data as a resource*has grown rapidly. Given appropriate technology, electronic information can be stored compactly, communicated easily and, in particular, searched quickly and efficiently. However, locating and accessing relevant electronic data may not be easy, and the range of data available is still, of course, socially determined. Cost may also be an issue. On the other hand, we would strongly recommend that researchers acquaint themselves with the on-line databases, CD ROMs, etc., which are available to them via their university libraries. We would also suggest that, while it should not be viewed as a panacea for a researcher's information problems, the Internet will increasingly play a key role in many research projects.

Documents

The proliferation of electronic information constitutes a recent stage in a longer historical process which has seen the volume of documents generated by societies expand rapidly as a consequence of printing, increased literacy, the dependence of organisations on written material, the development of the mass media, etc. In this sense industrialised societies in the contemporary world are undoubtedly 'information societies', even if the degree of centrality of information to what goes on within contemporary societies remains debatable (Lyon, 1987). However, an observer might easily infer from the visibly greater emphasis on documents within historical research, and from the sparseness of discussions of documents in the social research methods literature, that documents play a very limited role in social research which has a contemporary focus. Such an inference would underestimate both the usage of documents within and the potential value of documents to such social research.

In its broadest sense, the term 'document' refers to any object which has been shaped or manufactured by human activity. Books and web pages on the Internet are clearly documents, but, from this perspective, so are wedding photographs and video-recordings of the 'happy day', paintings in art galleries and posters on bedroom walls in halls of residence, worn steps in churches and whole cathedrals. Thus, while documents frequently consist of written text (and/or numbers) inscribed on some medium, this is not always the case: documents can be audio-visual, pictorial or even traces left behind by human behaviour. Plummer (1983: 33) notes that personal possessions can also be viewed as documents.

The range of documents available can be categorised in a variety of ways. One obvious and important distinction is between private and public documents. Personal documents such as diaries and letters are particularly useful in the context of life-history research. Documents generated by the state include official statistics (see Scott, 1990; O'Connell-Davidson and Layder, 1994), which will be discussed later in this chapter. In addition to the legal and political documents generated by the state (and, for that matter, documents generated by international organisations such as the United Nations), many documents are produced by other organisations for administrative, educational or commercial purposes. Scott sub-divides administratively generated documents into those that are recurrent, those that are regular and those that are special (1990: 83), and organisations clearly produce documents for both internal and external audiences. The mass media and literary/artistic communities act as sources of documents of an overtly cultural nature, and it is worth noting that documents can either reflect dominant ideologies and cultural norms or constitute evidence of resistance to them. It is also worth noting that documents are sometimes the work of single 'authors', but may equally have been moulded into shape via some form of collective authorship.

Scott has put forward a 12-category classification of documents (1990: 14) which not only takes account of the authorship of a document (personal, official private, official state), but also takes into consideration the important issue of access (closed, restricted, open archival, open published). As is the case in both qualitative and survey fieldwork, documentary research can involve travel and negotiations before access to the desired data is (with luck) obtained. However, the most prominent typology of documents, of key importance to historians, relates neither to access nor to authorship *per se*, but instead to the proximity of the author to the events described in a document. Historians prefer primary sources (which contain first-hand, witness accounts) to secondary sources (wherein the author discusses events that they did not actually witness). Tertiary sources is a term applied to abstracts, indices, etc. Unfortunately this use of the word 'secondary' sits awkwardly alongside the way that it is used elsewhere in this chapter, where 'secondary analysis' implies the re-examination of what historians would presumably view as primary sources. This ambiguity in terminology reflects in part the limited scope for primary data collection in most historical research, a notable exception being oral history (Thompson, 1988).

So far in this section documents have been viewed as a form of existing data. However, documents such as diaries and letters blur the boundaries between this chapter and other parts of the book, since they can be and have been solicited within primary research. Clearly, however, such documents do not benefit from the same lack of reactivity as unsolicited material. The distinction between carrying out a literature review and analysing documents is also a blurred one: for example, in this text we implicitly evaluate the contents of other research methods texts, which in a sense is a form of documentary analysis.

Types of documents

Documents can be:

- written   (e.g. books and web pages)
- visual   (e.g. photographs and films)
- physical   (e.g. buildings and clothes)
  artefacts

- primary   (witness accounts of events)
- secondary   (second-hand accounts of events)
- tertiary   (abstracts, indices, etc.)

- private   (e.g. personal letters and diaries)
- public   (e.g. published official statistics).

Documents may be produced by:

- the state   (e.g. political and legal documents)
- organisations (e.g. university prospectuses and advertisements for cars)
- the mass   (e.g. newspapers)
  media
- artists   (e.g. paintings and sculptures)
- anyone   (e.g. personal address books).

Documents may be:

- published
- publicly available via archives
- in private archives
- unarchived and located within organisations or households.

Uses and types of documents

Documents can be used on their own, or in combination with other forms of data. They can provide information about a substantive issue, or information about the way in which a substantive issue is discussed/conceptualised, or they can themselves constitute the focus of study rather than acting as information sources. While documents may on occasions provide the only source of information about a topic, they more often form part of a broader research design: for example, they may constitute the basis of a contextual or historical section in a thesis or a research report. At an early stage of the research process documents may provide the researcher with an insight into a topic or a setting, may stimulate theorising, or may contribute to practical aspects of the research: for example, a school roll might act as a framework for the selection of respondents.

Documents can be triangulated with each other, or with other forms of data, as a way of cross-checking validity (Denzin, 1970). Triangulation of this sort may also highlight theoretically interesting contradictions. For example, documents laying out the official policies of an organisation may tell a different story to documents generated as a by-product of day-to-day practice within that organisation, and may be even less consistent with individuals' personal accounts, assuming such accounts are available. Bryman (1989) notes that the effective use of archival information in organisational research is often achieved through its use alongside data from other sources, such as interviews. Reinharz (1992) notes Luker's use in her research on abortion of semi-structured interviews alongside the textual analysis of documents.

Documents and the life-history approach

Documents, both solicited and unsolicited, frequently play an important role in biographical/life-history research. In his evangelistic but convincing discussion of this 'humanistic' style of research, Plummer (1983) notes that its main concern is to 'give voice' to those being researched, though this emphasis on the subjective viewpoints of human actors is often complemented by interpretation and contextualisation. Thus the documents used in biographical research can relate to the individuals' subjective perceptions, to events in their lives, and to the historical and structural contexts of their lives.

A classic study in this context is Thomas and Znaniecki's *The Polish Peasant in Europe and America* (1958). This study of a Polish migrant to the United States involved extensive use of personal documents, including letters, along with newspaper archives and the records of courts and social agencies (Plummer, 1983: 39–63). These documents complemented the individual's own life-history account. This study illustrates the emphasis on the self and on subjective perceptions within symbolic interactionism, which was prevalent within the Chicago School of Sociology in the

1920s and which continues to be of significance. Researchers within the Chicago School frequently used other documentary and statistical material to complement and contextualise personal documents and accounts within life-history research. It is unfortunate that this willingness to combine both primary and secondary data, and also quantitative and qualitative data got lost at some point during the twentieth century. However, as Plummer notes, the life-history approach does typically involve the use of a combination of sources: an individual's own account, observation, interviews, the examination of personal documents, etc. (1983: 14). He also advocates the complementary use of the life-history approach alongside other methods, as an exploratory/sensitising preliminary, or more generally because of the value of its subjective, experiential nature (1983: 72).

Personal documents

Ironically, while personal documents relating to powerful and high-status people are more numerous and easy to come by, personal documents corresponding to ordinary and 'marginal' people are frequently more useful than public documents for the study of such people's lives. It may, however, be difficult and time-consuming to assemble a suitably extensive range of such documents (see Burnett *et al.*, 1984, in relation to working-class autobiographies) and their coverage may well be patchy and biased. The existence, availability and typicality of personal documents are issues which feed into the broader issue of representativeness, which will be discussed later in the chapter. Considerations of representativeness, however, may take second place to 'giving voice' to a category of individuals.

When diaries are used in social research, the subjectivity and self-presentation of the diary-keeper may be of more concern to the researcher than the 'truth' or comprehensiveness of the diary's content. While the researcher may be interested in the diary's 'factual' content (which is likely to be patchy), they may be less interested in what the diary-keeper says than in why they say it and the way in which they say it. However, the diary still needs to be evaluated in the context of the diary-keeper's personal characteristics and reasons for keeping a diary. Like personal accounts more generally, diaries are sometimes solicited by researchers (as in the research on supply teachers by Morrison and Galloway, 1996), in which case their contents are likely be more structured and focused (e.g. as in time-budget diaries). Plummer notes that diaries have the advantage over retrospective accounts of being more or less contemporaneous with events (1983: 17).

As mentioned earlier, letters were an important data source in Thomas and Znaniecki's *Polish Peasant*. While letters may usefully complement other data sources in life-history research, issues of survival and accessibility (and hence representativeness) are important if letters written by a variety of individuals are to be used as a key resource in the study of a particular group of people. Representativeness may also be an issue if, like Thomas and Znaniecki, the researcher attempts to obtain existing letters via an advertisement. Locating and obtaining access to a sample of letters may be arduous and time-consuming, but in some instances collections of letters may already be available, as in Stacey's use of letters written to a film magazine (Stacey, 1994). Letters written to magazines might be viewed as one of a range of 'sub-genres' of letters (Plummer, 1983: 21), and highlight the need to evaluate letters with reference both to their authors and to their recipients. In some sub-genres of letter the proportion of the content which is of value to the researcher may be frustratingly low. For example, if a researcher is using ordinary, personal letters, written by friends to each other, to examine the concept of friendship, then the detailed content of a letter (in relation to events, third parties, etc.) may be of markedly less interest than its tone and thematic content. Of course, letters, like other forms of document, can be solicited by the researcher, in which case the 'dross rate' (Webb *et al.*, 1966: 105) should be less of a problem.

In contemporary society some of the historical roles of letters are now played by even more ephemeral communication media, i.e. telephone calls and electronic mail, which has inevitably reduced the prominence of letters as a resource for social researchers. However, the wider dispersal across society of photographic and audio-visual technology means that photographs and video-recordings have become common documents of family life, increasingly capturing aspects of day-to-day life as well as long-standing photographic magnets like weddings and holidays, and thus may provide an important insight into self-image and norms (Scott, 1990: 182–196; Plummer, 1983: 31). Visual data, which can be used both for illustrative purposes and also as the basis of analyses, have arguably been under-utilised by social researchers, though there is a growing trend towards the use of such material (Ball and Smith, 1992; Pole *et al.*, 1999; Prosser, 1998).

Using visual data provides some fairly distinctive challenges for the researcher, such as interpreting the images without the reassuring presence of words, and integrating them into the research report. Visual data such as photographs also need to be contextualised: who took them, when and why? Do they belong to a particular 'genre' (e.g. 'holiday photos')? As with letters, both the author and the audience are of significance (even when they are the same person). As noted by Becker (1981) among others, the context in which a photograph is interpreted is as significant as the photograph itself. With respect to visual data, accessing them, assessing their representativeness, and contextualising them may all be challenging tasks.

Official and public documents

Scott (1990) views official documents (including official statistics) as the most important category of documentary sources. Such documents can cast light upon the organisation and interests of state agencies: for example, highlighting their roles in surveillance and social control. However, official documents are arguably just as important as sources of 'factual' information, so long as the researcher always remembers that the 'facts' are to a greater or a lesser degree social constructions, and is cautious to avoid letting the availability and nature of the documents misdirect their research agenda. As with other documents, both their content and what can be learnt from them about their authors (and society more broadly) may be of interest; Scott notes that official documents often have more to say about men's lives than about women's lives but that they can convey important messages about patriarchy and the sexist nature of officialdom.

Documents generated by the mass media have frequently been the objects of attention of researchers working from a cultural studies perspective but are also of interest to social researchers more broadly (Seale, 1998). Depictions of women in magazine articles, advertisements and other products of the mass media have been a popular source of material for gender-related analyses (see, for example, various articles in recent volumes of the journal *Sex Roles*). Such documents can clearly act as a source of information about ideology and cultural norms, but can also provide an insight into the commercial concerns and organisational structures of the individuals and bodies that created them. It is rare for documents such as television programmes to be used by social researchers as sources of 'factual' information; however, the makers of some TV documentaries are in effect engaged in 'oral history'. The interpretation of the products of the mass media raises issues relating to authors' intentions, audience responses, 'genre', etc., which are discussed later in this chapter.

Publicly available documents produced by non-governmental organisations may act as an important stepping stone via which researchers can familiarise themselves with some basic aspects of the organisations in question. Relevant material can include, among other things, marketing materials (such as prospectuses), annual reports and yearbooks, and directories of members. However, Scott (1990) discusses problems of credibility and inclusiveness in relation to the use of directories as sampling frames, or as de facto censuses of people/organisations.

Some practicalities of using documents

As we saw earlier, Scott's classification of documents is based in part on their accessibility. In order to be able to use a document a researcher needs to:

- be aware of its existence
- identify its location
- gain access to it in that location.

Even then, the nature of the access gained needs to be considered: can the researcher borrow the document and/or take copies from it? Is the researcher limited to examining the document or can he or she also publish material from it?

Making oneself aware of the existence of relevant documents echoes the process of searching for literature more generally, inasmuch as the process is likely to involve the consultation of bibliographies, citation indices, abstracts, etc. However, more specific searches of specialist catalogues, archival guides, directories, etc., are also likely to be necessary. Following in the footsteps of other researchers may be an effective approach, either via lists of references in their published work or by contacting other researchers directly. Where documents are uncatalogued, or where the catalogues are not widely available, word of mouth is of particular importance; just as journalists seek information by ringing up people whom they perceive to be 'experts', researchers may need to contact other researchers, librarians, information officers, appropriate points of contact in organisations, etc.

The interpersonal aspect of access to documents may involve formal applications and negotiations, or may be more a question of forming and maintaining a good relationship with a gatekeeper. As in qualitative fieldwork, it is worth remembering that gatekeepers often lack neutrality; biographers negotiating with the relatives of their subjects for access to materials are well aware of this. (For example, David Lean had to tread carefully when gathering material for his biographical film about T.E. Lawrence; see Brownlow, 1997.) Plummer points out that while it is non-reactive, documentary research offers plenty of scope for violations of privacy (1983: 145).

The contents of collections of documents, the conditions of access to them, and the extent to which they are properly catalogued, are all determined by a mixture of legal constraints and obligations, organisational resources and priorities, the actions of individuals, and chance. Government archives contain documents which are unavailable for public consultation because of the UK Official Secrets Act, whereas equivalent documents in the US would be available as a reflection of the Freedom of Information Act (assuming that the researcher was aware of their existence). Documents produced by non-governmental organisations may be even less accessible (Scott, 1990), and the Data Protection Act has implications for the availability of many documents. Books published in Britain are easier to access than visual media, because of the legal obligation of publishers to (offer to) deposit copies at designated copyright libraries. The private papers of a notable individual may have been donated to a library, but there is no guarantee that resources will have been dedicated to cataloguing them, and resources can also dictate the duration of access permitted and level of support provided to a researcher by an archive.

Archives of note include the Mass Observation archive at the University of Sussex (website: http://www.sussex.ac.uk/library/massobs/) and the Qualidata archive at the University of Essex (website: http://www.essex.ac.uk/qualidata/).

Documents are not just located in libraries and archives, but also in organisational settings and homes. In a sense, all these locations are archives. In many cases accessing the documents will cost the researcher time and money travelling and will also involve time and effort on the part of librarians,

archivists or other gatekeepers. Good preparation and the systematic and effective consultation of documents is an important way of avoiding a need for return visits. More generally, irrespective of whether a researcher is using organisational documents located in dusty archives or web pages on the Internet, effective searching and adequate record keeping are vital. In terms of searching, the researcher needs to strike a balance between drowning in a sea of tenuously relevant documents and missing interesting documents because their search is too narrowly defined. When searching electronic catalogues (or searching for web pages on the Internet) the researcher should have to hand a list of synonyms for their key concepts/topics of interest; it is also worth experimenting with combined searches (e.g. 'divorced' *and* 'parenting').

Continually updating their own bibliography/ catalogue of documents helps the researcher avoid the frustrating process of trying to track down the details of a half-remembered item at a later stage. Taking full and accurate notes from documents, keeping a record of when and where the notes were taken, and organising the resulting sets of notes systematically are also good practice. Note taking is a skill acquired with practice; the apparent 'short cut' provided by photocopying may just put off to a later date the process of 'boiling down' material, though photocopying may on occasions keep a researcher's options open as to what may turn out to be relevant. Finally, it is a brave researcher who has enough confidence in their assessment of the material that they have accumulated to risk losing relevant material by inadvertently disposing of it within the course of a 'spring clean'.

Assessing documents

In order to be able to make full use of the documents that she or he has located and accessed, the researcher needs to assess their validity and value to her or his research. To some extent such assessments are contingent on the researcher's agenda and approach; what is relevant and valuable to a positivistic historical sociologist may be of less interest to a feminist utilising a literary approach, and vice versa. However, there are a number of themes which apply to most or all uses and types of documents: for example, Scott (1990: 6) puts forward four (overlapping) validity criteria:

- authenticity
- credibility
- representativeness
- meaning.

The sections that follow echo Scott's last two criteria by considering the important issues of sampling and interpretation, but before this his authenticity and credibility criteria are briefly considered.

Documents lack authenticity if they are not what they implicitly or explicitly claim to be. Forged letters and diaries are not unknown (e.g. the Hitler diaries publicised by newspapers in the early 1980s and subsequently found to be forgeries; see Harris, 1986); forged paintings are perhaps proportionally more common. Assessing the authenticity of a document may involve examining both its internal consistency and also its consistency with external sources of information (Platt, 1981). However, credibility is perhaps more likely to be a pertinent issue: the author of a document may intend to be misleading, or may unintentionally be inaccurate. There are a range of economic, ideological and social motives for insincerity (e.g. in the context of documents such as publicity materials, political propaganda and letters to family members), and the author's sincerity may be negated by 'honest mistakes', or by false inferences, or by their deception by a third party. The researcher needs therefore to reflect on factors which may have affected the author's desire and/or ability to convey accurate information via the document.

However, Scott (1990: 123) notes that where earlier researchers have already assessed documentary sources, the authenticity and/or credibility of the documents may not appear to be a problem. There are also occasions when the lack of credibility of an author may in itself be of interest. Howard (1996)

notes in his biography of the film director Michael Powell that Powell's own autobiography (Powell, 1986) contains accounts of non-existent social encounters and therefore lacks credibility in a way that can arguably be viewed as illustrating the director's penchant for 'fantasy'. This example thus relates to an important issue that we have already touched upon: are documents being used as sources of information about past events, or about the author, or is it the document's text itself that is of central interest?

Sampling documents

The researcher should select documents in a systematic fashion, perhaps theoretically if they wish to develop theoretical ideas via a Grounded Theory approach (see Chapters 3 and 8), perhaps using something akin to random sampling if generality is an issue, and they should make explicit in their research output what they have done. This process of sampling will, of course, be constrained by the availability of documents and by the time and resources available to the researcher. There are clear echoes here of the discussions of sampling in Chapter 3. As suggested in that chapter, it is likely that the researcher will need to assess the extent to which their 'sample' of documents is representative of a broader 'population' of documents. However, there are a number of different 'populations' which might be taken as points of comparison. For example, a selection of diaries could be compared to:

- the diaries to which the researcher has access
- the diaries that she or he knows still exist
- the diaries that have ever been written by the relevant category of people
- the diaries that would have been kept by the members of the group of interest to the researcher (had all of them kept diaries).

The fourth of these 'populations', albeit a hypothetical one, may unfortunately be the most appropriate point of comparison if the researcher intends to use the documents as a source of information about a broader group of people than just diary-keepers. In this situation, if the research has a contemporary focus, it may be appropriate for the researcher to solicit diaries from a range of individuals, possibly providing incentives for their completion, in an attempt to achieve an adequate degree of representativeness. The third of the above 'populations' may, however, be of more relevance to a researcher whose interest lies primarily in the documents themselves. In general, the researcher needs in the first instance to have developed a good knowledge of the first two 'populations', i.e. accessible and existing documents, though the constraint of inaccessibility may mean that the researcher has to make inferences about the latter.

The relationship between accessible/existing documents and the full range of relevant documents which have ever existed needs to be assessed in a fashion broadly analogous to that used when assessing survey non-response, or, more precisely, attrition in longitudinal studies. Documents may have been lost or mislaid, or destroyed within a process of selective 'weeding'; conversely, documents may have survived because of a deliberate choice that someone has made to deposit them in an archive. It is thus possible that surviving documents may be disproportionately 'unusual' ones. While people may have chosen to preserve documents which seemed likely to have some enduring value or to be of historical interest in the future, documents relating to day-to-day life which might have been of interest to the researcher are likely to have been discarded. Finally, it may be useful for the researcher to reflect upon the selective process of creation which led to the range of documents that ever existed; Reinharz (1992) notes that the absence of female-authored novels among novels written at certain times and in certain places can be informative about gender and power.

While a researcher will often want to generalise from a selection of documents, this does not mean that strict representativeness is necessary, since the generalisations that they wish to make may be theoretical rather than statistical, and the typicality and coverage of the documents used may thus be of more relevance. Plummer suggests that a handful of good life histories may give adequate coverage of a cultural world (1983: 100). In Reinharz's study of personal documents relating to miscarriage, she used documents corresponding to a range of times, places and socio-economic situations in order to identify the existence of different or invariant meanings across these dimensions (Reinharz, 1992). However, in order to guarantee the coverage, diversity or typicality of a selection of documents, a comparison still needs to be made with an underlying 'population'. On occasions, documents are used within a case study where generalisability is not an issue, but the scope for generalisation is more often than not something that the researcher should reflect upon, irrespective of whether their sampling approach is theoretical or is geared towards a more stereotypically statistical notion of representativeness.

Establishing meanings: the interpretation of documents

At the time of writing the British government has just put forward proposals relating to a new policy geared towards reducing teenage pregnancy (Brindle, 1999). A document containing such proposals might be used by researchers in a number of different ways:

1 as a 'factual' statement of government plans
2 as an example of government self-marketing (more specifically, an attempt to advertise its support for 'traditional family values' to the electorate)
3 as raw material for an analysis of power and ideology in contemporary society.

Thus the role of the document as a measuring instrument or indicator relates in each of these three examples of uses to a different concept: policy, party politics and ideology. Note also that in the first of the above uses the focus of attention is more on the policy than on the document *per se*.

The meanings ascribed by researchers to documents are thus not only a function of the documents themselves but also of a researcher's agenda and approach to interpreting them. Researchers who view documents as information resources will inevitably interpret them differently from both researchers whose primary concern is the process of social construction of the documents, and also researchers who are only interested in the discourse(s) and internal meanings embedded within the text. There are a number of key themes and issues relating to the interpretation of documents which are useful both in themselves and also as a way of highlighting differences between some of the approaches to interpretation.

Historians have long recognised the need to take account of a document's context and process of production when interpreting it. Documents are constructed by social actors within social structures and hence need to be viewed in their cultural, organisational and historical contexts. This applies as much to visual documents as it does to written documents: for example, paintings are produced within temporally and spatially specific artistic contexts. One implication of this is that the researcher will need to familiarise herself or himself with the 'language' used in the relevant context in order even to establish the superficial, 'literal' meaning of the text in a document. Furthermore, documents are likely to belong to a context-specific 'genre' (e.g. 'newspaper article', 'undergraduate essay') and their style of presentation is also likely to reflect context-specific norms.

Viewing the 'meaning' of a document simply as the meaning consciously intended by an (appropriately contextualised) author is, however, unduly restrictive. Documents have intended and unintended audiences, including the researcher. The interpretation of a document by a reader is a subjective process, with meanings thus being established within subjective and varying frames of reference. Readers may also interpret documents in a way that uncovers unconscious messages sent by authors, and authors may have consciously endowed documents with more than one intended meaning: for example, a film may have been intended both as a work of art and as a political statement. (For related material on photography, see Becker, 1981.) Some multi-authored documents may reflect the varying intentions of a number of different authors. Some films serve as examples of documents with respect to which the audience's interpretations do not necessarily match the author's intentions, with both the intended interpretation and a 'subversive' reading being possible. However, in addition to the intended and received meanings of authors and audiences, some researchers view documents as having internal meanings which are divorced from both author and audience.

The subjective viewpoint of the author is central to some forms of documentary research. Indeed, Plummer suggests that within life-history research capturing the author's subjective reality is more important than the factual accuracy of the material in the document (1983: 106). More generally, understanding the frame of reference of the author is an important step towards properly contextualising a document's content. However, the researcher cannot avoid approaching the document from within their own frame of reference. This issue is central to the hermeneutic approach to interpretation. Hermeneutics involves the contextualisation of a document's meaning via a merging of the author's and researcher's frames of reference, leading to an interpretation which is still from within the researcher's frame of reference but which is also consistent with the author's intentions and context. Scott (1990: 31) describes the 'hermeneutic circle', wherein the researcher initially approaches text purely from within their own frame of reference, but uses the text to achieve an understanding of the author's frame of reference, which in turn is reconciled with their own frame of reference, hence allowing them to understand the text from within the author's frame of reference as well.

A hermeneutic approach requires that the researcher grasps the language, 'genres' and literary forms of the author's cultural and social context. To some extent this may be achieved via a dialogue with the text of the document, but contextual knowledge from other sources is also likely to be important, especially where interpretation would otherwise initially be very reliant on the researcher's own frame of reference: for example, in the case of visual images, where the author's intentions and frame of reference are not embedded within written text. Note also that in situations where a researcher is interested in the shared meaning of documents to author and audience, for example where documents from the mass media are being analysed, the researcher will need to engage with the common frame of reference of author and audience.

A rather different approach to the meaning of documents is taken by writers who have been influenced by semiotics. Such writers tend to view the meaning of a text as being contained within the text, and thus as being independent of the author's intention and the interpretations of audiences. Semiotics, which draws upon work by Saussure in the field of structural linguistics, focuses on the relationship between 'signs' (words, phrases and 'systems of rules' embedded within the text) and ideas/concepts. According to Barthes (1967), the underlying meaning of a text can be decoded using such a set of rules which structures the text. Other writers such as Althusser and Foucault have also focused upon the internal, hidden meanings of texts in a fashion which does not involve the consideration of linkages to anything external to the text. We share the view of Giddens (1979, 1982) and Scott (1990: 33) that the absence of such a consideration can lead to relativism, and that authors' intentions, audiences' perspectives and documents' contexts are frequently of vital significance for the adequate interpretation of the meanings of documents. The meanings of documents reflect both structure and agency (the latter being the agency of both author and audience); 'internal meanings' may be of considerable interest, but they are only part of the story. In addition, while Barthes suggests that the validity of an interpretation of the 'internal meaning' of a document can be assessed in terms of its coherence, it is not clear how a researcher is meant to assess the relative merits of competing semiotic interpretations of a comparable degree of coherence. As will be discussed further in the next section, interpretations cannot really be disentangled from the situations and perspectives of researchers; it is thus not straightforward to separate 'internal meanings' from 'received meanings'.

Issues and practicalities when using documents

Documents can be used:

- in combination with other data (e.g. where different sources of data are triangulated with each other, or where other data are used to contextualise the documents)
- within life-history research (e.g. to help illustrate actors' subjective viewpoints)
- to help familiarise the researcher with a topic, organisation or setting.

The use(s) to which a researcher puts document(s) may be one or more of the following:

- an examination of factual information contained within the document(s)
- an examination of the process of social construction of the document(s)
- an examination of the discourse(s) and ideology embedded within the document(s).

Documents may be viewed as having:

- intended meanings (reflecting the author's intentions)
- received meanings (within interpretations by audiences or by the researcher)
- internal meanings.

The researcher needs to:

- identify the existence of, locate and negotiate access to the documents

- use an appropriate sampling approach and assess the representativeness of the sample of documents used relative to a relevant population
- assess the authenticity and credibility of the documents
- take careful notes from, and keep full and accurate records of, the documents
- bear in mind when interpreting the documents their own frame of reference, the author's frame of reference and the frames of reference of relevant audiences
- situate the documents in their historical, cultural and organisational contexts and be aware of relevant language, genres and literary forms.

Analysing documents: methods and approaches

The methods used to analyse documents vary considerably, in ways which reflect the broad theoretical frameworks of researchers as well as reflecting some of the issues raised in the previous section. This section will first consider content analysis, which is often positivistic in tone, before moving on to qualitative, interpretative approaches, with their more phenomenological slant. The section then looks at critical analysis and discourse analysis, whose emphasis on power and structurally rooted oppression has led to their frequent adoption by, among others, feminist researchers and Marxists.

Content analysis (Weber, 1990) is an approach which has been used widely in the field of media studies; in its 'conventional' form it is very much a quantitative technique. For example, Jagger (1998), in her content analysis of a sample of (heterosexual) dating advertisements, counted occurrences of various categories of characteristics desired in a partner, and carried out statistical tests to establish the existence of gender differences. One of her aims was 'to determine the extent to which men and women market the self and describe their partner in bodily terms' (1998: 799). She therefore counted

occurrences of references to the body, both in terms of attractiveness and also specific physical characteristics. For example, she found that references to body size/height (using terms such as 'tall', 'short', 'small' and 'petite') were made by 23% of 670 men, as compared with 11% of 424 women, a statistically significant difference ($P < 0.001$).

Content analysis echoes many of the issues which arise in quantitative analysis more broadly; the researcher needs to reflect on sampling and representativeness in the context of data collection, and on coding and reliability in the context of data analysis. Hypotheses can be tested, or generated, and the systematic nature of the coding and quantification leads to an apparent 'objectivity', an impression which may be reinforced by the scope for computer-based analysis.

However, this style of content analysis has some potential limitations, which follow on to some extent from its standardised, quantitative nature. The treatment of documents is atomistic, especially where the unit of analysis is small, e.g. words or phrases. A word which occurs in many places within a document may be of no more substantive importance than a word which occurs a few times; without consideration of intention, meaning and context the weight that should be attached to words is simply implicitly assumed. The standardisation necessary for counting to take place imposes an assumption of comparability on material which may not be consistent in nature between documents, or even within a document. The focus on patterns within the documents may lead to context being neglected, and the quantified data do not necessarily tap intentions and meanings.

In a classic work on content analysis, Holsti (1969) demonstrates an awareness of the above kind of issue. While promoting a rigorous approach to the classification process central to content analysis, for example by advocating the derivation of a set of precisely defined, mutually exclusive categories into which all of the data items fall, Holsti also discusses the use of a secondary, contextual level of analysis, whose units facilitate the researcher's understanding of the meanings of the units at the primary level. This use of two nested levels of units of analysis is arguably an important step towards a more holistic, interpretative approach.

> MacMillan and McLachlan (1999) discuss their analysis of education news in the press, in which they used both content analysis (via the qualitative data analysis software NUD*IST) and discourse analysis approaches. Their content analysis showed how often certain terms (such as 'yob' and 'tearaway') were applied to pupils, and by which newspapers. It also allowed them to examine how often and to whom or what 'blame' for problems in education was ascribed. However, they felt that a more detailed textual analysis was needed to analyse how such descriptions and ascriptions of 'blame' work in the newspaper text, and to situate the detailed content of stories within a larger, more persistent meta-story relating to society in general. According to MacMillan and McLachlan, discourse analysis provided a 'theoretical basis for showing how news . . . is rhetorically managed' (1999: Section 7.2). (Note that discourse analysis is discussed in more detail in the next section.)

It would be a mistake to assume that content analysis is 'objective' and independent of researcher interpretations. Once a rigorous classification system has been developed, it can be tested for internal reliability and replicated in other studies. However, the process of category derivation is inevitably dependent on the researcher's theoretical framework and interpretations of the material; hence there is an inherent subjectivity involved. As a consequence, content analyses of the same documents by different researchers could produce dissimilar-looking findings which were, however, equally valid within the researchers' respective frames of reference (Scott, 1990: 57). Different researchers constitute different audiences, and differences between their analyses of documents reflect this. This statement is not intended to indicate an acceptance of relativism; rather it points out that any reading of a document, whether by a researcher or by any other audience, needs to be assessed with reference to that audience's context and perspective.

A quantitative style of content analysis arguably shares with semiotic approaches a tendency to focus on 'internal meanings' in a way which neglects not only authors' intentions but also the meanings of documents to audiences. Conversely, a more interpretative approach need not limit itself to focusing on the author as a conscious social actor, but can also look at the audience as an active agent interpreting a document from within a particular social context. In qualitative content analysis the author is generally viewed as communicating with an audience or audiences; the concepts and categories emerge from the documents via a Grounded-Theory-like approach, and the emphasis is on intended and received meanings, albeit that additional data over and above the documents themselves are needed to grasp and contextualise audience readings of the documents. (It is surprising that it has only been relatively recently that mass media research has recognised the need to research the active and context-specific role of audiences in determining received meanings (Scott, 1990: 148; Stacey, 1994). Arguably this reflects the influence of semiotics in past studies of the mass media.)

The methods used in qualitative content analysis are in essence analogous to methods of qualitative data analysis more generally: for example, there are parallels between the analysis of documents and the analysis of interview transcripts. As in qualitative analysis more generally, the emphasis is on the actor's own perspective, and the themes generated from the documents reflect both the author's subjectivity and also a degree of conceptual input from the researcher. Furthermore, not only are documents and their authors viewed holistically within the qualitative approach to content analysis, but they are typically also situated within a historical and spatial context: for example, in ethnographic research, documents both reflect settings and inform researchers about them (Hammersley and Atkinson, 1995: 165–174). The qualitative analysis of documents does not only lend itself to the documenting of specific actors' subjective viewpoints; individual documents, like other qualitative data, can collectively contribute to the generation of theory via analytic induction (Plummer, 1983: 120–125).

Critical analysis and discourse analysis

We now turn our attention away from those methods and approaches to analysing documents which broadly parallel other quantitative and qualitative methods and towards some forms of textual analysis which have been applied to documents. Such forms of analysis include semiotic approaches, as discussed earlier in the chapter, and linguistically orientated approaches borrowed from feminist literary criticism; however, the remainder of this section focuses on critical analysis and discourse analysis, Foucauldian or otherwise. Central to the discussion that follows is the notion that the ideas and knowledge contained within documents can reflect or constitute a form of power which is used by one group within society to oppress or control another group or groups.

- The **critical analysis** of documents involves analysing their social structural roles, especially in relation to power, control and conflict. Documents are seen as vehicles for ideologies which present society from the viewpoint of particular social groupings; the discourses contained within official documents can thus be seen as an attempt by the state to maintain the status quo (Jupp and Norris, 1993).

- **Discourse analysis** focuses on the way in which language is used, the purposes for which it is used, and the social context of its usage. It attempts to uncover the internal structures and 'rules' of discourses; these discourses are both shaped by and shape their broader socio-cultural context. Different discourses may be in conflict with each other and they are frequently viewed as being tied to the exercise of power (Potter and Wetherell, 1994; Van Dijk, 1985).

- **Semiotics** focuses on the relationship between the **signifier**, such as a word, picture or object, and the **signified**, which is the mental image or meaning associated with that thing. The signifier and the signified together constitute a **sign**. Apparently simple signifiers can convey subtle meanings and a collection of signs can constitute a complex system of communication (Lapsley and Westlake, 1989).

- **Feminist literary criticism** focuses on 'the ways [in which gender] ideology is inscribed within literary forms, styles, conventions, genres and the institutions of literary production' (Greene and Kahn, 1985: 5). The ideology of gender is seen as inscribed in discourse, and produced and reproduced within literature specifically and in cultural practice generally.

The critical analytic approach (Jupp and Norris, 1993) sees many documents as attempting to impose specific understandings of society on their audiences. Inequalities within the social structure (e.g. those relating to class, gender and 'race') are seen as structuring the ideas and knowledge which are dominant within a given society at a given point in time. Documents thus convey/are ideological messages; critical analysis focuses on the ideological dimensions of documents and provides alternative readings of them by breaking down, or **deconstructing**, the knowledge that is contained in the documents, and **reconstructing** it in a way that demonstrates its structural origins and oppressive nature. Official documents are an obvious source of material for critical analysts, since they contain views of society legitimated by the state. For example, Hickman (1998) deconstructs the content of British official documents and political records to demonstrate how the 'forced inclusion' within a 'myth of homogeneity' of the Irish in Britain, evident in their exclusion from immigration controls, contributed to the invisibility of the Irish as members of an ethnic minority suffering racialisation, problematisation and discrimination (1998: 305).

In an analysis of photographs of working-class women taken in the 1930s and 1940s on behalf of two official US bodies, the Farm Security Administration and the Office of War Information, Ellis (1996) argues that the photographs typically portray poverty in a way which is non-threatening to a middle-class audience, bringing deprivation to their attention in a way which justifies intervention by a socially concerned, liberal government, including agricultural re-organisation in the context of a technocratic, capitalist economy. However, Ellis identifies a specific photographer whose images are subversive, portraying social marginality in a disturbing way and showing working-class women in ways which are in opposition to the ideological impositions of wartime propaganda. Ellis thus deconstructs and reconstructs the information contained in the photographs to show how they reflect both state ideology and opposition to state ideology.

Documents containing the views of 'experts' – for example the medical and legal professions – who have a certain amount of power over other people's lives, are also ripe for deconstruction, as are documents produced by academic 'experts' which feed research findings into the social policy literature (see, for example, Leonard, 1996). Critical analysts often see the state as central to oppression within society, but some, such as those who have been influenced by the work of Foucault (1977, 1979, 1980), see power and control as being exercised in other contexts as well (Jupp and Norris, 1993: 49): for example, within commercial organisations.

In examinations of the ways in which official documents shape the agenda in relation to particular social issues, critical analysis operates by:

- focusing on the 'problems' identified by the documents
- considering the explanations of and solutions to these problems which are contained within the documents

- considering competing explanations and solutions which are absent from the documents.

Like interpretative approaches to documentary analysis, the critical analytic approach is more holistic than quantitative content analysis in its treatment of documents, and is orientated towards general theoretical development rather than specific hypothesis testing. The technical procedures employed within critical analysis are not as well defined as its objective, i.e. the examination of how knowledge is used as a mechanism via which power can be exercised. However, critical analysis often involves some form of discourse analysis, an approach to which we now turn.

A discourse can be thought of as a collection of ideas or 'knowledge' about society, or about groups of individuals within it, which is in common use within some group (or groups) of people, or within society in general. Discourses are not only visible within documents and speech but can also be seen within actions and behaviour. Discourses are intrinsically linked to power, but nevertheless may be common to both the oppressors and the oppressed. However, there may be resistance to discourses (e.g. to 'expert' medical discourses), and different, competing discourses may exist, of which one may be dominant at a given point in time.

The meanings attached to discourses need to be identified with reference to their temporal and social contexts; in addition to the content of documents, both authors and their intentions and also audience interpretations need to be considered if the researcher is to be able to link the application of power via discourses back to its structural roots. However, not all styles of discourse analysis acknowledge the importance of specific authors and audiences. The Foucauldian approach to discourse analysis views authors and audiences simply as occupants of positions constructed by and present within the discourse itself; according to this approach everything that matters is contained within the discourse and individual social actors and human agency are seen as irrelevant. However, while Foucault's work has much to offer in terms of its theoretical sophistication, we share with a number of other authors (e.g. Plummer, 1983: 131) a concern that his approach neglects human agency and is hence of limited value to many empirical social researchers.

Jupp and Norris (1993: 50) use insights from discourse analysis to draw up an agenda for the critical analysis of discourses within documentary analysis. The agenda calls for:

- the identification of dominant and alternative discourses, and of key groups and key documents
- an examination of the pervasiveness and consistency of discourses across society
- an evaluation of the ways in which discourses tie in with conflict, power relationships and resistance within society
- an assessment of the extent to which the state is of central underlying importance.

As befits this book's general message that different research approaches (quantitative, qualitative or otherwise) need not be seen as mutually exclusive, it is worth us noting that quantitative content analysis and textual analysis can and have been used in combination with each other within research projects (for example, Reinharz (1992) discusses such a study by Cancian and Gordon, which focuses on changing norms in relation to emotions within marriage).

Mohr (1999) analysed a sample of medical charts corresponding to individuals hospitalised in psychiatric hospitals in the United States in the 1980s. Her quantitative content analysis established that while the majority of chart entries (56%) were descriptive (of patient behaviour), more than 20% were in categories that she labelled as 'pejorative' (9%), 'punitive' (5%), 'inane' (8%) and 'nonsense' (1%). Her second level of analysis was Foucauldian: for example, she observes that the juxtaposition of a 'pejorative' entry about a patient's behaviour and a 'punitive' entry about a nurse's response to the behaviour is illustrative of the process of surveillance, labelling as abnormal, and punishment of non-conformity which can be found within Foucault's analysis of power relations and the 'disciplinary gaze' (Foucault, 1977; 1980).

Whichever style or styles of documentary analysis a researcher adopts, there is a common need to document the link between the research findings and the documents from which they have been derived, and more generally for the researcher to validate their conclusions.

In quantitative content analysis adequate documentation of the classification and coding process goes a long way towards establishing the reliability of the findings and their validity within the context of the researcher's theoretical framework. However, in the textual analysis of documents, it is important that an adequate amount of the original documentary material is included for the reader to be able to assess for herself or himself the validity of the researcher's interpretations. Illustrative material, such as quotations, may have been chosen selectively, and may not constitute sufficient information for the reader to be able to establish the extent to which the findings have been shaped by the researcher's theoretical input. Of course, whether the form of analysis is quantitative or qualitative, the findings are potentially contingent upon, and need to be evaluated with regard to, the frame of reference of the specific researcher in question.

The validity of quantitative and qualitative findings from documentary research can also be assessed in relation to external sources of information, whether these are findings from other analyses of documents, or other forms of data (e.g. actors' behaviour). Plummer (1983: 104) notes the possibility of an autocritique by the subject of life-history research; the consistency of interpretations with the views of social actors more generally may also be worth examining. As noted earlier, the representativeness of the documents analysed may have implications for the validity of the interpretations in terms of their generalisability. Assessing the validity of interpretations derived from documents is in many ways analogous to assessing the validity of interpretations based on other forms of quantitative or qualitative data; however, the validity of interpretations generated via literary or semiotic approaches is more difficult to assess (Scott, 1990: 32–33), perhaps because of the lack of overlap between these approaches and other social research methods.

Official statistics

In 1980 Bulmer wrote that there was 'relatively little interest in the potentialities of official statistics for sociological analysis' (Bulmer, 1980: 505). However, we know from our own sociological research in the fields of education and marriage that official data can form a vital contextual backdrop against which to analyse qualitative data. Furthermore, as will be discussed later in the chapter, official data have been used by sociologists in a range of valuable and interesting secondary analyses. So why did Bulmer make the above comment?

In the 1950s the use of official statistics was seen as a way of bolstering the credibility of sociology as an academic discipline (Levitas and Guy, 1996: 1), but scepticism of or even hostility towards them grew in the 1960s alongside the development of phenomenology and other interpretative approaches. Thus Bulmer's observation needs to be viewed in the context of the critiques prevalent in 1970s sociology of both quantitative methods and also the state. Unfortunately the damage that was done to the reputation of official statistics within the academic community has only partially been repaired, in part because of the public distrust of official statistics which developed in the 1980s, and in part because of the after effects of the sceptical view of official statistics presented by research methods teachers and the sociological research methods literature around the time when Bulmer was writing. The view, discussed in more detail later in this chapter, that official statistics are fatally flawed as information sources, because they are

socially constructed in a way which leads them to reflect the values of those who produced them, has also led to a tendency for published official statistics to be viewed as material more suited to critical analysis than to use as a resource. However, a recognition that official statistics are not objective or theoretically 'neutral' does not necessitate their rejection as a resource.

While deep suspicion of official statistics has to some extent stretched beyond the boundaries of sociology into other social science disciplines, researchers in neighbouring disciplines such as demography take for granted the potential value of official statistics as a resource, while recognising that, as social products, their value is something that needs to be reflected upon rather than accepted without question in an empiricist fashion. However, such reflections can perhaps be facilitated by ideas drawn from the sociological critiques of official statistics, including both ideas from phenomenological critiques, which echo the more general scepticism of many qualitative researchers about quantitative data, and also the emphasis on the role of the state central to the work of critical analysts. On the other hand, we believe that the critiques of official statistics exaggerate their limitations, perhaps in part because they tend to focus on data based on administrative records rather than on data generated by social surveys, and on topics such as suicide and crime rather than on topics like, say, work or the family. The notion that official statistics are of minimal value to radical critiques of the status quo (Miles and Irvine, 1979: 127) sits rather uncomfortably alongside the fact that official statistics can be and have been used to document the persistence and growth of social inequality.

Critiques of official statistics

As industrial capitalism has developed, official statistics have flourished over the last two centuries (especially in the post-war period) as tools for economic management and social policy making. The range of areas covered by official statistics is diverse, including, for example, the economy, agriculture, crime, the population, property ownership and poverty. It is unsurprising that economic statistics are particularly well developed, but according to critics such as Miles and Irvine (1979: 126), the state's uses of official statistics stretch well beyond straightforward economic and social policy purposes. The state is also seen by such critics as facilitating capitalist production by creating appropriate social conditions; official statistics are thus seen as a means of supporting state dominance via their use in the following contexts:

- surveillance
- the justification of the activities of state agencies
- the preservation of social cohesion
- the generally favourable presentation of the state and of capitalism
- the reproduction of the dominant ideologies of capitalist society.

(Presumably such criticisms could also be levelled at the state in communist societies.) In the context of the use of official statistics for policy purposes, economic and political priorities determine the quantity and range of data available in different policy areas; Miles and Irvine suggest that this can, for example, lead to better data on housing than on homelessness.

It is more or less inevitable that state agencies are the only source of certain forms of statistical information, given the resources needed to generate them and the element of compulsion sometimes required (e.g. with regard to Census data). However, critics such as Miles and Irvine, and Hindess (1973), argue that official statistics are presented as conceptually neutral products of a 'neutral technocracy', and that, from the perspective of the producers of the statistics, official statistics are 'objective facts' whose limitations are confined to 'technical' flaws. The state is argued as presenting itself as serving the public interest neutrally; thus official statistics are presented by the state as being of equal value to all political standpoints (Miles and Irvine, 1979: 124).

While we agree that official statistics reflect the functions and goals of the state, and that the concepts and categories used reflect to some degree the ideological framework(s) of those with power within the state, we view the extent to which this limits the value of official statistics to the researcher (radical or otherwise) as something which needs to be evaluated. Though the concepts used are not neutral, and may be asociological, sexist, etc., they may nevertheless be close enough to the conceptual framework of a researcher for official statistics based on those concepts to be of some value. We would also agree with Miles and Irvine's observation (1979: 116) that state agencies (in Britain at least) are more often guilty of empiricism (and on occasions, perhaps, a lack of conceptual sophistication) than of conscious political manipulation, though it needs to be acknowledged that Miles and Irvine were writing before the apparent political interference of the 1980s (Levitas and Guy, 1996: 3).

The various critiques of official statistics emphasise different dimensions of their production. Sometimes the emphasis is on social structure: Marxist and feminist critiques see official statistics as reflecting underlying power structures, and Miles and Irvine view as crucial structures within capitalist society and the role of the state. Conversely, some critiques arguably neglect structural factors because of their emphasis on decision making by individual actors: phenomenological discussions of official statistics focus on the ways in which the statistics reflect the meanings of concepts to those constructing the data. (In between these 'extremes', critiques typically recognise the relevance of an institutional level of analysis, and the importance of organisational practices and structures to the ways in which official statistics are constructed.)

Atkinson (1978) examines the categorisation of deaths as suicides, a process which underpins official statistics on suicide. His analysis situates decision making by individual actors (coroners) within a legal–organisational context, and more broadly within a cultural context, i.e. a society in which particular shared definitions of suicidal situations prevail. The definitions of suicide used by coroners are viewed as both being affected by and also affecting the societal definitions. While Atkinson's analysis situates social actors in a cultural context, there is no emphasis on power, capitalism and the state, though he does cite US President Eisenhower's hypothesis that a high suicide rate in Sweden was a consequence of too many years of social-ist government (1978: 53), which suggests that a capitalist state (or, for that matter, a socialist one) would have an incentive to present a low suicide rate, to indicate a society at ease with itself.

Writers have often attempted to incorporate both individual decision making and structural context into their accounts of the production of official statistics:

- Hindess (1973) views official statistics as in essence reflecting culturally/organisationally determined conceptual instruments, but allows social actors some discretion in the imple-mentation of those instruments.
- Cicourel (1964) views this as too deterministic, but is concerned to 'situate' the decisions made by individuals and to take account of structures.
- Miles and Irvine see as important both the actions of individuals and also organisational practices within state agencies, albeit that they appear in the final analysis to see these as rooted in capitalism, exploitative class relations, and the operation of the state within a given historical instance (1979: 121–127).

We share with these various authors a concern with the ways in which official statistics are shaped con-ceptually by power relations and the meanings of concepts to social actors, but we view official stat-istics as a resource rather than just as a topic for crit-ical analysis, and see this 'shaping' of the statistics as leading to a set of conceptual limitations to be considered alongside any technical limitations when a researcher is assessing the value of official statistics to their research.

As noted earlier, critiques of official statistics have often focused on statistics relating to deviant behaviour derived from administrative sources, which Bulmer notes as often being difficult to adapt for research purposes (Bulmer, 1980: 508). The existence of conceptual differences between the perspectives of administrators and researchers in this context is unsurprising, and the kinds of con-cepts arising in the area of deviance are particu-larly likely to be contested and difficult to measure, leading to problems of validity and reliability. It is clear that data relating to deviant behaviour are socially constructed by individuals operating within organisational and legal contexts. Hence Durkheim's classic research on suicide (1952) has been subjected to extensive criticism (see Scott, 1990: 48–52), in part because of the obvious difficulties involved in 'measuring' the intentions of the dead, and in part because of the scope for cross-cultural variations in definitions of suicide.

Crime statistics date back as far as the late eigh-teenth century and are frequently central to critiques of official statistics. The view of ethnomethodo-logists, which is that such statistics do not convey any useful information about the occurrence of criminal activity, is easy to relate to, if a little over-stated. Kitsuse and Cicourel (1963) view official statistics as defining crime rather than measuring it; they held similar views about much educational data. A less clear-cut view is that the process of social construction leads to crime statistics which paint a very distorted picture of reality. Scott dis-cusses the involvement of social actors in the see-ing, reporting and recording of crimes, and the role of 'situated decisions' and administrative routines in the construction of crime statistics (1990: 91–94). Changes in reporting/recording practices or in administrative routines can clearly induce trends in the statistics which do not reflect vari-ations in the pattern of criminal activity.

Reiner (1996) notes the continuing prominence and misinterpretation of crime statistics in public and political debates, and points out that 'health warnings' and technical advances are largely nullified by the tendency for the debates to focus on crude figures which are especially prone to measurement distortions.

The introduction of a new counting method in Britain in 1999 highlighted both measurement issues and media responses in relation to crime statistics. The changes, which involved some multi-faceted offences (which had previously been counted as single offences) being counted more than once, created an artefactual jump in the recorded crime rate. Newspaper responses to this jump varied. Some headlines noted the artefactual nature of the increase ('New rules push up crime figures', *Financial Times*, 13 October 1999, p. 3); some concentrated on the 'underlying' change ('Crime still falling but at slower rate', *Guardian* 13 October 1999, p. 4); some frankly appear misleading ('Statistics shake-up shows rise in crime', *Daily Telegraph*, 11 October 1999, p. 6; 'Violent crime figures set to soar', *The Times*, 11 October 1999, p. 10). The last headline quoted above was followed after a couple of days by 'Violent crime falling for first time in years' (*The Times*, 13 October 1999, p. 11). What is clear from the above is the newsworthiness of the trend in the overall figure for recorded crime, and also the trend in the more specific figure for violent crime. On this occasion the artefactual nature of the 'trend' was difficult for the media to ignore, but the limitations of the crude figures rarely receive such critical attention.

O'Connell-Davidson and Layder (1994) focus specifically on rape statistics, which can be used to highlight a range of issues relating to the validity, reliability and process of construction of official statistics. Official statistics on rape provide very poor estimates of 'actual numbers', but provide useful information in relation to police and court practices. They are shaped by both cultural norms and gender/sexuality ideologies and also by the actions of rape victims, the police, judges, juries, etc., within this cultural/ideological context.

In recent critiques of official statistics unemployment statistics have become very prominent. Where such statistics are generated administratively, and first and foremost for the internal purposes of government, it is more or less inevitable that they will differ conceptually from what is ideally required by academic researchers and radical commentators. However, criticisms of unemployment statistics in the 1970s evolved in the 1980s into concerns about deliberate political manipulation, which were picked up by the media and continued into the 1990s (Levitas, 1996a). Between 1979 and 1989 30 changes were made to the count used, including a shift from counting those registered for work to counting those in receipt of benefit, inducing an artefactual decrease in the count. In a way unemployment as an issue highlights the worst and best of official statistics, since critiques of official, administratively based unemployment figures can make (and have made) use of data from the Labour Force Survey, an official government survey (Levitas and Guy, 1996: 4). This highlights the value of the secondary analysis of official data, within which it may be possible to operationalise concepts differently to how this has been done in published official data. Of course, any differences between competing sets of unemployment figures must reflect underlying conceptual or technical differences, which need to be understood before the greater validity of one set of figures or another can be established. Comparison with a second set of figures may in itself help to highlight the practices which generated a set of official statistics.

The emphasis on crime, suicide and unemployment within critiques of official statistics no doubt reflects both ideological and political aspects of these issues and also the comparative ease with which these topics can be incorporated within such critiques. However, while some of the forms of official data referred to later in this chapter (e.g. demographic data), may present fewer measurement problems (Bulmer, 1980: 508), later sections of this chapter refer to official data relating to 'race' and disability which highlight the need for all researchers to evaluate official statistics with reference to their own conceptual frameworks.

In defence of the use of official statistics

Concerns about the validity and reliability of official statistics are not unique to the authors of critiques; both those involved in the production of official statistics and those who use them are typically aware of and reflect upon the scope for and existence of limitations. In his defence of official statistics, Bulmer (1980) accepts that they are contingent on both social structural factors and the actions of officials, and stresses the need for an understanding of the process which produced them. Similarly, Scott suggests that official data (e.g. medical records) need in the first instance to be studied as a topic, i.e. in their own right, but can then be used as a resource, once they have been contextualised within the process that generated them (1990: 129). Official statistics thus need to be approached with a degree of scepticism and their meaning needs to be interpreted before they can be used. Once an understanding of their meaning has been achieved, the crunch issue is the extent to which the official concepts and the researcher's own concepts correspond to each other, assuming that the data are valid with reference to the official conceptual framework (1990: 95). Bulmer notes that the fit between sociological concepts and official data is often poor (1980: 520), but questions whether the gap between the conceptual standpoints of government statisticians and of sociologists is fatally wide (1980: 509). He suggests that the common-sense assumptions of statisticians may match up quite well to the theoretical constructs of sociologists, as exemplified by the 'key variables in social investigation' discussed in Burgess (1986). In addition, while published official statistics present data in a fixed form, secondary analyses of official data allow the researcher to minimise the impact of the official conceptual framework. For example, the re-analyses of the General Household Survey by Arber (1990) used a modified class schema more appropriate than the existing official schema to the examination of the impact of women's occupations on their health.

As noted in the previous section with reference to unemployment statistics, some form of triangulation may be useful, whereby administratively based official statistics are complemented by data from another source, official or otherwise. O'Connell-Davidson and Layder (1994) note that the under-reporting of sex offences within official statistics has been established by comparisons with survey data. Reiner (1996: 201) suggests that the use of multiple sources reduces the need for scepticism, citing the use of data on victimisation from the British Crime Survey and data on burglary from the General Household Survey as a way of establishing the extent to which official crime statistics are misleading. However, the statistical 'benchmarks' used for such comparisons, of course, have their own limitations. West (1996) discusses a slightly different form of triangulation, i.e. the use of workplace data and case study research to complement data from the Labour Force Survey.

Another strand of Bulmer's defence is the suggestion that findings of substantive value have been derived from official statistics. He focuses on the relationships between class and health which have consistently been shown to exist using official statistics. In this context 'health' is, strangely enough, often operationalised as mortality, and the unreliability and lack of accuracy of occupational data on death certificates have long been a cause for concern. However, mortality, while not ideal, seems in the view of many medical sociologists to be an adequate indicator of a more sociological conceptualisation of 'health', and Bulmer noted (1980: 514) that official statisticians were concerned about the limitations of death registration data. Indeed, Wilkinson (1996: 69) has pointed out that this concern contributed to the development of the OPCS (Office of Population Censuses and Surveys) Longitudinal Study (LS), which strengthened the occupational information available to researchers by linking death certificates back to earlier Census data. Since the publication of Bulmer's article in 1980, observed class-related inequalities in health have generally been accepted as mirroring genuine differences rather than being artefactual, data relating to the relationship have improved in quality, and official statistics have been used in critical discussions of health inequalities (Guy, 1996).

Bulmer also mentions the use of official statistics by social researchers in the Chicago School, within a 'sociographic' strand of research complementing their ethnographic work (1980: 521–523). This highlights the possibility of combining the use of official statistics with qualitative material, and it also highlights the value of official data corresponding to local areas (typically Census data). In Britain, recent research using deprivation measures for local areas based on 1991 Census data has shown a relationship between local deprivation and mortality (McLoone and Boddy, cited in Wilkinson, 1996).

The value of official data on class-related inequalities in health rests upon the acceptability of the official operationalisation of class. As noted in Chapter 5, Registrar General's Social Class is conceptually flawed and is being replaced. However, as noted by Bulmer (1980: 517), for all its conceptual inadequacies Registrar General's Social Class produces similar relationships with health to those produced by, for example, Goldthorpe class (see Chapter 5). Thus the considerable overlap between the empirical patterns produced using different operationalisations of class demonstrates that they have much in common, and, arguably, enough in common to render Registrar General's Social Class acceptable, at least in the absence of something better. The review of official social classifications (Rose and O'Reilly, 1997) has received considerable input from sociologists with a neo-Weberian perspective, which is consistent with Bulmer's recommendation that there should be greater academic involvement with the conceptual development of official statistics (1980: 520); the classification superseding Registrar General's Social

Class will thus presumably render official statistics more acceptable to researchers with this perspective. However, some will no doubt regret the absence of a neo-Marxist slant in the collapsed version of the new classification (Nichols, 1996), since the cleavages between categories do not correspond in a straightforward way to differences relating to ownership, credentials and managerial/supervisory responsibilities, as in the schema of Wright (1985), and the ordering of the categories markedly separates routinised non-manual and routinised manual work. The review's emphasis on the term 'classification' as opposed to the more politicised term 'class' is also rather disconcerting.

The revision of the official social classifications is to an extent illustrative of broader attempts to improve official statistics, both conceptually and technically. In addition to addressing some of the issues raised by critiques, government statisticians have worked collaboratively with academia, have sought user feedback, and have engaged in consultation processes with researchers in specific fields. No doubt this will only result in a proportion of official statistics becoming more conceptually acceptable to some but not all researchers, but it is indicative of the fact that official statisticians see themselves as something more than servants of the capitalist state and perhaps share Levitas and Guy's view that the dissemination of such information is an essential feature of an informed democracy (1996: x).

It is clear that official statistics can be treated as a topic of study: for example, rape statistics and the process that generated them can be used to examine the operation of ideology and power relationships within society. However, official statistics can also be used to document social inequalities which governments would prefer not to exist (or at least prefer to remain unseen). Thus, like the self-styled Radical Statisticians, Dorling and Simpson (1999), we see official statistics as something to be used as well as to be critiqued; official statistics may be social products but they can still be a resource for social research, 'radical' or otherwise. For example, Staines (in Dorling and Simpson, 1999) uses death registration data and Census data to highlight a widening gap between rich and poor in relation to life expectancy in Yorkshire in the 1980s.

Developments in official statistics

This section looks briefly at developments in official statistics over the last two decades of the twentieth century, and uses the concepts of disability and 'race'/ethnicity to illustrate some of the issues relevant to the analysis of official statistics. While there have been some advances in the nature, volume and availability of official data, there is an ongoing need for researchers to approach official statistics with caution and to avoid taking them at face value. In their assessment of changes in official statistics since 1980, Levitas and Guy (1996) highlight problems of funding cuts, distortion and suppression, and a loss of public confidence. They also point out that positive changes in the quality of data available for secondary analyses may benefit academic researchers, but that it is published official statistics which are of more direct relevance to the general public. Should it be official statisticians or academic researchers who bear the responsibility for documenting, say, increasing social inequality?

Levitas and Guy note that Bulmer's 1980 defence coincided with a turning point for official statistics (1996: 2). The 1970s had seen improvements in official statistics, including, ironically enough (Levitas, 1996b: 9), a shift away from data generation for the purposes of the state towards data production for wider, public consumption. However, the government's Rayner review of official statistics in 1980/1 required cuts, potentially (but not in practice) including the loss of the General Household Survey, and prioritised government purposes and 'value for money' over public service. Levitas (1996b) and Townsend (1996) discuss how the period following the Rayner review saw a decline in the coverage of inequality and poverty within official statistics, and apparent government manipulation with respect to statistics in areas such as unemployment.

From the beginning of the 1980s onwards opposition to the above came less from the sociological community than from the statistical community. The Royal Statistical Society (RSS) opposed reduced accessibility and an emphasis on government needs. A desire on the part of the Government Statistical Service to be 'neutral' and 'objective' was mirrored by RSS demands during the 1980s for an independent National Statistical Commission and an Official Statistics Act to underwrite the autonomy of official statistics. Concerns about political interference, public confidence and data quality continued to be voiced during the 1990s; undercount problems with the 1991 Census were of particular concern in the latter context.

Recent trends, however, have been more encouraging; Tim Holt, appointed head of the revamped Office for National Statistics (ONS) in 1996, stressed the importance of freedom from political interference and of improved public confidence, in part to be achieved via better access to official statistics (Holt, 1998). The current government and ONS both seem orientated towards methodologically well-grounded, independent official statistics, though the government is hesitant to allow independence in some potentially controversial areas. However, from the point of view of the sociological community, methodological improvements may well lean more towards the 'technical' rather than towards the 'conceptual', and it would seem probable that a supposedly 'neutral' approach by ONS will still generate official statistics which reflect the interests of the state more than they reflect the conceptual frameworks of academic social researchers.

Disability and ethnicity: the value and limitations of two official data sources

In the mid- to late 1980s a number of disability-related surveys were carried out by OPCS to facilitate the planning of benefits and services. In a critique of the surveys, Abberley (1996) suggests that their conceptual framework locates the source of disability in individuals rather than in society. Hence the role of individual impairments is emphasised relative to the role of structural and environmental constraints. Abberley suggests that, given that state welfare exists within the broader context of industrial capitalism, it was the concerns of the state which led the surveys to focus on the ability and willingness of disabled people to work rather than on the 'disabling environment' (1996: 182).

More specifically, Abberley criticises the 'spurious objectivity' of the severity scale used, which was rooted in the subjective conceptual framework of a panel, of whom an unspecified number of members were themselves disabled people, and who were asked, among other things, to compare one form of impairment with another: for example, the inability to walk with the inability to see (1996: 168–169). Abberley views the results of this process as reflecting a crude version of any pre-existing cultural consensus with respect to beliefs about disability. He also highlights the problematic use within the surveys of the concept of 'difficulty', pointing out that finding an activity 'difficult' is a subjective assessment, which reflects an individual's expectations as well as their interpretation of whether being able regularly to carry out an activity successfully (e.g. through practice) means that it cannot be difficult. This conceptual flaw can be assumed to have led to an under-estimation of the problems of disabled people; Abberley also notes that comparisons with other data sources indicate that the OPCS surveys under-estimated the costs attached to disability (1996: 181).

Abberley does, however, acknowledge that the OPCS surveys are of some use, albeit limited, to academic researchers like himself, and he notes the existence of useful secondary analyses of the OPCS survey data by other researchers (some of which are discussed later in this section). His principal concern appears to be that the 'medical model' adopted by the surveys individualises disability in a way which not only limits the value of the data but also renders the research ethically questionable (1996: 174–175), though he is also concerned

about the lack of attention to issues of class, gender and ethnicity. Overall, Abberley's critique provides a good example of a situation where the gap between the conceptual framework embedded within official statistics and a specific researcher's own conceptual framework is close to being fatally wide.

A sizeable gap also exists between the conceptual frameworks of academic sociologists and the categories of the ethnic group question included (for the first time) in the 1991 Census. Analyses of 'ethnicity' using the 1971 and 1981 Censuses were reliant on data relating to country of birth, but the growing number of second-generation members of minority ethnic groups rendered this kind of 'approximation' useless. A self-identification question on 'ethnicity' was introduced within the 1979 Labour Force Survey, but plans to introduce such a question in the 1981 Census were abandoned due to unsuccessful trials and opposition from some minority groups (Fenton, 1996: 149). After further trials, and in spite of both a degree of continued opposition and also disagreements regarding the most appropriate form of classification, a question was included in the 1991 Census, with the justification for its inclusion being that it was needed for planning purposes and also for the monitoring of disadvantage and discrimination. The categories used in the question were as follows:

- 'White'
- 'Black – Caribbean'
- 'Black – African'
- 'Black – Other'
- 'Indian'
- 'Pakistani'
- 'Bangladeshi'
- 'Chinese'
- 'Any other ethnic group'.

They thus appear to be a strange mish-mash of phenotype/'colour' and (ancestral) nationality/geographical location. The conceptual limitations of the categories mean that researchers will typically need to use them in combination with country of birth data. However, even bolstered in this way, the above categories are far from providing a wholly valid measure of people's membership of distinct cultural groups. The absence of any differentiation within the 'White' category means that groups who have often been economically disadvantaged or discriminated against racially are rendered invisible, which does not seem consistent with the monitoring objective mentioned above. In particular, the absence of an 'Irish' category has been widely criticised (Fenton, 1996: 159–162). The 2001 Census will address this specific issue, and will also include a question on religion, but debates on this issue continue (see the chapters by Ahmad and by Southworth, in Dorling and Simpson, 1999), and in any case the ethnic group question included in the 1991 Census is still a useful example of the conceptual limitations that are often to be found in official data (see Dale and Holdsworth (1997) for a discussion of the implications of the ethnic categorisation for analyses of ethnic differences).

Both the OPCS Disability surveys and the data on ethnic groups within the 1991 Census SARs have, however, been used extensively by secondary analysts; the examples given below of analyses using these sources arguably demonstrate that their utility outweighs their conceptual limitations. (Secondary analysis is discussed more generally as an approach to research later in this chapter.)

Secondary analyses using the OPCS Disability surveys

Many secondary analyses of these surveys focus on resource issues: for example, Kavanagh and Knapp (1999) used them to estimate health and social care service costs for elderly people with cognitive disability. However, other secondary analysts have focused on the experience or social consequences of disability: Astin *et al.* (1996) examined the prevalence of pain among disabled people, finding that 30% of disabled adults experience pain which severely affects their daily activities, and they consequently suggest that pain is a major public health problem;

Hirst (1992) showed that mothers of severely disabled young people are less than half as likely as comparable mothers to be in paid work, controlling for other relevant factors.

Ethnicity-related secondary analyses using the 1991 Census SARs

Holdsworth and Dale (1997) explored variations in patterns of employment and occupational attainment among women from different ethnic groups, finding, for example, that the presence of a partner has the greatest impact on Pakistani and Bangladeshi women's employment, whereas the presence of a pre-school child is most significant for White women's economic activity.

Model (1999) examined ethnic inequalities with regard to a variety of socio-economic outcomes (including unemployment and both the economic and social dimensions of occupations). She combined the ethnic group and place of birth information to improve the substantive value of the ethnic categories. She found, for example, that on several outcomes Indian males outrank Black Caribbean males, whereas Black Caribbean females outrank Indian females.

Official statistical data: their value, usage and availability

We have suggested that the researcher needs to make an assessment of the validity of official data for the purposes of their research, based on the degree to which the definitions and categories of the concepts operationalised within the official data are consistent with the researcher's own conceptual framework. However, given that there will often be an adequate degree of consistency, there is an extensive range and massive volume of official statistical data available to researchers. The technical quality of official data in Britain is on the whole very good, published material is likely to be freely available within university libraries, and even secondary analyses of official data are inexpensive relative to other forms of research. The distinction between the use of published data and secondary analysis (which usually makes use of microdata, i.e. 'raw' data about individuals) is an important one; published official statistics can provide important background information to provide a context, say, for a small-scale qualitative study, but secondary analysis can enable the researcher to carry out a sophisticated, explanatory analysis of a social phenomenon, which might act as the core element of a research study. Access to microdata from official surveys, and secondary analysis more broadly, are discussed later in this chapter.

A researcher wishing to use official statistics as background information within a UK-focused research project will typically find herself or himself looking at a table of figures containing aggregated information about the population of interest to her or him, located within a volume published by The Stationery Office (which used to be Her Majesty's Stationery Office or HMSO). Such a table can often give the off-putting impression of being a sea of figures, and as such may help to confirm the prejudices of a researcher who is sceptical about official statistics. However, extracting the relevant information can in practice be straightforward.

Suppose that a researcher (whose study focuses on Wales) is interested in finding out what proportion of women who live with dependent children in households in which there are no other adults are students. This information can be found in a table within a volume containing 1991 Census data relating to household composition (OPCS, 1993). However, the relevant table is a cross-classification of four variables (i.e. the economic position of the household head, the composition of the household, the age of the household head, and the specific country), and it stretches across 35 (A4) pages. On the other hand, there are only four numbers in the table which are of interest to the researcher, and these are shown below:

WALES:	All economic positions (p. 428)	TOTAL HOUSEHOLDS
	1 adult female with 1 dependent child	2017
	1 adult female with 2+ dependent children	1483
	Economically inactive: students (p. 433)	TOTAL HOUSEHOLDS
	1 adult female with 1 dependent child	260
	1 adult female with 2+ dependent children	307

Extracted from Table 12 in OPCS (1993), Crown Copyright.

Thus the figure that the researcher is interested in is as follows:

$$(260 + 307)/(2017 + 1483) = 16.2\%$$

For another example of simplifying tabular data (which includes the original table in full) see Sapsford (1996).

Once the researcher has come to terms with the layout of a table, scepticism becomes more healthy, since the figures in the table need to be interpreted in relation to the process which constructed them, and the researcher should have in mind the range of issues relating to surveys, documents and official statistics which have been discussed in this and earlier chapters. More specifically, the researcher needs to establish a sufficiently full and clear picture of the data-collection process, the operationalisation of concepts, etc., for him or her to be able to assess the validity and reliability of the figures in the table. In particular, figures derived from survey data are not always accompanied by standard deviations, and the researcher thus needs to bear in mind that such figures are subject to sampling error.

Published official statistics may not correspond precisely to the geographical areas of interest to the researcher, and the categories used may not be fully consistent with the researcher's conceptual framework. The researcher may therefore be forced to make some assumptions, and may also need to manipulate the data to achieve a correspondence that is as close as possible to their specific requirements. Often, the scope of the researcher's objectives will stretch further than the published figures: for example, the researcher may wish to look simultaneously at the ways in which behaviour varies according to age, gender and socio-economic situation, but it is quite likely that none of the tables available will cross-classify the behaviour by all these three factors at the same time. It is in this kind of situation that secondary analyses of official data become highly desirable, since they allow the researcher to carry out customised, multivariate analyses and to minimise the mismatch between what the researcher wants and what the data have to offer.

What official statistics are available?

Researchers in the UK may be aware via looking at earlier studies of the key official data sources in their substantive field, but they can also consult the *Guide to Official Statistics* produced by the Office for National Statistics (ONS, 1996a). Additionally, electronic databases listing ONS-published statistics and UK Official Publications more generally have been produced, and should be accessible via university libraries. ONS, like the US Census Bureau, now has its own website on the Internet (http://www.statistics.gov.uk/), via which an on-line database, Statbase, can be accessed, which contains information about all the statistics produced by the Government Statistical Service (GSS). Information about government surveys is also available from other sources on the Internet. For example, the Data Archive at the University of Essex, via which survey data can be obtained for secondary analyses, has many official surveys in its on-line catalogue, and the ESRC Question Bank (mentioned in Chapter 5) contains on-line information about the

research instruments (concepts and indicators, questionnaires, etc.) used in some important government surveys. Note that there is inevitably a delay between the collection of data and the availability of published figures and of data for secondary analyses.

Looking beyond the UK, both national governments in advanced industrial societies and also international organisations such as the United Nations, the World Bank, the Organisation for Economic Cooperation and Development (OECD) and the International Labour Organisation (ILO) publish extensive statistical material (e.g. demographic and socio-economic statistics) which may be of value to researchers doing cross-national research or focusing on countries other than the UK. However, data corresponding to less-developed countries are more scarce, and may be of poor technical quality; researchers making cross-national comparisons should also be aware of the risk of non-comparability as a consequence of inconsistencies in measurement between countries and/or across time.

Turning back to the UK, the wide range of topics covered by official statistics is visible in the *Guide to Official Statistics*. Demographic data (e.g. data from the Census) are considered in more detail below, but in addition material is available corresponding to a wide range of topics such as the following:

- the labour market (e.g. data on unemployment derived from administrative records; data from the Labour Force Survey)
- health and social care (e.g. data based on cancer registrations; data from the Health Survey for England)
- crime (e.g. data from the British Crime Survey; data based on the administrative records of family courts)
- transport (e.g. data from the National Travel Survey; data derived from police reports on road accidents).

It is clear from the above examples that official statistics are based on Censuses, on surveys and also on administrative records.

The value of demographic data to researchers

Official data on the population of Britain have a long history. Vital registration (i.e. the registration of births, marriages and deaths) at parish level dates back a number of centuries, and the decennial Census and centralised vital registration date back to the first half of the nineteenth century. Scott has assessed the validity of historical vital registration data, and is upbeat about their value to researchers (1990: 97–107). More generally, Bulmer notes the extensive use of official statistics in demographic research, and also points out that demographers typically reflect carefully on the limitations of demographic data, notwithstanding their relative reliability (1980: 508–513). While many British sociologists have been hesitant to use official statistics because of their perceived inadequacies, the small but active demographic community and various interdisciplinary researchers have instead focused on minimising any limitations. Bulmer notes the involvement of sociologists in work on Census under-enumeration in the United States in the 1970s (1980: 514); similar work in Britain in the 1990s has not involved the sociological community to the same extent.

The 'taken-for-granted' value of demographic data to those who use them may perhaps explain in part why discussions of official statistics are sometimes dominated by substantive topics such as crime. (However, for a discussion of the 'demographic method', see Cicourel, 1964.) Examples of the use of vital registration data are very easy to find: for example, as a backdrop to the study of early motherhood (Phoenix, 1991), in the study of marriage breakdown (Gibson, 1994), and in the study of health inequalities (Townsend *et al.*, 1988). Aggregate-level data from the Census are even more widely used, within research on topics such as migration as well as as a source of information on the population structure of specific geographical areas. Developments such as the Samples of Anonymised Records (SARs), which contain microdata from the Census, and the Longitudinal Study

(LS), which links Census and registration data at the individual level, have enhanced the value of the Census to researchers (Dale and Marsh, 1993; Dale *et al.*, 1999). Other official data sources contain demographic data of value to social researchers: for example the General Household Survey contains marital history data which can be used in analyses of repartnering after divorce (Lampard and Peggs, 1999).

Accessing existing statistical data: data archives and broader issues

Published official statistics for the UK can be accessed via libraries, and official data which are available for secondary analysis can on the whole be obtained at minimal cost (by academics and students) through the Data Archive at the University of Essex. However, much of the existing statistical data which are of interest to social researchers is not produced by government agencies, and some of these data have not been deposited in a generic archive. Accessing such data is analogous to accessing other forms of document, as discussed earlier in the chapter, and is likely to involve negotiation with gatekeepers. The Data Archive holds data from some cross-national surveys; data for other countries can also be obtained via libraries or via the Data Archive's links with similar organisations overseas (e.g. ICPSR, the Inter-university Consortium for Political and Social Research archive at the University of Michigan in the United States; website: http://www.ICPSR.umich.edu/). Social researchers have sometimes ignored the potential of data generated by commercial organisations such as market research companies; the cost of obtaining data from such sources may be higher than the cost of accessing official data, but it is still likely to be markedly less than the cost of primary research, especially where the data in question are commercially redundant. Of course, issues of quality and validity are still as pertinent, and perhaps more pertinent, than they are in relation to official data.

For the UK-orientated researcher who wishes to establish what data on their research topic are readily available for secondary analysis, the on-line catalogue of the Data Archive at the University of Essex is the obvious starting point (http://www.data-archive.ac.uk/). The holdings of this archive include data from many government and academic surveys (including all ESRC-funded surveys) and also from some market research surveys. However, not all the data held come from surveys, and the archive also runs a historical data service. Furthermore, a parallel archive of data from qualitative studies (QUALIDATA) has recently been established (http://www.essex.ac.uk/qualidata/).

Secondary analysis

Secondary analysis (as distinct from the term 'secondary sources', as used by historians in relation to documents) refers to empirical research using data which already exist, i.e. the secondary analyst was not involved in the data collection/compilation process. In the case of many surveys, secondary analyses of the data are as important as the analyses carried out by the original researchers; the potential of the data collected by a survey almost always outstrips the time and resources available to the original researchers, and some surveys (e.g. the British Social Attitudes Surveys) are explicitly geared towards secondary analysis. The discussion of official statistics earlier in this chapter has already indicated that secondary analyses of official data can be used to critique official analyses; in addition, the published reports based on official surveys are often primarily descriptive, leaving a lot of scope for secondary analyses of a more explanatory nature. More generally, debates between researchers can be fuelled by competing secondary analyses of the same data source.

In view of the latent potential of existing survey data and the relatively low cost of secondary analysis-based research, one might reasonably have expected secondary analysis to be a very popular form of research, at the very least among researchers who do not like to see resources 'wasted'. However, in the context of the UK, Dale *et al.* (1988) describe it as a useful but 'neglected' form of research. The extent of this neglect has probably declined over the last decade or so, as a consequence of easier access to a wider range of material, increasingly user-friendly statistical software, and more widespread possession or acquisition of the necessary technical skills. A decline in the level of scepticism among British sociologists about the value of quantitative methods may also be relevant; secondary analysis has been used more widely in the United States where such scepticism was less prevalent in the 1970s than it was in the United Kingdom. It is interesting that Devine and Heath (1999: 19) do not include a secondary analysis-based study among the eight examples of research studies whose uses of research methods they discuss; they explain this in terms of the absence of a suitable study, i.e. a study which reflects explicitly upon the methods that it uses, but the omission arguably also indicates that secondary analysis is still viewed as lying outside the 'core' set of research methods, even by writers who view quantitative methods positively.

So far in this discussion, secondary analysis has been characterised as a quantitative research method. However, the previous section noted the existence of a qualitative data archive. Secondary analyses of qualitative data are, of course, possible, but the extent to which the original qualitative researcher is part of the research process poses a number of problems, including with respect to the provision of appropriate documentation for secondary analysts. Furthermore, there may be marked ethical problems in making qualitative data available for secondary analysis: for example in relation to confidentiality and anonymity. It is perhaps more relevant to think of quantitative secondary analysis as something which can be profitably used in combination with primary qualitative research: for example, secondary analysis could be used to identify gender differences, which could be analysed further using ethnographic data or data from qualitative interviews. Clearly, secondary analysis is susceptible to the criticisms which are directed at quantitative methods in general, and a combined quantitative/qualitative approach may help deflect some of these. For example, quantitative secondary analysis might be used to establish the existence of relationships, and qualitative data might help uncover the motivations and meanings underpinning those relationships.

More generally, research involving secondary analysis often makes use of more than one data source. While some secondary analyses constitute self-contained pieces of research – for example, sophisticated multivariate analyses which aim to extend the researcher's understanding of previously researched issues – on many occasions secondary analysis is used only as a subsidiary method to provide a quantitative benchmark or backdrop: for example, to contextualise a case study or a qualitative sample. Sometimes a primary survey is complemented by the secondary analysis of an existing survey, with the latter either providing some form of benchmark or allowing an examination of trends over time to take place. Sometimes secondary analyses involve the use of existing quantitative data from more than one source:

- Findings from different surveys can be compared or combined (e.g. within cross-national analyses or meta-analyses).
- Data from a cross-sectional survey can be complemented by longitudinal data.
- Data from different years of a repeated survey (or even from different surveys, assuming an adequate degree of comparability) can be used to examine trends over time (and/or to boost the overall sample size).
- Survey data on individuals can be complemented by geographical data relating to the locations in which those individuals live, obtained from other sources.

It should be clear from the above that secondary analysis allows lone researchers to tackle issues that they simply could not address properly via primary research of their own:

- Cross-national and historical research becomes more of a practical possibility.
- Secondary analyses of longitudinal data facilitate studies of change over time (e.g. within life-course-related research using a cohort study such as NCDS or a panel study such as BHPS; see Chapter 2).
- Large, nationally representative samples allow sophisticated and generalisable analyses to be carried out, and may enable the researcher to look at small and relatively inaccessible minorities.

Secondary analysis has a range of other advantages, some of which relate to the benefits that secondary analysts obtain via the expertise of others. The technical quality of data from sources such as government agencies and professional social research organisations like the National Centre for Social Research (formerly SCPR) is likely to be good; such data are also likely to be well documented. The researcher may also profit from exposure to the experiences of other researchers who have analysed or are also analysing the data; in the case of a study like the British Household Panel Study (BHPS; Buck et al., 1994; website http://www.iser.essex.ac.uk/bhps/), which is heavily used for secondary analyses, occasional research workshops may take place. Using one of the major sources of data within their secondary analysis will also help provide the researcher with an entrée into a research network/community.

While secondary analysts should, for example, maintain the anonymity of survey respondents, secondary analysis is non-reactive and hence the ethical issues involved are somewhat more limited than in primary research. It is debatable, however, whether an adequate version of informed consent is generally obtained by the original researchers with respect to the use of survey data in secondary analyses, especially given that the research objectives of future secondary analysts cannot necessarily be anticipated. More generally, no research which generates published output is free from an ethical dimension.

Perhaps the most obvious potential disadvantage of secondary analysis is its reliance on data which are inevitably somewhat out of date, though this may not be a serious problem if the research area is relatively unchanging, or if the researcher's objectives have a historical focus. Many of the other significant disadvantages of secondary analysis relate to the constraints that it can place on the researcher's agenda. Before considering this issue in more detail, it may be helpful for us to outline some 'varieties' of secondary analyst:

- Some secondary analysts have clearly defined research agendas involving the testing of some quite specific hypotheses.
- Other secondary analysts have rather less precisely defined sets of research objectives, which involve focusing on some sub-issues in relation to their research topics but which do not involve the testing of highly specific, predetermined hypotheses.
- A third type of secondary analyst adopts a more exploratory approach and aims primarily to discover what a data source has to offer in relation to a broad research topic.

While all secondary analysts need to be aware of the potential for mismatches between the conceptual framework of the original researchers and their own conceptual framework, researchers in the first of the above three categories of secondary analyst are most vulnerable to this sort of mismatch. Furthermore, the coverage of sub-topics within and the specific indicators available from a data source are of greater importance to researchers in the first two categories than to those belonging to the third. The degree of flexibility in the aims of the research thus determines how much the researcher will be prepared to let the existing data's nature, and the coverage that these data provide, direct the research and dictate its agenda. Of course, as is the case with documents, the lack of availability of any relevant data for secondary analysis may render the use of existing data impossible and make primary research a necessity.

While it is impossible to compensate for the failure of the original researchers to collect a specific type of data, it may nevertheless be possible to sidestep their conceptual framework. For example, as noted by Lampard and Peggs (1999), the failure of the General Household Survey to collect fertility-related data corresponding to men parallel to those collected from women makes gender comparisons in this context impossible. However, as noted by Dale *et al.* (1988: 77), the tendency for official statistics to select a male as the 'head of household' can be circumvented within secondary analyses by defining the household head in a different, less sexist way. More generally, the construction of new indicators from existing data is a creative process which can sometimes succeed in shifting the conceptual balance a long way towards the secondary analyst's own conceptual framework.

The extent to which secondary analyses of official data are constrained by an official conceptual framework varies markedly, as does the extent to which the indirect involvement of the state justifies criticisms of the analyses' credibility. Some of the secondary analyses of the disability surveys discussed earlier in this chapter may be fatally constrained by the individualisation of disability within the surveys (Abberley, 1996), but the existence of secondary analyses of official data documenting politically embarrassing social inequalities demonstrates the scope for the application of a critical conceptual framework.

Other disadvantages of secondary analysis relate to technical limitations and practicalities. Surveys may have used an inadequate sampling frame or even non-random sampling, or may have had a high level of non-response. Such limitations may also not have been adequately documented. The researcher may require the technical skills, software and hardware needed to handle a large, awkwardly structured and badly documented dataset. Even in relation to a relatively straightforward dataset, secondary analyses require a degree of technical proficiency and can be extremely time-consuming. A student doing a secondary-analysis-based doctoral thesis will save time on fieldwork, but the balance of their thesis will be pushed towards data ana-lysis as opposed to data collection, and more extens-ive and sophisticated statistical analyses may be expected of them.

Secondary analysis in practice: a step-by-step approach

One thing which makes secondary analysis time-consuming is the need to get to know both the dataset to be analysed and also the research process that generated it. This process of familiarisation is one of the key requirements for a successful sec-ondary analysis. Useful questions for the researcher to ask herself or himself when getting to know a dataset are given by Stewart (1984: 23–30) and Dale *et al.* (1988: 19–31). The following set of questions for secondary analysts to consider draws upon these sources:

- Is secondary analysis an appropriate approach given the researcher's objectives?
- Does the secondary analyst know the topic area well enough to be able to interpret and evaluate the information available?
- Who collected the information, when, how, and for what purpose?
- Are the original researchers and the information that they collected credible and of good quality, and technically sound?
- What similarities and differences are there between the conceptual frameworks of the original researchers and of the secondary analyst?
- What information was collected, how was it coded, and what do the categories mean?
- Is the information collected sufficient for the secondary analyst to be able to address their research questions and/or test their hypotheses?
- How consistent is the information with in-formation from other sources (and should it be weighted to correct for unrepresentativeness)?
- Is the information representativeness enough to support generalisations?

Another key requirement for a successful secondary analysis is good record keeping; it is not just qualit-ative researchers who need to keep research journals. As well as reflecting upon the contributions to the research process made by the researchers who originally collected the data, the secondary analyst needs to document properly their own contribu-tions to the process. These contributions date back to the point in time when the researcher first started thinking about the research topic; it therefore makes sense for the researcher to keep a record of their thoughts about the topic from the word go. This need for self-awareness on the part of the secondary analyst demonstrates that reflexivity is an issue in secondary analysis as well as in qualitat-ive research.

Before a researcher engages with the practical-ities of secondary analysis he or she also needs to acquire an adequate level of knowledge of the sub-stantive area of his or her research. An examination of existing literature in this area will develop the researcher's awareness of relevant concepts and the-oretical ideas, thus helping him or her to develop his or her own conceptual framework and enabling him or her to assess the conceptual specificities and limitations of existing data sources. In addition, an awareness of what is already known about the topic will help the researcher identify issues to be explored by his or her own research. While adopt-ing an exploratory approach to secondary analysis would mean that such research questions would not necessarily need to be very precisely defined at this early stage, the researcher would still need to consider whether the questions could be answered using existing quantitative data, or whether, say, a qualitative study would be more appropriate.

Step 1 – Locating and accessing a data source
If secondary analysis is felt to be an appropriate approach, the next stage is to locate potential sources of data. The researcher may already be aware of some of these from their perusal of the literature, but an examination of relevant catalogues and guides can also highlight possible additional sources. The on-line catalogue of the

Data Archive at the University of Essex allows the researcher to carry out keyword-based searches, which lead them to brief summary descriptions of potentially relevant studies. With luck the researcher will be able to identify one or more recent, accessible studies whose coverage of material appears consistent with their agenda and conceptual framework. However, it is unlikely that a brief summary of a study will tell the researcher all that she or he needs to know. If the researcher is lucky, a cost-free examination of further documentation will be possible via a library copy of the study report, or on-line (e.g. where the study in question is one of those whose research instruments are available via the ESRC Question Bank). However, some of or all the relevant documentation (e.g. documentation on coding; technical reports) may need to be ordered from the Data Archive (and paid for), or even obtained directly from the original researchers.

Reading study documentation is a central aspect of the familiarisation of the researcher with the data source, and as such is likely to lead to entries in the researcher's research journal. The documentation is a means by which the researcher can get a retrospective insight into the process by which the data were constructed. This insight should relate to the original study viewed as a whole as well as to specific details of the data collected, and hence should be based on an assessment, via the documentation, of the original researchers, researcher sponsors and fieldwork organisation, as well as of specific aspects of the research instruments. For example, poor-quality documentation may indicate that the organisation which conducted the fieldwork has significant limitations, which in turn may raise questions about the quality and credibility of the data. If little documentation is available, the researcher should also be very cautious about using the data source.

A study's research instruments provide the secondary analyst with knowledge about the range of topics covered and the specific questions asked. The researcher can then assess whether data have been collected in relation to all the concepts which are fundamental to their research agenda. For concepts in relation to which data have not specifically been collected, the researcher will need to assess whether new indicators can be derived/constructed from the data which were collected. In addition, questionnaires or interview schedules, together with any instructions to interviewers, will also help the researcher to get to grips with the interpersonal dimension of the data-collection process and with the ways in which some of the concepts have been operationalised. Coding notes will throw light upon practical and conceptual aspects of the coding of the data, possibly including coding variability.

An account of the sampling methods used in a study and the non-response rate allow the secondary analyst to assess the representativeness of the data and hence the scope for generalisation. The researcher needs to examine whether the population which is of interest to him or her and the sampling frame used in the study are mismatched geographically or in other ways. Note also that, though an overall non-response rate is often quoted, the adequacy of a response rate of, say, 70% depends on the extent to which the non-response is differential; the kind of detailed discussion of non-response which is sometimes included in survey reports by major research organisations is not always available. Details of the sampling method used may also be crucial at the analysis stage: for example, many surveys (e.g. the National Survey of Sexual Attitudes and Lifestyles; Johnson et al., 1994) sample addresses or households but only interview one respondent per household, which can mean that weighting is necessary at the analysis stage if distortion of the findings as a consequence of the sampling method is to be avoided.

The researcher may also find useful discussions of a data source in earlier published secondary analyses using that source. Such discussions may highlight some of the idiosyncrasies of the source and how the earlier secondary analyst(s) dealt with them. A list of earlier published analyses may constitute part of the available documentation corresponding to the data source; the researcher can also carry out searches of citation indices to locate such analyses (perhaps by using the title of the original study within a keyword search). In general, examining past analyses allows the researcher to avoid needlessly repeating both the substantive and the methodological work of earlier researchers.

Having examined the available documentation relating to the data source, the researcher needs to assess whether the source is suitable for her or his purposes. This assessment can be very difficult; there may be no clear-cut way of assessing whether the data are too dated, whether any potential biases or apparent flaws are too serious, whether the operationalisation of concepts is close enough to the researcher's own conceptual framework, etc. Furthermore, it may be necessary for the researcher to carry out exploratory analyses of the data herself or himself before the value of the source can be completely determined. However, where good-quality, up-to-date survey data are available, which conceptualise the research topic in a way that parallels the researcher's own perspective, the suitability of the data may be self-evident.

Step 2 – Acquiring and setting up the data

The next stage is to obtain permission to use the data and then either order a copy of them or arrange on-line access, if the data are available in that way. Obtaining access permission from the Data Archive at the University of Essex takes longer if the archive has to refer back to the original researchers (as in the case of requests to use official data sources); it may be worth starting to obtain access to the data some time before the researcher anticipates actually using them, to take account of the anticipated lag from the time of the application to access being granted. In the case of the Data Archive, application forms can be downloaded via the Internet from their website.

In the past, the huge volume of data within some existing sources meant that secondary analysts sometimes had to work with sub-sets of data. However, the advent of CD ROM technology has made it much easier to transport and store large quantities of data, and at the time of writing an up-to-date PC with a CD ROM drive constitutes an adequate platform for most secondary analysis purposes, both in terms of hardware and the ability to run relevant software such as SPSS for Windows. Smaller datasets can be supplied on a disk or transferred electronically via the Internet. Access to appropriate software is clearly essential; many data sources are available in SPSS format, or are available as ASCII data/in text format and hence can be read into both SPSS for Windows and also other statistical software packages. Where data are only available in a software-specific format, access to the relevant software or to software for transferring data between formats may be necessary, though packages such as SPSS for Windows can convert data from some other formats. It is important that the researcher has access to software which can carry out both the necessary statistical analyses and also any manipulations of the data which are required. For this reason software such as SPSS or SAS is preferable to less sophisticated software, with the scope to write ad-hoc programs (e.g. by typing commands into an SPSS syntax window) being essential in some circumstances. It is sometimes necessary to use more specialised software: for example, MLwiN might be used to fit multi-level models (see Chapter 9), or SIR might be used to handle complex manipulations of hierarchical data (see Dale et al., 1988). For a student doing an empirically based dissertation, the costs of carrying out a secondary analysis should not be prohibitive, since their institution should have adequate hardware and software available, and the costs of documentation and data supply, while they may not be negligible, are now relatively low.

Assuming that the researcher has acquired a copy of the data, the next stage is to read it into a software package such as SPSS for Windows. If the data have been supplied in a format specific to the software (e.g. as an SPSS system file), then this should be very straightforward. If the data have been supplied in text format/as ASCII data, then the researcher may need to input (via menus, or by setting up a file of commands) the location and details of each variable (which should be specified in the accompanying documentation), though if the researcher is lucky a 'set-up' file will have been supplied with the data. Once the data have been successfully read into the software package, a software-specific version of the data (e.g. an SPSS system file) will be created, and should then be saved. Irrespective of whether such a software-specific version of the data was supplied or was created by the researcher, a copy of this initial version of the data should be set aside, so that later amendments to the data do not render the original form of the data unrecoverable. From this point onwards it is vital that the researcher keeps an accurate record in their research journal of the ways in which they manipulate and analyse the data; the researcher can waste much time at a later date trying to work out exactly how and why he or she created a new version of one of the variables.

Step 3 – Getting to know and manipulating the data
Before creating any new (versions of) variables, the researcher should get to know them in their original form. The first step is to look at the frequencies in each category of each variable of interest. Not all the categories' meanings may be obvious from the questionnaire or interview schedule, and the researcher may have to refer to coding notes to establish their meanings (or may even have to contact the original researchers: for example in the case of a variable which was derived from a number of questions in the interview schedule, and for which the process of derivation is not well documented). The researcher should take note of the existence of any categories which correspond to missing or otherwise problematic data, as these categories will need to be excluded before analyses are carried out. Occasionally, an examination of the frequencies for a variable brings to light a bizarre spread of values; this may indicate that the data have been corrupted, or that some other error has occurred.

At this point the researcher will probably wish to move on to bivariate analyses, perhaps to test specific hypotheses or perhaps as part of a more exploratory approach. In either case, theorising, whether explicit or implicit, is taking place, and it is

important that the form of the variables involved in the analyses meets the requirements of the researcher's conceptual framework. It is possible that existing variables in the data source operationalise the relevant concepts adequately, but it is perhaps more likely that the researcher will need to recode some of the existing variables (see the companion web pages) or derive completely new ones.

For example, the researcher may wish to use a variable indicating whether or not there are any children under the age of 5 years in a respondent's household. If no such variable exists, it may still be possible for the researcher to construct one. For example, if a variable exists corresponding to the age of each individual in the respondent's household, the objective could then be achieved by recoding each of these age-related variables into two categories: 1 = 'Under 5' and 0 = '5 plus', and then computing the sum of the recoded variables, which would consequently be a count of the number of individuals in the household aged under 5 years. This summary variable could then be recoded into two categories: 1 = 'One or more people aged under 5' and 0 = 'No one aged under 5'.

As can be seen in the above example, derived variables sometimes draw upon existing variables corresponding to a number of different individuals. In this example the relevant unit of analysis corresponding to the new variable is the household, not the individual. Dale *et al.* (1988) note the scope for the derivation of such variables provided by the hierarchical structure of household surveys, and discuss in detail the secondary analysis of hierarchical surveys, including the derivation of various types of new variable.

It is good practice to examine the frequencies of recoded or newly derived variables and to cross-tabulate each new variable against the original variable or variables from which it was derived, to ensure that the recoding or derivation process has achieved what the researcher intended it to achieve. The new variables may need to be further refined:

for example, they may need to be recoded if the number of categories is unduly large. Descriptive labels will need to be linked to every new variable and to each of its categories. Once again, the researcher's journal plays an important role, as it is essential that a precise record is kept of the ways in which variables are recoded and in which new variables are derived.

Some of the above issues are not specific to secondary analysis, and in many ways secondary analysis is analogous to other forms of quantitative data analysis (see Chapter 9). To be a good secondary analyst a researcher needs to be a competent (or better) data analyst, which in turn requires both an adequate understanding of statistical testing and also lots of practice at analysing data. The presentation of the statistical findings from a secondary analysis parallels to a large extent the presentation of findings from primary research, though the researcher needs to be sure to reference the data source properly. Some of the methodological points which might otherwise have needed to have been raised explicitly by the researcher can be covered by pointing the reader towards such a reference corresponding to the data source. However, as has been suggested above, the secondary analyst still needs to reflect upon the suitability of the data source for their purposes, and such reflections should be presented alongside the statistical analyses when the researcher writes up the secondary analysis. Note that a well-kept journal should facilitate the writing-up process.

Secondary analysis: examples

This section discusses as examples two secondary analyses carried out by one of the authors, one using data from the British General Election Surveys and the Social Change and Economic Life Initiative (Heath *et al.*, 1994; Gallie *et al.*, 1994; Lampard, 1997), and the other using data from the General Household Survey (Lampard and Peggs, 1999). Examples of secondary analyses using the OPCS Disability surveys and the 1991 Census

Samples of Anonymised Records (SARs) were discussed earlier in this chapter.

The use of the General Household Survey (GHS) for secondary analyses is discussed in detail by Dale *et al.* (1988: 70–75); it continued to be used extensively in this way in the 1990s, for research on a diverse range of topics such as health, employment and the family. The popularity of the GHS for secondary analyses reflects a number of factors:

- a large sample size
- the fact that it has been repeated more or less annually since the early 1970s, which allows trends to be examined
- a broad agenda which means that relationships between concepts belonging to different policy areas can be examined
- a hierarchical structure, which allows linkages between different members of the same household to be examined (Dale *et al.*, 1988: 223).

The GHS is also a classic example of an official data source which is ripe for external analyses; the official usage of GHS is in the first instance primarily descriptive, leaving a lot of scope for more analytical work, and the conceptual framework embedded within the survey is adequately close to the conceptual frameworks of many social researchers.

Unfortunately the extensive nature and hierarchical structure of the GHS can make the practicalities of secondary analyses using it more technically demanding, as can be seen in the first of the two examples which follow.

Secondary analysis example no. 1: *the General Household Survey and repartnering*

The analysis of repartnering among the formerly married carried out by Lampard and Peggs (1999) used the retrospective marital history data collected by the 1991/2 GHS, alongside a range of other demographic and socio-economic variables. These data can be found in different locations (records) within the main GHS data file. Permission from ONS to use data from the GHS was obtained via the Data Archive at the University of Essex, and a copy of this data file was accessed remotely via a computer located at the University of Manchester, which runs a national on-line data service (MIMAS). The file was manipulated using the software package SIR in order to produce a smaller file of relevant data which could be transferred electronically and read into SPSS for Windows on the author's PC.

A significant conceptual limitation of the GHS marital history data used in the secondary analysis was that cohabitation was not treated as equivalent to marriage by the GHS, and as a consequence completed periods of cohabitation which did not lead to marriage were not recorded. Consequently, the fact that this omission could distort the findings of the research had to be accepted if the GHS data were to be used. Similar compromises had to be made elsewhere in the secondary analysis. For example, data on the timing of births from the recorded fertility histories (which were only available for female respondents) were used to create a count of the number of children born to a woman by the end of her first marriage. This somewhat crude measure was the best (retrospective) indicator available of the presence of children in a formerly married woman's household. The models of repartnering behaviour used in the secondary analysis necessitated the construction of new variables, including the duration from the end of a respondent's first marriage until the start of their next cohabiting or marital relationship (if there was one). Durations were calculated from the existing marital history variables, which were in the form of dates, and the new variables were checked for problems such as negative durations.

Secondary analysis example no. 2: *the British General Election Study and party political homogamy*

The analysis of party political similarity between spouses (party political homogamy) carried out by Lampard (1997) mainly used data from the 1987 British General Election Study (BES). These data were obtained from the Data Archive at the University of Essex on a CD ROM, and were made available in the form of an SPSS export file, which could be read into SPSS for Windows very easily. The BES surveyed individuals, rather than all the members of a household (as the GHS does), which meant that the data to be analysed had a simple structure, but which also had conceptual implications for the secondary analysis. Specifically, the statistical analyses made use of data relating to respondents' spouses' party political identifications which were provided by the respondent rather than directly by their spouse. The party political identifications may thus have been misreported. Furthermore, the data were only available for some of the respondents' spouses. The validity of the findings based on the 1987 BES thus had to be bolstered by comparisons with data from the SCELI Household and Community Survey, which collected party political data from both partners within couples, and data from the 1992 BES, which collected some additional relevant data. Various new variables were derived during the course of the research, including a measure of spouses' similarity to each other in occupational terms, which combined data from variables relating to the respondent's occupation and to their spouse's occupation.

Secondary analysis using SPSS for Windows

A secondary analyst needs to have or to acquire an adequate degree of familiarity with some form of data analysis software. SPSS for Windows is perhaps the most obvious software to use for secondary analysis, since many of the datasets held by the Data Archive at the University of Essex are available as SPSS system files (which can be transported as SPSS export files or portable files). SPSS also has the benefits of wide availability and usage, and of increasingly good coverage of statistical techniques, with its ability to handle complex file structures improving with the introduction of new versions. Examples showing how existing data can be read into SPSS for Windows, and how SPSS for Windows can be used to manipulate existing variables to create new ones, can be found within the web pages corresponding to this text.

Conclusion: some questions for the researcher to consider

This chapter has discussed various forms of existing data which can be used in social research (though there is a degree of overlap with forms of data that the researcher might collect herself or himself). The following list of questions helps summarise the issues raised within this chapter:

- Are there existing data which I can use within my research?
- For what purpose(s) can I use the existing data?
- What characteristics of the existing data do I need to reflect upon?
- Are the existing data suitable for my purposes?
- What skills or knowledge do I need to have in order to be able to use the existing data effectively?

Are there existing data which I can use within my research?

We have shown that there is a wide variety and huge volume of existing data available to social researchers, in the form of documents, official

statistics and survey data available for secondary analysis. The researcher thus needs to carry out a **data review** to acquaint herself or himself with what is available, via visits to libraries, examinations of archive catalogues, searches of on-line databases and the Internet, etc. The researcher should also bear in mind that not all the relevant existing data need be in the form of text or numbers: for example, visual data may be useful to some researchers. Using existing data can be a creative process; it may be the researcher's manipulation or interpretation of the data which demonstrate their relevance.

For what purpose(s) can I use the existing data?

Existing data can, of course, be used for the same purposes as primary (qualitative and quantitative) data, assuming that appropriate data exist. However, for some purposes (e.g. within research on the media and popular culture) existing data are uniquely valuable, and social historians are also clearly heavily dependent on existing data. Existing data and primary data can also play complementary roles: for example, existing data relating to a setting, organisation or group of people may be used to contextualise the primary qualitative data collected by a study.

Existing data can be used as a source of factual information or as a way of accessing discourses and ideologies, or the subjective perspectives of social actors, or as evidence of the power structures within society.

What characteristics of the existing data do I need to reflect upon?

It is important that the researcher is aware of relevant aspects of the context in which the existing data were generated. The researcher needs to be familiar with the language used in documents, and with the documents' authors and audiences;

secondary analysts need to examine survey documentation in order to assess the context of production, technical quality and degree of representativeness of survey data.

The researcher needs to get to grips with the frame(s) of reference of those who created the data. The concepts used within the text of documents and operationalised within survey data reflect the conceptual frameworks of the people who produced the documents and data, and may also reflect the interests of, say, the state.

Whenever the researcher is considering using existing data as a source of 'factual' information, the impact of any gap between conceptual frameworks needs to be evaluated. Fortunately, the impact of any gap that exists is frequently insignificant, or can be side-stepped by manipulations of the data. In addition to assessing the conceptual suitability of the existing data, the researcher also needs to assess their credibility, reliability, representativeness, coverage, etc.

Are the existing data suitable for my purposes?

While an understanding of the frame(s) of reference of those who created the existing data is vital, it is also crucial that the researcher is aware of the relevance of their own perspective and conceptual framework. While textual analysis involves a 'dialogue' between the frames of reference of the researcher and of the document's author (Scott, 1990: 31), secondary analysis involves an assessment by the researcher of whether the gap between their own conceptual framework and that of the original researcher is too wide for the existing data to be valid for the researcher's purposes. (In a way this is a form of 'comparative reflexivity', wherein the secondary analyst is reflexive both about their own role in the research process and also, as a proxy, about the role of the original researcher.)

What skills or knowledge do I need to have in order to be able to use the existing data effectively?

Many of the skills needed for research using existing data are the skills which are needed for (qualitative or quantitative) primary research: for example, a knowledge of sampling issues or the interpersonal skills needed to negotiate access successfully. Efficient, careful and systematic record keeping is valuable both to documentary research and also to secondary analysis; return visits to archives and the re-running of statistical analyses are equally frustrating ways of wasting time. Of course, there are some specific forms of knowledge or skill which are needed for specific uses of existing data; a researcher carrying out textual analyses may need to know about semiotics (and Foucault), whereas a secondary analyst may need to develop data-management skills.

Chapter 8

Making it count: approaches to qualitative data analysis

Introduction

The title of this chapter, 'Making it count', is intended to convey the importance of data analysis to the research process. The implication of the title is that without analysis the research process discussed thus far can achieve little in terms of explaining social phenomena. Whilst we do not wish to undermine the significance or importance of anything we have said so far about research design and the various approaches to data collection, it is important to recognise that unless data are subjected to careful analysis, then their potential to facilitate explanation and understanding cannot be realised. We would go so far as to say that the reason for collecting data and ensuring this is done sensitively and carefully is to facilitate analysis, as without good data meaningful analysis is impossible.

If this view is accepted then it is immediately clear that there is a close and mutually dependent relationship between the data collected and the analysis to which they are subjected. We are at the same time suggesting both that the capacity for effective analysis relies, largely, on the quality of the collected data and that without analysis there is no real reason for collecting the data in the first place.

The relationship between data and data analysis is indeed complex. The reason for this is that analysis is something which occurs both after the data have been collected and also as they are collected. Indeed, the assignment of data analysis to separate chapters in this text, as in many other methods texts, may at one level be seen as an unhelpful separation of process and product, which are inextricably linked. We would argue that analysis is an integral and inevitable aspect of the entire research process. Our view is that as the research process progresses from initial ideas and design, through to the development of findings and conclusions, a form of analysis is necessary at every stage, and although this chapter is located towards the end of this book, its content is also highly relevant to many of the issues discussed in the earlier chapters.

Stages of analysis

Having stressed the centrality of analysis to the research process we would argue that as the research progresses there are a number of different types of analysis that occur.

Preliminary analysis

At the outset, the identification of an area or a topic as appropriate for research entails a form of analysis. As the researcher(s) locate and evaluate previous research on their topic, as they search for relevant literature and identify research questions which, as we have already seen, begin to shape and focus the research, they engage in an analytical process. As the research progresses, researchers identify appropriate data-collection methods, which again involves a process of analysis wherein the nature of the data, their location and its epistemology are considered alongside particular collection techniques. Analysis at these early stages of research is central to the progress and success of the study. It is what might be termed **preliminary** analysis, required to ensure that the research is based on sound methodological and theoretical foundations.

Preliminary analysis therefore involves:

- identifying the topic area
- reading previous research
- examining past findings and existing data
- formulating research questions
- considering research tools.

Processual analysis

As the research progresses from the planning stages analysis moves from preliminary to **processual.** In using this term we wish to convey a sense of continuous engagement with the data as they are collected. Where interpretative methods are employed, such as in-depth interviewing or loosely structured observation, processual analysis is in a sense inevitable, since analysis in part dictates the trajectory of the data collection as it progresses.

What we refer to, therefore, is the ongoing interpretation of the data as they are collected. For example, at its most basic, this occurs during the conduct of an unstructured or loosely structured interview, where the interviewer is constantly thinking about the information provided by the interviewee and is framing subsequent questions accordingly. The researcher needs to interpret the data as they are collected and to frame the next question or topic for discussion on the basis of this ongoing interpretation or analysis. However, in a more tightly structured interview, where there is a strict order of questions to be followed, this level of interaction between data collected and questions posed is not possible.

The process of question posing, response and analysis may be represented as a circular motion, thus:

$$\text{Question/Discussion} \quad \rightarrow \quad \text{Answer/Response}$$
$$\uparrow \qquad\qquad\qquad\qquad\qquad \downarrow$$
$$\leftarrow \quad \text{Analysis} \quad \leftarrow$$

Similarly, research based on observation relies on an ongoing analysis of what is seen and/or experienced in order for the researcher to plan for and conduct the next set of observations.

In studies which use a range of research methods, processual analysis takes place between the application of the different methods. For example, a study utilising survey and qualitative interview methods may require some analysis of the survey data in order for the researcher to devise an appropriate interview schedule which will complement those questions posed on a printed questionnaire. Alternatively, a study based on observation followed by interview relies upon ongoing analysis of the observation data to inform the conduct of the interviews.

Processual analysis is important, therefore, in informing data collection and in shaping the direction of the research. For example, processual analysis may reveal a range of issues which the researcher wishes to explore or test out through further data collection. This may result in original ideas or hypotheses being reviewed or discarded. The role of processual analysis, therefore, may be to provide momentum to the research by constantly posing questions and redefining the research focus where it is appropriate.

Summative analysis

Whilst the research process involves a number of different forms of analysis at different stages and, furthermore, these forms of analysis are inextricably linked, it is perhaps the form of analysis that occurs after the data-collection phase of the research process which is often regarded as the most important form of analysis. In some respects this may be true, as it is at this stage that conclusions are drawn from the research. However, we hope to have indicated that summative analysis is reliant on the successful accomplishment of preliminary and processual analysis.

We have chosen the term summative analysis to convey a sense of analysis as a means of drawing conclusions from the research. In addition it is intended to imply that summative analysis is the vehicle for the research findings. It should be clear by now, however, that it is not possible to achieve effective findings without an integrated research process where each of the constituent parts is completed effectively in relation to the project in its entirety. It should also be clear by now that analysis is not a stage of the research process which can be left until the end, but one which is ever present, from the planning stages through the collection of data and the drawing of conclusions. Despite what might be seen as the almost endemic nature of analysis, many researchers continue to refer to data analysis as a distinct stage in their research, which occurs after data collection. In this sense, they hold a view of analysis which accords with what might be seen as a fairly stereotypical, hypothesis-testing approach to research. However, even with such an approach, the form of the analysis needs to be planned before the data-collection process begins; hence the analysis, as an idea at least, in this sense comes first. Similarly, many Ph.D. students continue to identify analysis as something which they will do during the third year, or equivalent if they are part-time students, of their doctoral research. What students usually have in mind is summative analysis. Often this is allied to what they term the 'writing-up' phase of their work. As we shall indicate in Chapter 10, however, we would also question the notion of a 'writing-up' phase, preferring to see writing, like analysis, also as something which occurs throughout the entirety of the research.

However, the notion of summative analysis being allied to writing is not in itself an entirely bad thing, as the two processes have much in common. For example, they seek to bring a sense of order to the information which has been collected, and to draw conclusions or make sense of things on the basis of that order. They both require a great deal of thought and may involve a degree of experimentation as ideas or forms of representation are tried out and evaluated. Ultimately they are both concerned with the conclusions which can be drawn from the research and the contribution which it makes to the stock of knowledge in the field in which it is located.

Key issues

- Analysis is ongoing throughout the research process.
- There are different kinds of analysis.
- Effective analysis relies on good data.
- Analysis involves trying out ideas.

Analysis in practice: entering the secret garden

Bryman and Burgess (1994) point out that recent years have seen a growth in the number of texts which address issues of data analysis. For example, Bryman and Burgess (1994), Dey (1993), Mason (1996), Miles and Huberman (1994), Strauss (1987), Strauss and Corbin (1990, 1997), Richardson (1996), although they vary in detail and approach, all include chapters or sections on how to conduct data analysis. These and other texts published during the last decade may be seen as offering the novice, and perhaps the not so much of a novice, researcher access to what previously may have been seen as the secret garden of data analysis.

Publishers have long been reluctant to encourage extensive methodological reflection in monographs which might have shed light on the process of analysis, and many general textbooks, whilst giving adequate attention to statistical techniques, have overlooked qualitative approaches to analysis. The result has been that data analysis, other than that which can be conducted using a calculator or a statistical software package, has become somewhat surrounded in mystery. The last decade has witnessed, therefore, a greater openness about research, as those writing the books have themselves become more practised in and sophisticated at conducting qualitative research and, indeed, as qualitative approaches to research have themselves become more common and accepted.

In outlining approaches to qualitative data analysis and describing their use in relation to particular pieces of research, authors of the more recent methods texts (e.g. Delamont, 1992; Devine and Heath, 1999; Coffey and Atkinson, 1996; Strauss and Corbin, 1997) have not only made the process of qualitative analysis more visible but have also contributed to their development by encouraging new generations of researchers to try them and to experiment with, evaluate and develop the methods. The situation which we now face, therefore, is that there are many approaches to the analysis of qualitative data open to the researcher which are well documented in the literature.

Whilst this openness and reflection are largely to be welcomed, we feel it is also important to avoid seeing data analysis in formulaic terms, where data are simply subjected to a standardised set of techniques. We are less than enthusiastic, therefore, about those texts which have attempted to standardise qualitative data analysis to the extent that the element of creativity or imagination (Mills, 1959), which the researcher brings to the process, is lost or significantly curtailed. Consequently we fully endorse those texts that have approached qualitative data analysis in an open and imaginative way, where the uniqueness of the data can be realised through the analysis. In discussing qualitative data analysis, therefore, our concern is to avoid the kind of approach which emphasises technique over creative social scientific insight or imagination.

In using terms like 'imagination', 'insight' and 'creativity', our intention is to stress the importance of the role of the researcher in data analysis. As with research design, data collection and writing, the researcher is the principal agent in the data-analysis process. Therefore, the analysis which is conducted, together with the conclusions which are drawn from it, are to some extent a reflection of the researcher who is responsible for it. In this respect, data analysis is no different from any other aspect of the research process.

Finding the key

The plot of Burnett's (1911) children's classic *The Secret Garden* relies on the heroine, Mary Lennox, finding the key to the door of the abandoned garden which she then enters and explores. Consequently the garden is magically transformed and returned to its former glory. Whilst qualitative data analysis has little to do with magic, it is concerned with finding a key and using it as a tool to bring order to what might be seen as chaos, and to nurture research findings.

Analysis and, in particular, summative analysis, is the key to research. It enables the researcher to make sense of the collected data and to advance explanations and understandings of the social phenomena to which they relate. Analysis is, therefore, an essentially creative aspect of the research process via which the social scientist contributes to the stock of knowledge about his/her chosen subject. In order to realise that creativity and to make that contribution, however, the researcher must first be destructive, breaking into pieces the thing that they wish to study.

Analysis as destruction

With most research projects the researcher starts with a complete or holistic situation. For the case-study researcher, for example, this may be an easily identifiable institution such as a factory or a hospital. For the life-history researcher it may be a person's life and career, or more generally it may be a set of circumstances, social interactions or social problems: say, for example, the nature of doctor–patient relationships or junior doctors' bedside manner. The researcher's task is to study the situation and as such he/she begins with something whole and then proceeds to take it apart, examining it in minute detail. For example, the life-history researcher may encourage his/her subject to talk at great length just about their first job or the birth of their first child. Similarly the researcher conducting a case study of a hospital may spend many hours observing the working of the laundry or accompanying a consultant on her rounds of the wards. The point being made here relates to a question of the focus and scope of the research. If the researcher wishes to understand the processes which shape whatever is identified as the focus of the research, then it is unlikely that this can be achieved holistically. However, a holistic understanding may be the ultimate objective of the research. To achieve it, the researcher engages in a process of identifying elements of the whole which can be studied effectively. In this sense, he/she engages in a set of activities which might be seen as destructive as, in order to understand the complexities of the whole, it is necessary to examine the constituent parts. We are not suggesting here that in order to understand the whole, the researcher merely fits the constituents back together in an amalgam of analysis, as in terms of advancing understanding of social phenomena we would subscribe to Durkheim's (1947) notion that the whole is greater than the sum of its parts. We would suggest, however, that in order to begin to understand social processes the researcher must look for a starting point and this can often be found in examining the constituent parts.

Key issues

- Analysis makes sense of the data.
- Analysis is creative.
- Analysis contributes to the stock of knowledge.
- Analysis must be thorough.
- Analysis is destructive.

Starting to analyse

When starting the process of analysis we find it is most useful to think first about the overall mass of data, which has been collected. In common-sense terms it may be useful to think of the data piled up in the centre of a room. Whatever might be seen to constitute data should be metaphorically, and possibly literally, piled up and viewed. This will, undoubtedly, be a daunting task as the extent of the collected information is observed and the need to make sense of it and to decide what is useful and what is not is realised. At this stage it is apparent that a strategy needs to be put into place which will allow the researcher to break down the mound and examine its constituents in a systematic fashion.

Data sorting

In deciding what to contribute to the data mound the process of analysis has begun. When constructing the mound, the researcher will need to decide what is to be considered as data and will thereby judge the merits of the information collected. A selection process begins. The researcher may have collected information from a wide range of sources, in line with and perhaps in addition to the specifications of the research design, but at the start of the summative analysis phase, the researcher has to make judgements about the quality of the data.

The judgements will be made not only in terms of the integrity of the different types of data collected, but also their capacity to relate to and be used alongside other data. Consequently, whilst most of the collected data will be added to the data mound some will be rejected.

Getting to know the data

In order to decide what should be added to the data mound and what should be rejected, the researcher needs to get to know the data in detail. Even where a data analysis package is to be used, it remains essential for the researcher to become familiar with the data in detail.

The means by which the researcher gets to know the data will vary with the nature of the data. For the most part, however, the familiarisation process will be a long one and will involve the researcher transcribing tape-recorded interviews, looking at photographs, reading documents, observation notes, fieldnotes and diaries and scrutinising anything else which has been included in the data mound. In addition, where there are tape-recorded interviews it may be useful to listen to these whenever possible. For example, whilst driving or if there is access to a personal stereo, the opportunities for this are numerous. Although we would not suggest listening as a substitute for transcription, there are, of course, things which the spoken word can convey which the printed word cannot. For example, tone of voice (whether a person sounds angry, sad, happy, confident, etc.) can say much about the interviewee's reaction to a question or a particular line of conversation, while pauses in the conversation can illustrate whether a person is unsure of him/herself or perhaps uneasy with the topic. This additional information which a tape-recording provides not only allows a richer picture of the interviewee to be constructed but also helps to provide a context for the interview. If a video-taped interview has been conducted then the detail and context can be further enhanced by the analysis of the visual, non-verbal information which the video-tape offers. Where notes have been kept alongside a tape-recording of the interview an account of the non-verbal information, such as facial expression, body language, location etc., may also provide some of this context. In addition, careful listening to a tape, use of the counter and careful note taking can reduce the amount of the interview that needs to be transcribed. Again, a process of selection is involved, where a decision is taken not to transcribe certain parts of a tape or even complete tapes. Similarly, visual data represented through photographs, video-tape, drawings or paintings, graffiti, etc., need careful attention to ensure that whatever information can be conveyed by the medium in question is recognised and accounted for by the researcher as the data are sorted.

Part of the process of getting to know and sorting the data also involves keeping a systematic inventory or data log of what has been collected. This data log can be compiled as the data are collected and the research progresses. Basic information about the collected data, such as the date and time, the place where they were collected, the names and status/role of those involved, brief notes on the focus of the data and of any particular circumstances which may have been influential in their collection (for example having to conduct an interview in a public place where the conversation could be overheard, being granted access only to particular documents but not others) will often prove beneficial to the process of analysis. A common system of labelling and logging data is particularly important where research is conducted by a team of researchers and where data are pooled.

Coding

Whilst there are numerous textbooks which offer approaches to data analysis based on different methods of data display or organisation (e.g. Dey, 1993; Miles and Huberman, 1994), and many of these are helpful for both beginning and experienced researchers as a source of ideas and techniques in data handling and analysis, we would argue that the basis of all qualitative analysis is effective coding of the collected data. Indeed, whilst many of the ever growing number of qualitative data analysis software packages make claims about data organisation, data management and theory building (Fielding and Lee, 1991; Dey, 1993; Richards and Richards, 1994; Seidel et al., 1988; Tesch, 1990), their effectiveness in all such tasks relies on comprehensive data coding. It is then, in our view, comprehensive and careful coding which provides the key to making sense of the data mound by providing a basis on which the researcher can sort and organise ideas.

In attempting to explain and come to a definition of coding, however, we are aware that it is in some ways an anathema to the very notion of qualitative data. If one takes the view that researchers engage in qualitative research because they are concerned to capture the detail of a situation, and that the strength of the approach lies in the detailed and rich data, then to reduce this to a series of codes, and on the basis of these codes to break up and sort the data, would seem to counter the very strengths of the approach. However, it is here that we return to the theme of research as a practical activity and to the compromise that this often involves.

By coding and sorting the data we are merely seeking to make them more accessible and easier to understand. Whilst it may be our objective to understand an institution, a set of interactions or a social phenomenon holistically, and this may have been the reason for opting for a qualitative approach in the first place, it is unlikely that we will be able to achieve such an understanding without first looking in detail at the individual characteristics which constitute that institution, those interactions or that phenomenon. The code is, therefore, a necessary tool to help us do that.

There is, then, an inevitable process of reduction involved as we seek to code and sort our data. By coding we attempt to summarise the words used by the interviewee, or the observation notes taken as we watched or participated in a set of events, or the contents of a diary. By looking for key words or phrases or examples of observed behaviour which summarise aspects of the data, we are looking to describe the data in a way which, although some of the richness and the detail are inevitably lost, the essence of what was said, observed or written remains. Moreover, the summary or the code acts as a signpost to the data which the researcher(s) can follow to access the richness and detail which the code can only suggest.

The best way to proceed here is to use an example. The following is an extract from an observation note taken as part of a study of postgraduate students in the social sciences (Burgess, Hockey and Pole, 1992) which we have already considered in relation to interviews in Chapter 6. The study involved detailed semi-structured interviews with students and supervisors as well as observation of the day-to-day activities of the university department (a business school in England) in which they were based. The observation note was made during and just after one of the present authors attended a meeting held for doctoral students, many of whom were from overseas. The note which we reproduce at length below records the event in the following way:

ESRC POSTGRADUATE PROJECT
Premier Business School Fieldnotes

22/11/92
Researcher: C. Pole
First Year Ph.D. Students' Meeting with Director of Doctoral Studies.
First meeting of academic year.
Scheduled start 12.00. Actual start 12.05.
All 16 remaining students present (2 having left the course). One member of staff (Alan Firth, Director of Doctoral Studies). One researcher (C. Pole), seated at the back of the group.

Alan Firth sits behind desk, students in rows in front of him. A.F. says this is too formal, moves to the side of the desk. A.F. says this is an opportunity for you to say how things are going, any problems, gossip, etc. (*How much of this is for my benefit?*) Tries to be jovial but is a little uneasy.

No response from students.

A.F. tells them about one student who has left – seeking to transfer to Northern – he's not pleased about this. Also another student who they have just traced – it seems he has also left.

A.F. tells them about Doctorate in Business Administration. Students ask if they can transfer, A.F. says probably if they have a good MBA. Student asks what's the difference between Ph.D. and DBA? A.F. hedges – he's pressed again. A.F. says 'Ph.D. is difficult, academic and exacting – so is the DBA. Ph.D. is for academics, DBA is for consultants and those wanting to teach in management. Ph.D. is for scholars, DBA is for those wanting money! Students ask again can we transfer? A.F. again says probably.

A.F. informs them about refurbishment of doctoral area. £4500 to be spent. Not much response from students.

A.F. asks again for questions from students. Hui Chang raises issues of standardisation of supervision. A.F. says this is human interaction – how can it be standardised? Another student Julian (young, male, English) asks Hui Chang how can it be standardised, it's down to human nature – asks has he read the paper by Peter Brown (member of this school) on this subject.

A.F. intervenes – tells Julian he has a point but is pushing it too far. Stresses his role is to monitor super-vision, he is available to talk to students about anything. Stresses he is discreet – supervisors talk to him about students, why shouldn't students talk to him about supervisors? Hui Chang says there are vast differences and some people are not receiving enough support. A.F. stresses again he's available to stu-dents for discussion about anything.

Beverley Mills changes the subject to the inefficiency of the printer in the doctoral area. A.F. says he'll get it fixed but has noticed that the printing expenses have increased this year by £3K whilst photo-copying has declined. Saudi student complains that there is only one lap top computer, can they have another one? A.F. says probably, says he will talk to Professor Murray about the budget. Sandwiches arrive and coffee. A.F. tells some students (Malaysians) to serve the others, adds 'if you fail your Ph.D. you can always open a Chinese restaurant'. General laughter.

A.F. informs students that he intends to hold a discussion on the topic of doing a Ph.D. in an Anglo-Saxon culture. Wants them to discuss the difficulties of assimilation to a different culture. Refers to Professor Sanders' course on philosophy, describes him as a crocodile, asks if students feel threatened by it. Beverley Mills (middle-class, middle-aged Anglo-Saxon) says she does, God knows how the others feel then.

Malaysian student raises the question of presentation of proposals for upgrading from M.Phil. to Ph.D. in June. He is concerned that there is a hidden agenda, refers to politics of the school and students being used as pawns in an academic/political game by different factions of Premier Business School who are on the panel which assess the proposals and decide on upgrading.

A.F. assures the student that the only criteria by which they are judged are academic ones. He admits that there are political and academic differences between 'scholars' but stresses these won't affect the way they are judged. He will ensure fair play.

Students seem unconvinced by his reply. A Saudi student asks if there are clear criteria by which pro-posals are deemed worthy of upgrading to Ph.D.

A.F. says yes, it has to be original, contribute to the stock of knowledge. M.Phil's can be clever but they don't require original work. Students are all quiet. (What does he mean by original? How do you become original? That's what I would want to ask him.)

Hui Chang says – in effect there are two Ph.D.'s at Premier Business School – one to get upgraded from M.Phil., the other to get the Ph.D. A.F. agrees. He says different universities have different standards. Premier Business School standards are high, 'and you'll be ever so pleased when you get your Ph.D.' He says 60% get upgraded first time but it's OK to have a second go at getting upgraded. Many people do. He reassures them that virtually all second years have now been upgraded and he expects 8 or 9 third years to graduate this year, then we'll have a party. He urges them to read other people's Ph.D.'s. This is the best way to appreciate what is required. Also, to talk to 2nd and 3rd years about what is required in the proposal. He says he's never seen a perfect proposal, they're not looking for perfection. They are looking for three things:

– 'What are you going to do?
– Why do you want to do it?
– How are you going to do it?'

Stresses the need to keep it simple, 3 sides. Says because it needs to be simple, that's why it's difficult to do.

Time now 12.35. A.F. says he must leave for another meeting. Two students try to ask him other questions – Hui Chang succeeds in trapping him for 2 more minutes about a reference. The other student is told to walk with him to the other meeting.

A.F. leaves the room, winking at me as he leaves.

I stay behind talking to students. I am quickly cornered by Hui Chang who wants to talk to me again next week. He is concerned that students are afraid to voice their opinions, afraid to criticise. He says the Orientals just say everything is OK, when it's not. Only he is prepared to stick his neck out. (He sees me as a means of voicing his frustration, I've already spoken to him for 1 and a half-hours, and his wife (also a first year Ph.D. student) for an hour. I shall have to be careful how I play this one.)

I also talk to a Peruvian who's just arrived on the course for a while. He's impressed that I'm from Warwick (Warwick rejected him). He's at Premier Business School because it has high status. The conversation is difficult, his English is not good. I move around the room, chatting to others about their work. Some are interested in my research, want to know how Premier Business School compares with other places, what the feelings of the students are towards their supervisors, where have I been conducting the research? I tell them I can't tell them where I've been working and make fairly bland statements in relation to the others. I begin to ask them questions. I feel a bit uneasy about this. They've all given me quite a lot of their time and are nice people. They want something back, but I can't give it at this stage.

The meeting has also acted as an important social event (the only one for a long time). What is amazing is that people are swapping addresses as though they are meeting for the first time – but this can't be the case, they've all been on the same course since September.

What I also find difficult to handle is that most of these students are experienced (5–6 years) teachers in universities in their own countries. In this meeting they have been treated not unlike first year undergraduates. They have also acted like it.

I hang around talking to people until there's no one left. The whole thing is over by 1.25 p.m. Lots of sandwiches and fruit left – pity I'm on a diet!

The note attempts to capture the content and format of the meeting from the position of an observer who is not a full participant in the proceedings. However, the note goes further than pure description, to include some judgmental comment from the observer, although we do not wish to imply that observation notes should necessarily do this. It is clear from the note that this is the observer's interpretation of what happened rather than an attempt at a pure description (if such a form of description is possible).

In terms of our typology of the analysis process, **preliminary analysis** took place early in the project when the research design was matched with the specific focus of the study. As a result, observation of meetings such as that described above was deemed useful as likely sources of relevant data.

In terms of **processual analysis**, this occurred at two levels. In the first place, as the students were given more than a full week's notice of the meeting by the postgraduate tutor, the researcher was able to plan for the observation, by seeking to locate the event in the context of what was already known about the student experience at the business school. Here the researcher drew on material collected earlier in the project by means of interviews, documents and other observations. From these data he was able to look for basic factual information like the frequency with which such meetings took place, the relationship of the meeting to other methods of communication between staff and students and also the numbers of staff and students likely to be involved, as well as the gender and ethnic mix of the meeting. In addition, the data already collected offered insight into the issues of current concern to the students and staff and hence the likely content of the meeting. In this instance, the processual analysis enabled a form of triangulation to occur as the researcher was able to compare the data collected from observation of the meeting with those collected via other means and in other situations. The note itself also provides evidence of processual analysis, as the judgemental comments made by the researcher, as the meeting progresses, are indicative of the ways in which he is thinking about the situation as it occurs and the way in which he is interpreting what he sees. This form of analysis is one which ties the researcher closely in to what is happening in the setting and is one which integrates what the researcher is observing with what he/she already knows about the situation from other sources. In this sense, processual analysis performs a role which is in some ways similar to Hammersley and Atkinson's (1995) notion of reflexivity in research in which the analysis is a product not merely of what is observed but also of the way in which the researcher engages with what is observed.

Our notion of processual analysis, therefore, eschews any possibility of wholly objective empiricism. The notion is based on a belief that it is impossible to separate the researcher from the data or to collect data in isolation from what is already known about the area being researched.

In the context of our example, therefore, the data collected at the beginning of the meeting were a reflection of the preliminary analysis conducted before the research began and also of what had been learnt from earlier stages of the study. The data collected towards the end of the meeting were influenced not only by the preliminary and processual analyses but also by the data collected at the beginning of the meeting and their ongoing, reflexive interpretation by the researcher.

For example, one of the very first observations in the note records that 'Alan Firth sits behind his desk.' These six words tell us much more than just their literal description of where the member of staff is sitting. In the light of the preliminary analysis which, for example, included some literature work on staff–student relations in universities in general and at doctoral level in particular, the relative positions of Alan Firth and the students begin to alert the observer to ideas about hierarchy: for evidence of a distance (social, structural, intellectual) between Alan Firth, the director of the doctoral programme, and his students. In addition the processual analysis of previously collected data from other observations and in particular from interviews with students, alerted the observer to a general sense of unease or tension between staff and students.

From this very simple, initial descriptive observation the researcher begins to interpret and interrogate the data in relation to particular issues and concepts. The concepts, here those of distance and tension, stay with the researcher and are operationalised as the observation of the meeting and its interpretation continue. For example, where the observation note records what happens in the room after Alan Firth leaves it is clear that one of the earlier emphases on distance and communication remains. The note states:

I stay behind talking to students. I am quickly cornered by Hui Cheng who wants to talk to me again next week. He is concerned that students are afraid to voice their opinions, afraid to criticise. He says the Orientals just say everything is OK when it's not. Only he is prepared to stick his neck out.

Given the number of people in the room and the content of the preceding meeting it seems likely that there would have been a range of issues which the researcher could have focused on in the observation note. It is clear, however, that the idea of distance between staff and students has become a theme in the observation and the researcher has emphasised this in the note.

So far the example has been helpful in demonstrating that analysis in its different forms occurs before any data are collected and is an integral part of the data-collection process itself. Whilst preliminary and processual analysis help us to understand the way in which the data are collected, it is our third form of analysis, **summative analysis**, which is of prime importance as a means of understanding whatever it is we are studying, of looking for connections with other research and drawing conclusions.

It is in relation to summative analysis that we return to the need to get to know the data in detail and to the issue of coding. Knowing the data means not only reading, viewing or listening to them until they become very familiar, but also means contextualising them in relation to preliminary and processual analysis. In relation to our example, this would mean making explicit the influences which are thought to have impacted upon their collection. Here Glaser and Strauss's (1967) ideas about memo writing are helpful. Writing an account of the data-collection phase in memo form addressed to yourself or to colleagues in the research team, in which the research can be contextualised, in which ideas can be introduced, tried out, rejected or signposted to be revisited in subsequent memos, can prove useful in coming to a fuller understanding of the data.

However, the essence of summative analysis is the process of coding to which the data are subjected.

Key issues

- Starting to analyse
- Sorting the data
- Evaluating the data
- Getting to know the data
- Writing memos
- Coding.

Coding in practice

In the first instance, coding can be characterised as an exercise in which the researcher seeks to summarise the detailed data through the identification of a series of descriptors which act as signposts to the collected data. Some researchers refer to this as 'open coding'. At the same time this initial or open coding allows the researcher to re-access the data in such a way that the richness and detail contained within can be realised. As such, coding is reductionist but at the same time has the capacity to be expansive.

However, various textbooks and guides to research discuss coding in different ways, applying different terminology to the process. Similarly, judging from researchers' accounts of their attempts at coding it would appear that there are as many different approaches to coding as there are researchers or indeed as there are research-based studies, because there is no guarantee that researchers always take the same approach to coding. Indeed Bryman and Burgess (1994) go so far as to say, 'Clearly there is the potential for considerable confusion regarding what coding actually is, so that it is doubtful whether writers who employ the term are referring to the same procedure' (p. 218).

Indeed, many research texts go into considerable detail about different stages of coding in which the researcher seeks to achieve higher and higher levels of understanding and explanation from the collected data. Whilst many of these texts are useful, providing a resource for the experienced and reflexive researcher, others seem unduly complicated and are likely to deter the less experienced researcher from attempting something which we feel is essentially straightforward.

Most accounts of data coding are based on the idea of 'Grounded Theory' developed in the 1960s by Glaser and Strauss (1967). The importance of this approach should not be under-estimated. Not only did it offer the first systematic account of the process by which qualitative research could yield theory, but it has also been the benchmark, quality assurance symbol and general security blanket for qualitative analysis ever since. Again, Bryman and Burgess (1994) have an interesting view on this.

> We suspect the influence of grounded theory has been twofold. First, it has . . . alerted qualitative researchers to the desirability of extracting concepts and theory out of data. Second, grounded theory has informed, in general terms, aspects of the analysis of qualitative data, including coding and the use of different types of codes and their role in concept creation (p. 220).

The essence of Grounded Theory is the discovery of theory from the data. Rather than identifying a hypothesis at the outset of the research, which is then tested by collecting data, and if confirmed is developed into a theory, Grounded Theory works in the opposite way. As the title of the celebrated 1967 publication implies, researchers first collect data and then look to identify or discover theory within them. The emphasis is upon the researchers to interrogate the data to the point of saturation in their efforts to discover theory. As such, the approach is one which rests on a process of induction rather than deduction.

The close reading of the data and the identification of codes is, therefore, an important part of theory discovery. In identifying codes we are seeking to give meaning to the research which goes beyond the detail of the data in a way which is both more abstract and conceptual. By this we mean that the codes enable us to develop general ideas about the specific content of the research. They are, then, what Dey (1993) sees as the building blocks of data analysis.

Miles and Huberman (1984) identify a number of different kinds of codes which may be used in the early stages of data analysis. For example, we may wish to attribute descriptive codes to the data relating to who is speaking, the status of the actors, the kinds of things they are talking about or the actions we have witnessed and recorded in our observation notes. Secondly, we may wish to take coding a step further by adding interpretation to the data. Rather than taking at face value what has been said or observed, we begin to infer meaning in the language and actions. For example, we may have collected data from a discussion in a staff-room amongst art and design teachers. They may have been talking about a lack of appropriate materials for their 'A' level students. In wider terms this may perhaps be interpreted as a concern about resource priorities, school finance or even the importance attached to their subject by those who decide on resource allocation in the school and beyond. Clearly this level of interpretative coding necessitates a level of abstraction on the part of the researcher as he/she interrogates not just the data from the teachers' discussions, but also from other things known about the school, art and design, resourcing priorities etc., from other data collected as the study progresses. Thirdly according to Miles and Huberman (1984) we may seek to apply codes which are explanatory. In the context of the example cited above, explanatory codes may relate to a reduction in the school's budget from the local authority, a failure to order sufficient stock by the head of department, or a strike by paint manufacturers. The categorisation of the data and the codes which are applied to them may overlap in terms of whether the codes are descriptive, interpretative or explanatory. The fact that this may happen is a reflection of the development of the codes from the literal to the more abstract. However, it should be obvious by now that all codes are based on interpretation or analysis by the researcher. They are not objective, uncontested artefacts. Rather, they are the result of the researcher's interaction with the data.

The codes operate, therefore, at a number of different levels. In the first place, they operate descriptively as a guide to what is contained in the data, though clearly they cannot convey the full detail.

Thus by reading through the codes, for example, from an interview transcript or a set of detailed observation notes, we are able to gather, in general terms, what the conversation or the observed action was about. At a 'higher' or more abstract level the codes act as ideas which can be linked back to preliminary analysis which focused on debates in the literature, findings from other research in the area and our ideas, the epistemology and ontology which shaped the research in the first place. At this higher level, the codes begin to operate conceptually in a way which helps us to understand and explain social phenomena. In some instances this form of coding has been referred to as 'axial coding'. At this stage, axial coding may also involve the comparison of codes and categories, attributed to different aspects of the data, with a view to establishing connections between the codes and between data from the different sources.

The codes help to identify issues and ideas which may have a role extending beyond the specific case that the data have described. At this higher level the codes may be used to move the analysis beyond descriptions to offer more complex[1] explanations of whatever is being studied and hence provide a bridge between descriptive and theoretical accounts of social behaviour.

It may now be helpful to return to our earlier example, the observation note made at the business school, and to consider some of the issues relating to data coding before going on to attempt some coding.

Technical issues

The example reproduced again on page 202 reveals a number of simple yet vital points. To begin with, the data have been clearly displayed. Here the note is carefully typed with simple articulation of what is happening, when it happened and who was involved. In some instances an observation note may also include a plan of the setting. In addition the display needs to provide ample space for codes to be written in the margins in such a way that it is clear to which sections of the data they relate. Here, double spacing has been used, together with wide margins on either side which provide room for codes to be written in and cross-referenced. Other more sophisticated forms of display may include numbering of the paragraphs or the individual lines. Such a form of display not only enables coding to be applied to the observation note or interview transcript, but also facilitates a more detailed annotation in memo form which is recorded in a separate file or notebook and can be read alongside the data. At the same time, the data can be clearly located by means of the numbered lines. Such a scheme also allows a more continuous sense of codes to be conveyed where the same code might be applied across several lines of data. For example, in the context of our example, numbering the lines would enable us to show that from line 001 to line 005 and from line 26 to line 32 the meeting is concerned with issues of rapport between staff and students. Indeed, the concept of attributing numbered lines to the data and then attributing codes to the lines forms the basis of all qualitative data analysis packages (Dey, 1993; Richards and Richards, 1991; Seidel, 1991; Seidel *et al.*, 1988; Tesch, 1990, 1991). Essentially, the specially designed package and the more traditional 'hands on' method rely on the same principles of data sorting, coding and categorisation. The aim remains the same: to produce an account of the collected data which will facilitate explanation and understanding of the social phenomena being studied.

Where the data are represented by an interview transcript taken from a tape-recording, in addition to line numbers, it can also be useful to include counter numbers from the tape-recorder which give the exact location of the data on the tape.[2] Counter

---

[1] The word 'complex' should not be confused with complicated. In this context its use relates to knowledge which seeks to be comprehensive and explanatory in relation to the phenomena with which it engages.

[2] It should be borne in mind, however, that all tape-recorders work at slightly different speeds. Therefore, playing the tape back on a machine different from the one on which the transcription was made will result in slight discrepancies in the exact location of data *vis-à-vis* the counter number.

numbers are particularly useful where an audio typist may not have been able to hear sections of the interview or to make sense of specific phrases. The interviewer may wish to listen to the tape in order to fill in the gaps. Alternatively, an interviewee may have used technical, scientific or other language with which the audio typist is unfamiliar. Being able to locate its exact place on the tape will, again, enable an accurate transcription to be produced. Many researchers will not, however, have access to an audio typist and some of you reading this text may already have spent many hours doing your own transcription. Whilst this can be tedious and laborious, it is an excellent way of getting to know the data. Doing your own transcription means that many of the problems of incomplete data or 'gaps' in the nature of those described above can be avoided. Nevertheless, recording the counter number remains good practice which will enable a particular section of the tape to be located and, if necessary, the data listened to, rather than merely read. Here the audio record provides access to data which a transcript is unable to capture, such as tone of voice, speed of speech, accent and hesitations.

Key issues

- Display data clearly by typing and leaving large margins.
- Include contextual information on location, time and number of participants, etc.
- Use line or paragraph numbering.
- Make a note of the tape counter number at the top and bottom of each page of transcription.
- Remember, doing your own transcriptions means you get to know your data.

Having satisfied yourself that there is sufficient technical information included alongside the data, you will now be in a position to begin attributing codes. Let us take the first two pages of the observation note as an example to work on:

Applying the codes

ESRC Postgraduate Project

Premier Business School Fieldnotes

22/11/92

Researcher: C. Pole

First Year Ph.D. Students' Meeting With Director of Doctoral Studies.

First meeting of academic year.

Scheduled start 12.00. Actual start 12.05.

All 16 remaining students present (2 having left the course).

One member of staff (Alan Firth, Director of Doctoral Studies).

One researcher (C. Pole), seated at the back of the group.

1 Alan Firth sits behind desk, students in rows in front of him. A.F. says this is too formal, moves to the side of the desk. A.F. says this is an opportunity for you to say how things are going, any problems, gossip, etc. *(How much of this is for my benefit?)* Tries to be jovial but is a little uneasy.

director speaks, position, barriers, hierarchy, status, rapport, uneasy/tension

2 No response from students.

rapport, students silent

3 A.F. tells them about one student who has left – seeking to transfer to Northern – he's not pleased about this. Also another student who they have just traced – it seems he has also left.

information, director speaks, student attrition

4 A.F. tells them about Doctorate in Business Administration. Student asks if they can transfer, A.F. says probably if they have a good MBA. Student asks what's the difference between Ph.D. and DBA? A.F. hedges – he's pressed again. A.F. says 'Ph.D. is difficult, academic and exacting – so is the DBA. Ph.D. is for academics, DBA is for consultants and those wanting to teach in management. Ph.D. is for scholars, DBA is for those wanting money! Students ask again can we transfer? A.F. again says probably.

qualifications, status, rapport, facilities, students question, academics vs. consultants, money vs. scholarship, student transfer

5 A.F. informs them about refurbishment of doctoral area. £4500 to be spent. Not much response from students.

resources, rapport, student passive

6 A.F. asks again for questions from students. Hui Chang (young, male, Malaysian) raises issues of standardisation of supervision. A.F. says this is human interaction – how can it be standardised? Another student Julian (young, male, English) asks Hui Chang how can it be standardised, it's down to human nature – asks has he read the paper by Peter Brown (member of this school) on this subject.

questions, supervision, defence, criticism, rapport, distance, student interaction

7 A.F. intervenes – tells Julian he has a point but is pushing it too far. Stresses his role is to monitor supervision, he is available to talk to students about anything. Stresses he is discreet – supervisors talk to him about students, why shouldn't students talk to him about supervisors? Hui Chang says there are vast differences and some people are not receiving enough support. A.F. stresses again he's available to students for discussion about anything.

rapport, supervision, criticisms, defence

In this example the paragraphs have been numbered and general codes written in the margins alongside the text. Already by this relatively simple process we can begin to see patterns emerging from the data. If we compare the codes paragraph by paragraph we get a feeling for the issues emerging from the data.

From this example of just seven paragraphs we can see a number of issues emerging from the data. The method of coding is one which is, to some extent laborious, but which does begin to bring the data alive by identifying themes which in this case seem to shape and organise the experiences of the students at Premier Business School. The process of coding succeeds in moving attention beyond the particular concerns of individual students and towards more general issues. For example, the themes of hierarchy and rapport begin to emerge and reoccur. Similarly the codes encourage us to ask questions about the information that students are given by the staff about their fellow students and why some have chosen to leave. They also start to open up ideas about the perceived value and utility of the qualifications being offered by Premier Business School and about distinctions drawn between scholars and consultants. Some of the codes are descriptive – for example, those relating to who is speaking and their location in the room – whilst others are interpretative – for example, those which relate to hierarchy, to the value attributed to qualifications and to observations of status. Rather than moving from the descriptive to the interpretative and then to the explanatory, our approach is one in which different kinds of codes and categories are applied simultaneously.

The process of coding, and in particular of coding as the data are collected, contributes to both processual and summative analysis. As codes are identified, they raise questions about actions or language in terms of their meaning and significance to the focus of the research. To explore further the meaning and significance, the researcher may need to collect more data and/or subject the data to more analysis in relation to literature in the area or in relation to other data.

The coding method is one which can be applied to many different kinds of textual data sources, such as interview transcripts, diaries or other written documents, or to the reading of a set of photographs. The method allows the comparison of data from various sources by highlighting key issues across different kinds of data. The attribution of codes to particular lines, paragraphs or 'chunks' of data which have been clearly displayed and identified allows the researcher to re-enter the text at relevant points and to access the detail to which the codes or 'signposts' relate. The method facilitates, therefore, a constant entering and re-entering of data and the identification of further codes.

From codes to concepts

Whilst the codes or signposts offer a map of the data which may of itself be useful as a précis of what has been collected, the purpose of qualitative data analysis is to construct a conceptual framework by which the researcher can make sense of the social world which he/she is studying. By conceptual framework we refer to a way of making sense of the data which takes us from the particular events or instances which constitute the data, to a broader understanding of the phenomena which constitute the focal point of the research. By engaging in coding which is at the same time descriptive, interpretative and explanatory, we are already well on the way to producing a conceptual framework.

As with analysis more generally, we believe that there is a large degree of unnecessary complication which adds an almost mythical tone to the process of conceptualising data. In simple terms we see the identification of a conceptual framework as the process of looking for connections between the attributed codes and in turn linking these back to our original ideas about the research, the preliminary analysis which shaped and helped to focus the study and to our literature work, that is the processual analysis. In terms of our example, therefore, the codes from the first four paragraphs, which are a combination of descriptive, interpretative and explanatory, begin to suggest themes which might be developed as a means of organising the data, providing a framework for an understanding of the situation. For example, paragraph 1 has been attributed codes which refer to position, barriers, hierarchy and status. These are codes which recur throughout the observation note. Meanwhile, paragraph 4 introduces issues of qualifications, status and scholarship. Again, these are issues which are found elsewhere in this observation note. Moreover, the codes in both paragraphs 1 and 4 are also to be found in other locations within the overall mound of data. They recur in interviews with staff and students, in other observations of events within Premier Business School and within documentation collected as the research progresses. There is, therefore, a process of confirmation taking place as the various data sources are examined and coded, revealing common issues. Gradually the common issues emerge as themes within the data and it becomes appropriate not merely to discover them, but also to actively seek them out. At this stage we are looking for confirmation that the themes have a resonance throughout the data and consequently can serve as a useful tool in the explanation and understanding of whatever constitutes the focus of the study. It is this resonance of themes throughout the data which we feel can most usefully be described as the conceptual framework. Its identification allows us to apply concepts developed from the coding process across the data as a way of organising and understanding social processes.

In terms of our example, what began as an interpretative code or hierarchy can now be used to explain the way in which the business school is organised in terms of its management, its staffing and staff–student relations. It may also be a useful tool for explaining the content of some of the courses offered by the school in terms of hierarchies of knowledge and in shedding light on issues of resource allocation (human and material)

within the school. The concept of hierarchy in this context becomes a versatile tool in explaining many aspects of the school. In its development from a code to a concept, there is movement from the particular, represented by a specific observation in a specific location and at a specific time, to the more general. Although we are limited to a consideration of Premier Business School at the time when the data were collected, the concept of hierarchy rather than the code is able to explain and hence help us to understand a range of issues within the school. Furthermore, we may also take the codes relating to, for example, position, barriers, and rapport from the observation of the meeting and look for these throughout the collected data. The identification of these and similar codes may have enabled us to group them together and, in this particular case, put forward a concept of distance – in this instance between staff and students, but in turn the concept of distance may prove useful in helping us to explain patterns of doctoral supervision or the use of space in the business school or patterns of student sociability. Distance, therefore, becomes a useful conceptual and explanatory tool which has been developed directly from this process of careful reading and coding of the data.

The idea is that by engaging in this process of coding and conceptual development, we gradually move to a situation where we are able to make sense of what we have observed in the research setting or heard whilst conducting an interview. We are looking to offer convincing explanations which whilst grounded in the detail of particular circumstances, help us to understand social behaviour on a broader canvas. In terms of our example, therefore, this process of induction has enabled us to move forward, from the observation of the doctoral students' meeting to the identification of concepts of hierarchy and distance in the data and the use of these to explain not just the organisation and experience of that particular meeting but many other aspects of the business school and the students' experiences of doctoral study.

Key issues

- Knowing the data in detail
- Knowing the context in which data were collected
- Thorough coding
- Looking for connections
- Looking for contradictions
- Linking to the literature
- Linking to original ideas about the research
- Identifying concepts.

How do we know it is true? Relativism, reliability and validity

Throughout this chapter it has been our intention to emphasise the importance of close reading of the data. In doing this we seek to ensure that research findings are grounded in the information that has been collected in the field. The process of analysis which we have described has its foundations in analytical induction and is based on Glaser and Strauss's (1967) *The Discovery of Grounded Theory*. We would argue that this approach allows for a comprehensive and thorough examination of the data, which is, as far as possible, unencumbered by explicit expectations about what the research might find, or by personal beliefs and philosophies. At the same time, it is an approach which leaves itself open to charges of relativism. By this we mean that the explanations which we advance on the basis of analytical induction – in our example, those of hierarchy and distance – are not the only explanations which this process of analysis might yield. Moreover, the charge of relativism in this context might also extend to a concern that, despite using the same method, different researchers may find different things. For example, different researchers may not have focused on hierarchy or distance as means of conceptualising some of what they had observed at the business school.

The problem seems to be at least two-fold. First of all there is the issue of the relative merits of the different conceptual frameworks and explanations that are advanced from the same data. How are we to judge them? Are we to assume that all findings or knowledge gained from the data are equally true or valuable? Secondly, how are we to know when data have been conceptually exhausted? Could it be that data can go on and on yielding different codes and concepts, perhaps boosted by different researchers working on them? A fresh pair of eyes may see things differently. Or is there a limit to the process of induction? Glaser and Strauss (1967) speak of reaching a point of saturation at which all possible explanations have been wrung out of the data. However, the problem remains of knowing when this point has been reached. Or will there inevitably be the feeling that there is still something lurking in the data which we have not yet seen?

At one level these concerns are a reflection of the richness of qualitative data and at another level they are indicative of the importance of the relationship between the researcher and the data. More so than quantitative data analysis, qualitative data analysis depends on an intimate relationship between researcher and data. In effect, the analysis – that is to say, the discovery of theory within the data – is a construction of the researcher, brought about by his/her knowledge of the data and the capacity to identify codes and concepts within it. In turn, the discovery of theory also depends on the capacity of the researcher to relate the codes and concepts to the epistemological and ontological questions which have shaped the research. Given the central role of the researcher in this process, critics could suggest that qualitative analysis is little more than a reflection of the creative ability of the researcher, who tells a story based on the data in a similar way to a novelist. Moreover, they could also assert that every account of a set of events that is produced is as good, or as true, as any other. It is here that questions of reliability and validity are important.

What distinguishes the social researcher from a writer of fiction is his/her capacity to produce accounts of social phenomena which are not merely good stories, but are valid and reliable. In doing this, the researcher hopes to avoid the charge of relativism and accusations that his/her findings are little more than a product of the imagination. Whilst reliability and validity are important to all researchers, we feel it is fair to say that these are terms which are associated most frequently with quantitative rather than qualitative research. This may be due to the relative ease with which quantitative researchers are able to assess the reliability of their findings in statistical terms. In addition, at least in theory, though rarely in our experience in practice, it is easier for quantitative studies to be replicated at a later date by the original researcher(s) or by others, in an attempt to test reliability by looking for a repeat of the original findings. For the qualitative researcher, however, such simple assessments of reliability and validity are not available and repetition of what may be a long, loosely structured, highly time- and location-specific study may simply be impossible. Although, as Bryman (1988) reveals, there have been attempts to replicate qualitative anthropological studies, they have usually met with little success.

Differences between qualitative and quantitative studies are, therefore, both technical and epistemological. They relate to the methods by which data are collected and to the nature of the knowledge which the studies yield. Nevertheless, the principles of reliability and validity remain equally important for both qualitative and quantitative research. In short, we may take reliability as referring to the extent to which repetition of the research will yield the same results, and validity as the degree to which the research has successfully measured the social phenomena upon which it has been focused.

Having characterised validity and reliability in this way, it may still seem that they are terms that can only be applied to quantitative data, where there is an emphasis on enumeration and measurement. However, Dey (1993) makes a convincing case for their reinterpretation in line with the nature of qualitative data. Whilst, as we have already established, repetition of qualitative studies is rarely possible, it is possible to open up a study

to public scrutiny. Dey calls for an openness in this respect, which includes allowing other researchers and interested parties to assess not only the findings of qualitative research but also the means by which they were reached. This point relates to those which we made in the opening chapter about diligence in research and the role of the research community in evaluating its output. Here, the concern is with the quality of the data, its richness and detail. In addition, any scrutiny of the research should include an examination of the fit between the research design and the substantive focus. That is, an evaluation should assess whether the conclusions are based on appropriate methodological and epistemological foundations. The scrutiny should include not only the way in which the methods were executed but also their relationship to the kind of knowledge which the research is seeking to advance. The context in which the data were collected is also relevant here, as is the relationship between the researcher(s) and the funder of the research. For example, to fully understand what is seen or heard within an institution it is necessary to understand the wider political, economic and cultural circumstances in which it operates. In relation to our example of Premier Business School, we could not fully understand the concept of hierarchy unless we were aware of issues concerned with its internal politics, its funding structure and some of its history. Similarly, in order to evaluate the research we would need to know who had funded the study and for what reason. If, for example, the Commonwealth Universities Association had commissioned the research with a view to placing more overseas students in the school, then we might have expected a closer relationship between staff and students to have been promoted by school authorities as they sought to convey a picture of a supportive and caring institution. In terms of reliability of the data and their analysis, therefore, it is this contextual information which is essential. Without this it would not be possible to explain properly how the research had been conducted or how the conclusions had been reached. Nor would it be possible to make sensible comparisons with conclusions drawn from studies in other similar settings.

Although the definition of validity in terms of the capacity to successfully measure social phenomena may sound more relevant to quantitative than qualitative approaches to social research, this is re-interpreted by Dey to refer to the extent to which an account is 'well grounded conceptually and empirically' (1993, p. 253). Dey's reference to the account being 'well-grounded' is, we believe, an obvious overture to Glaser and Strauss (1967) and the Grounded Theory approach to qualitative analysis. By this we take Dey's notion of validity to refer to the extent to which an account is embedded within the data, and to the capacity of the researcher to support his/her findings with relevant, detailed examples from those data. Consequently, the validity of research rests not only on the richness and the detail of the collected data, but also on a number of quantitative and structural issues. For example, in attributing significance to what is heard in an interview or whilst engaged in observation, the researcher will need to take into account who is speaking, what position they hold in the organisation and, therefore, what is likely to influence their particular perspective on whatever is being discussed. This is not to suggest that the views of people in senior positions are inevitably more valid than those in more junior positions. The example merely serves to emphasise that in order to judge the validity of research findings, as with reliability, we have to understand the context in which the data upon which they are based are collected. In addition, the frequency with which something is heard or observed is also relevant to validity. Again, this is not an issue about which there is a hard and fast rule. We are not suggesting, for example, that the more times something is said or observed the more valid it is likely to be. Neither are we suggesting that analysis or validity can be reduced to a matter of totalling the number of times a particular code is attributed to a section of data. The relationship between data collection, analysis and validity is more sophisticated than either of these two examples suggests. It may be, for example, that the

significance of frequency with which something is observed can only be fully understood in the context of the specific behaviour being observed and of who is involved in it. There may, for example, be an event which is deemed highly significant in spite of the fact that, or even because, it occurs infrequently. Again, our example of the doctoral students' meeting is useful here. Given that such meetings rarely took place, the one which is recorded in the observation note may be seen to have considerable significance, not least because of its rarity.

Reliability and validity are relevant to both qualitative and quantitative research. Moreover, they are themselves both qualitative and quantitative in nature. They are of central importance to qualitative research as a means of avoiding relativism and subjectivity. Without them, the social researcher may just as well be a novelist. They are, however, difficult concepts to define precisely in the context of qualitative research and even more difficult to realise. Their relevance to quantitative research is just as important, although perhaps slightly more straightforward to define, and this is discussed in Chapter 5.

In the context of qualitative research, we have proposed a route to reliability and validity which is firmly based on getting to know the data, on engaging in thorough analysis of the data, which takes account not only of their specific content but also their social context, of searching for connections between different parts of the data, and in the subsequent identification of concepts which are grounded in the data. This approach does not allow the application of a statistical formula that will tell us the extent to which our research findings are correct. It does, however, offer a means of establishing confidence in our findings by ensuring that it is the data which come first and that any claims for the research can be traced back directly to the data. In this sense, reliability and validity serve as a challenge to the researcher to ensure that there is comprehensive collection of data, which are then thoroughly analysed in terms of what we have described as the preliminary, processual and summative processes.

Key issues

- Knowing the data
- Thorough coding
- Identification of concepts
- Grounding the concepts in data
- Knowing the context
- Opening the findings for scrutiny.

Conclusion

Above all, this chapter has sought to emphasise that data analysis is an integral aspect of the research process. It is not something which occurs only after data have been collected, but is part of every stage of research from its inception to the production of the final report, thesis or publication and beyond.

Analysis can be one of the most exciting aspects of research, bringing together the technical expertise of data collection, theoretical insight and creative aspects of writing. The products of this synthesis of different activities are the research findings. It is these findings which allow the researcher to contribute to the knowledge base in his/her chosen field.

We have outlined an approach to qualitative data analysis which we feel is thorough, efficient and at the same time entirely commensurate with the richness and detail of qualitative data. Above all, the approach emphasises the importance of getting to know the data, of the researcher being able to immerse him/herself in what has been collected and to reflect not only on its substantive content but also on the context from which it has been collected and on the means by which this was done. There is, then, a continuous interaction between the researcher and the data. Hammersley and Atkinson (1995) identify this researcher–data relationship as an important aspect of reflexivity. In our view, it is this relationship which is central to the process of analysis and the production of research findings.

The approach which we have outlined and the examples we have used to illustrate it are based on analytical induction and Grounded Theory methods. Whilst we have not slavishly adhered to the procedures advocated by Glaser and Strauss (1967), we have, nevertheless, taken the essence of their approach and applied it in a less restrictive way to our research. In doing this we have stressed the importance of discovering concepts and theory from within the data. Our approach also places the researcher at the centre of the process. In this we recognise that data analysis is itself a social process.

Underlying everything that we have said about data analysis is a concern for reliability and validity. We stressed that in order to avoid charges of relativism and subjectivity, which might seriously undermine their findings, researchers need to be open about their work. They need to submit it to scrutiny by their peers and, above all, to ensure that everything they put forward can be traced back not only to the data themselves, but also to the context in which they were collected. In doing this we also believe that researchers will achieve a degree of confidence about their work which will enable them to defend it against the charges of subjectivity and relativism which we have already mentioned.

Data analysis may at times be difficult; it may also be tedious and a chore. Ultimately, however, it should be the most rewarding and exciting aspect of research as it is here that things start to make sense, and we begin to understand social relationships, interactions and structures. It is also here that we identify further questions about our topic and generate ideas about further research.

Chapter 9   Quantitative data analysis: knowledge from numbers

Introduction

This chapter builds upon the statistical material relating to samples in Chapter 3, and focuses on the analysis of a case-variable matrix (see Chapter 5) containing survey data, which have either been collected by the researcher or which were collected by other researchers and have been obtained from them either directly or via a data archive (see Chapter 7, which also considers the analysis of tabulated official statistics and other published tables/quantitative material).

In an ideal world, a social researcher analysing quantitative data would have the technical skills and software needed for him or her to be able to select and implement the most appropriate statistical technique for the specific analysis that they have in mind, given the form of the data available to them, and for him or her to present their findings in as clear and informative a way as possible. Relative to this ambitious goal, the aims of this chapter are modest:

- to equip the reader with a theoretical and practical understanding of some statistical techniques for the analysis of cross-tabulated data
- to enable the reader to present categorical and cross-tabulated data in a straightforward but appropriate way
- to mention, or discuss relatively briefly, a range of other analytical and presentational

techniques, directing the reader to appropriate further reading and sources of reference.

In attempting to achieve the first two aims we hope to demonstrate that quantitative analysis is not only useful to the researcher but is also an approach which is readily accessible to them. Our third aim reflects a desire to give the reader a starting point and resource for developing their quantitative skills further. Material on the web pages corresponding to this book is intended to give the reader a degree of familiarity with a statistical software package (SPSS for Windows).

Quantitative data analysis is far from being simply a technical exercise. It involves a process of decision making and data manipulation, which is guided by a mixture of the following:

- theoretical ideas
- the researcher's substantive insight
- her or his degree of experience as a data analyst
- the data themselves.

A major objective of this chapter is thus to equip the reader with a basic set of tools with which they can carry out simple but useful statistical analyses, and to encourage them to learn the skill of data analysis the only way it can really be properly learnt, i.e. by practising analysing real data. Good data analysis reflects practical experience as much as it does knowledge of techniques; it is for this reason that survey data have been made available via the web pages corresponding to this book.

Forms of data, levels of measurement

So why does this chapter focus on techniques for the analysis of cross-tabulated data such as those in Table 9.4? The answer is that a two-way cross-tabulation displays the relationship between two variables with the simplest possible form, i.e. variables at the nominal level of measurement.

A **nominal-level** variable consists of a set of (mutually exclusive) categories that are not hierarchical or ordered in any way. For example, undergraduate students' degree subjects would constitute a nominal variable.

Similar to, but slightly more complex than nominal-level variables are variables at the **ordinal level** of measurement. Ordinal-level variables consist of categories that are ordered in some way. For example, highest educational qualification (judged in terms of whether people have degrees, 'A' levels, GCSEs, or none of these) is an ordinal-level variable.

In fact, ordinal-level variables have another property, or, to be more precise, another limitation. This can be illustrated by considering the substantive differences or 'distances' between degrees and 'A' levels, and between 'A' levels and GCSEs. Is the difference in value between the first two types of qualification greater or smaller than the difference in value between the second two types of qualification? There is no watertight answer to this question. Ordinal-level variables are not **metric**, i.e. the distances between neighbouring categories do not have fixed meanings which allow the gaps between categories to be compared in a meaningful way.

Variables that have the property of being metric are at the **interval level** of measurement. Many such variables are also at the **ratio level** of measurement, i.e. they have an obvious zero point. Two examples of ratio-level variables are the number of children in a household and the amount of time per week (in hours) a person spends doing housework. In both these examples the intervals between neighbouring (whole number) values of the variables have a consistent meaning: for example, the difference between two children and three children is equivalent to the difference between six children and seven children, and the difference between zero hours and one hour of housework is equivalent to the difference between 25 hours and 26 hours of housework.

An extra child or hour of housework may certainly be experienced differently according to the starting point and might in some situations be the proverbial (and unpleasant) straw that breaks the camel's back, but mathematically the differences between neighbouring values have the same meaning. The existence of a zero point means that ratios of values are meaningful: for example, eight hours of housework is twice as much housework as four hours of housework.

An important difference between the last two examples is that the number of children can only take a **discrete** range of (whole number) values, whereas, in theory at least, time spent doing housework is a **continuous** variable which can be measured to any level of accuracy from whole hours down to fractions of a second and beyond. However, when discrete variables are summarised, the restriction of meaningful interpretations to the discrete set of values may disappear, as in the famous example of 2.4 children, which, though an apparently perverse value, has a sensible meaning at the aggregate level, since, for example, a rise from 2.4 children per family nationally to 2.5 children per family may necessitate more schools, teachers, etc.

In practice, the level of measurement of a variable is not always clear-cut. An attitudinal question which uses the range of answers 'Strongly agree', 'Agree', 'Neither agree nor disagree', 'Disagree' and

'Strongly disagree' is often treated as generating an interval-level variable (see Chapter 5) when in fact this range of answers strictly speaking only constitutes an ordinal-level variable. Similarly, social class categories are in practice sometimes 'upgraded' from ordinal to interval level. Conversely, age-related variables are often collapsed into a set of age bands, which may then be treated as an ordinal-level variable, or even as a nominal-level variable. Variables with only two categories, which are often referred to as **dichotomies** or **dichotomous variables**, are simultaneously both nominal-level variables and also interval-level variables, as the single gap between the two categories means that these variables automatically have the property of being metric.

In fact, by splitting a variable with any level of measurement into a set of categories and ignoring any natural ordering of these categories, the researcher can always obtain a nominal-level variable. Thus, after this simplification of the variables, all relationships between variables can be represented by cross-tabulations. There is, however, a price to be paid for this 'simplification' of the form of data analysed. Basically, the process of simplification involves throwing away information, and this loss of information makes it more difficult to assess whether an observed pattern or relationship in data from a sample is a genuine reflection of the situation in the broader population. In other words, converting interval-level data into nominal-level data before analysing them reduces the researcher's power to learn from his or her data.

For example, condensing a variable corresponding to respondents' ages in years into the two categories 'Under 50' and '50 and above' may make it more difficult to identify a relationship between age and ill health, since any differences between people aged 50 and people aged 80 are lost from the analysis.

The use of nominal-level variables may necessitate the loss of a certain amount of information. However, for the novice quantitative researcher, concentrating in the first instance on a narrowly

defined but all-encompassing set of techniques which equips them to carry out useful analyses may be more appropriate than trying to benefit from the extra power offered by a broader range of techniques. It is also important to recognise that the logic of the process of testing for the existence of relationships between variables is fundamentally the same whatever the form of the data (see Blalock, 1981: 154–166).

To recap, this process of statistical testing (which was introduced in Chapter 3) consists of comparing the data that the researcher observes with the figures that they would have expected to have seen given certain assumptions, often including the assumption that the variables involved are unrelated in the population. The researcher asks the question: 'Could the observed pattern have occurred by chance (given the assumptions)?' and then calculates a P-value, i.e. the probability that it would have occurred by chance (that is as a consequence of sampling error; see Chapter 3), given the assumptions. If the P-value is small (conventionally, less than 0.05 or 5%), then the researcher concludes that the observed pattern is unlikely to have occurred by chance, and therefore that the assumptions must be incorrect. This conclusion often involves the rejection of the assumption that there is no relationship between two variables, i.e. the acceptance that such a relationship exists.

The logic of statistical testing and the practical and technical aspects of analysing cross-tabulated data are illustrated in the sections that follow, in which we work through examples of the kind of straightforward but interesting data analyses which can be carried out by researchers with a relatively basic set of skills and with access to statistical software.

A cross-tabulation-based analysis of class identification

This section uses data from the 1991 British Social Attitudes Survey (BSAS; Jowell et al., 1992) to examine the relationship between a respondent's occupational class (operationalised in the form of Registrar General's Social Class) and their subjective (i.e. self-rated) social class. The analysis can be recreated (and extended) using the data provided on the web pages corresponding to this book (and the SPSS for Windows commands used are also included on the web pages). The data were obtained on a CD ROM from the ESRC Data Archive, along with the relevant technical report (Brook *et al.*, 1992). The technical report notes that analyses using these data should weight the data to take account of the sample design (see Chapter 3). The illustrative examples that follow are, however, based on unweighted data; this avoids some complications in the presentation of the examples. (As it happens, there are no differences of consequence between the weighted and unweighted findings in this case.)

It is good practice when reporting analyses of survey data to give the reader as good as possible an idea of the origins and nature of the variables involved. In keeping with this, the question on self-rated social class leading to the variable used here was as follows:

'Most people see themselves as belonging to a particular social class. Please look at this card and tell me which social class you would say *you* belong to? . . . And which social class would you say your *parents* belonged to when you started at primary school?'

The categories listed on the card were 'Upper middle', 'Middle', 'Upper working', 'Working' and 'Poor'. If your reaction to the question is anything like that of the authors, you will already be reflecting on its strengths and limitations, which demonstrates the importance of reporting question wordings (perhaps in a footnote or an appendix). The other variable in the analysis that follows, Registrar General's Social Class, is a standard measure of occupational class (see Chapter 5). However, an important point that can be gleaned from the BSAS documentation is that it is operationalised here on the basis of the respondent's own current occupation, or their last occupation.

Table 9.1 Self-rated class

Class	Frequency
Upper middle	27
Middle	400
Upper working	263
Working	682
Poor	58
Don't know	30
No answer/Refused	13
Missing	1445

Before looking at the relationship between two variables it is sensible to get a feel for the distribution of values for each variable separately. In the case of a pre-coded question this is simply the spread of answers given by respondents to the question. Table 9.1 shows this information for the self-rated class variable.

The first thing to note about the set of figures in Table 9.1 is that there are three categories of answer which were not included on the card shown to respondents. Two of these categories relate to a small number of respondents who could not, did not, or would not answer the question. A decision has to be made at some stage by the researcher as to whether this small proportion of respondents is best excluded from more elaborate analyses of the data. In this case the numbers involved are arguably sufficiently small that excluding these categories does not make the data markedly less representative. However, in situations where many respondents do not give 'concrete' answers to a question, or where respondents' reasons for not providing such answers are felt to be of potential theoretical importance, excluding this kind of category is less easy to justify. In general, when presenting results, it is important to let the reader know how many respondents have been excluded from consideration and why. Note that the large number of 'Missing' answers is simply a reflection of the fact that the 1991 BSAS used two overlapping but different questionnaires, and hence the questions examined here were only asked of half the

Table 9.2   Self-rated class

Class	Percentage
Upper middle	1.9
Middle	28.0
Upper working	18.4
Working	47.7
Poor	4.1
	N = 1430

Note: This excludes 43 respondents who did not provide one of the above answers.

Table 9.3   Occupational class

	Frequency	Percentage
RGSC I	134	4.8
II	672	24.3
III NM	644	23.3
III M	578	20.9
IV	515	18.6
V	221	8.0
	N = 2764	

Note: This excludes 92 respondents who had never had a job and 62 who were impossible to classify.

respondents. In fact, missing answers often reflect questions that were only asked of a sub-set of respondents.

The numbers of respondents who answered 'Upper Middle' or 'Poor' are quite low. Should these categories be retained as separate entities, or should they be aggregated with the 'Middle'-class and 'Working'-class answers? It is often useful to reduce the number of categories of answer to simplify analyses and to enable the findings to be presented in a clear and striking way. However, aggregating categories results in a loss of information. To keep the analysis that follows simple, the two middle-class categories are added together, as are the two working-class categories and the 'poor' category. However, simplicity is achieved at the cost of a loss of detail.

Meanwhile, you may have been looking at Table 9.1 and saying to yourself things like 'Nearly half of the people who were asked the question rated themselves in an unqualified way as being working class.' If so, congratulations on your mental arithmetic. If not, then you probably have an even better understanding of why it is important to convert raw frequencies into a more easily comprehensible form, such as percentages.

Table 9.2 converts the figures in Table 9.1 into a relevant set of percentages. Note that the total number of answers (N) should always accompany a set of percentages, so that the reader can, if they want to, re-create the original frequencies. Table 9.3 contains both frequencies and percentages corres-

ponding to the occupational classes of the BSAS respondents.

Questions relating to occupation were asked of all the BSAS respondents. However, when the two variables are cross-tabulated against each other, as in Table 9.4, the effective sample size is constrained by self-rated class only having been established for half the sample.

The totals below and to the right of the main body of Table 9.4 are often referred to as the **marginal** totals, and would be equal to the original frequencies if some categories of respondent had not been excluded. Once again, Table 9.4 is much easier to take in when converted into percentages, as shown in Table 9.5.

The percentages in Table 9.5 suggest that there is a strong relationship between occupational class and self-rated class, with much higher proportions of respondents in the top three, non-manual classes seeing themselves as middle class than in the bottom three, manual classes. Only respondents with occupations in Class I are more likely to see themselves as middle class than as working class. While, according to Table 9.5, most Class I people see themselves as middle class, the percentages in Table 9.5 do *not* show that most people who see themselves as middle class have Class I occupations! This is a reflection of the use of percentages which add up to 100% across the rows (**row percentages**) rather than percentages which add up to 100% down the columns (**column percentages**). The

Table 9.4   Occupational class by self-rated class

Occupational class	Frequencies		
	Self-rated class		
	Middle*	Working*	TOTAL
RGSC I	46	18	64
II	150	172	322
III NM	106	223	329
III M	41	258	299
IV	44	199	243
V	19	82	101
TOTAL	406	952	1358

Note: (*) Middle includes Upper Middle; Working includes Upper Working and Poor.

Table 9.5   Occupational class by self-rated class

Occupational class	Percentages		
	Self-rated class		
	Middle	Working	*N*
RGSC I	71.9	28.1	(64)
II	46.6	53.4	(322)
III NM	32.2	67.8	(329)
III M	13.7	86.3	(299)
IV	18.1	81.9	(243)
V	18.8	81.2	(101)
TOTAL	29.9	70.1	(1358)

relevant column percentage would be $100 \times 46/406$ = 11.3%. So, only a small minority of self-rated middle-class respondents have Class I occupations. The choice between row percentages and column percentages depends on whether we are more interested in how people with Class I occupations see themselves, or more interested in what kinds of occupations people who see themselves as middle class have. We might even be interested in what percentage of all people both have Class I occupations and also see themselves as middle class, in which case we would need a third type of percentage, and the relevant figure would be $100 \times 46/1358 = 3.4\%$. In general, the researcher needs to

think carefully about which set of percentages is most relevant to the questions that they want to answer.

While the pattern visible in Table 9.5 is a marked one and suggests the existence of a relationship between occupational class and self-rated class which makes substantive sense, the possibility remains that the pattern visible in Table 9.5 is simply a coincidence (i.e. a consequence of sampling error) and therefore cannot be generalised from the sample to the broader population of Britain. Hence it is necessary to demonstrate that the observed pattern is unlikely to have occurred by chance and can therefore be safely assumed to reflect what is going on in the broader population. This is achieved by the calculation of a **chi-square** statistic.

An individual's self-rated social class may depend on their family background and/or lifestyle as well as, or instead of, on their current or last occupation. However, it would seem reasonable to expect an individual's own occupation to typically have an impact on how they see themselves in class terms, and hence to expect occupational class and self-rated class to be related.

Testing for the existence of a relationship using the chi-square statistic

What would one have expected the figures in Table 9.5 to have looked like if there was no underlying relationship between a respondent's occupational class and their self-rated class? If there was no relationship then one would expect the distribution of respondents' self-rated classes to be the same for each occupational class. In other words, one would have expected the percentages in each row of Table 9.5 to have been the same as those in the TOTAL row, as in Table 9.6.

It is, in effect, the differences between Table 9.6 and Table 9.5 which we earlier interpreted as a relationship between respondent's occupational class and their self-rated class. Comparing the tables we can see, for example, that the percentage of respond-ents with Class I occupations who rated themselves as middle class was more than twice as big as would have been expected if there was no underlying relationship. In other words, 71.9% of respondents with Class I occupations rated themselves as middle class, whereas if there was no underlying relationship we would have expected the same percentage for respondents with Class I occupations as for respondents in general, i.e. 29.9%. What does this comparison look like in terms of actual numbers of respondents? We can find this out by converting Table 9.6 from percentages into (expected) frequencies, using the row totals: for example, 29.9% × 64 = 19.1. The results are shown in Table 9.7.

By comparing Table 9.7 with Table 9.4 we can see that 46 respondents with Class I occupations rated themselves as middle class, whereas one would have expected less than 20 (19.1) respondents to have done so if there was no underlying relationship between occupational class and self-rated class. Similarly, 258 respondents with Class III M occupations saw themselves as working class, compared to an expected figure of 209.6 if there was no underlying relationship. Comparing each figure in Table 9.7 with the corresponding figure in the original cross-tabulation (Table 9.4) gives the results in Table 9.8.

The differences in Table 9.8, which have been obtained by subtracting the frequencies that would have been *expected* if there was no underlying relationship from the *observed* frequencies, can be

Table 9.6   Expected percentages

| | Self-rated class | | |
Occupational class	Middle	Working	N
RGSC I	29.9	70.1	(64)
II	29.9	70.1	(322)
III NM	29.9	70.1	(329)
III M	29.9	70.1	(299)
IV	29.9	70.1	(243)
V	29.9	70.1	(101)
TOTAL	29.9	70.1	(1358)

Table 9.7 Expected frequencies

| Occupational class | Self-rated class | | |
	Middle	Working	TOTAL
RGSC I	19.1	44.9	64
II	96.3	225.7	322
III NM	98.4	230.6	329
III M	89.4	209.6	299
IV	72.6	170.4	243
V	30.2	70.8	101
TOTAL	406	952	1358

Table 9.8 Differences*

| Occupational class | Self-rated class | | |
	Middle	Working	TOTAL
RGSC I	26.9	−26.9	0
II	53.7	−53.7	0
III NM	7.6	−7.6	0
III M	−48.4	48.4	0
IV	−28.6	28.6	0
V	−11.2	11.2	0
TOTAL	0.0	0.0	

Note: (*) Observed frequencies minus expected frequencies.

viewed as a summary of the relationship between the two variables. The positive differences in the top left-hand quadrant of Table 9.8 indicate that more respondents with non-manual occupations rated themselves as middle class than would have been expected by chance. Conversely, the positive differences in the bottom right-hand quadrant show that more respondents with manual occupations rated themselves as working class than would have been expected by chance.

The differences in Table 9.8 also constitute the evidence provided by the sample of there being an underlying relationship in the population. In this context it is the existence and magnitude of the differences that matter, not whether they are positive or negative differences. If one decided to sum-

marise the differences in Table 9.8 to give an over-all measure of the evidence that there is a relationship, then summarising the differences by simply adding them all together would not work, as it is clear that the sum of the differences in Table 9.8 is zero, since the positive and negative differences in each row and column cancel each other out. Since a positive difference and a negative difference of the same magnitude provide the same amount of evidence of a relationship, a solution would appear to be to convert all the differences into positive values by simply ignoring the minus signs. However, for technical reasons, it turns out to be more appropriate to remove the minus signs by squaring all the differences, i.e. by multiplying each difference by itself, remembering that a negative value multiplied

Table 9.9   Squared differences

Occupational class	Self-rated class	
	Middle	Working
RGSC I	723.6	723.6
II	2883.7	2883.7
III NM	57.8	57.8
III M	2342.6	2342.6
IV	818.0	818.0
V	125.4	125.4

Table 9.10   Squared differences divided by expected frequencies

Occupational class	Self-rated class	
	Middle	Working
RGSC I	37.9	16.1
II	29.9	12.8
III NM	0.6	0.3
III M	26.2	11.2
IV	11.3	4.8
V	4.2	1.8

by a negative value gives a positive value. (In effect, this process of squaring places a greater emphasis on larger differences than on smaller differences.)

Table 9.9 shows the squared differences. At first sight, these could be added together to give a summary measure of the evidence of a relationship. However, we need to backtrack and think a little more about the differences in Table 9.8. There was an excess of 26.9 respondents with Class I occupations who saw themselves as middle class and an excess of 48.4 respondents with Class III M occupations who saw themselves as working class. However, the first of these two excesses relates to an expected figure of 19.1 and the second to an expected figure of 209.6. In other words, proportionally, the first excess is bigger than the second excess, since there were more than twice as many self-rated middle-class respondents with Class I occupations as would have been expected by chance ($46/19.1 = 2.41$), whereas there were less than a quarter too many self-rated working-class respondents with Class III M occupations ($258/209.6 = 1.23$). Sometimes proportional differences are more important than absolute differences: for example, a 'punch-up' between a group of five youths on one side and two youths on the other side seems rather more one-sided than a street fight between groups of 35 and 32 youths respectively! To take account of the importance of the proportional aspect of the differences, the squared differences in Table 9.9 can be divided by the expected frequencies in Table 9.7, giving the figures in Table 9.10.

Adding the figures in Table 9.10 together to give a summary measure of the evidence of a relationship results in a value of 157.1. To recap, we have:

- calculated the figures that we would have expected (on average) to have seen if there was no underlying relationship between the two variables (i.e. the **expected frequencies**)
- subtracted them from the figures that were actually obtained from the sample (i.e. the **observed frequencies**)
- squared the resulting differences to make them all positive
- divided the squared differences by the expected frequencies to take account of the importance of the proportional aspect of differences
- added the resulting values together to give a summary measure.

In fact, what we have in effect done is to implement the following formula, which is the formula for a **chi-square statistic** (as represented by the notation χ^2):

$$\chi^2 = \Sigma \frac{(O - E)^2}{E}$$

In the above formula, Σ stands for 'the sum of', O is an observed frequency and E is an expected frequency. Hopefully it is clear from the above discussion that the statistic generated by this formula is an intuitively sensible measure of the amount of evidence of a relationship provided by the data in Table 9.4. However, does a chi-square statistic of 157.1 provide enough evidence for one to conclude that there is an underlying relationship between occupational class and self-rated class? Could a value as big as 157.1 have occurred by chance if there was actually no underlying relationship?

The chi-square statistic and statistical significance

Before assessing whether the chi-square value obtained in the last section provides sufficient evidence for one to be able to conclude that there is an underlying relationship, we need to think a little more about the process via which the value was generated. At the final stage of this process, the 12 values in Table 9.10 were summed to give the chi-square statistic. If the table had had only three rows instead of six, we would have only added six values together. Unsurprisingly, therefore, chi-square statistics come in different varieties, or 'denominations', depending on the shape of the cross-tabulation being examined.

Common sense would seem to suggest that the chi-square statistic corresponding to Table 9.4 is of a '12-component' variety. However, looking at Table 9.8, it is clear that half of the differences which contribute to the chi-square statistic are 'mirror images' of the other half, i.e. each difference in the 'middle-class' column in Table 9.8 is paired with a difference of the same magnitude but with the opposite sign in the 'working-class' column. Furthermore, adding up the first five differences in the 'middle-class' column gives a total of 11.2, the 'mirror image' of the final value in the column. Thus, while there are twelve differences in Table 9.8, knowing the values of five of them enables one to work out the values of the remaining seven.

More generally, a chi-square statistic corresponding to a cross-tabulation with R rows and C columns is said to have $(R - 1) \times (C - 1)$ **degrees of freedom**. The number of degrees of freedom corresponds to the number of 'independent' differences contributing to the chi-square statistic, i.e. to the minimum number of differences which need to be specified before one can figure out all the remaining differences. Thus the chi-square statistic

calculated in the last section is an example of one with $(6 - 1) \times (2 - 1) = 5$ degrees of freedom.

Thus our example chi-square statistic has a value of 157.1 and has 5 degrees of freedom. But does this value constitute too much evidence of a relationship for it to have occurred by chance, i.e. is it plausible that a value of chi-square this big would have occurred (as a consequence of sampling error) if there was no underlying relationship between occupational class and self-rated class? This question can be answered by identifying what kinds of values of chi-square would have been likely to have occurred if there was no relationship. One way of doing this is to carry out a simulation corresponding to this hypothetical situation.

The following 100 chi-square values were obtained from cross-tabulations based on 100 random samples of 1358 people drawn from a hypothetical population in which 29.9% of people rated themselves as 'middle class' and 70.1% rated themselves as 'working class', and in which these figures were the same for each occupational class:

0.5	0.8	0.8	0.9	1.2	1.4	1.4	1.4
1.6	1.7	1.7	1.8	1.8	1.8	1.9	1.9
2.1	2.2	2.3	2.7	2.8	2.9	3.0	3.1
3.1	3.1	3.2	3.2	3.2	3.3	3.4	3.5
3.5	3.6	3.6	3.7	3.8	3.9	3.9	3.9
4.0	4.0	4.1	4.3	4.4	4.5	4.6	4.7
4.9	4.9	5.0	5.0	5.0	5.2	5.2	5.3
5.4	5.4	5.4	5.6	5.7	5.7	5.8	5.8
5.9	6.3	6.5	6.5	6.6	6.7	6.7	6.7
6.7	6.9	7.0	7.0	7.1	7.2	7.2	7.2
7.3	7.8	8.3	8.5	8.5	8.9	9.1	9.2
9.2	9.3	9.5	9.5	10.1	10.4	11.5	11.8
12.1	13.5	13.7	21.0				

Comparing 157.1 with the above set of values makes it very clear that the value of the chi-square statistic corresponding to Table 9.4 is much bigger than the kinds of values which are likely to have occurred by chance if there was no underlying relationship between occupational class and self-rated class. Given a choice between either (i) concluding

that there is no relationship, and that the unusually large value of the chi-square statistic is a coincidence, or (ii) concluding that there is a relationship, and that the large value of the chi-square statistic simply reflects this, it seems reasonable to opt for the latter conclusion.

As discussed in Chapter 3, it is standard practice to conclude that any observed relationship (in a sample) which is sufficiently strong that it would have occurred less than 5% of the time by chance provides significant evidence of a genuine relationship (in the population). The above 100 values suggest that in a situation where there are 5 degrees of freedom, chi-square values of more than about 12 happen by chance less than 5% of the time. The average (mean) of the 100 values is about 5.4, with a corresponding standard deviation of about 3.3. More generally, for a chi-square statistic with v degrees of freedom, the distribution of values occurring by chance (i.e. if there is no underlying relationship and the statistic simply reflects sampling error) has a mean of v and a standard deviation of $\sqrt{2v}$. The exact distributions of values for such **chi-square distributions** can in fact be derived mathematically (rather than approximated as in the above illustrative simulation). Furthermore, **critical values** for specified levels of significance – for example, values which are only exceeded 5% of the time – can be calculated exactly. For a chi-square statistic with 5 degrees of freedom, the critical value at the 5% level, which is only exceeded by chance 5% of the time, is in fact 11.07.

The conclusion of a formal statistical test focusing on the relationship between occupational class and self-rated class in Table 9.4 might thus be as follows:

The chi-square statistic corresponding to Table 9.4 is 157.1, which is greater than 11.07, the critical value at the 5% level of significance for a chi-square statistic with 5 degrees of freedom. Table 9.4 thus provides evidence of a statistically significant relationship between occupational class and self-rated class.

Critical values corresponding to chi-square statistics with various numbers of degrees of freedom and to different levels of significance (5%, 1%, 0.1%, etc.) are often presented in tables at the back of statistics texts (Appendix B of this text contains a limited number of critical values of this sort). However, statistical software such as SPSS for Windows calculates an exact level of significance, or **P-value** (see Chapter 3) to accompany each chi-square statistic. Hence, while one way to evaluate the significance of a chi-square statistic is to compare it with a relevant critical value or values, an alternative but equivalent approach is to look at its accompanying significance level or P-value. For the value of 157.1 calculated in the last section, the accompanying P-value (as generated by SPSS for Windows) is 0.00000, or 0.000%. In other words, the probability that a chi-square statistic as big as 157.1 would have occurred by chance (as a consequence of sampling error) is less than 0.00001, or one in a hundred thousand. Quoting a P-value is more satisfactory than simply comparing a chi-square statistic with the relevant critical values, because, for example, stating that a chi-square statistic is bigger than the relevant critical value at the 5% level of significance is equivalent to saying that $P < 0.05$, a much cruder assessment of the rarity of the value of the chi-square statistic than its exact P-value.

The statistical significance of a chi-square statistic (at the 5% level) can be established in two different but exactly equivalent ways: first, by seeing whether it is bigger than the relevant critical value at the 5% (0.05) level, and, second, by seeing whether its P-value, or significance level, is less than 0.05 (5%).

The limitations of the chi-square statistic

The use of chi-square statistics to test whether relationships in cross-tabulations are statistically significant (i.e. provide adequate evidence of the existence of relationships in the population) is often pivotal within social research involving categorical data. However, there is much more to analysing a cross-tabulation than just significance testing via the chi-square statistic; in addition, the chi-square statistic is not without its limitations. When looking at a cross-tabulation like Table 9.4, three related questions should come to mind:

- Is there (adequate) evidence of a relationship?
- How strong is the relationship?
- What is the form of the relationship?

The chi-square statistic usually allows us to answer the first of these questions, but does not help us much with the second and third questions. In other words, while there is little point in discussing the pattern visible in a cross-tabulation if a chi-square statistic has not been used to identify whether there is adequate evidence of a relationship in the population, such a significance test legitimates a discussion of the observed pattern but does not contribute to the analysis beyond this.

The third question can only be answered by looking at the various cells of a cross-tabulation in more detail: for example, using percentages (Table 9.5), or differences between observed and expected frequencies (Table 9.8). As will be shown in the next section, there may be a case for homing in on sub-tables, for example, to answer the question 'Does self-rated class vary between the manual occupational classes (IIIM, IV and V)?' The second question requires the use of a **measure of association**, i.e. a measure of the strength of the relationship between two variables, as opposed to a measure of the evidence for the existence of a relationship, such as the chi-square statistic. One such measure of association, Cramer's V, is introduced in a later section.

There are some situations in which the chi-square statistic is even limited in its ability to answer the first question properly. It should go without saying that the sample on which the cross-tabulation is based should ideally be random. However, problems also arise when one or more of

the expected frequencies, as in Table 9.7, (*not* the observed frequencies, as in Table 9.4) are small. Small expected frequencies can increase the likelihood of getting large chi-square values simply as a consequence of sampling error. Different texts give different rules of thumb, but the researcher should definitely be worried about the validity of the chi-square test if more than a fifth (20%) of the expected values are less than 5, and should also be worried about its validity if *any* of the expected values are less than 5 when the number of degrees of freedom is small, or if any values are less than 10 when there is only one degree of freedom, i.e. in the case of a 2×2 cross-tabulation (i.e. a cross-tabulation with two rows and two columns).

In general, the calculation of the chi-square statistic for a 2×2 cross-tabulation should arguably be adjusted using **Yates's correction for continuity**, which involves reducing the differences between the observed frequencies and the expected frequencies by 0.5 before squaring them, and which hence results in a smaller value than the unadjusted chi-square statistic. Yates's correction has also been proposed as a suitable response to the existence of expected frequencies of less than 5 (Walsh, 1990), but a more usual response to this is to reduce the size of the cross-tabulation by aggregating categories, though this needs to be done in a theoretically informed way if the cross-tabulation is not to be rendered less informative or even meaningless. Where small expected frequencies cannot be avoided in this way, the use of more precise **exact tests**, such as Fisher's exact test for 2×2 cross-tabulations, may be appropriate. The phrase 'exact test' also highlights why the expected frequency limitation of the chi-square statistic exists; the chi-square test is an approximation which is vulnerable when expected frequencies are small.

A less frequently mentioned limitation of the chi-square statistic, in the context of cross-tabulations with a medium-to-large number of rows and columns, relates to the way in which a large number of degrees of freedom can 'swamp' the evidence of a relationship. For example, consider a cross-tabulation (Table 9.11) of the occupational classes

Table 9.11   Occupational class by attitude to sex roles

Occupational class	Response				
	Strongly agree	Agree	Neither	Disagree	Strongly disagree
RGSC I	2	7	15	16	11
II	16	30	31	47	28
III NM	10	16	13	13	8
III M	27	47	51	44	17
IV	11	15	20	17	8
V	5	10	5	5	2

of male BSAS respondents against their responses to the statement 'A husband's job is to earn money; a wife's job is to look after the home and family':

The chi-square statistic corresponding to Table 9.11 has a value of 27.2 and 20 degrees of freedom (P = 0.131), and is thus not statistically significant.

However, the situation becomes rather different if Table 9.11 is collapsed into a 2 × 3 cross-tabulation:

	Agree	Neither	Disagree
RGSC I to III NM	81	59	123
RGSC IIIM to V	115	76	93

The value of the chi-square statistic for the collapsed version of the cross-tabulation is 11.4 and the statistic has 2 degrees of freedom, giving a *significant* P-value of 0.003. In other words, the process of collapsing Table 9.11 has revealed a significant relationship whose existence the chi-square statistic for the original cross-tabulation did not identify.

This analysis of Table 9.11 highlights the inability of the standard (Pearson) chi-square statistic to capitalise on the inherent ordinality of the two variables. An alternative variant of chi-square, named after Mantel and Haenszel, is more suited to testing for a relationship between two ordinal-level variables. This alternative statistic has a value of 17.2 for Table 9.11, with 1 degree of freedom and a corresponding P-value of 0.00003. However, the problematic 'swamping' effect of a large number

of degrees of freedom is not restricted to cross-tabulations based on ordinal variables. A possible general solution is to look at (theoretically meaningful) collapsed versions of large cross-tabulations, and perhaps also to look at relationships in specific parts of cross-tabulations. Both of these tactics are appropriate ways of getting to know cross-tabulated data better.

Examining cross-tabulations in more detail: Disaggregating chi-square

A rather crude summary of the relationship visible in Table 9.5 would be as follows:

As one moves down the occupational class hierarchy the probability of someone rating themselves as middle class decreases significantly.

However, this leaves open questions such as 'Does the probability of rating oneself as middle class vary significantly between different *non-manual* occupational classes?' and 'Does the probability of rating oneself as middle class vary significantly between different *manual* occupational classes?' Since the chi-square statistic calculated earlier relates to the whole of Table 9.4, these questions can only be answered by calculating separately chi-square statistics for the upper and lower halves of Table 9.4.

It can be seen from the chi-square statistics in Table 9.12, which both have 2 degrees of freedom

Table 9.12 Chi-square statistics for the two halves of Table 9.4

46	18			
150	172	$\chi^2 = 39.1$	2 d.f.	P = 0.00000
106	223			
41	258			
44	199	$\chi^2 = 2.5$	2 d.f.	P = 0.28303
19	82			

Table 9.13 Chi-square statistic for a collapsed version of Table 9.4

302	413	$\chi^2 = 108.5$	1 d.f.	P = 0.00000
104	539			

(d.f.), and from their accompanying P-values, that there are significant differences in self-rated class between the non-manual classes (P < 0.05), but that the differences in self-rated class between the manual classes are not significant (P > 0.05). It is reasonably clear from the percentages in Table 9.5 that there are differences in self-rated class between the non-manual classes taken collectively and the manual classes, but this can be confirmed by calculating the chi-square statistic for a collapsed version of Table 9.4, as shown in Table 9.13.

Note that the sum of the values of the three chi-square statistics calculated in this section is of a similar magnitude to the overall chi-square statistic for Table 9.4. This more focused examination of Table 9.4 can be viewed as a process of disaggregating the overall chi-square statistic, which seems primarily to reflect non-manual/manual occupational differences, and to a lesser extent internal differences between the non-manual occupational classes.

Measures of association: Cramer's *V* and the odds ratio

Measures of association are used to assess the strength of the relationship in a cross-tabulation.

There are many such measures, each of which has its own advantages and disadvantages (Walsh, 1990). The rationale for focusing on Cramer's *V* in this section is simply that Cramer's *V* is based on the chi-square statistic. However, we need to consider why the chi-square statistic itself is not a useful measure of the strength of the relationship in a cross-tabulation.

- First, if there is a relationship, chi-square depends on sample size, increasing as the sample size increases. However, while an increasing sample size should provide more evidence of any relationship, it should not affect the researcher's estimation of the strength of any relationship.
- Second, chi-square depends on the shape of the cross-tabulation, growing in magnitude as the numbers of rows and columns grow. A measure of relationship strength should clearly be independent of how large a cross-tabulation is, among other reasons because comparisons between different-shaped cross-tabulations are then appropriate.

Cramer's *V* is defined as follows:

$$V = \sqrt{\frac{\chi^2}{N(R-1)}}$$

where *N* is the sample size, and *R* is the smaller of the number of rows and the number of columns.

Cramer's *V* is thus an adjusted version of the chi-square statistic, with the adjustments taking account of the effects on the chi-square statistic of sample size and the shape of the cross-tabulation.

In fact, $N(R-1)$ is the maximum value that the chi-square statistic can take for a given cross-tabulation, and Cramer's *V* thus has a minimum of zero, corresponding to no evidence of a relationship, and a maximum of 1, corresponding to a 'perfect' relationship.

The value of Cramer's *V* corresponding to Table 9.4 is 0.340. Whether this constitutes a 'strong' relationship or a 'weak' one is a difficult question to answer, as 'strength' is a relative concept, and is established by comparisons or with reference to some kind of norm. The utility of Cramer's *V* is thus best demonstrated by comparing the values that it takes for two cross-tabulations. As noted earlier, BSAS respondents were asked to rate their parental social class in a similar way to the way that they rated their own class. A cross-tabulation of this parental class variable with self-rated class has a value of Cramer's *V* of 0.627. A comparison of the two values of Cramer's *V* indicates that self-rated class is more strongly related to the respondent's rating of their parental class than it is to their own occupational class. Arguably, this suggests that self-rated, 'subjective' class has more to do with cultural identity than socio-economic circumstances.

Another measure of association, which focuses on the strength of the relationship in a 2 × 2 cross-tabulation, is the **odds ratio**. Focusing on the collapsed 2 × 2 version of Table 9.4 used in the last section (Table 9.13), it can be seen that the odds of someone with a non-manual occupation rating themselves as working class as opposed to middle class are 413/302 or about 4 to 3. Conversely, the odds of someone with a manual occupation rating themselves as working class as opposed to middle class are 539/104, or about 5 to 1. The odds ratio is simply the ratio of these two sets of odds, i.e. (539/104)/(413/302) = 3.79. If there were no relationship, and the cross-tabulation had reflected this, then the two sets of odds would have been equal, and the odds ratio would have been 1.

More than one odds ratio is needed to summarise the relationship in a larger cross-tabulation; in fact the number of odds ratios needed is equal to the number of degrees of freedom of the chi-square statistic. For example, five odds ratios are needed to summarise the relationship in Table 9.4. Comparing RGSC I with each of the other occupational classes in turn gives the following set of odds ratios: 2.93, 5.38, 16.08, 11.56 and 11.03. Odds ratios are

thus not the best way of summarising the strengths of relationships in larger cross-tabulations, since a correspondingly large number of odds ratios is required. However, odds ratios are a structurally important feature of log-linear models, which are discussed later in this chapter.

Elaboration: cross-tabulations with more than two dimensions

The relationship between two variables may be interesting in itself, but it is often the case that a researcher's questions will necessitate their moving from a **bivariate analysis** (involving two variables) to a **multivariate analysis** (involving more than two variables). This process of **elaboration** can take a number of different forms depending on the nature of the research question. For example, if the starting point is the bivariate relationship between occupational class and self-rated class, three forms of elaboration corresponding to different types of research question are as follows:

- The introduction of a **prior** variable: 'Is the relationship between occupational class and self-rated class a reflection of the dependency of both variables on parental class?'
- The introduction of an **intervening** variable: 'Does occupational class determine economic rewards which in turn determine self-rated class?'
- The introduction of a third variable that **interacts** with the bivariate relationship: 'Is the relationship between occupational class and self-rated class the same for men as for women?'

The last of the above three questions gives us another opportunity to look at Cramer's *V* in action. Focusing for simplicity on Table 9.13, which has a value for Cramer's *V* of 0.284, we obtain the values in Table 9.14 when it is sub-divided by sex.

Looking at the chi-square statistics in Table 9.14 (which apply Yates's correction), it is clear from their P-values that the relationship between

Table 9.14   Chi-square statistics for Table 9.13 sub-divided by sex

Women	163	267			
	53	247	$\chi^2 = 33.8$	1 d.f.	P = 0.00000
Men	139	146			
	51	292	$\chi^2 = 83.2$	1 d.f.	P = 0.00000

occupational class and self-rated class exists separately for each sex. However, calculating Cramer's V gives values of 0.218 for women and 0.367 for men. (The corresponding odds ratios are also rather different, being 2.85 and 5.45 respectively.) Thus the relationship between occupational class and self-rated class appears weaker for women than for men.

As is often the case, there is more than one plausible hypothesis that could account for this difference. Supporters of the 'conventional', or 'malestream' view of women's social class (Goldthorpe, 1983) might argue that the self-rated classes of many of the women are likely to be dependent on the occupational classes of male partners, thus weakening the relationship with their own occupational classes. However, Registrar General's Social Class is not unproblematic (see Chapter 5), and it is possible that the above difference relates to its inadequacy as a schema when applied to occupations held by women. In particular, its treatment of women in routine non-manual occupations as homogeneous and occupationally advantaged may be problematic.

However, it is jumping the gun a little to start interpreting the above gender difference. While the two values of Cramer's V look rather different to each other, we have done nothing to show that the difference is not a coincidence. Perhaps the difference is just a reflection of the particular sample involved, i.e. a consequence of sampling error. In other words, we need as usual to answer the question 'Could it [i.e. the observed pattern or difference] have occurred by chance?' In order to answer this question we need to go beyond the comfortable and relatively unsophisticated world

of chi-square and use a log-linear model. Like some other statistical techniques which are seen by social researchers who lack quantitative expertise as advanced, log-linear models are in fact the most appropriate way of answering some relatively straightforward types of question: for example, in this case, 'Does the relationship between occupational class and self-rated class vary significantly in nature or strength according to gender?'

Modelling relationships within cross-tabulations: hierarchical log-linear models

Marsh (1988) and Gilbert (1993a) discuss how data analysis can be viewed as a process of fitting models to data. Researchers use theoretical ideas and specific hypotheses about the social world to build a model consisting of the relationships between concepts that their theorising suggests should or might exist. The next step is to identify what the data might typically have been expected to have looked like if the model were correct. These predicted or expected data are sometimes referred to as the fit of the model. The actual data will invariably differ to some extent from the predictions of the model; Marsh introduces the following formula:

Data = Fit [of model] + Residual

The 'Residual' part of the above equation corresponds to the inaccuracy of the model's predictions, i.e. the differences between the observed data and the expected data. The plausibility of the model is thus a function of the 'Residual' part of the equation. The smaller in magnitude it is, the better the model fits the data.

It can be seen that the chi-square analysis carried out earlier in this chapter is consistent with this model-fitting process. Specifically:

Table 9.4 = Table 9.7 + Table 9.8

The differences, or **residuals**, in Table 9.8, were in effect used to assess the fit of a model to the data. The way this was done was to calculate the chi-square statistic, which can thus be seen to be a measure of **goodness-of-fit**. But what was the nature of the model that was fitted? It was, in fact, a very basic model, often referred to as the **independence model**, which is based on the hypothesis that variables are unrelated.

The independence model and its obvious counterpart in this context, i.e. the model which specifies a relationship between occupational class and self-rated class, can both be described neatly using a notation introduced by Fienberg (1980). If occupational class is denoted by [O], self-rated class by [S], and the relationship, or interaction, between them by [OS], then the independence model is simply denoted by the following:

[O][S]

The above implies that the data in the cross-tabulation are simply a reflection of the distributions of respondents across the occupational and self-rated classes. Conversely, the alternative model is denoted by the following:

[OS]

The above implies that the data reflect both the distributions of respondents across the categories of the two variables and also an interaction, or relationship, between the variables.

The above notation becomes really useful in the context of cross-tabulations based on more than two variables. If we introduce sex/gender into the analysis, and denote it by [G], then for the three-way cross-tabulation of occupational class by self-rated class by sex there are various possible models, including the following three examples:

1 [O][S][G]
In this first model there are no relationships between any of the variables.
2 [OS][OG]
In this second model self-rated class is related to occupational class, and there is also a relationship between occupational class and sex.
3 [OSG]
In this third model the three variables interact with each other in a simultaneous and complex way: for example, the relationship between self-rated class and occupational class may vary according to sex.

Fienberg's notation can be used when a researcher applies **hierarchical log-linear models** to cross-tabulated data. The term 'log-linear' reflects the mathematical transformation underlying such models (specifically, a linear additive equation for such a model is obtained by transforming mathematically the two sides of a multiplicative equation by taking logarithms). The term 'hierarchical' relates to the way in which progressively more complex models can be obtained by the addition of a hierarchy of components, for example: [O], [OG], [OSG].

For example, the second of the example models listed above is further up the hierarchy of complexity than the first example model, because the former contains the additional components [OS] and [OG] corresponding to relationships between self-rated class and occupational class, and between occupational class and sex.

Within log-linear models relationships between variables are quantified in terms of odds ratios. The inclusion of a two-variable component, such as [OG], means that the odds ratios corresponding to the relationship between the two variables are allowed to vary in accordance with the data in the cross-tabulation, rather than being restricted to taking the value 1, which signifies no interaction (relationship). In the model [OS][OG][SG] the odds ratios corresponding to the interaction between occupational class and self-rated class are constrained to take the same values for each sex, whereas in the model [OSG] these odds ratios can vary according to sex. In general, the inclusion within or exclusion from the model of components is paralleled by the presence or absence of constraints on the values that can be taken by odds ratios.

The goodness-of-fit of log-linear models is usually assessed using a different form of chi-square statistic. So far we have been using **Pearson chi-square**, a long-established and straightforward measure. However, for log-linear models, the standard measure of goodness-of-fit is **likelihood ratio chi-square**, sometimes referred to as the model's **deviance**, which is calculated in a more complicated, but also more appropriate, fashion. While in the analysis of a two-way cross-tabulation the researcher's main question is usually 'Does the independence model fit or not?', in the analysis of higher-dimensional cross-tabulations the question is more typically 'Which model fits best?' Likelihood ratio chi-square statistics are used to identify a model that fits the data significantly better than any of the other models. Since different models are compared, the differences between the goodness-of-fit statistics for the various models are thus crucial.

Table 9.15 gives details of a number of different log-linear models fitted to Table 9.14. The first of the two columns of P-values shows whether the model in question fits the data. Where $P < 0.05$ in this column, there is a significant difference between the model and the data, i.e. the residual component of the observed data is unlikely to be a reflection of sampling error and to have occurred by chance. In other words, $P < 0.05$ indicates that there is some form of pattern in the observed data which the model does not account for. The second column of P-values compares pairs of models, with $P < 0.05$ in this column indicating that the more complex model fits the data significantly better than the preceding model. The deviance figures, to which the P-values correspond, are very similar to Pearson chi-square statistics: a large value in the first deviance column indicates poor goodness-of-fit, and a large value in the change in deviance column indicates a sizeable improvement in fit.

The most complex model of Table 9.14, [OSG], is a **saturated model**, which fits the observed data perfectly by definition, since it allows for all the possible relationships between the three variables. None of the other models in Table 9.15 fits the data properly. The [OSG] model also fits the data significantly better than the next most complex model, [OS][OG][SG]. The [OSG] model is therefore the most appropriate model of the cross-tabulation.

The superiority of the fit of the [OSG] model to the observed data confirms that the gender difference in the values of Cramer's V noted in the last section is unlikely to be a coincidence (reflecting sampling error), i.e. there is statistically significant evidence that the relationship between occupational class and self-rated class varies according to sex. However, the verification of the existence of complex interactions of this sort is not the only useful task that can be accomplished using log-linear models. Log-linear models can also enable a researcher to identify whether relationships

Table 9.15 Details of various log-linear models fitted to Table 9.14

Model	Deviance	d.f.	P	Change	d.f.	P
[O][S][G]	147.7	4	0.000			
[OS][G]	34.0	3	0.000	113.7	1	0.000
[OS][OG]	9.2	2	0.010	24.8	1	0.000
[OS][OG][SG]	6.0	1	0.014	3.2	1	0.076
[OSG]	0.0	0	1.000	6.0	1	0.014

Table 9.16 Parental class by party political identification

Parent's class	Conservative identifier	
	Yes	No
Middle	161 (51.6%)	151 (48.4%)
Working	365 (32.2%)	770 (67.8%)
$\chi^2 = 39.2$	1 d.f.	P = 0.00000

between variables persist when they **control** for other relevant variables, as will be shown in the example that follows.

Suppose that a researcher is interested in the effect of class background on party political identification. Cross-tabulating the rating of parental class used earlier against a (dichotomous) variable indicating whether BSAS respondents identified with the Conservative Party or not gives Table 9.16.

The relationship between Conservative identification and the rating of parental class is clearly statistically significant (P < 0.05). However, is this relationship simply a reflection of the respondent's own class, self-rated or otherwise? If log-linear models are applied to a four-way cross-tabulation defined by the above two variables (denoted by P and C), together with the respondent's self-rated and occupational classes (denoted by S and O), then the details of some relevant models are as shown in Table 9.17.

All three of the models detailed in Table 9.17 fit the observed data (P > 0.05). However, the third model, which contains the term [PC], corresponding to the interaction between parental class and Conservative identification, does not fit the data

significantly better than the second model, which does not include that term. The first model is, in fact, the best model, indicating via the inclusion of the [OSP] term that occupational class, self-rated class and parental class interact in a complex fashion, and also indicating via the inclusion of the [OC] and [SC] terms that Conservative identification is related both to occupational class and to self-rated class. The nature and form of these relationships need to be established by an examination of the four-way cross-tabulation, but an important point arising from the set of models in Table 9.17 is that once the researcher has controlled for occupational class and self-rated class, the parental class rating no longer has a significant effect on Conservative identification.

In conclusion, multivariate analyses using log-linear models allow us to answer a broader range of research questions than can be answered via straightforward chi-square analyses of two-way cross-tabulations:

- Log-linear models can be used to show whether the nature/strength of a relationship between two categorical variables varies significantly according to the value of a third categorical variable.
- Log-linear models can be used to show whether the relationship between two categorical variables can be explained in terms of their relationships to other categorical variables.

However, tests for the existence of relationships within cross-tabulations should always be complemented by descriptions of the nature and form of any relationships which have been shown to be statistically significant.

Table 9.17 Details of various log-linear models of a four-way table

Model	Deviance	d.f.	P	Change	d.f.	P
[OSP][OC][SC]	5.3	5	0.381			
[OSP][OSC]	3.2	4	0.521	2.1	1	0.150
[OSP][OSC][PC]	2.0	3	0.582	1.2	1	0.260

Interval-level variables: bivariate and multivariate analyses

We now move on from looking at cross-tabulated data to consider a broader range of statistical techniques applicable to analyses where one or more of the variables is interval-level. The sections that follow draw upon the material on sampling distributions in Chapter 3, and make use of some statistical terminology and formulae. However, the reader needs to recognise that the techniques discussed are, as was the case with chi-square, first and foremost sensible ways of addressing questions about differences and patterns within survey data.

Many of the statistical techniques used in analyses that involve interval-level variables require the researcher to think in terms of the dependence of one variable, the **dependent variable**, on one or more explanatory variables, the **independent variable(s)**. The choice of technique to be used depends to some extent on whether it is the dependent variable that is interval-level, or the independent variable(s), or both.

- If the dependent variable is interval-level and (each of) the independent variable(s) is nominal-level – for example, where a researcher is interested in the way in which age at marriage depends on ethnic group – then the most likely techniques to be used are the t-test and analysis of variance (ANOVA).
- If both the dependent and independent variables are interval-level – for example, where a researcher is interested in the dependence of daughter's age at marriage on mother's age at marriage – then the most usual techniques to be used are correlation and (linear) regression.
- If the dependent variable is a dichotomy (i.e. two categories) and one or more of the independent variables is interval-level – for example, where a researcher is interested in the dependence of separation or divorce on age at marriage – then a standard technique to use is logistic regression.

The choice of statistical technique to use is not, however, simply a question of the levels of measurement of the variables involved. Many of the most commonly used statistical techniques make assumptions about the distribution of values of the dependent variable in the population. Very often it is assumed that the values are **normally distributed** (see Chapter 3). Statistical techniques that make assumptions of this sort are referred to as **parametric**. In situations where assumptions fundamental to the validity of a statistical technique are clearly questionable, researchers should instead use a 'distribution-free' or **non-parametric** technique (Neave and Worthington, 1988; Siegel, 1956). However, parametric techniques are used more frequently than the non-parametric ones and the next few sections discuss the standard parametric techniques mentioned above.

Comparing means: the (two-sample) t-test

The examples used in this section, and in the sections that follow, are based on data from the ESRC-funded Social Change and Economic Life Initiative, or SCELI (see Gallie et al., 1994), and can be reproduced using data provided on the web pages corresponding to this book. Suppose that a researcher wishes to know whether there is a gender difference in the average (i.e. mean) age at marriage of graduates.

The mean ages at marriage according to sex of a random sample of graduates living in the Coventry area were found to be as follows:

Men $\quad (n_1 = 18)\quad \bar{x}_1 = 299.9$ months (24 years 11.9 months)
$s_1 = 33.5$ months

Women $(n_2 = 14)\quad \bar{x}_2 = 265.7$ months (22 years 1.7 months)
$s_2 = 40.1$ months

$\bar{x}$ is the sample mean, n is the sample size, and s is the sample standard deviation (see Chapter 3).

If the mean ages at marriage look surprisingly low to you, then bear in mind that in the past graduates used on average to marry at a rather earlier age than they do nowadays. The difference between the two sample means, 34.2 months (or nearly three years), appears, in substantive terms, to be large. But we still need to ask ourselves the usual statistical question, i.e. is such a difference likely to have occurred by chance (as a consequence of sampling error)? More specifically, we need to establish the range and distribution of values that we would obtain for the difference between the groups if we took a number of random samples from a (hypothetical) population in which the two means were identical. (In fact, rather than assessing the kinds of differences between sample means that would have occurred 'by chance', we instead convert the difference between the two means into a *t*-**statistic** and assess how likely a *t*-statistic of the observed magnitude would have been to have occurred 'by chance'.)

When using two sample means to assess whether the corresponding population means might be equal, there are three factors that the researcher needs to consider:

1 If the sample comes from a population in which the means for the two groups are equal, then it would be reasonable to expect the difference between the sample means to be fairly close to zero. Thus, the larger the difference between the two sample means, the more implausible it is that the two population means are equal.

2 Larger samples, on average, provide more accurate results. Thus the difference between the two sample means needs to be evaluated in the light of the sample size, as a larger sample is less likely to generate a difference of the observed magnitude, or greater, 'by chance' (i.e. as a consequence of sampling error).

3 The more variation that there is in the variable being measured, the more scope there is for variation in the sample means, and hence the more scope there is for variation in the differ-

ence between the sample means. In other words, the more 'noise' that there is in the variable being measured, the more likely it is that there will be a difference of the observed magnitude or greater between the sample means 'by chance'.

As implied in (3) above, the scope for variation in the difference between the sample means is dependent on the amount of variation in the variable being measured. The latter quantity is measured by the sample standard deviations. If the two groups are assumed to vary to the same degree in the population (i.e. to have the same population standard deviation), then the two sample standard deviations can be combined to give a single measure (estimate) of how much variation there is in the variable. The formula for this estimate is as follows:

$$s = \sqrt{\frac{(n_1 - 1)s_1^2 + (n_2 - 1)s_2^2}{(n_1 + n_2 - 2)}}$$

The above formula may look complex, but it in effect just calculates a weighted average of the variation in each of the groups. The estimated scope for variation in the difference between the sample means, i.e. **the standard error of the difference**, is dependent on the overall estimate of variation in the variable and on the sample sizes in the following way:

$$s_{\text{diff}} = s \sqrt{\frac{1}{n_1} + \frac{1}{n_2}}$$

The *t*-**statistic**, which is used to evaluate whether a given difference between two sample means is likely to have occurred by chance, and which takes into account all of the three factors listed above, is simply the difference between the means divided by the standard error of the difference:

$$t = \frac{\bar{x}_1 - \bar{x}_2}{s_{\text{diff}}}$$

For the example considered here the various quantities can be calculated as follows:

$$s = \sqrt{\frac{(18-1)(33.5)^2 + (14-1)(40.1)^2}{18+14-2}} = 36.5$$

$$s_{\text{diff}} = 36.5\sqrt{\frac{1}{18} + \frac{1}{14}} = 13.0$$

$$t = \frac{299.9 - 265.7}{13.0} = 2.63$$

Having calculated a t-statistic, we need to answer the questions 'What kind of values for the t-statistic typically occur by chance?' and hence 'Is it likely that a t-statistic of the observed magnitude (or greater) would have occurred by chance?' As was the case for the chi-square statistic discussed earlier in this chapter, we need to know what the distribution of t-statistic values occurring 'by chance' is. The relevant distribution for the t-statistic, given that we are prepared to assume that the variable being considered has a normal distribution (see Chapter 3) within each of the two groups (in the population), is the appropriately-named *t*-distribution.

If we are not prepared to make the above assumption (of normality), then the non-parametric Mann–Whitney U-test is preferable to the t-test. Similarly, if the assumption made earlier that the standard deviations of the two groups are the same is implausible, then a slightly different test is required. The assumption that the standard deviations are the same can, in fact, be tested formally (e.g. using Levene's test); in the example considered here the standard deviations do not differ significantly. However, the assumption that age at marriage among graduates is normally distributed (for each sex) is more problematic: for example, the distribution can be expected to be skewed to the right, since few students out of those graduating in their early twenties will be married yet, but there is no equivalent 'barrier' to marriage at higher ages.

Just as there were a number of different chi-square distributions, there are a number of different t-distributions, depending on the number of degrees of freedom that the t-statistic has. The number of degrees of freedom for a t-statistic in this

context is, in fact, $(n_1 + n_2 - 2)$. Degrees of freedom can be thought of as sources of variation; hence the number of degrees of freedom reflects the number of individuals in each group. The subtraction of 2 reflects the fact that, for each of the two groups, if we know the sample mean for the group and all but one of the values in the group, we can work out the remaining value.

t-distributions are similar in shape to the normal distribution (see Chapter 3 for a diagram), i.e. they are symmetric and approximately bell-shaped, but they have fatter tails and a slight flatter central 'bump'. In fact, as the number of degrees of freedom involved grows larger, the t-distribution becomes indistinguishable from the normal distribution. Thus, for very large sample sizes, the **critical value** of t (at the 5% level), which needs to be exceeded for the researcher to be able to conclude that the difference between the two sample means is statistically significant, is 1.96, the 'magic number' introduced in Chapter 3. In other words, for large samples from populations in which the two groups being compared have identical means, 95% of t-statistics are less than 1.96 (and greater than -1.96).

Critical values of t for t-statistics with smaller numbers of degrees of freedom are given in Appendix B. In the above example, where the statistic has 30 degrees of freedom, the critical value of t at the 5% level is a little bigger than 1.96, i.e. 2.04. The value of the t-statistic in our example, 2.63, is bigger than this, and it can thus be concluded that the average ages at marriage of male and female graduates are significantly different from each other. A t-statistic with 30 degrees of freedom and with a value of 2.63 has a corresponding P-value of 0.013, i.e. values of t as big as this would occur by chance (as a consequence of sampling error) on less than 2% of occasions.

Note that the above t-test is a two-tailed test (see Chapter 3); if we had wanted to test whether male graduates had a higher mean age at marriage than female graduates then we would have carried out a one-tailed test and hence would have used a different critical value.

t-tests are useful when we want to compare the means of two groups. However, if we want to compare the means of three or more groups – for example, to see whether ages at marriage differ between social classes – then, rather than carrying out a number of *t*-tests, we can compare all the means simultaneously using a technique discussed in the next section: analysis of variance. Note that carrying out a large number of *t*-tests involves a risk of spuriously significant results, as does carrying out a large number of significance tests more generally; it is important to realise that, on average, you only need to carry out 20 significance tests for one of them to be statistically significant 'by chance'.

Comparing means: analysis of variance

A number of related techniques come under the broad heading of **analysis of variance**; for the purposes of this book we are interested in the most basic variant; hence in this section it is one-way, between-subjects analysis of variance that is discussed. Central to the use of analysis of variance as a tool for identifying significant differences between group means are the concepts of **between-groups** and **within-group** variation, measured in the form of **sums of squares**. The first two terms are illustrated by the (hypothetical) example that follows.

Suppose that a researcher finds that in a small sample of male graduates the mean age at marriage is 28 years for those with a postgraduate qualification, but is 24 years for those without a postgraduate qualification. This difference between the two means could reflect rather different patterns of age at marriage in each of the two groups, as shown in the following scenarios:

Scenario 1:	*Ages at marriage*	*Mean*
Postgraduates:	27 27 27 28 28 28	28
	29 29 29	
Graduates:	23 23 23 24 24 24	24
	25 25 25	

Scenario 2:	*Ages at marriage*	*Mean*
Postgraduates:	20 22 24 26 28 30	28
	32 34 36	
Graduates:	20 21 22 23 24 25	24
	26 27 28	

The between-groups variation, i.e. the difference between the two means, is the same in each scenario. However, the within-group variation, i.e. the extent to which age at marriage varies within each group, is much greater in the second scenario. Perhaps more to the point, the first scenario provides stronger evidence than the second does of a relationship between whether or not an individual has a postgraduate qualification and age at marriage, because the ages at marriage of the two groups do not overlap in the first scenario. In other words, holding the amount of between-groups variation constant, a smaller amount of within-group variation seems to be linked to more convincing evidence of a genuine difference between the groups in the population. As will be shown below, analysis of variance tests whether the observed amount of between-groups variation is too great to have occurred by chance given the observed amount of within-group variation.

Analysis of variance can be used for comparisons of any number of means from two upwards, though it is perhaps more usual to use a *t*-test to compare two means. However, since both techniques can be used to compare two means, we can make use of the same example as analysed in the last section, this time looking at it in a rather different way.

The actual ages at marriage (in months) of the 18 male and 14 female graduates are as follows:

Men:	256	260	269	270	270	274
	282	285	289	295	313	314
	316	318	322	338	350	378

Women:	170	224	235	235	246	271
	276	282	283	284	290	292
	303	329				

The first value corresponding to a female graduate neatly reminds us of three laws of data analysis:

1 The researcher should look at their data in some detail before subjecting them to sophisticated analyses.

2 The researcher should be careful not to make unjustifiable assumptions about the origins of their data and the range of values which are valid (e.g. in this case the potentially false assumption that all married graduates living in the Coventry area were married in Britain at an age of at least 16).

3 The researcher needs to recognise that data analysis is a dirty business, and that there may be errors in the data that they are analysing.

In general, data analysts need to keep their eyes open for **outliers**, i.e. cases that appear distinctive relative to the other cases (Marsh, 1988: 107).

How can the researcher quantify the between-groups and the within-group variation? A sensible way of looking at within-group variation is to look at how much the values in each group differ from the relevant group mean. The first male value, 256, is 43.94 months less than the male mean of 299.94. The within-group variation for men could be quantified by summing the differences between each value and the mean. However, some of the differences are negative and some are positive, so (just as in the calculation of the standard deviation; see Chapter 3) in practice the squared differences are summed to produce a sum of squares.

The sum of squares for the men is thus:

$$(256 - 299.94)^2 + (260 - 299.94)^2 + \ldots + (350 - 299.94)^2 + (378 - 299.94)^2 = 19\,124.9$$

The sum of squares for the women is thus:

$$(170 - 265.71)^2 + (224 - 265.71)^2 + \ldots + (303 - 265.71)^2 + (329 - 265.71)^2 = 20\,884.9$$

Hence the overall within-group sum of squares is

$$19\,124.9 + 20\,884.9 = 40\,009.8$$

The between-groups sum of squares is calculated in a similar way, by comparing the means of each group with the overall mean (which in this case is 284.97 months), then squaring the resulting differ-ence, and then weighting each squared difference by the size of the relevant group.

The between-groups sum of squares in this case is thus:

$$[18 \times (299.94 - 284.97)^2] + [14 \times (265.71 - 284.97)^2] = 9227.2$$

Note that if the squared differences between each of the 32 values and the mean of all 32 values are summed, a value of 49 237.0 is obtained for the total sum of squares, a measure of the overall amount of variation in the data. Note that the three sums of squares are interrelated:

$$49\,237.0 = 40\,009.8 + 9227.2$$

i.e. the total sum of squares can be sub-divided into the within-group sum of squares and the between-groups sum of squares. In other words, the overall variation in the 32 values reflects a combination of variation within each of the two groups and variation between the two groups.

As was noted earlier, the evidence of a difference between the two groups is provided by the amount of variation between the groups (the between-groups sum of squares) relative to the amount of variation within the groups (the within-group sum of squares). However, the amount of between-groups variation is to some extent dependent on the number of groups being compared, and the amount of within-group variation is dependent on the number of cases within each of the groups. Thus, as was the case in chi-square tests and t-tests, the researcher needs to take account of the number of sources of variation, or **degrees of freedom**, involved. In the case of analysis of variance, since there are two amounts of variation, there are two sets of degrees of freedom. The value corresponding to the degrees of freedom of the between-groups sum of squares is $(n - 1)$, where n is the number of groups, and the value corresponding to the degrees of freedom of the within-group sum of squares is $(N - n)$, where N is the overall sample size. (The minor adjustments to the 'obvious' values, n and N, are needed because the number of sources of variation relates to the number of comparisons between groups or cases, which is always one less than the number of things that are being compared.)

Each of the sums of squares is divided by its number of degrees of freedom to give a **mean square** value (per source of variation). The resulting mean square values are compared to give an F-statistic. In other words, the calculation of the F-statistic is as follows:

$$F = \frac{\text{Between groups sum of squares}/(n-1)}{\text{Within group sum of squares}/(N-n)}$$

Thus, for the example considered here:

$$F = \frac{9227.2/(2-1)}{40009.8/(32-2)} = \frac{9227.2}{1333.7} = 6.92$$

The F-statistic can be used to answer the question 'Is it likely that the means would have been as different from each other as they are "by chance" (i.e. as a consequence of sampling error)?' The way in which this is achieved is by a comparison of the value of the F-statistic with the relevant F-distribution, which indicates the spread of values of F that would be expected to occur 'by chance'. If there is no underlying difference between the group means, then the value of F will on average be about 1. So is a value for F of 6.92 too big to have occurred 'by chance'? The critical value (at the 5% level of significance) of an F-statistic with 1 degree of freedom and with 30 degrees of freedom is 4.17. (See Appendix B for a list of critical values of F.) Hence it can be concluded from the above F-statistic that the mean ages at marriage of male and female graduates differ significantly.

In fact, an $F_{1,30}$ statistic with a value of 6.92 has a P-value of 0.013, i.e. a value as big as 6.92 would happen by chance on less than 2% of occasions. These figures may give you a sense of *déjà vu*, since you read something very similar in the last section. Specifically, the P-value for the t-statistic calculated in the last section was also 0.013. This is not a coincidence. Squaring the value of t, which was 2.63, gives a value of 6.92, i.e. the value of the F-statistic. Given that in this section and in the last section we have analysed the same data, it should be reassuring that we have obtained the same result! The two-

sample t-test and the F-test in the between-subjects one-way analysis of variance are, in effect, mathematically equivalent tests for a difference between two means.

Given this equivalence between the two techniques, it is unsurprising that the assumptions made by analysis of variance mirror those made by the t-test, i.e. both assume that the standard deviations of the groups being compared are the same (in the population), and also that the variable under consideration is normally distributed within each group.

The following application of analysis of variance involves a comparison between three groups, and looks at the way in which age at marriage depends on women's pre-marital occupational classes:

Occupational class	Mean age at marriage	Standard deviation	Sample size
RGSC I or II	286.0	54.1	45
RGSC IIINM	263.6	47.2	192
RGSC IIIM to V	259.2	42.1	183

	Sum of squares	d.f.	Mean square	F
Between groups	26 008.7	2	13 004.3	6.19
Within group	875 721.8	417	2100.1	
Total	901 730.5			

In this case the critical value of $F_{2,417}$ at the 5% level of significance is 3.00 and the P-value corresponding to the F-statistic of 6.19 is 0.002. Hence the ages at marriage of women vary significantly according to their pre-marital occupational classes ($P < 0.05$). However, is the difference between the second and third means, 263.6 and 259.2, too big to have occurred by chance? This specific difference needs to be examined separately (e.g. via a t-test), since analysis of variance has indicated that the three population means are not all the same, but has not indicated which of the means differ from each other. In fact, the second and third means do not differ significantly from each other ($t_{373} = 0.95$;

$P = 0.341 > 0.05$), suggesting that it is the first mean which is distinctive.

The relationship between two interval-level variables: correlation

The relationship between two interval-level variables is best visualised by plotting the pair of values for each case on a **scatterplot** or **scattergram**. Suppose that a researcher is interested in the potentially protective effects of economic resources on psychological well-being. Figure 9.1 displays, for a sample of 42 graduates living in the Coventry area, the relationship between household income and a measure of psychological well-being (specifically, a scale based on a four-item version of the GHQ, as described in Chapter 5). The scatterplot was produced using SPSS for Windows; where there was more than one case with a given pair of values, the values were adjusted slightly so that all the cases are visible on the plot. The spread of cases suggests that there may be a tendency for higher incomes to be associated with lower GHQ scores (i.e. with a greater degree of psychological well-being).

But could this observed pattern have occurred by chance, i.e. as a consequence of sampling error? The relationship visible in Figure 9.1 can be summarised and tested for significance using a (Pearson) **correlation coefficient**.

Let us consider the evidence of a relationship provided by some specific cases. One graduate has a household income of £375 and a GHQ score of 2. The mean income for the sample is £229.4, and the mean GHQ score is 3.36, so this graduate has a higher than average income and a lower than average GHQ score, thus providing some evidence of a negative relationship between the two variables. Another graduate has an income of £45 (below average) and a GHQ score of 10 (above average), hence providing additional evidence of a negative relationship. Conversely, a third graduate has an income of £110 (below average) and a GHQ score of 0 (below average), thus providing evidence of a positive relationship. Does the evidence of a negative relationship outweigh the evidence of a positive relationship? Is there conclusive evidence of any sort of relationship? The first step in calculating a correlation coefficient is to summarise the evidence provided by all the cases.

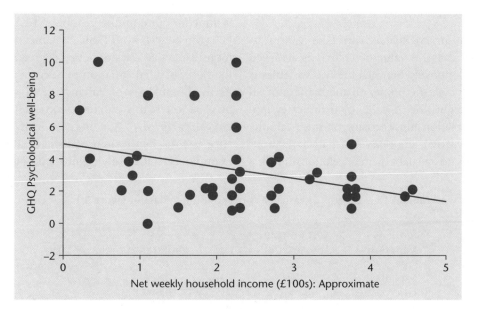

Figure 9.1 Scatterplot of well-being against income.

The evidence provided by the three graduates mentioned above can be quantified as follows:

$$(375 - 229.4) \times (2 - 3.36) = -198.0$$

$$(45 - 229.4) \times (10 - 3.36) = -1224.4$$

$$(110 - 229.4) \times (0 - 3.36) = 401.2$$

Repeating this approach to quantifying the evidence for all 42 cases, and summing the 42 values produced, gives a total of −3686.1. Thus overall, if anything, there is evidence of a negative relationship. However, the quantity of evidence needs to be adjusted to take account of the number of cases. Dividing the above total by $(n - 1)$, the number of cases minus 1, gives a quantity called the **covariance**, i.e. a measure of the extent to which the variables vary together. In this example the covariance is $-3686.1/(42 - 1) = -89.9$. However, the magnitude of the covariance depends on the amount of variation in each of the variables, as quantified by their standard deviations, which in this example are respectively £114.0 (income) and 2.46 (GHQ score). The correlation coefficient, r, is the result of dividing the covariance by the product of the two standard deviations; hence in this example:

$$r = \frac{-89.9}{114.0 \times 2.46} = -0.321$$

The correlation coefficient can take values of between −1 and 1. A value of −1 or 1 is achieved when the relationship between the two variables is perfect, i.e. when the points on the scatterplot all lie on a straight line. A value of 0 indicates that there is no relationship. Focusing on this example, a value of −0.321 indicates a negative relationship, but by no means a perfect relationship. Is a correlation coefficient with a value as big in magnitude as −0.321 likely to have occurred by chance (i.e. as a consequence of sampling error) if there is no underlying relationship?

In order to answer this question we need to make use of the fact that the square of the correlation coefficient, r^2 (r-squared), is a measure of the amount of variation in one of the variables explained by the second variable. In this example, $(-0.321)^2 = 0.103$ or 10.3%, so income explains just over a tenth of the variation in GHQ score. Is a value this big likely to have occurred by chance? This can be assessed by comparing the explained variation and the unexplained variation, in a way similar to the comparison of between-groups and within-group variation in the analysis of variance.

If 0.103 (10.3%) of the variation in GHQ score is explained by income, then 0.897 (89.7%) is left unexplained. In the above analysis, there is one source of explanation (i.e. income), hence the explained variation has 1 degree of freedom. There are 42 cases and hence 41 degrees of freedom (sources of variation) in total; hence the unexplained variation has 41 − 1 = 40 degrees of freedom. The mean explained variation per degree of freedom and the mean unexplained variation per degree of freedom can then be calculated, and this is done for our example in Table 9.18.

As can be seen from Table 9.18, there is markedly more explained variation per degree of freedom than unexplained variation per degree of freedom. As in the analysis of variance, an F-statistic can be used to test this difference for significance. The critical value of $F_{1,40}$ at the 5% level of significance is 4.08, hence the F-statistic of 4.59 for this example is statistically significant. (The P-value

Table 9.18   Analysis of variance corresponding to data in Figure 9.1

Variation	Proportion of variation	d.f.	Variation/d.f.	F
Explained	0.103	1	0.103	4.59
Unexplained	0.897	40	0.0224	
Total	1.000	41		

corresponding to the *F*-statistic is 0.038 < 0.05.) In essence, it is unlikely that income would have 'explained' as much of the variation in GHQ score as it has done if the two variables had been unrelated in the population. Hence the fact that income has explained significantly more than its 'fair share' of the variation in GHQ score (given its 1 degree of freedom) leads us to conclude that a relationship exists between income and GHQ score.

The correlation coefficient does not, however, tell us everything that we might want to know about the relationship between two interval-level variables. We know from the above analysis that the relationship between income and GHQ score is significant and negative, but as yet we have not quantified the magnitude of the effect of income on GHQ score. How much of a reduction in GHQ score does an extra £100 per week generate on average? The technique that can be used to answer this sort of question is **regression**.

The relationship between two interval-level variables: regression

Regression, like analysis of variance, comes in different forms: the standard form of regression, as outlined below, is **Ordinary Least Squares (OLS)** linear regression, which minimises the squared distances between the cases and a straight line, as described below.

Looking again at Figure 9.1, it can be seen that a (straight) line has been drawn across the scatterplot. Linear regression involves fitting a straight line to the plotted data, the line chosen being the one that best summarises the positions of the various cases. But why is the straight line in Figure 9.1 a better summary of the data than a line which is marginally steeper or shallower, or a line which is a millimetre or two further up or down the page?

In fact the straight line in Figure 9.1 has been chosen in such a way as to minimise the sum of the squares of the vertical distances between the line and the positions of the various cases. This sum of squares is, if you think about it, a measure of that part of the variation in the GHQ scores which is not explained by the regression line. The vertical distances between the positions of the cases and the regression line are **residuals** (i.e. differences from the 'predictions' of the regression line); hence the sum of squares is referred to as the **residual sum of squares**.

Straight lines can be represented by formulae of the form $y = mx + c$, where y is the variable corresponding to a scatterplot's vertical axis (or *y*-axis), x is the variable corresponding to a scatterplot's horizontal axis (or *x*-axis), m is a measure of the slope of the line, and c is a constant value. Thus, in this example, the regression line can be represented by the following formula:

$$GHQ = (-0.69 \times income) + 4.94$$

The **constant term**, 4.94, is the regression line's prediction of what the GHQ score for an individual with zero income would be. The **slope** of the line, −0.69, is the change in GHQ score that the regression line indicates is consistent with an extra unit of income, i.e. an extra £100. Note that this value, or coefficient, for the slope is often labelled as *B*. The above formula can be used to predict the typical GHQ score that a graduate with a given income would be expected to have: for example, an income of £300 pounds would generate a predicted GHQ score of $(-0.69 \times 3) + 4.94 = 2.87$.

Descriptions of regression analyses usually involve more information than is contained in the above formula. Such descriptions typically include a measure of the proportion of the variation in the dependent variable which is explained by the regression line. For this example, the relevant value is 0.103. Note that this is the value of *r*-squared generated earlier from the correlation coefficient.

Links between correlation, regression and other techniques

The correlation coefficient and OLS linear regression (involving two variables) are, in fact, linked mathematically, and the proportion of variation in the dependent variable explained by the regression line is indeed r-squared, the square of the correlation coefficient. The F-test of the squared correlation coefficient, as outlined earlier, can alternatively be viewed as a test of whether the independent variable in a (bivariate) regression analysis has a significant effect on the dependent variable.

Furthermore, the slope of the regression line, B, is usually accompanied by a t-statistic. In our example, the t-statistic corresponding to the slope of −0.69 is −2.142, which is statistically significant, with a P-value of 0.038. This is the same P-value as that in the earlier test of the correlation coefficient for significance, and $(−2.142)^2 = 4.59$, the value of the F-statistic corresponding to that test. The t-statistic corresponding to B is thus an alternative way of checking whether the variable in question has a significant effect on the dependent variable.

Regression also has fundamental similarities to the two-sample t-test and the analysis of variance. This can be seen if we revisit our earlier example of the ages at marriage of male and female graduates, to which we applied both these techniques. The data for this example can also be analysed using regression, since, as we noted earlier, a dichotomous categorical variable can also be viewed as an interval-level variable. If we carry out a regression analysis with age at marriage as the dependent variable and sex as the independent variable (coded as Male = 0 and Female = 1), then we obtain the results in Table 9.19.

If you look back to the analyses earlier in this chapter you will find that all the regression-related figures in Table 9.19 occurred within either the t-test or the analysis of variance (the value of r-squared, 0.187, is the ratio of the between-groups variation to the overall variation in the latter). In fact, all of the techniques relating to interval-level variables discussed above belong to a family of statistical models known as **generalised linear models** (see Lindsey, 1995; Dobson, 1990), as do log-linear models. Underlying similarities between the techniques should thus, perhaps, be unsurprising.

As was the case for the t-test and the analysis of variance described earlier, the validity of OLS linear regression rests on a number of assumptions:

- Crucially, a straight-line relationship is assumed to exist between the variables. This assumption is not always reasonable: for example, at younger ages, income may on average rise with increasing age, but it may remain relatively constant (or even fall) at older ages. Such a relationship is more **curvilinear** than linear.

- Regression also involves the assumption that the residuals (i.e. the vertical distance for each case between the value of the dependent variable and the regression line) are normally distributed.

- Finally, regression assumes that the amount of variation in the dependent variable is the same for all values of the independent variable (**homoscedasticity**).

These assumptions parallel those made by the t-test and the analysis of variance. Problems of non-linearity, non-normally distributed residuals and **heteroscedasticity** (the opposite of homoscedasticity) can sometimes be resolved by **transforming** the data: for example, by using the logarithm of the dependent variable instead of the variable in its original form (see Marsh, 1988).

Table 9.19 Ages at marriage of male and female graduates

Regression line:	AGE = (−34.2 × SEX) + 299.9
	t-statistic corresponding to B of −34.2 = −2.63 (P = 0.013)
Variation explained:	r-squared = 0.187
	$(F_{1,30} = 6.92; P = 0.013)$

Multiple regression

Bivariate regression, as discussed above, is both a way of looking at how much of the variation in a dependent variable is explained by a single independent variable and also a way of quantifying the effect of the independent variable on the dependent variable. However, since the researcher is often interested in explaining as much of the variation in the dependent variable as they can, and is also usually interested in the effects of more than one independent variable on the dependent variable, **multiple regression**, i.e. regression involving two or more independent, explanatory variables, is usually used.

Suppose that the researcher felt that the protective effect of household income on GHQ score identified earlier might be related to graduates' lifestyles and economic resources more generally. Another variable which relates to lifestyle and resources is housing situation. Might being an owner-occupier also have a protective effect on the psychological well-being of graduates living within a 'nation of people who desire home ownership'?

A multiple regression of GHQ score on both household income and housing situation (coded as 1 = Owner occupation and 0 = Other) generated the results in Table 9.20 for the sample of graduates.

The value of B corresponding to household income has decreased in magnitude from −0.69 to −0.47, and is no longer statistically significant ($P = 0.139 > 0.05$). The value of B corresponding to housing situation is, however, statistically significant. Being an owner-occupier thus has a significant protective effect on psychological well-being (reducing GHQ score on average by nearly two points).

Multiple regression allows the researcher to look at the effect of one variable **controlling for** the effects of other variables. In this example, an overlap between the effects of housing situation and of household income means that the effect of income, net of the effect of housing situation, is not statistically significant. The researcher, therefore, cannot safely conclude that income has an independent effect on psychological well-being (though it is possible that such an effect exists but that the sample of 42 graduates is too small to verify its existence).

Note that a **partial correlation** is a measure of the strength of the relationship between two variables once one or more other variables have been controlled for. Hinton (1995) discusses the relationship between partial correlations and the r-squared value for a multiple regression.

The results from a series of linked multiple regressions can sometimes be put together to form a **path analysis**. For example, consider the relationship between someone's current occupation and their parents' occupations. The path from class origin to class destination proceeds via type of school, educational performance, first job, etc. To complement a regression analysis with current occupation as the dependent variable, each of these intermediate stages can be used as the dependent variable within a separate regression analysis. When presented in combination, the results from the various regression analyses can then be used to give an idea of the roles and the relative importance of the various factors affecting the social mobility process. (For a more detailed example see Reid, 1987: 137.)

Table 9.20 The psychological well-being of graduates

Regression line:	GHQ = (−0.47 × income) + (−1.95 × housing) + 5.74
	t-statistic corresponding to B of −0.47 = −1.51 (P = 0.139)
	t-statistic corresponding to B of −1.95 = −2.60 (P = 0.013)
Variation explained:	r-squared = 0.236
	($F_{2,39} = 6.01$; P = 0.005)

Logistic regression

Many interesting research questions involve a dichotomous or **binary** dependent variable. For example, a researcher might be interested in identifying the factors that have led to some people becoming graduates rather than others. Since, as noted earlier, any variable with two categories can be treated as an interval-level variable, a binary variable can in theory be used as the dependent variable within a standard linear regression analysis. However, such an analysis would have a number of major flaws, not the least of these being that the assumption that the residuals were normally distributed would inevitably be false.

Logistic regression is a technique which has as much in common with log-linear models as it does with standard linear regression, and which is more appropriate than conventional regression in analyses where there is a binary dependent variable. Suppose that we are interested in who becomes a graduate. Instead of focusing on the probability, p, of somebody becoming a graduate, logistic regression focuses on the odds, $p/(1 - p)$, of them becoming a graduate. However, if we are interested in the way in which explanatory factors such as school qualifications may double or halve the odds of becoming a graduate, then we are concerned with multiplicative effects, rather than additive effects like those found in a linear regression equation. On the other hand, additive models are arguably easier to grasp, and logistic regression allows us to focus on the odds of becoming a graduate within an additive framework by focusing on the logarithm of the odds. Thus the equation for a logistic regression involving one independent variable, x, is:

$$\log\left[\frac{p}{1 - p}\right] = mx + c$$

The transformation of p into $\log [p/(1 - p)]$ is called the **logistic transformation**. $\log [p/(1 - p)]$ is also sometimes referred to as the **logit** of p. The effect of a change of one unit in the independent variable, x, is to multiply the odds, $p/(1 - p)$, by e^m

(i.e. m exponentiated, where **exponentiation** is the reverse of taking logarithms).

Suppose that we are interested in the effect of age at (first) marriage (in months) on whether or not somebody has separated or divorced within the first 10 years of marriage. If d is the probability of separation or divorce, the results of a logistic regression analysis, using the SCELI sample of Coventry adults, are as follows:

$$\log [d/(1 - d)] = (-0.0112 \times \text{age at marriage}) + 0.613$$

The P-value corresponding to the B coefficient (-0.0112) is 0.0046. Since $P < 0.05$, the effect of age at marriage on the probability of separation or divorce is statistically significant. Suppose that we wish to compare the odds of separation or divorce of two people who at marriage were aged 20 and 30 respectively.

$$30 - 20 = 10 \text{ years, or } 120 \text{ months}$$

$$-0.0112 \times 120 \text{ months} = -1.34$$

$$e^{-1.34} = 0.262$$

Thus the odds of the second person having separated or divorced are only about a quarter (i.e. 0.262) of the odds of the first person having separated or divorced. The actual predicted odds of separation or divorce for the two people are about 8:1 against and 31:1 against respectively. These odds of separation or divorce may appear quite low, but note that most of the SCELI respondents married when separation or divorce early in marriage was very much the exception.

Data analysis using SPSS for Windows: relevant material on the web pages corresponding to this book

The analyses used as examples in the preceding sections of this chapter were all carried out using SPSS for Windows, and can be duplicated using the instructions and data provided on the web pages corresponding to this text. Alternatively, the techniques discussed in this chapter and the SPSS data files on the web pages can be used to carry out exciting new analyses of your own. For further details of the implementation of the various techniques within SPSS for Windows, see Bryman and Cramer (1997), Fielding and Gilbert (2000), or the various SPSS user manuals (Norusis, 1994a; 1994b).

Discussing findings from statistical analyses: some words of warning

Carrying out statistical analyses can be an exciting activity, and students and researchers can sometimes become so engrossed in the practicalities of quantitative data analysis that they lose sight of the assumptions that they have made, of the limitations of their analyses, and of the theoretical relevance of what they are doing. The following points, which to some extent echo issues discussed in Chapters 3 and 5, are worth bearing in mind:

- A statistically significant finding is not necessarily a substantively significant or theoretically interesting finding. For example, a small but statistically significant difference may not be large enough to be of substantive importance. Similarly, the fact that there is conclusive evidence of a relationship between two variables does not in itself mean that the relationship is relevant or worth discussing.

- Statistical findings do not 'speak for themselves': they are only as relevant and convincing as the interpretations that are made of them and the explanations of them that are provided by the researcher.

- Correlation is not causation: the causal direction of an observed relationship may in fact be the opposite of what is assumed within a statistical model.

- Variables are indicators of concepts, rather than being the concepts themselves, and there is no guarantee that the variables used in a statistical analysis are valid indicators of the concepts of interest.

- It is an intrinsic feature of statistical inference that statistically significant findings (at a given level of significance, such as 5%) are occasionally coincidences (i.e. 5% of the time). A large number of statistical tests will inevitably generate an occasional 'significant' result which is, in fact, not a reflection of a genuine underlying relationship or effect.

- Conversely, a relationship which an analysis does not show to be statistically significant may nevertheless be a substantively significant relationship which, however, is not strong enough to be identified as existing, given the sample size involved in the analysis.

- The scope for generalisation is constrained by the fact that statistical analyses are in general based on samples collected at specific times and in specific places from specific groups of respondents. For example, the relevance to the adult population of contemporary Britain of generalisations based on findings relating to graduates living in the Coventry area in 1986 needs to be carefully assessed by the researcher.

- The assumptions that need to be correct for statistical analyses to be strictly valid are usually false. Non-response undermines the randomness of samples, and social phenomena are not, on the whole, precisely normally distributed. While in practice flawed assumptions are not necessarily fatal, researchers should not be complacent about their effects.

- Findings from a multivariate analysis are likely to rest on much more solid foundations if the researcher has 'got to know' their data beforehand, i.e. has started by looking at the frequencies for each of the variables involved and has built up to the multivariate analysis in a step-by-step fashion, rather than simply bunging a dependent variable and umpteen explanatory variables straight into a multiple regression!

A good discussion of the results of a statistical analysis thus locates the findings within a plausible theoretical account and reflects on the limitations of the analysis and the assumptions made within it, demonstrating the relevance and robustness of the findings while remaining suitably cautious and qualified in its conclusions.

Further reading

Analysing cross-tabulations

Many social statistics texts (e.g. Hays, 1973; Reid, 1987) contain technical descriptions of the chi-square statistic; good material on the practicalities of data analysis and data presentation in the context of cross-tabulations is less common. Marsh (1988) contains interesting material on data analysis but does not cover the chi-square statistic and significance testing. Walsh (1990) contains relevant chapters on chi-square tests, measures of association and elaboration. Discussions of partitioning (disaggregating) chi-square can be found in Everitt (1992) and Blalock (1981). A description of how to enter published cross-tabulations into SPSS for Windows, and analyse them using chi-square, is given by Kinnear and Gray (1994: 163–168).

Discussions of log-linear models have until recently been confined to advanced texts. Gilbert (1993a) focuses exclusively on analysing tabular data and includes a discussion of log-linear models. In addition to Fienberg's classic book (1980), rather more technical accounts of log-linear models than the one given here can also be found in Rose and Sullivan (1996), Lindsey (1995) and Loether and McTavish (1993). Fielding and Gilbert (2000) provides a brief technical account accompanied by details of log-linear modelling using SPSS for Windows.

Analyses involving interval-level variables

Most of the material in the sections focusing on analyses involving interval-level variables is covered in some detail by Walsh (1990), Wright (1997), Hinton (1995) and many other texts. More

specifically, Loether and McTavish (1993) contains a good, broad account of multiple regression and path analysis, and there is a chapter on logistic regression in Gilbert (1993a). More detailed material on regression can be found in Lewis-Beck (1993) and Draper and Smith (1981), and path analysis is well described in Asher (1976). For a more general, technical overview of the analysis of binary data see Cox and Snell (1989). Material on the relationship between experimental design and statistical techniques, which this book does not have the scope to cover, can be found in John (1977).

It is important to have a good grasp of basic statistical ideas such as sampling distributions and significance testing before tackling the relevant material in the above references, so it may be worth the reader first consolidating their knowledge of such material via an accessible text such as Rowntree (1981) or Reid (1987).

Describing and summarising data

The emphasis of this chapter has very much been on statistical testing and inference. However, exploring and graphing data are also important tasks for the researcher. Material on graphing data can be found in Loether and McTavish (1993: Chapter 4), Henry (1995) and Tufte (1983). In addition, Chapman and Wykes (1996) is a very useful guide to presenting data in tabular and graphical form. There are a number of texts (e.g. Marsh, 1988; Erickson and Nosanchuk, 1992) which have been influenced by Tukey's Exploratory Data Analysis (EDA: Tukey, 1977), an approach which places a strong emphasis on the visual display of data. Marsh's text also contains advice on the presentation of tables and on effective plotting. Finally, Huff (1954) is the classic text on misleading statistics and displays. Statistical software such as SPSS for Windows can be used to produce a range of graphical displays.

In this chapter and in Chapter 3 we have seen how data can be summarised using means, standard deviations, percentages, measures of association (such as Cramer's V and the odds ratio), and correlation coefficients. However, some social research topics involve data that are best summarised in some other way: for example, using indices, rates and ratios, or other more specialised measures. Horn (1993) discusses a range of statistical measures relevant to the social sciences.

In some situations a researcher will need to summarise the information contained in a number of related variables. The construction of scales was discussed in Chapter 5. However, information from a single variable can also sometimes be summarised in a more appropriate fashion than via the standard measures of location and spread. For example, a common summary measure of inequality with respect to an interval-level variable, such as income, is the **Gini coefficient**. Marsh (1988) discusses both a good example of a composite score (the Retail Prices Index) and the derivation of the Gini coefficient.

Demographic research, with its emphasis on mortality and fertility, has generated a range of useful aggregate measures (Pressat, 1978; Pollard *et al.*, 1981; Hinde, 1998). One of these, the **standardised mortality ratio (SMR)**, is in effect a death rate adjusted to control for a third variable, age (see Marsh, 1988, for discussions of the SMR and of standardisation more broadly). Another important demographic method for summarising and displaying data is the **life table**. The life table summarises both death rates at different ages and also the way in which a population experiencing those rates diminishes in size as it ages. As will be discussed further in the next section, demographic measures and methods relating to mortality can be used in the analysis of any social process which can be viewed as a 'survival' process.

Advanced statistical techniques and related literature

This section mentions briefly a wide range of techniques and issues within social statistics. It is useful for researchers to be aware of these techniques and issues, partly because they may on occasions wish to use the techniques themselves, but primarily because analyses using such techniques may be an important feature of the literature in their substantive research areas. Many techniques are discussed in a relatively accessible way within a series of short papers, published by Sage, on Quantitative Applications in the Social Sciences (QASS).

A range of sophisticated techniques can be implemented using standard statistical software such as SPSS for Windows. (Examples of analyses using SPSS for Windows to apply some of the techniques discussed below can be carried out using the instructions and data provided on the web pages corresponding to this book; the techniques are described in more detail in the various SPSS manuals.) It is worth, however, noting that there are a range of other statistical software packages available, some of which are more flexible than SPSS for Windows and thus better suited to the fitting of relatively unusual and sophisticated statistical models, and some of which are dedicated to specific types of model. For example, researchers fitting models belonging to the GLM (Generalized Linear Model) family, such as log-linear models, often use a software package called GLIM (see Healy, 1988; Aitkin *et al.*, 1989). Minitab, another statistical package commonly used for teaching purposes, can be used to implement a more limited range of techniques (Bryman and Cramer, 1996).

Many advanced techniques are similar to techniques discussed earlier in this chapter. A technique that can be viewed as an extension of both analysis of variance and regression is **analysis of covariance (ANCOVA)**. This technique, like analysis of variance, allows the researcher to compare the means of a variable for different groups, but ANCOVA also allows the researcher to control for the effects of variation between the groups with respect to other, interval-level variables which affect the dependent variable (see Anderson *et al.*, 1980). Another extension of correlation and regression is **canonical correlation analysis**, in which a pair of indices is constructed from two sets of interval-level variables in such a way that the correlation between the indices is maximised.

While canonical correlation analyses are relatively unusual, many frequently used and interesting techniques fall under the same broad heading of **multivariate analysis**. A good overview of many of these techniques is provided by Everitt and Dunn (1991); alternative, relatively technical accounts are given by Manly (1986) and Chatfield and Collins (1980). One of these techniques, **cluster analysis** (Everitt, 1993), can be used to develop typologies by classifying cases into relatively homogeneous groups according to their values on a range of variables. Another multivariate technique, **discriminant analysis**, uses differences between the characteristics of members of different groups to develop a procedure for predicting group membership. Hence in discriminant analysis a dependent variable (group membership) is analysed in relation to a number of independent variables (predictors of group membership). Kinnear and Gray (1994) illustrate the implementation of this technique with SPSS for Windows.

Bailey *et al.* (2000) discuss how cluster analysis, applied to data from the 1991 Census relating to 37 socio-economic and demographic variables, has been used to classify the local authorities of Great Britain into groups containing 'similar' authorities. This classification is useful, for example, to researchers who wish to compare areas which are similar in socio-economic and demographic terms.

A number of multivariate analysis techniques are geared towards uncovering the underlying structure of a set of related variables, or of a cross-tabulation. **Principal components analysis** and **factor analysis** are both oriented towards identifying the common dimension or dimensions underlying a set of interval-level variables. For example, if a researcher wishes to use a set of questionnaire items to produce a scale (see Chapter 5), then ideally the items will tap a single underlying dimension (the concept of interest). However, children's marks on a series of school examinations may reflect a number of distinct underlying dimensions (hard work, writing ability, numeracy, etc.). Principal components analysis and factor analysis allow the researcher to assess how many important underlying dimensions there are. Note that such techniques identify empirically important underlying dimensions; the substantive meaning of the dimensions identified relies on the researcher's interpretations. Walsh (1990) contains a brief discussion of factor analysis; Kinnear and Gray (1994) and Bryman and Cramer (1997) illustrate how it can be implemented with SPSS for Windows.

Fraser (1994) uses factor analysis to analyse data on 15 human rights indicators for 82 countries, and identifies five underlying human rights dimensions, relating, among other things, to political rights, constitutional rights, and social and economic rights.

Two techniques which generate 'maps' showing which cases, or which categories of respondent, are 'close' to each other, and which are 'further apart', are **multidimensional scaling** and **correspondence analysis**. Multidimensional scaling (Coxon, 1982) generates a map from a matrix of distances. When cases are being compared, these distances are calculated using the values for each pair of cases of a range of variables. When categories are being compared, the matrix is derived via the calculation of distances between the rows and/or between the columns of a cross-tabulation. In the correspondence analysis of a contingency table (Weller and Romney, 1990), the results of the analysis relate to the relative positions of the categories on underlying dimensions, which once again are derived from distances between the cross-tabulation's rows and/or columns, this time implicitly. Multidimensional scaling has been used to generate the values for each occupation on the Cambridge Scale used in social stratification research (Prandy, 1990; see Chapter 5).

Ennis (1992) and Cappell and Guterbock (1992) both use multidimensional scaling, applied to categorical data relating to the joint areas of interest of members of the American Sociological Association, to produce 'maps' of the relationships between sociological sub-fields. (Perhaps unsurprisingly, 'demography' and 'ethnomethodology' lie at opposite extremes of one of these maps, implying that few US sociologists are interested in both these areas!)

Correspondence analysis has similarities to various ordinal models that have been used to look at the relationship within a cross-tabulation by relating the relationship to one or more underlying dimensions. For example, the relationship between husbands' and wives' educational levels can be modelled in terms of the spouses' positions on an underlying educational dimension. Gilbert (1993a) discusses such models, and also discusses the way in which the association in cross-tabulations can be modelled using theoretically generated **topological models**. For a more extensive discussion of ordinal models of cross-tabulations, see Clogg and Shihadeh (1994); for a general discussion of the modelling of relationships within cross-tabulations, see Agresti (1990).

Some of the techniques discussed above – for example, factor analysis – are based on the assumption that there are theoretically relevant **latent variables** which have not been measured explicitly but which underlie the observed data. A technique known as **structural equation modelling**, or as the **LISREL** approach, developed among others by Jöreskog, involves regression-like analyses where one or more of the variables involved are latent variables (Saris and Stronkhorst, 1984). Models involving categorical latent variables have also been developed (Everitt, 1984).

Burholt and Wenger (1998) use a **latent class analysis**, applied to four-way cross-tabulations based on indicators of intergenerational solidarity, to identify a two-class typology of older peoples' relationships with their children and siblings (the classes being labelled 'close knit' and 'loose knit' by the authors).

In recent years there has been an increasing interest in social research utilising techniques for examining change over time (e.g. Dale and Davies, 1994). Research on **time series** (Chatfield, 1996) has long been the focus of much economic research, and log-linear models are often used to examine social trends (Payne et al., 1994). However, more interesting to many social researchers, partly because of a growing emphasis on longitudinal data (see Chapter 2), are the techniques that have been developed in the area of **event history analysis** (Allison, 1984; Tuma, 1994). Such techniques are used extensively in socio-demographic research, wherein **survival analyses** (e.g. the analysis of first-marriage durations) and analyses of series of events (e.g. births) are common. Such techniques include extensions of logistic regression (Gilbert, 1993a) and an extension of the life table, the **proportional hazards model**, which allows the researcher to identify differences between groups in the ongoing risk, or hazard, of an event (such as death) occurring (see Plewis, 1997; Anderson et al., 1980; Cox and Oakes, 1984).

Lampard and Peggs (1999) use a proportional hazards model both to assess the effect on formerly married women's likelihood of repartnering of the number of children that they have had, and also to look at the way in which the relationship between the likelihood of repartnering and the duration that someone has spent as a formerly married person is gendered.

Not all quantitative techniques of interest to social researchers fit within a conventional framework of descriptive and inferential statistics. For example, researchers interested in **social network analysis** can call upon a relatively distinctive technical literature (Scott, 1991). The same to some extent applies to researchers interested in the **simulation** of social processes (Gilbert and Doran, 1994). Furthermore, some statisticians take a distinctive **Bayesian** approach (Gelman et al., 1995), which can lead to rather different interpretations of data to those generated by a conventional or **frequentist** approach.

Some recent developments relating to multi-level models

A recently developed approach, which has generated considerable interest among social researchers is **multi-level modelling** (Plewis, 1997; Goldstein, 1995). Such models, which have been used extensively in educational research but which have many other applications, take account of the different units of analysis, or levels, which are found in some research topics. For example, a quantitative study of schoolchildren may involve individual pupils within classes within schools within geographical areas. The software available for multi-level modelling includes the dedicated package, MLwiN.

> Dryler (1999) applies multi-level models to the choices of educational field of female and male school pupils, with the pupils being nested within classes within schools. She demonstrates that choices vary significantly between schools and between classes once pupils' characteristics have been controlled for, and that pupils' choices are correlated with those of their same sex classmates, but not with those of their opposite sex classmates.

Sophisticated statistical techniques are continually being developed to deal with awkward problems within quantitative social research. One such problem is the effect of complex sample designs on the precision of findings (see Chapter 3). Researchers often treat survey data as if they come from a simple random sample. However, this can lead to a situation, known as **over-dispersion**, where the sampling error is greater than it is assumed to be, and where any statistical tests are, as a consequence, subject to an increased risk of Type I errors (i.e. spuriously significant results). The literature relating to this issue is quite technical (e.g. Skinner *et al.*, 1989), and at this point in time it can be difficult for social researchers to routinely take account of the problem, since the necessary adjustments to the test statistics of interest may be difficult to estimate. However, cluster samples are multi-level in structure (individual respondents being nested within clusters), and hence for such samples the effect of sample design can be accounted for within multi-level models.

Another problem, which occurs in the context of analyses of longitudinal data, is the problem of omitted variables, or **unobserved heterogeneity** (see Dale and Davies, 1994). Consider, for example, the relationship between divorce rate and marriage duration in a sample of marriages examined over time. The divorce rate peaks after a number of years of marriage, and then diminishes thereafter. This declining rate might be interpreted as providing evidence that marriages that have survived for a certain number of years become more stable. However, an alternative explanation for the declining rate is that the more unstable marriages have tended to end in divorce relatively quickly, which induces a declining divorce rate, as the surviving marriages are disproportionately the more stable ones. In other words, the declining rate may simply reflect an omitted (i.e. unmeasured) variable, such as 'marital stability'. The techniques that have been developed to take account of unobserved heterogeneity build assumptions about the existence and form of the omitted variables into models. Again, it is difficult at present for social researchers to make routine use of such techniques.

However, where the longitudinal data to be analysed relate to repeated events, information about the omitted variables is embedded within the differences between individuals; for example, an individual who has had a series of short cohabiting relationships can be assumed to have some characteristic or characteristics which increases their risk of relationship breakdown. Data about repeated events, such as those contained within cohabitation and marriage histories, are once again multi-level in structure, with specific cohabitations and marriages being nested within individuals; hence such data can once again be analysed using multi-level models.

Chapter 10   Approaches to writing: the craft of communication

Introduction

Many study guides provide advice about the best way of writing. They usually include information on how to structure your writing, how to reference, how to lay out your written output and what stylistic features to incorporate (e.g. Becker, 1986; Sharples, 1998). In addition, many people will give you advice about writing and how to approach what is often a daunting task. All of this advice will be well meant and based on their own experience of trying to make the task easier and more enjoyable and the output generally better. In many respects, this chapter is similar to those guides and those people. It provides advice based on our experiences of writing, not least of which has been writing this book. However, without suggesting that you should close the book now, we feel that it is important to realise the limitations of the guidebooks and the advice.

Many people find writing difficult. This must be the case or there would not be a market for guidebooks or such ready imparting of advice by those who have experienced this difficulty. It is our view that no matter how long you spend reading study guides, planning your writing or listening to advice, the principal difficulty remains: that is, as far as writing is concerned, *you just have to do it*. Until you actually begin the task of writing

it is difficult to appreciate the level of difficulty entailed.

It seems to us that the difficulty comes from a number of different sources. In the first place, there is the physical aspect of writing: that you have to sit, usually in one place, notwithstanding the growing availability of portable computers, for reasonably long periods of time and apply yourself to this one task. Another source of difficulty is that writing is usually a solitary activity. Although many books, papers and a variety of forms of written output are jointly authored – again this book can serve as a case in point – this usually means that the writing has been divided up into chapters, topics, or some other clearly defined set of units for which individual writers take responsibility. Given that social research is rarely a solitary activity, the act of locking oneself away and writing may seem particularly strange and isolating. For some, however, this may be a welcome opportunity to gather their thoughts away from the distractions of fieldwork or of colleagues. Writing may also be seen as difficult because it brings together all the different elements of the research process, from research design through data collection to analysis, and seeks to represent them in a way which is not only accurate but also interesting to the reader. Moreover, the very idea of the reader can also contribute to the difficulty of writing, as the writer anticipates the reactions of his/her reader.

When to write

As with analysis there is often an assumption made that writing is something that occurs primarily towards the end of the research process. Again, as with analysis, such a view may be correct but it also fails to take account of the different kinds of writing that social research requires. We would argue that it is desirable and important for all researchers to write throughout the entire research project. Indeed, we would go so far as to say that research is as much about writing as it is about fieldwork or data analysis. What we mean by this is that there is a mutual dependence of these activities on one another. We cannot do fieldwork effectively unless we write about it in fieldnotes, memos, research diaries and so on. Writing is central to the reflexivity demanded of research which is based on fieldwork. In addition, as we saw in Chapters 8 and 9, the process of analysis depends on the quality of the data collected during fieldwork, and without data there would be nothing to write about. Consequently, we can say that writing is central to the conduct of fieldwork, data collection and data analysis.

The research process demands that we write different things at different times. However, there is a tendency for researchers to talk about **writing up** their research. Traditionally Ph.D. students, who have tended to think of their third year as the 'writing up' year, have exemplified this. This would not imply that they did not write anything until their final year; rather it implies that the type of writing that occurred at this time was different from other types. Writing up implies that the researcher was seeking to make some kind of statement from their research which would be their contribution to their field of study. To get to this stage they will inevitably have already written a considerable amount. Writing is, therefore, integral to research.

What to write

Different stages of the research process demand different kinds of writing. Some of these will be for an external audience, others only for those involved in or close to the research and some only for the researcher's personal use. Some forms of writing will be required which contribute to the conduct of the research and are allied to different stages of the research process. We refer to these types of writing as **process writing** as they relate directly to the effective collection and manipulation of data. In effect, process writing is an essential precursor to the second type of writing, which we call **product writing**. Here, the emphasis is on the output from the research and the term refers to the kind of writing which has typically been seen as constituting the writing-up phase of research. Product writing is oriented towards producing a specific end product such as a report, a thesis or a paper.

In more detail, process and product writing might include some, or in some cases all, of the following.

Process writing

Research proposals and plans

Writing a research plan is an integral part of any research programme. We have already discussed the importance of research design to successful research. Usually, it is in the preparation of the research design that process writing first occurs. We refer here not to the formalised research proposal but the more informal formulation of ideas, questions and research plans. As we outlined in Chapter 1 the ideas underpinning a study may come from a wide range of sources and the first task of the researcher is to collate these ideas, to evaluate them and to pose questions about them. The writing associated with this embryonic stage of research may take the form of notes on literature: the jotting down of ideas and questions with which to interrogate the literature or to talk about with colleagues. The writing may be informal, e.g. a series of notes or memos and will usually be for personal use by the researcher.

What follows this initial personal writing will be a more formal research plan or proposal in which the aims and objectives of the research will be outlined along with the proposed methodology. Not only is this a more formal kind of writing but it will also be shared with other people. At this stage, the writing has progressed from process writing to product writing as it is a form of writing which has a particular audience in mind. This may be a colleague, a funding body or a supervisor. Any of these audiences will be looking for a research plan or proposal which requires the researcher to bring together his/her ideas about the research, formulated as a result of earlier process writing, in a clear and unambiguous way. The formal research proposal will need to show what the research will achieve, how it will be achieved and what the rationale for the research is. It will also need to include detailed financial and time costings, along with justifications for proposed expenditure.

Research journal

We would strongly recommend that all researchers keep a research journal or diary. This can be an invaluable source of support: a friend and a comfort throughout the research process. The diary or journal is another form of personal process writing which may include the kinds of ideas, questions and plans described in the previous section. In addition it may be the place where the researcher records his/her personal feelings about the research, the progress made, anticipated difficulties, notes on how a particular piece of fieldwork went, details of and results from preliminary or exploratory statistical analyses and almost anything which is seen to be relevant to the progress of the study. In this way, the journal can help to document the research process and to understand the context within which the research is conducted. The journal may be the place where ideas about analysis and concept formation are tried out and the place where notes on relevant reading may be made or references may be noted. In effect, the journal has the potential to be the Mary Poppins bag of the research process from which many useful and surprising objects may be pulled. The journal may also be something which the researcher compiles in

longhand rather than being a word-processed document. The advantages of this are that notes can be made anywhere and at any time. Indeed, buying a new journal can become part of the ritual of starting a new research project. Ring binders with paper and pockets inserted in them, along the lines of a Filofax, offer portability and a degree of flexibility. Alternatively, the word processor's capacity to move material around and the ability to print a particular section of the journal in order to work on it can outweigh the perhaps romantic idea of the secret journal. Whatever method is chosen, we would urge researchers to ensure that the journal is kept secure, particularly if there are personal thoughts and experiences or confidential information about research participants recorded within it.

Fieldnotes

Fieldnotes represent a more formalised form of writing and may often be shared with colleagues. Whilst their principal role is to record what happens in the field, they may go beyond merely describing what has been witnessed to include some initial on-the-spot analysis of what is being seen and/or heard. Again, they may be an appropriate location for ideas about analysis and may include cross-references to other data. The fieldnote written shortly after the meeting at Premier Business School used in Chapter 8 is a fairly typical example of a fieldnote which incorporates essential descriptive information about what was happening, together with a number of questions and some interpretation, which help to focus the observation and relate it to other data.

There are usually two kinds of fieldnotes. It may be that we wish to make very rough notes whilst we are actually in the field (**real-time fieldnotes**) which we would write up in more detail later on (**reflexive fieldnotes**). If this is the case, and in our experience it usually is, it is important to ensure that sufficient detail is taken down as events unfold, to provide an adequate basis for later elaboration. It is not possible to re-run an observation and rarely possible to ask for clarification of what happened. Writing a fuller account of events as soon as possible after the observation has been conducted is also a good idea. This means that any shorthand notes made in the field can quickly be made sense of and elaborated upon. The two kinds of fieldnotes serve two different but related purposes. Whilst the real-time fieldnotes are made with the primary intention of giving an account of what is happening and in this sense are largely descriptive, the reflexive fieldnotes seek to flesh out the description and to form the first stage of data analysis. Real-time fieldnotes may, therefore, be very brief and include lots of abbreviations and diagrams which are meaningful only to the note taker, whereas reflexive fieldnotes are more carefully constructed, contain much more detail and are intended to make sense both to the researcher and others who may be involved in the research. In situations where a single researcher conducts a study, as is the case with many undergraduate research projects and particularly with doctoral work, we would recommend that this is not seen as an opportunity to rely solely on real-time fieldnotes. The point of producing reflexive fieldnotes is that the process by which this is achieved will provide practice in writing and, perhaps most importantly, will contribute to data analysis.

Memos

By memos we refer to notes written about specific aspects of the research. These may be a series of questions about the data, about the research site or about particular participants. Memos may be written to colleagues or to oneself as a reminder of something to come back to later in the research. They are a means of trying out ideas and providing a commentary on the data and on the analysis as it emerges. Memos may be written as part of the research journal or, if they are for consideration by colleagues, they are best written as stand-alone items to which colleagues may wish to write responses. In this way a dialogue may be built up as the research progresses. As with the research journal,

memos offer an opportunity for the researcher to reflect upon and experiment with data, literature and analysis and their general thoughts about the work in progress.

Documenting datasets

In Chapter 5 we encouraged researchers to document adequately the various stages and aspects of survey research. As is evident from Chapter 7, there is a tradition of opening up survey data for use by other researchers. This is also becoming much more common with all kinds of qualitative data. Documenting and depositing data are, for example, conditions of receiving research funding from the Economic and Social Research Council. A well-documented dataset is a must for the secondary analyst; hence as the research progresses the original researcher needs to generate clear descriptions of aspects of the research design such as sampling, copies of the research instruments, annotated or accompanied by commentaries on their use, interview instructions, coding notes, etc. It is important that such material is compiled as a form of process writing as the research progresses. This will then allow the researcher to provide more detailed notes on the dataset as a form of product writing, before it is deposited in a data archive.

Summary

The types of writing outlined above are essential components of research. They illustrate quite clearly that writing takes place throughout the research process and is not something that the researcher encounters for the first time after data collection has been completed and analysis conducted. If the researcher engages in these different types of writing as the research progresses, we believe that not only will the research itself benefit, but also the researcher will become more familiar with the data and with their manipulation. As we have already seen, familiarity with the data is essential for effective data analysis. In addition, the researcher will get essential practice in writing about the research, which will pay dividends when it comes to the research product writing.

Product writing

Having emphasised the importance and inevitability of writing throughout the research process to the extent that writing should not be seen as something which is novel or limited to the later stages of the research process, we do not wish to detract from the importance of product writing. This will yield tangible output from the research by means of reports, papers, monographs and books. The principal reason for engaging in much writing is to produce a summation of the research, bringing together analysis and reflection to produce well-grounded, thoughtful and well-written conclusions. In this way, social scientists contribute to their disciplines and advance knowledge in their particular fields. The way in which researchers choose to do this may be allied to the nature of the work that they are undertaking. For example, a doctoral student is required to produce a thesis, an undergraduate may be required to produce a project report or dissertation and a contract researcher may be required to produce a specific type of report for the sponsor of his/her research. Alternatively, the researcher may be free to decide on the most appropriate type of product or combination of products him/herself.

We will now go on to provide examples of product writing in greater detail. As you read through the examples, however, you may think that your present research project is unlikely to generate such products. This may well be the case. Nevertheless, we felt it was important to provide a reasonably comprehensive list of the kinds of product writing that researchers engage in for two reasons. First of all, as we stated in the preface to this book, we hope that some readers will return to these chapters at different stages of their research careers. Consequently, whilst writing a book, a journal article or a conference paper may seem unrealistic when, as an undergraduate, you plan your first ever piece of

research, however, if you decide to progress to post-graduate work or you take up a career where product writing is important, then what we have to say will hopefully be of greater relevance at that time. Secondly, as the world of publishing can often seem distant and mysterious, we thought that some readers would simply be interested to know how books, journal articles and reports, etc., get into the public domain.

Research reports

Research reports are amongst the most common forms of product writing. Academics, undergraduates, contract researchers, market researchers and many different kinds of personnel from various branches of industry and commerce are required to produce reports of their research. Whilst reports usually need to meet specific requirements laid down by whoever is to receive them, there are a number of general, technical issues to be borne in mind.

Reports need to be clearly focused. They need to identify the terms of reference which directed the research in the first instance and to make explicit the aims and objectives of the research. They need to be easily accessible and will benefit from the effective use of sub-headings and, in some instances, numbered paragraphs. It is common for reports to include a brief account of the research methodology and an equally brief discussion of some of the existing research in the same field. References may not necessarily be extensive but must, as always, be relevant and accurately cited in the bibliography. The main part of a research report will be devoted to a discussion of the results or findings of the research. Again, this needs to be clearly and unambiguously written, with data included in order to support the discussion. Data may be included within the narrative of the report or, if this is deemed to inhibit its readability, it may be better accommodated in an appendix. Irrespective of whether data are to be included in tabular, prose, diagrammatic or photographic form, they should always be carefully labelled to ensure that they can be read in combination with the appropriate narrative.

For many readers, the conclusions will be the most important part of the report. Again these need to be clearly articulated, to be supported with data and to address directly the focus of the research. Allied to conclusions are recommendations. Whilst these may not always be required, and will usually be most appropriate in policy-focused research, the recommendations, like the conclusions, can be seen by some readers as the most important aspect of the report. Here, our advice remains the same. Recommendations should be clearly articulated, unambiguous, well supported by appropriate data and directly relevant to the focus of the study.

It may be that you feel that the research report does not do justice to the time and effort put into the research. From our own experiences this is often the case: for example, when writing final reports for the Economic and Social Research Council (ESRC). Here the 5000 word limit may seem unduly restrictive for a research project which may have taken several years to complete, have cost hundreds of thousands of pounds and have involved a team of researchers. However, the message in this case, as with all reports, must be to remain focused, to write with a style that is as economical as possible and to ensure that the main points you wish to convey are given a high profile in the document. It is, then, the product rather than the process that is the most important aspect of report writing. Rather like the artist commissioned to paint a portrait, the thousands of individual brush strokes are not seen, but the finished product, in this case the portrait, is what is most important to the client or audience and hence in some ways to the artist. However, the portrait would not exist without the thousands of brush strokes.

Whilst we do not intend to go into technical details of layout and presentation here, it is nevertheless essential to emphasise the importance of an attractive, high-quality finished product. The versatility and increasing availability of high-specification word processors usually puts this objective within reach of most researchers.

Conference papers

A useful way of bringing your work into the public domain is to present a paper at a conference. Most of the very many conferences which take place each year, both in the UK and overseas, operate in a broadly similar way. A call for papers is made, usually via journals, newsletters, internet sites and mailshots, some months, and often up to a year, before the conference. The call, which usually details the overall theme of the conference along with the areas in which the organisers would wish to receive papers, invites would-be participants to submit an abstract of the paper they wish to present for consideration by the conference committee. Once your paper has been accepted you should receive details of the conference programme which shows where and when your paper is to be delivered.

Most conferences are organised so that participants have the choice of listening to one of several papers which are presented simultaneously. These are known as parallel sessions. As a presenter you will be told how much time you have for your paper. This may be quite limited. For example, many conferences, in trying to maximise the number of papers presented, restrict presentations to 20 minutes. Moreover, the time you are allowed usually includes time for questions and discussion. Consequently, you will not be able to use all your time for presentation and a careful chairperson will ensure that your slot does not over-run. However, most conferences require presenters to write and submit a full paper, rather than merely a 20-minute presentation, and to make the full paper available to the audience. There may be a temptation, therefore, to produce two documents: one for the 20-minute presentation and another fuller paper for distribution. Our advice would be to concentrate on the full paper and once you are happy with that, to write a brief distillation of its main points to present at the conference. Whilst the full paper may be similar in style and content to a journal article or book chapter (see below), the presentation requires a different approach. In 20 minutes you cannot hope to convey the full detail of your research. Our advice is to put together a presentation using overhead projection transparencies or using a software package such as PowerPoint which states the topic or focus of your research, briefly outlines the methodology used and raises any particular issues in relation to this which the audience may wish to pick up on. Something like 10 minutes of your 20-minute presentation should be given over to a discussion of the findings of your research and to drawing some conclusions in relation to its principal focus. The intention is that the presentation provides a précis of the full paper, with the intention that this will stimulate people to read the full paper which you, or in some cases the conference organisers, can make available upon request.

The presentation needs to be economical, tightly focused and well grounded in the data. Questioners may wish to take issue with some of the things you say, and for many presenters, particularly first time or inexperienced presenters, this can be daunting. The best way to defend yourself and your research is to be able to point to data which support your findings and to demonstrate that your research has deployed rigorous methodology.

Journal articles

Most research will have the capacity to yield a number of papers, which you may wish to submit for publication to journals. By the time you come to write an academic paper it is likely that you will have a good grasp of your data and a sound knowledge of the literature in the area to which it relates. Up-to-date knowledge of the literature will help you to identify where you might make a contribution to current debate in the area, perhaps by drawing on your research to fill gaps that you have identified about what is known in your area, or by using your work to provide a critique of existing research and knowledge.

In order to write a paper which is likely to be accepted for publication, it is essential to familiarise yourself with the range of journals which publish material in areas relating to your topic.

Your university subject librarian should be able to help here and keyword searches of indices of journal articles may also be useful. Having done this it is a good idea to get to know, in general terms, the style in which academic papers in your area are written by reading a selection from the relevant journals. It is then just a question of writing the paper! It may be that you wish to target your paper at a particular journal and you should, therefore, write with this in mind. However, given that you can never guarantee that a specific journal will accept your paper, it is probably better to write it keeping in mind a range of relevant journals, leaving your final choice of where to submit it until you are happy with the content. At this stage you can review the range of possibilities once more, decide on the most appropriate journal, make any changes to the content of the paper which you feel are necessary to produce a better fit with the focus and orientation of that journal and submit it. All journals have their own house styles which relate to page layout, total number of words, presentation of diagrams and tables, referencing and footnoting and a range of other technical issues. Whilst these requirements are broadly similar across journals, it is essential that you conform to what is required by the editors of the journal to which you submit your article. Most journals give clear instructions under the heading of 'notes for contributors' within each issue. However, if you are not sure whether you are conforming to the requirements, a phone call to the editor(s) should resolve any ambiguity.

It is important to send your papers to refereed journals whenever possible. This means the editor(s) of the journal will send your article out to a number of people, often three, who are known to work and publish in your field. They will be asked by the editor to comment on the suitability of your paper for publication. The referees send their comments back to the editor(s) who will then inform you of their decision. The refereeing process usually takes around three months, although this will vary according to how popular the journal is with contributors and, in the UK, how close we are to the Research Assessment Exercise. You should receive an acknowledgement on submitting your paper and if you have heard nothing from the editor(s) after three months we would recommend that you contact them and enquire politely about the paper's progress. You should also bear in mind that editors are usually full-time academics who do not receive large payments for their efforts with a journal. Similarly referees are usually full-time academics who are not paid at all for commenting on papers.

There are generally three kinds of outcomes to the refereeing process. The best you can hope for is that the editor accepts your paper for publication as it stands without the need for any alterations or modifications whatsoever. Decisions like this are rare. Alternatively, and what is more likely, if the editor decides to accept your paper, he/she will agree to publish it providing certain changes are made. These changes may range from minor issues like the labelling of diagrams or ensuring that you comply with house-style requirements, to major rewrites of particular sections of the paper. Sometimes editors invite the resubmission of a revised paper without any clear indication that it will definitely be accepted for publication once the revisions have been made. However, a thorough approach to the revisions, together with a detailed commentary on how you have tackled the recommendations of the referees, can make it difficult for the editors to reject a resubmitted paper. Thirdly, the decision that no writer wants is a straightforward rejection of the paper. A rejection may occur because referees deem the paper to be below the required standards of the journal, or it may occur because the focus of the paper does not fit with that of the journal or because there are too many smaller concerns about the content of the paper for rewriting to seem worthwhile. Rejection is, unfortunately, quite common and however experienced at writing you are it is usually disheartening.

Editors will usually send you the anonymised comments of the referees. These will be essential if you decide to rewrite your paper for resubmission and they can be helpful in offering another view of your work, although they may make painful reading if your paper has been rejected. If this is the case, you should try to take heart from the facts that everyone receives rejections from time to time, and that most journals receive far more papers for consideration than they could ever publish, so that the acceptance rate is never very high, and that the referees' comments can be a useful resource if you decide to rewrite the paper or when you come to write another one. It is also worth remembering that there are many journals. Although your paper has been rejected by one this does not mean it will be rejected by all. There is nothing to stop you revising the paper in line with the comments received with the rejection and submitting it somewhere else.[1] Our advice would be to start by submitting your paper to a high-status journal[2] and, if this is not successful, to work your way down the hierarchy. If a journal which rejects your article has a particular emphasis it can sometimes be advisable to send the revised version to a journal with a different emphasis. If, however, you keep receiving rejections on the basis of what are perceived by referees to be serious flaws in the paper it is probably time to admit defeat and relegate it to the back of the filing cabinet.

If your paper is accepted for publication the editor will inform you of the issue in which it will appear. This may be as much as a year after it has been accepted. Again this will vary between journals. Before publication you will receive proofs which need to be checked very carefully and quite quickly for typographical errors. The editor is likely to reject any substantive changes you wish to make

---

[1] As a matter of academic courtesy to editors and referees we would not advocate submitting the same paper to more than one journal simultaneously. In fact notes for contributors often explicitly state that this practice is unacceptable.

[2] In some disciplines such as economics there is a clear and formally acknowledged hierarchy of journals. In others, hierarchies operate more implicitly. International journals and those supported by a learned society tend to enjoy high status, whilst those which do not referee submissions or are in-house journals, perhaps internal to an institution, tend to be of lower status. Talking to your supervisor or a more experienced colleague should help to establish the best place to try to publish your paper. It is also worth noting that submitting a paper to the most prestigious journal may not be the best tactic to get the paper published quickly.

to the text at this stage, as these can be very expensive for the publisher. On publication you should receive a number of copies of your paper (offprints). Some publishers send you a copy of the entire issue, and offer you a chance to buy more at a discounted rate. You may then wish to send copies to people who work in your field and who you think would be interested in your work, and to your friends, family and colleagues. At this point, we recommend that you sit back and enjoy the thrill of publication, before starting the whole process again.

Chapters in books

From time to time, and as your work becomes known through publications such as those outlined above, you may be invited to contribute a chapter to an edited book. This involves a process similar to that associated with a journal article. However, such chapters tend not to be refereed in the same way as journal articles. In place of this process, the editor of the volume will comment on the paper when it is submitted and may require redrafts and modifications to be made before agreeing to include it in the publication. Edited books usually focus on a specific topic, which may be addressed from different perspectives by the various contributors. In preparing a chapter it is a good idea to get to know as much as possible about the focus of the book and the content of the other contributions. This will enable you to refer to the other chapters and therefore a greater degree of coherence will be achieved throughout the book.

Books

If you are engaged in your first piece of research then you may regard the prospect of ever writing a book as remote. We would guess that most researchers felt like that at some stage. However, the fact remains that research projects of one sort or another, including those conducted for doctoral study, frequently give rise to books. Moreover, within the present system of higher education in the UK where the Research Assessment Exercise is influential in determining not only the status enjoyed by an academic department but also its income, books are of great importance. They are also very important for individual researchers' and academics' career prospects in general.

Books fall into two main categories. Those attracting the most status are 'authored' books where one person or sometimes two, three or more (though in the social sciences it is rarely more than three), are responsible for writing the entire content of the book. Alternatively, there are also edited books which are usually collections of chapters written by different authors (see 'Chapters in books' above) focusing on a particular theme, in line with guidance provided by its editor(s). If you decide to produce an edited book, then you take on the responsibility for finding a publisher, assembling the group of contributors, reading and commenting on their work, ensuring that the volume has a substantive and stylistic coherence and making sure that deadlines are met. The volume is then attributed to you as the editor and subsequently referenced as your publication.

Whether you are writing or editing a book, our advice is the same. It is important to get a contract with a publisher before you do a significant amount of writing. Many publishers have specially designed proposal forms which they require would-be authors to complete. Others take a more flexible approach. However, all publishers require a great deal of detail about the proposed book before they will agree to a publication contract. Moreover, as with journal articles, publishers will often send book proposals out for other academics to referee. The proposal is, therefore, of vital importance to the procedure associated with producing a book and like many other forms of writing it demands careful attention.

Our advice would be to construct a proposal around several essential sections. These are as follows.

Rationale for the book Here you need to outline briefly the field to which the book will contribute. The section needs to be concisely written and to outline the major debates to which your work will contribute and, most importantly, it should highlight the gaps in the existing literature which your book will address. The publisher needs to be convinced that there is a need for the book within a particular well-defined substantive area. Consequently this opening section of the proposal needs to be written in an upbeat and persuasive style.

Type of book This brief section needs to say whether the book is authored or edited. If it is authored you simply name the authors. If it is edited you should name the editors and give a list of the contributors. It is a good idea to get the agreement of as many of the individual chapter authors as possible before sending off the proposal. Not only is this regarded as required etiquette, but it also enables you to make a stronger case to the publisher by demonstrating that the project has gone beyond the stage of a mere idea. In this section you should also state the anticipated length of the book. However, it is also useful to remember that the optimum length of many academic books is around 70 000 words. Many publishers are reluctant to go beyond this length due to the concomitant increase in price that longer books necessitate.

Outline of proposed contents Working systematically through each chapter, this section should provide details of the content of the volume. Providing a paragraph on each of the chapters and indicating their individual lengths will enable the publisher and the referees to gain a clear idea of the content of the volume. This will help them to judge its academic merit and assess its chances of selling well.

Market for the book This is a very important aspect of the proposal. For the publisher it is probably the most important consideration. Publishing houses need to make a profit from their books, which means that they are unlikely to take a chance on publishing something for which there is not a buoyant and clearly identifiable market.

Consequently, decisions about whether or not to award a contract to an author are often as much about commercial and business concerns as they are about the content and academic credibility of the book. This means that publishers are unlikely to agree to publish a book in an already crowded subject area unless the author can provide a different angle on the topic, which is likely to result in good sales figures for the title. Similarly, publishers are equally unlikely to agree to publish a book in a highly esoteric area within which sales would be small. Our advice here is to identify the kinds of courses that the book would be recommended for, both at undergraduate and postgraduate level, along with any policy- or practitioner-related areas that might attract sales. International sales are particularly important for publishers, so reference to these, if relevant, is a good idea. Whilst you need to be optimistic about likely sales, we would not encourage exaggeration or fiction in this section. Referees are also likely to have a good idea of probable sales and therefore 'over-enthusiasm' in this area may lead them to question other aspects of the proposal.

Relation to other books in the field Reference to the rationale and the market for the book is useful here. It is important that there is already a literature in the area to which you intend to contribute, but at the same time you should avoid giving the impression that there already exists a large number of texts on your topic. If it seems likely that your book will be merely one more text on an already well-stocked shelf, then we would advise you to look for a different angle or style or something to make your text distinctive. Outlining the relationship to the field is not simply a question of saying that your book will fill existing gaps in the literature. This may be the case, but it may also be that your book challenges what already exists, or updates arguments in existing books. Alternatively, as is often the case with edited collections, the book may bring together a particular set of debates or authors for the first time. Ultimately you are looking to be able to promote a text which is different in some way to what already exists, will make a significant contribution to its field and, on this basis, will realise significant sales figures.

Time-scale and delivery Again our advice here is to be realistic. Publishers prefer to have a date for delivery of a manuscript that authors can realistically meet rather than promises of something quick that will not be kept. In addition, from the author's perspective, it is also important to have sufficient time to produce a high-quality manuscript with which publishers will be happy to progress. Having said this, it is also important to keep in mind developments in the discipline and the area to which your book will contribute. A time-scale which is too long may result in your book being seen as already out of date or surpassed by others soon after it is published. In our experience, it is rare for authors to propose a time-scale which is shorter that one year, but equally rare for it to exceed two.

Clearly, there can be no magic formula for producing a book proposal and each case will require its own variations. However, we hope the framework suggested above will at least shed a little light on what often remains a somewhat mysterious process, about which little is written or explained.

In some instances, particularly with new authors, publishers may request some sample material which will also be sent out to referees. Where this occurs it is often the case that one full chapter is requested or a number of chapter overviews. This not only gives the publisher a more detailed sense of the book, but also demonstrates writing style. However, once a proposal has been accepted the publisher will usually produce a draft contract which covers the process of producing the manuscript in addition to copyright and royalties. Although contracts are usually fairly standard, you should read what the publisher is offering very carefully before signing. If you are unsure of anything, check with a more experienced colleague but always be prepared to go back to the publisher for clarification. Royalties are also fairly standard across publishers at somewhere between 8% and 10%. It is unlikely that you will make a huge amount of money from an academic publication. Remember also that certain items of expenditure incurred by the publisher during the preparation of the manuscript may be deducted from your royalties. For example, these can include any advance you were paid at the time the contract was signed, any indexing work conducted by the publisher's staff, payments to other contributors in the case of edited books and changes made to the text at the proofreading stage. Taking all of these into account may mean that your first annual royalty statement could indicate that you actually owe the publisher some money! Hopefully this will be cancelled out as sales of the book increase over time. In addition, the book remains valuable for research assessment purposes for your department, will be beneficial to your career and is something to show your grandchildren!

Summary

It has been our intention to raise awareness of the different types of writing that a research project might engender. In addition, we have sought to stress that writing is an integral part of the research process, not something that occurs solely towards its end. However, we recognise that what we have presented is only a selection of the different kinds of both process and product writing in which researchers engage. We also recognise that for many of our readers the idea of writing a book, presenting a paper to a conference or submitting an article to a journal is something that they have no wish to do, or is something much further on in the research process to which serious thought cannot be given at present. However, we hope that this brief guide to different forms of writing will act as a resource for when and if the time comes to consider writing a book, a report, a paper or whatever. Having identified several different forms of writing, it is not our intention to suggest that researchers limit themselves to what we have highlighted here. We hope merely to have increased awareness of the many possibilities and outlets that exist and at the same time to have gone some way towards de-mystifying what may often seem a closed world of publishing.

Raising awareness and de-mystifying in this way may be useful in helping you to see the potential in your material, but it is unlikely to assist you in the actual process of writing. We will now turn briefly to this issue.

How to write

This is probably the most difficult part of this chapter and that is probably why we have left it until last. Like many writers we have put off attempting something difficult until we really have to. Attempting to give guidance as to how to write is difficult, not least because every writer has his/her own style, and in this sense writing is a reflection of the individual doing the writing as much as it is of the substance of what is being written. This diversity of styles is in our view a positive aspect of the writing process which is to be encouraged. In attempting to give guidance on how to write it is certainly not our intention to encourage a standardised approach or an homogenised output. What we do wish to suggest, however, are a number of common-sense tips on how to get the job done.

As a means of getting you started and keeping you going, we would suggest the following:

- Try not to see writing as a chore. Look on it and talk about it positively. This will help you to enjoy the process and to reach the stage where writing becomes a natural activity. Writing is at the same time both a form of work and a form of self-expression; it can be boring and can make you feel exposed and self-conscious, but it is a fundamentally creative activity which can also generate a great deal of personal satisfaction.
- Find somewhere comfortable to write. Choosing a location in which you feel at ease will help you to spend long periods of time there without becoming sick of the sight of the same four walls or the same dated posters on those walls. However, if boredom sets in, and it probably will at some stage, switching between locations may be useful.
- Start by making a plan of whatever it is you are going to write. This may start off as a very brief skeleton to which you add detail as you think about the task and as you try out the ideas contained in the plan. The plan should include details of the overall focus of the writing and a brief summary of what you want the piece to say, what the argument is that you wish to advance and what the conclusions are that you wish to reach. Clearly, in order to do this you will need to have given a great deal of thought to what it is you are writing. You will probably already have written memos about this and tried out some of the ideas. Having made this general statement of objectives it is then useful to work your way through the different sections that you envisage writing. Whilst doing this you should keep in mind the focus and the overall objective of the piece. The intention is to articulate how each of the individual chapters or sections will help you to achieve this overall objective. You will need, therefore, to give detail on the content of each of the sections and attempt to show how they link together.
- Try to see what you are writing as a set of linked stages which are held together by a clearly and simply articulated focus. This will help to give coherence to the writing whilst at the same time breaking it down into manageable pieces for you to write and for the reader to digest. With this in mind, it is important that your writing plan gives attention to structure as well as to content.
- Set yourself a target of how much you intend to write or for how long you intend to write in a day or whatever portion of the day is available to you. For example, one of the present authors tries to produce 1000 words per day whilst the other prefers to work on the basis of an average number of daily words achieved across a longer period of time, dependent on motivation,

competing tasks and the pressure of deadlines. Whatever method you use to identify your target, it is important that this is both realistic for you to achieve and achievable in the context of all the other things that go on in your life. For example, setting a target of 50 words per day towards a thesis of 100 000 words would not be realistic unless you intended to make it your life's work! Similarly you may not be able to achieve a target of 1000 words per day if you have childcare commitments and are only able to write when the children are in bed. Everyone will have different targets and will work towards them in different ways. Do not be put off by this. Concentrate on what works well for you. If it does not work, try a different strategy.

- Do not spend too long on the first draft of any particular section of whatever you are writing. Sara Delamont's (1992) advice 'Don't get it right, get it written' is something we wholly endorse. Rather than striving for perfection at an early stage, we take the view that it is better to get into place the general idea or shape of the piece that you are writing before worrying too much about the detail of the finished product. To use an analogy from sculpture, in order for Michelangelo to produce the *David* he had to start at some point with a block of marble. Until he had the block he could not begin to shape what was arguably to become an artefact of great beauty. Your chapter or thesis or research report is in many ways similar to this. Once you have produced the first draft, you can then begin to work on the detail, ultimately producing something, if not of great beauty, then of which you can be confident and proud.

- Make use of helpful feedback. Having someone whose opinion you trust to read and comment on your work can be enormously helpful as the process of writing progresses. In order to move from first draft to something that you think is more like a finished product it is necessary to do two things. First, it is important to look at each chapter or section in relation to the whole document. Whether it is a research report, a journal article or an entire thesis, individual sections need to be evaluated in the context of the thesis as a whole. At a purely instrumental level it is important that cross-references are made between sections or chapters but, more fundamentally, there needs to be an integrity to the piece which sees the substantive focus or thread sustained and developed throughout. To help you achieve this we would encourage you to seek out comments from two sorts of people. These are your peers and your supervisor, tutor, mentor or more experienced colleagues. In asking for comments from peers you are looking for an honest reaction from someone who is at a similar stage in their career, who may, therefore, be able to provide you with critical comments in a way which is non-threatening and with whom you will feel able to talk openly about your feelings towards your work. Comments from your supervisor, tutor or more senior colleague may have a more 'official' quality. It is important that you respect the judgement of whoever you ask to comment on your work and that you are confident that he/she knows the area in which you are writing and understands what you are trying to achieve. If this is the case then you should take the comments they make seriously and act on them accordingly when it comes to producing the second draft. However, we are not suggesting that simply because a more experienced colleague or supervisor has made comments that they should be accepted unquestioningly. It is important that as the author of whatever is being written you have a sense of ownership of it. Although you may quite sensibly decide to follow the advice of supervisors and colleagues, we would argue that it is the author who ought to make decisions as to what changes are made and what the final version looks like. After all, it is your degree result, doctorate or professional reputation that may rest on the final product.

- Keep full bibliographical records throughout the research process. This will avoid your having to spend hours in the library trying to track down something which you read 18 months ago, but forgot to record its full details.

- Know when to take a break. The more experienced that you become as a writer, the more you will get to know about your personal approach to writing and what makes you productive. It may be that some times or days are just not good for writing. If this proves to be the case then it may be better to have a break and do something different before returning to write later in the day, the next day or even after a few days' complete break, after which you may return to the task refreshed and with rekindled enthusiasm.
- When you come to the end of a writing session try to end at a point from which it will be easy to pick up next time. Getting into the swing of writing is often the most difficult part of the process. Therefore, leaving yourself an easy re-entry can be helpful. Another strategy to assist in picking up where you left off is to make a few brief notes about what you intend to write when you next return to the piece. It may be that on reading the notes you change your mind

about the next step. However, the notes will have served their purpose of getting you back into the discipline of writing by engaging you with the content at the place where you left off.

Conclusion

We could go on with other tips and further discussion of different kinds of writing. However, there is a limit to which such tips are useful in the abstract. The most important piece of advice which we can give is to urge you to begin writing as soon as possible in the research process and to keep writing throughout. Ensure that writing becomes a habit and an integral part of research. Moreover, in recent years, published work has become one of the principal means by which individuals and institutions are judged in academia. Therefore, developing a competent writing style and a disciplined approach to writing is likely to pay dividends not only in relation to your early research endeavours, but also in terms of your future career.

Introduction

This final chapter considers in detail two examples of research projects. The examples are hypothetical but draw upon the authors' experience of supervising numerous student projects. Our aim is to use the example projects to weave together many of the issues raised in earlier chapters. One of our reasons for doing this is to emphasise the point that topics such as sampling, interviewing and data analysis should not be viewed in isolation from each other; all take place within a broader research process which is thus perhaps best illustrated holistically. We also recognise that it is not always easy for students to relate discussions of methodological and technical issues to research practice; our examples, therefore, are of the kind of research project that undergraduates might carry out as the basis for final-year dissertations (which are often of about 5000 to 10 000 words in length); however, much of what follows is also of relevance to Master's degree dissertations, and to shorter undergraduate projects.

We start by outlining basic ideas for projects, with which two students might in the first instance come to their dissertation supervisors:

Example project 1: Single mothers out on a limb?
Mark wishes to do a project that investigates the suggestion that single parents are marginal to, or lie outside of, the mainstream of contemporary British society. His initial plan is to carry out in-depth interviews with a small number of lone mothers living in his local area.

Example project 2: Men of science?
Alex wants her project to examine the impact of gender on the subject choices that young people make at school. Her initial intention is to circulate a questionnaire to all the sixth-formers at her old school.

The rest of this chapter looks at a range of issues that might (and in many cases should) be discussed in relation to the above projects in a small number of meetings between the students and their dissertation supervisors. At an early stage Mark and Alex may be required to submit written research proposals to their supervisors; this example of process writing (see Chapter 10) highlights the point that writing, like analysis, should ideally occur throughout the research process.

Initial planning and information gathering

An important issue to consider is why Mark and Alex intend to do the research projects specified above. One possible answer is a purely instrumental one: they have to do dissertations based on empirical research as part of their degree courses.

This may be an obvious answer, but it does have implications for the goal that they are working towards and the amount of time and energy that they can (and should) devote to the research. An over-ambitious project may be praiseworthy in some ways but its positive attributes in this context may not always be the most important determinants of the mark awarded at the end of the year. Hence, as discussed in Chapter 2, the scope of the project needs to match the time and other resources available, which in turn has implications for the methods adopted.

Furthermore, the existence of a fixed submission deadline means that any research design which is interesting, but which proves not to be feasible, needs to be jettisoned at an early stage: for example, Alex's and Mark's research designs respectively need to remain flexible until access to a particular school is obtained and until an adequate sample of an appropriate category of lone parent can be guaranteed. In addition, as noted in Chapter 2, flexibility in the early stages of the research process allows the researcher to respond constructively to new information. Alex's and Mark's initial outline project ideas are quite likely to be amended in response to the background reading that they do after their first meetings with their supervisors. More generally, the agendas of their projects will no doubt be clarified via a process of progressive focusing, starting at the design stage and potentially continuing throughout the duration of the projects, including the analysis stage (see Chapters 2 and 8).

As stressed in Chapter 1, research is a creative activity and good projects typically reflect a motivation-sustaining interest in the subject matter as well as the desire to achieve a good mark. Fortunately, in addition to the instrumental dimension of their dissertations, Mark's and Alex's chosen topics are very likely to reflect a desire to know about the issues in question. Reflecting on why they are interested in these topics may help them crystallise their projects' aims and directions. Furthermore, clarifying exactly what it is that they would be interested in finding out may help uncover their implicit epistemological positions (see Chapter 6),

and in turn cast light on whether their proposed methods are appropriate.

Mark's orientation towards in-depth interviews perhaps reflects a desire to discover lone parents' subjective feelings about their positions within society as opposed, for example, to his wanting to carry out a more quantitative assessment of lone parents' socio-economic situations. However, generalisability may in any case be an issue, as Mark may be interested in the degree of uniformity of the lone parents' subjective feelings. Alex's aim may be to examine the extent to which masculinity and femininity explain the different patterns of subject choice of young women and young men. Her aim can certainly be addressed quantitatively (e.g. by examining whether women who are more 'feminine' disproportionately choose stereotypically 'feminine' subjects), but she may also be interested in individuals' subjective decision-making processes. Thus while Mark's and Alex's respective orientations towards qualitative and quantitative methods appear to be consistent with their objectives, there is scope for each of them to make constructive use of the other approach.

There can, however, be a tension between the complementary use of different methods and/or forms of data, as advocated in Chapter 2 and elsewhere in this book, and the constraints of an undergraduate dissertation. Similarly, the kind of longitudinal comparisons advocated in Chapter 2 are frequently impractical given the time period available, although there is sometimes scope for comparisons with the results of earlier research. However, examples of other forms of comparison discussed in Chapter 2 are visible in Alex's and Mark's outline ideas. Alex's project outline centres around a gender-based comparison, and Mark's involves an implicit comparison between lone parents and other members of society. Furthermore, there might be scope to extend Alex's project to encompass a comparison between schools and to extend Mark's to encompass a comparison between lone mothers and lone fathers.

Mark's and Alex's chosen topics may reflect personal and political interests as much as they reflect academic interests. It is not unusual for students to carry out projects on issues which are in some sense 'close to home'; Mark may have grown up in a lone-mother family and Alex may have studied physics at 'A' level. Furthermore, Mark's rejection of 'traditional family values' and Alex's feminism may have influenced their choices. The important point here is that both Mark and Alex, like all researchers, need to reflect on the impact that they have as individuals on the way that they conduct their research projects. As noted in Chapter 7, rather than being a capitulation to relativism, this self-awareness in relation to the research process makes it easier for the epistemological and conceptual determinants of the researcher's agenda to be made explicit. Hopefully, Mark's and Alex's supervisors would encourage them to reflect both on their own roles within their research and also on the roles of the researched; ethical issues within such projects should as far as is possible be anticipated and considered in advance.

Using existing information

In the early stages of their research projects Mark and Alex need to make use of existing information in a number of different ways. Searching for and digesting existing literature was noted in Chapter 2 as being an important way for the researcher to develop a conceptual framework and to focus their research agenda. However, as discussed in Chapters 2 and 7, existing data such as documents and official statistics may also extend the researcher's knowledge of their substantive topic and act as a source of ideas.

Alex and Mark may have accumulated a certain amount of relevant material from the lecture notes and reading lists of courses that they have taken or are taking, but they will inevitably need to carry out further computer-based searches for information, whether using library catalogues and databases or via the Internet. Keyword searches of a university library catalogue may identify some potentially relevant material: for example the terms 'lone' and

'parent' or 'lone' and 'parenthood' might generate items such as books (e.g. Hardey and Crow, 1991), research reports (e.g. Bradshaw and Millar, 1991) and the publications of relevant organisations (e.g. the Gingerbread Lone Parents' Manual). The volume of material generated may be sufficiently large that searches using more specific terms or combinations of terms are appropriate. On the other hand, relevant material may be more sparse: for example, a keyword search using 'gender' and 'subject' might only generate one reference, and this relating to higher education rather than secondary education (Thomas, 1990). Clearly, a great deal of relevant material in relation to Alex's and Mark's topics may exist within more generic books on 'secondary education' and (the) 'family', but students should also not hesitate to search for relevant material contained within journal articles, including those within the increasing number of on-line journals.

A search of the Social Science Citation Index (using the Web of Science service; see the website at http://wos.mimas.ac.uk/), using keywords like those in the previous paragraph, would generate a range of potentially relevant references, some of which might be highly relevant but in journals which were not immediately accessible (e.g. Middleton (1995) considers the 'peripheral' nature of lone parents), and some of which might appear to be of tenuous relevance but could perhaps be worth following up (e.g. Greif (1992) considers lone fathers from the perspective of social work practice in the United States; Watson (1997) examines the relationship between discourses of femininity and discourses around single-sex schooling). However, some of the references generated might be in readily accessible journals and relate closely to the subject of interest (e.g. Stables and Stables (1995), Wikeley and Stables (1999) and Ashworth and Evans (1999) all relate to studies of gender and subject choice).

Searches for current or recent research projects may also be productive. A visit to the website of the Economic and Social Research Council (ESRC; http://www.esrc.ac.uk/) can lead on to a website listing research funded by the ESRC, including a research project on gender and subject choice by Stables and Wikeley. In addition to the projects themselves, this website (http://www.regard.ac.uk/) also lists related references (reports, journal articles, etc.).

References generated by literature searches

Hardey, M. and Crow, G. (1991) *Lone Parenthood: Coping with Constraints and Making Opportunities*, London: Harvester Wheatsheaf.

Bradshaw, J. and Millar, J. (1991) *Lone Parent Families in the UK* (Department of Social Security Research Report No. 6), London: HMSO.

Thomas, K. (1990) *Gender and Subject in Higher Education*, Buckingham: Society for Research into Higher Education and Open University.

Middleton, D. (1995) 'In What Ways can Lone Parents be Regarded as Peripheral in British Society?', *Health and Social Care in the Community* 3(3): 151–161.

Greif, G.L. (1992) 'Lone Fathers in the United States: An Overview and Practice Implications', *British Journal of Social Work* 22(5): 565–574.

Watson, S. (1997) 'Single-Sex Education for Girls: Heterosexuality, Gendered Subjectivity and School Choice', *British Journal of Sociology of Education* 18(3): 371–383.

Stables, A. and Stables, S. (1995) 'Gender Differences in Students' Approaches to A-Level Subject Choices and Perceptions of A-Level Subjects: A study of 1st Year A-Level Students in a Tertiary College', *Educational Research* 37(1): 39–51.

Wikeley, F. and Stables, A. (1999) 'Changes in School Students' Approaches to Subject Option

Choices: A Study of Pupils in the West of England in 1984 and 1996', *Educational Research* 41(3): 287–299.

Ashworth, J. and Evans, L. (1999) 'Lack of Knowledge Deters Women from Studying Economics', *Educational Research* 41(2): 209–221.

Taking Hardey and Crow's edited book as an example, by perusing it Mark would be able to establish that when considering the marginality of lone parents he might usefully reflect on issues of housing, health, employment and poverty as well as social contact/loneliness. Furthermore, and very importantly, the book would bring it home to him that lone parents are a heterogeneous group. The book also contains demographic information about lone parents in contemporary Britain that Mark might find useful, and its bibliography might lead him on to more specific references. Digesting material from this book would thus enhance both Mark's knowledge of his topic and also his conceptual framework.

Some of the documents relevant to Alex's project will need to be accessed during the fieldwork itself: for example, documents providing contextual information about the schools which act as settings for her fieldwork and also information about the pupils within them. Similarly, Mark may make use of personal documents relating to his respondents at a later stage in his research. However, there may be relevant publicly available documents which can be accessed immediately. Some of these may be accessible via the Internet: for example, the lone-parenthood-related organisation Gingerbread has a website (http://www.gingerbread.org.uk/), and school inspection reports are available via an official website (http://www.ofsted.gov.uk/). Official publications and official statistics more generally can be located by searches of guides and catalogues, which are increasingly electronic in form rather than hard copy volumes (see Chapter 7). The Department of Social Security has published a number of research reports relating to lone-parent families, and the official ONS journal

Population Trends contains many articles focusing on lone parents which are based on official data. Statistics relating to 'A' level entries and achievements, broken down by subject and gender, are published in the Department for Education and Employment's annual volume *Education and Training Statistics for the United Kingdom*.

As noted in Chapter 7, documents can constitute topics for research as well as or instead of being research resources. Hence Mark might have decided to base his dissertation on a critical analysis of documents (official or otherwise), focusing on their portrayal of lone parents. It is certainly the case that discussions of lone parenthood in the media and in official material 'problematise' lone-parent families, and it would therefore be interesting to subject such material to a discourse analysis. Similarly, Alex might have chosen to examine the gendering of teaching materials within school subjects, perhaps carrying out content analyses and/or adopting a semiotic approach (see Chapter 7). However, even if documents do not constitute the primary focus of Mark's and Alex's projects, the students still need to be aware of the ways in which the availability and nature of the documents reflect their authors' agendas and frames of reference (which in turn may reflect organisational or state concerns), and consequently to view the documents as something other than simply neutral information sources.

A mismatch between Alex's and Mark's frames of reference (and/or conceptual frameworks) and the frames of reference of the documents' authors may be more problematic if the students want to use the documents as information sources rather than as topics for critical analysis. In general, it is important that Alex and Mark evaluate the documents that they use in terms of the documents' validity for their purposes, coverage, representativeness, datedness, accuracy, etc.

Chapter 7 showed that secondary analysis can allow researchers to (partially) escape the constraints placed on published official statistics by those who produced them. If Mark had been orientated towards quantitative research, he might have planned his dissertation to take the form of a secondary analysis of lone-parent-related survey data. A keyword search of the catalogue of the Data Archive at the University of Essex would show that the survey on which Bradshaw and Millar's report is based is available to secondary analysts, as are many other surveys which contain sufficient information for lone parents and their families to be identifiable as such. For example, Mark could have chosen to compare the health and well-being of lone parents with the health and well-being of other categories of people, using data from the 1984/5 Health and Lifestyle Survey (Blaxter, 1990).

However, while the secondary analysis of a survey is no longer exorbitantly costly, combining it with extensive fieldwork is perhaps too demanding for an undergraduate dissertation; if Mark had chosen to re-analyse a survey he would have had to have spent a long time getting to know the dataset (via the documentation and exploratory analyses), and it would have been important for him at as early a stage as possible to have applied for access to and obtained a copy of the dataset on a disk or CD ROM. It perhaps should go without saying that Mark would need a basic level of technical proficiency in order to cope with the statistical computing required for a competent secondary analysis, since without this proficiency the research would not be feasible; developing this proficiency further would constitute another time-consuming aspect of secondary-analysis-based research.

Whatever forms of existing information Alex and Mark used in their projects, it would be important for them to keep adequate records of and/or take adequate notes from the material that they examined. Their examination of existing information is part of the broad process of building up a bibliography and accumulating a 'mound' of data; in addition, it forms part of the ongoing process of analysis (i.e. 'preliminary analysis': see Chapter 8), so along with their notes they would additionally need to keep a record of their analytical thoughts. (Note that some of the documentary information accumulated early in the research process might end up in appendices within their dissertation reports, though padding out their reports with irrelevant material could well be counterproductive.)

Sample design and access considerations

Alex's initial plan to focus on sixth-formers at her old school reflects both the target population in which she is interested (she wants to focus on the choices of 'A' level subjects that sixth-formers have made) and a pragmatic recognition that she will have to negotiate access to a sample of respondents. However, even obtaining access to her old school may not be unproblematic and thus needs to be taken seriously, and the fact that the school is mixed-sex means that she will not be able to generalise from it to sixth-formers across the full range of coeducational and single-sex schools. More generally, she needs to reflect upon the extent to which the experiences of sixth-formers at her old school are representative of the experiences of sixth-formers across Britain as a whole. Sampling sixth-formers across a wide range of schools is unlikely to be a practical possibility, but Alex might consider researching two (rather different) schools, and at the very least should reflect upon the idiosyncrasies of her own old school.

Since Alex wants to analyse the results from her questionnaires statistically, she needs a sufficiently large sample size for the findings from her analyses to be adequately precise. Her old school is large and has about 200 sixth-formers; if she restricts herself to this school then it may be possible for her to administer questionnaires to everybody, but if she researches two schools then she may need (for reasons of time and cost) to use a cluster sample of sub-groups of students within each school, perhaps stratified in some way (e.g. according to years and administrative groups; see Chapter 3 for discussions of clustering and stratification). Stratification may increase the representativeness of her sample, and it may be simplest to administer the questionnaires to clusters of students. Alex should be able to obtain a list of sixth-formers at the school(s) which

she can use as a sampling frame, and hence may be able to establish the extent (and nature) of non-response.

Alex expects her positive existing relationship with the headteacher at her old school to facilitate access; however, she will also need to present her research in a credible way which makes it clear that it will involve minimal disruption to the life of the school. She also needs to be careful not to assume that the good-will of the headteacher removes the need to obtain the willing cooperation of other teachers and her student respondents; gatekeepers may occupy hierarchical positions which are as much a hindrance to the researcher as a help. As far as a second school is concerned, she may benefit from discussing with her supervisor the most effective way of approaching the school to gain access; a letter from her supervisor confirming that she is who she claims to be may, for example, be useful.

Issues of sampling and access are also central to Mark's project. A key question for him to consider is the composition of his sample. Should he attempt to interview a diverse range of lone mothers – for example, in terms of class, employment status, number and ages of children, etc. – or should he aim for a more homogeneous sample? A diverse sample may generate a more extensive range of accounts and experiences, but a more focused sample may make it more straightforward both to identify recurrent themes and also to pin down explanations for differences between respondents. Generalisations from a more focused sample at first sight appear more risky, but, either way, Mark's small sample and the fact that he needs to use a non-random approach to sampling have implications for the generalisability of his findings.

Practical considerations may in any case make it difficult for Mark to construct a sample with a pre-determined range of characteristics or to engage in theoretical sampling (i.e. to select sequentially respondents in such a fashion as to help him develop his theoretical ideas; see Chapter 3). There is no specific social setting frequented by all lone mothers and exclusive to them; recruiting respondents via a relevant organisation such as

Gingerbread would have implications for the kind of respondent sampled, this being especially pertinent in the light of Mark's theoretical focus on social marginality. Snowball sampling would also risk generating a sample of respondents who belonged to (potentially supportive) social networks. Advertising for volunteers via strategically located posters might (or might not) tend to attract particularly marginal respondents. It might be useful for Mark to consider locating respondents via a school; after all, lone mothers all have children. However, access would then be needed to a setting rather than simply to respondents on an individual-by-individual basis. It seems likely that Mark's sample will in many ways be an opportunistic one, though he may be able to use some crude 'quotas' (e.g. to achieve a balance of lone mothers in and out of paid employment).

The size of Mark's sample should reflect both the extent to which he wishes to generalise from his findings and the nature of the interviews that he carries out; a small number of successful in-depth interviews can generate a wealth of data, but the emphasis would then be on individual accounts rather than on any commonalities or diversities in lone mothers' situations. Either a handful of life-history interviews or more focused interviews with a markedly larger sample of lone mothers would be of value, but these two alternatives correspond to projects with rather different aims and objectives.

Primary data collection

Learning about the 'world of the researched'

While both Alex and Mark intend their core data to be generated by specific research instruments, namely questionnaires and in-depth interviews, both may still be able to gather useful additional data by observing, in an unstructured and opportunistic way, the social worlds and physical environments in which their respondents live. Alex is

likely to be able to observe relevant aspects of the school(s) that she researches; Mark may be able to observe the homes of some of his interviewees, and may perhaps be able to observe at least part of the broader socio-geographical locations of their lives (especially if he recruits interviewees from a narrowly delimited geographical area). Neither is likely to become a participant observer (see Chapter 4), but it is possible that they might be able to become 'observers as participants' if this seems relevant to their research (e.g. by 'helping out' in school science practicals, or by participating in an activity organised by a branch of Gingerbread).

The desirability of a general alertness to the possibility that they will observe things relevant to 'gender' and 'marginality' means that Alex and Mark are likely to make 'fieldnotes' to supplement the data generated by their core research instruments. In addition, during the fieldwork process Alex and Mark may make opportunistic observations of the behaviour and conversations of people who are unaware that they are being watched or overheard by researchers, which could arguably be viewed as a covert aspect of otherwise overt research. However, while both Alex and Mark may have other roles in their research settings (i.e. as an ex-student and as a local resident), both are there primarily and explicitly as researchers, and as such the reactive effects of their presence thus constitute an issue that needs to be considered in relation to their observations.

Constructing and administering research instruments: questionnaires and interviews

Generating a questionnaire which respondents understand and to which they are able and willing to respond requires a good deal of preliminary reflection and preparation (see Chapter 5). Alex must think very carefully about the data that she needs to collect to achieve her research objectives, since the data collected will place bounds on her later analyses and theorising. (It may be that she decides after all that her objectives are too exploratory and too orientated towards the views of individual social actors for a survey to be appropriate; sometimes 'doing a survey' can be an automatic response to a research problem rather than one that has been properly thought through.)

Alex also needs to ensure that her questions are expressed in language that is familiar and comprehensible to the sixth-formers to whom she administers the questionnaires. Background reading and 'brainstorming' may be helpful in this context, but it would also be sensible for her to carry out some preliminary qualitative research (e.g. some unstructured interviews or perhaps a focus group) to generate issues and appropriate terminology that can be embedded in her questionnaire (see Chapters 5 and 6).

The dependent variables and one of the explanatory variables that will feature in Alex's later analyses are fairly self-evident, i.e. subject choices at 'A' level (and also, before that, at GCSE level) and the respondent's sex. Constructing questions to collect these data may be reasonably straightforward. However, operationalising other relevant concepts may be more of a challenge. Alex's background reading and preliminary qualitative research may have suggested to her that the respondent's self-perception in terms of femininity and masculinity may be of importance, but may in addition have suggested to her that both the views, behaviour and characteristics of friends, teachers and parents and also societal norms more generally may be of relevance. Alex's questionnaire is therefore likely to contain clusters of questions corresponding to these various possible factors.

It may be possible for Alex to find appropriate measures or questions which have been developed by earlier researchers: for example, within the research on gender and subject choice located above, or within past research on masculinity/femininity. She might, for example, make use of the Bem Sex Rolé Inventory (see Annandale and Hunt, 1990). The use of existing measures can facilitate comparisons with earlier research (see Chapter 5);

more generally it would make sense for Alex to collect some forms of data in a standard way: for example, standard questions relating to parents' occupations would allow her to classify her respondents' class backgrounds according to a standard schema.

Once Alex has assembled a range of new and existing questions within a draft questionnaire she will need to pilot it. Administering the pilot questionnaire to a small number of sixth-formers may identify specific problems with question wording, may indicate which (if any) of a number of questions on a particular issue look likely to generate useful data, and may suggest ways in which open-ended questions can be converted into closed questions, i.e. questions with a fixed range of possible answers. The experience of administering the pilot questionnaire, together with feedback from the pilot respondents, is likely to be very valuable to Alex. She needs to be careful to use a questionnaire which is short enough to be tolerable to her respondents and which will be relatively easy to process when she prepares the data for her statistical analyses. A compact questionnaire consisting of closed, pre-coded questions would be best from this point of view, though it will inevitably place restrictions on the range and depth of her analyses. (Careful planning may also result in a questionnaire which can be scanned, though it is more likely that Alex will have to transcribe the data from the questionnaires into a spreadsheet, or into statistical software such as SPSS for Windows.)

The most effective way for Alex to administer her final questionnaire may be for groups of students to fill it in while she is present, since administering it on a one-to-one basis will be impractical but 'mailing' it to students could result in considerable non-response. If she administers it in this way, her presence will also allow her to 'introduce' the questionnaire and to clarify the meaning of questions where necessary, thereby reducing her dependency on the effectiveness of the questionnaire as a self-contained research instrument. However, a well-laid-out and attractive questionnaire will still be advisable.

While Mark's interviews lean towards exploration rather than statistical hypothesis testing, and are likely to be less strongly structured than Alex's questionnaire, they will still be structured to some extent by his research agenda. The focus on 'marginality' within his research will dictate a range of topics on which he will want to collect data from his respondents: for example, he will want the interviews to generate data which can be tied in with the various possible social and material dimensions of marginality (as indicated by the literature). However, his interviews are likely to be loosely structured around a list of topics, so that a degree of standardisation in terms of content will probably not result in a similar degree of standardisation in terms of the order in which the topics are covered and in terms of the length of the interview.

Mark needs to be careful to collect systematically any data that he needs to have in a consistent form for each and every interviewee: for example, the concept of class is relevant to many qualitative projects, but it is not unusual for students doing such projects to have difficulties assigning interviewees to social classes because of inadequacies in the range and form of occupational information that they have collected.

Mark's interviews are likely to be shorter than unstructured, life-history interviews, but, though semi-structured, his interviews will still be sufficiently flexible and non-directive for the lone mothers' own individual perspectives to become evident, and for the data from the interviews to be analysed using a Grounded Theory approach (see Chapter 6). It may be the case that in early interviews topics arise that Mark can follow up in later interviews; as such the first few interviews that Mark carries out may act as an intentional or de facto piloting process. Assuming that there is a fair degree of consistency in the material covered by his interviews, Mark may also be in a position to make some cautious generalisations.

Mark will need to be reflexive about his role within the research process. Clearly, the data generated by the interviews will to an extent reflect how visible within the questions that he asks his focus on marginality is, though his questions may seem, at least superficially, to relate to the lives of lone mothers in general. More generally, the kinds of question that he asks will in part determine the nature of the data collected (e.g. just as in questionnaire-based research, more 'open-ended' and less specific questions will allow the interviewee more control over the course and content of the interview). In addition, Mark may perceive himself as 'neutral', but he still needs to realise that his visible characteristics, manner, reactions to what an interviewee says, etc., may have reactive effects and hence shape the data generated. Arguably this is bound to be the case.

A degree of reflexive self-awareness may also be an important attribute for Mark to possess in relation to effective qualitative interviewing; he needs to have the self-discipline to listen actively and to monitor and control his own desire to talk. Interviewing is a form of social interaction; Mark may like or dislike an interviewee (both of which can be equally problematic), but he will be better able to make sense of the interview data if he can put himself in his interviewees' shoes and understand how they feel about and respond to being interviewed.

Developing a rapport and even empathising with respondents may be as much pragmatic as appropriate ethically; there are good, instrumental reasons for 'getting on' with gatekeepers and respondents. However, the social nature of social research brings with it responsibilities as well as practical and epistemological problems: Mark and Alex need to reflect continually on ethical aspects of their research. For example, there is clearly an important ethical issue for Mark to be aware of in relation to his interviews; conversations can be enjoyable but they can also be damaging, and the concept of 'marginality' could very easily turn out to be a sensitive one which leads to the interviews being a disturbing experience for some interviewees and/or for Mark.

Practicalities may dictate when and where each of Mark's interviews takes place, and can also affect how long each interview lasts. The social and physical context of an interview may affect the data collected (e.g. does the interviewee feel comfortable? does Mark feel 'at home'? are the interviewees' children in the house, and potentially within earshot?). There is much to be said for an interview in a private setting in which the interviewee feels relaxed and where there is no time pressure; however, this can sometimes be an unachievable ideal. A lone mother may have left her children with a baby-sitter who is impatient or who is paid by the hour; time constraints inevitably have implications for the coverage and/or pacing of interviews (see Chapter 6). Finally, in relation to the time and place of interviews, even a large, physically powerful person like Mark should take into account their own safety and, of course, the safety and well-being of interviewees.

Mark needs to prepare conscientiously for each interview: for example, by making sure that he arrives on time, and is equipped with his interview schedule/list of topics. Assuming that he is tape-recording his interviews, which needs the consent of interviewees but which preserves a more satisfactory record than note taking, he should be equipped with spare batteries and blank cassettes. (This may seem obvious, but it is surprisingly easy to make simple mistakes, such as failing to turn a microphone on.) The taped interviews can be listened to later at his leisure, though he needs to remember that transcribing interviews is a time-consuming exercise so he should avoid leaving himself too little time to process and analyse his data.

While still at the data-collection stage of their projects, Alex and Mark should engage both in processual analysis (see Chapter 8) and also in process writing (see Chapter 10). Feeding the results of the process of piloting a questionnaire into the design of the final questionnaire can be regarded as a form of processual analysis, as can allowing the findings from earlier interviews to influence the selection of later interviewees. Keeping a field journal is a form of process writing, and both Alex and Mark need to make notes about various aspects of the data-collection process so that they can contextualise the data generated. For example, Mark might usefully supplement his interview transcripts with contextual notes about the interview setting, etc., written as soon as possible after the interviews. However, the research process may also generate more analytical or methodological reflections: for example, Alex may be stimulated by the piloting process to make some notes about the pros and cons of using questionnaires to research gender and subject choice.

Data preparation, data analysis and writing

Preparation

In both Alex's and Mark's projects, the early stages of their data analyses will be in parallel with a process of data preparation. In Mark's case, the transcription of his early interviews may be interspersed with his later interviews. Transcribing taped interviews, while good experience, is a time-consuming process, perhaps taking six or more times the duration of the original interviews (half a dozen two-hour interviews could thus generate a couple of weeks' worth of solid transcribing), so Mark may prefer to be, or be forced to be, selective about the material that he transcribes. In this sense a process of interpretation and analysis is already taking place, since he is deciding which material is of theoretical relevance.

The process of transcription will certainly help familiarise Mark with his data; interesting quotes may 'stand out' from the flow of conversation, and common themes and issues may resonate across a number of interviews (see Chapter 8). Of course, Mark's perception of quotes as interesting and his identification of recurring themes are to some extent a reflection of his own research agenda and conceptual framework; it may be the case that a number of his interviewees do express a pride in their independence and self-sufficiency as lone mothers, but it is Mark who chooses to present and interpret this aspect of what his interviewees have said.

For Mark, transcribing his interviews directly into a word processor has obvious advantages with respect to the later manipulation of the data (whether within the word processor itself or within dedicated qualitative data analysis software such as NUD*IST or Atlas-ti). For Alex, building up a 'data matrix' that she can analyse statistically (see Chapter 5), by inputting her questionnaire data into a spreadsheet or directly into statistical software such as SPSS for Windows, is a necessity. This process of data entry, like interview transcription, takes time; even if her questionnaire is a short one, the sample size will ensure that the data entry constitutes a day or two's work, and a longer questionnaire could take a week or more to process. Entering data from pre-coded questions can be gratifyingly rapid; however, Alex may find the flow of her typing repeatedly interrupted by questions whose answers require coding: for example, when she codes her respondents' parents' occupations into social classes (which may involve flicking through the pages of the Standard Occupational Classification schema). To avoid these interruptions, Alex might usefully work through her pile of questionnaires beforehand, coding the parents' occupations and the answers to other, open-ended questions. This will also help her to build up a codebook containing a coding frame for each question, so that she can ensure that the answers to each question are coded consistently across the full range of questionnaires.

Analysis

As noted above, Mark's analysis of his interview data will in a sense be well under way by the time he moves on to a more self-conscious, systematic form of analysis (though Mark should probably start this latter form of analysis before he has finished carrying out all his interviews). Being thorough and 'systematic' when analysing qualitative data, however, does not imply a mechanical adherence to set procedures as might be outlined in a rather more prescriptive research methods text. As noted in Chapter 8, qualitative data analysis is an individualised, creative process requiring reflexivity and insight. On the other hand, a Grounded Theory approach (see Chapter 8), or, for that matter, any credible approach to analysing qualitative data, necessitates strong linkages between data and reported findings and interpretations.

The bulk of the 'data mound' on which Mark's analyses will be based consists of his interview transcripts. He will need to sort through that mound, breaking it down into digestible chunks, setting aside (at least temporarily) chunks which do not seem of immediate relevance, and labelling and rearranging the more overtly relevant material. As Mark attaches codes to chunks of data, he will be engaged simultaneously in processes of data reduction, data description and data interpretation; his codes may reflect the raw data but they are also shaped by processes of selection and interpretation determined by his conceptual framework.

As noted in Chapter 8, codes can be descriptive, interpretative or explanatory. For example, suppose that one of Mark's interviewees has commented that she does not go out socially very often. This could be coded descriptively as a lack of social activity, interpretatively as indicating a sense of social marginality, or explanatorily as a reflection of implicit comparisons made by the interviewee between her current social life, her past social life, and social norms relating to social activity. More generally, Mark might start, via a process of axial coding, to make linkages between chunks of interview transcript relating to 'social marginality' and chunks relating to 'the importance of relationships with children'. Note that, while grounded in his interview data, Mark's analysis will also be tied to the broad concept of 'marginality', and hence his analysis will be linked to a conceptual framework whose origins are outside and pre-date his own data. However, Mark's conceptual framework will no doubt in turn be amended and developed in the light of his interview data.

When presenting his findings Mark needs to be reflexive about his role within the research process, both in terms of his conceptual framework and also in terms of the specificities of his data analysis. Viewed from the perspective of (crude) relativism, the validity of his findings will be wholly content-specific and researcher-specific. However, for readers who view generalising from his specific findings as a possibility, the validity and reliability of his findings can only be properly assessed if he has adequately documented both the conceptual and the procedural dimensions of his research. As noted in Chapter 8, Mark should be open about the research process culminating in his written report, and should not shy away from exposing the process to external scrutiny.

The analysis stage of Alex's research will to an extent have been pre-determined in nature and scope by the questions that she included in her research instrument. Before she tests any hypotheses, however, it makes sense for Alex (like Mark) first to 'get to know' her data. This in practice will involve examining the ranges (and frequencies) of different answers given to each of her questions. There is a good chance that Alex will need to manipulate the data generated by a question before they can be used in an analysis; it is likely that the number of categories of answer will need to be reduced to produce a variable which has both a manageable number of categories and adequate numbers of cases in each category; furthermore, data from a number of questions may need to be combined. The implementation of this recoding process may require a degree of technical expertise, but Alex also needs to be aware of the conceptual dimension and implications of this process (see the companion web pages).

Once she has examined, and where necessary manipulated, the individual variables that she has generated, Alex can move on to examine bivariate relationships between (pairs of) variables. At minimum, Alex needs to have enough technical expertise to summarise relationships in some appropriate way, and to test whether observed relationships are statistically significant (i.e. are not simply coincidences). The level of measurement of some of Alex's variables may be interval-level (e.g. her masculinity/femininity scale), but if she recodes all her variables into sets of categories, she can use cross-tabulations and chi-square tests for all her bivariate analyses (see Chapter 9), though this will involve losing some of the detail in her data.

Alex might, for example, cross-tabulate individuals' choices of 'A' level subjects (recoded into categories such as 'sciences', 'arts', 'social sciences', 'mixed', etc.) against their levels of femininity or masculinity (recoded into categories such as 'high', 'medium' and 'low'). Alex could then look at the chi-square statistic for the cross-tabulation (and its P-value, i.e. level of significance) to see whether there was adequate evidence for her to conclude that a relationship exists between subject choice and level of femininity. It would probably be sensible to do this analysis for each sex separately, which would in effect necessitate looking at a three-way (three-dimensional) cross-tabulation. Alex might also find other ways of elaborating the bivariate analysis to make it multivariate: for example, by seeing whether the relationship existed, and was of the same magnitude, in two different schools.

When presenting her statistical analyses, Alex should recognise that the reader needs to know enough about what she has done to make sense of and interpret properly the figures that she presents (see Chapter 9). Hence she needs to make explicit both how variables were constructed (both in terms of the original questions and in terms of subsequent recoding), and also who is included in (and excluded from) each of her cross-tabulations. Her cross-tabulations should contain both percentages and Ns (sub-sample sizes), as well as including appropriate headings and labelling. Alex should also not be afraid to reflect in the accompanying text on the conceptual limitations of her variables; variables are, after all, rarely ideal indicators of the concepts of interest. More generally, Alex needs to discuss the size and composition of her sample to contextualise her detailed findings. The characteristics of her data and her sample have obvious implications for the generalisability of her findings; overall, like Mark, Alex needs to be open and communicative about her research, to enable readers to subject it to informed scrutiny.

Writing (up)

Let us assume that time has moved on, and that Alex and Mark are in the latter stages of their research. It will be easier for Alex to 'write up' her dissertation if she has been writing short accounts of her statistical analyses as she has carried them out. Mark's analyses of his qualitative interview data could also have been usefully done in parallel with a certain amount of process writing. Furthermore, there is no reason why both Alex and Mark should not have been generating other pieces of written material as their projects have progressed: for example, reviews of relevant literature, discussions of aspects of their research designs and of the research process, 'memos' that they have written to remind themselves of pertinent thoughts that they have had as the research has progressed, etc. However, there will be a point at which the data analysis reaches a summative analysis stage (see Chapter 8), where the form of writing shifts completely from process writing to product writing (see Chapter 10), and where the emphasis is on drawing together the material already written and the research findings and conclusions. At this point the material written earlier may need to be partially rewritten, so that the text generated during the process writing and product writing stages forms a coherent and fluid whole.

Writing and rewriting sections of a research report may not seem the most efficient way of generating the required volume of text, but a series of drafts of 'chapters' will have given Mark and Alex the opportunity to get feedback from their dissertation supervisors, and/or from their fellow students. Indeed, since Mark and Alex are on the same degree course, have known each other for a couple of years, and get on well, they have been able to use each other as sounding boards throughout the research process. Fortunately, they trust and like each other enough to be able to handle the constructive criticisms with which they provide each other. Mark is not as happy with the feedback from his supervisor, whom he regards as pedantic, and on occasions unnecessarily destructive; Alex could in theory get feedback from her partner Robin, but feels that this might be dangerously 'close to home', and be too much of a case of mixing business with pleasure. Alex gets on well with her supervisor, though she treats some of his advice with a pinch of salt.

Mark's and Alex's approaches to writing differ markedly, though each recognises the importance of a degree of self-discipline: Alex sets herself a daily target of 1000 words (written sitting on her orthopaedic chair in front of her PC), but is flexible enough to realise that this may turn out to be too optimistic on some days – for example, on a day when she realises that she needs to slightly alter some of her cross-tabulations; conversely, Mark has bursts of academic activity and is quite capable of spending a few hours after midnight lying on his bedroom floor writing, but he will force himself to be more systematic if he feels that he is falling behind schedule, even if it means that there is a risk that he will need to revise extensively what he has written at a later date. When Mark loses concentration, he takes a break, boils a kettle, and makes himself a herbal tea; when Alex has an academic off-day, she shrugs her shoulders and goes to the cinema, since she sees no point in banging her head against a brick wall if she does not absolutely have to.

Both Alex and Mark monitor carefully how much they have written: Alex because it comes naturally to her to do so, and Mark because he tends to end up having written too much and hates editing it down to meet specified maximum word lengths. Alex sympathises with Mark, because her tendency is to want to include very detailed accounts of the literature that she has read; she has recently become more ruthless in terms of leaving things out which are interesting but which are of limited relevance. Between them Mark and Alex have come to the conclusion that they need to include the following in their dissertation reports:

- an abstract
- an outline section (specifying the aims and objectives of the research)
- a review of the relevant existing literature (to provide a background/context for the research)
- material on methodological and technical issues (including the research design, ethical issues, etc.)
- data analyses and findings
- a discussion and conclusions section
- a bibliography
- various appendices
- 'accessories' to improve the report in presentational terms (e.g. plastic covers and a spiral binding; diagrams and illustrations; coloured sheets between sections, etc.).

In drawing up the above list both Alex and Mark have been influenced by examples of various relevant forms of research product that they have read; in particular, they have both studied the format of journal articles, chapters in books and research reports in the respective substantive fields of their dissertations. Given that their dissertation reports are meant to be 10 000 to 12 000 words in length, whole books do not seem to be that relevant a point of comparison, though Mark quite likes the idea of splitting his report into various 'chapters'.

Alex also likes the idea of having a number of sections with appropriate headings, but she is a little worried that her report will end up appearing to be rather fragmentary. She recognises that planning the written account of her dissertation is as much about aiming for a coherent whole as it is about planning the report's detailed content. Good dissertation reports are strong on analysis as well as on data and description; interesting empirical material which is not drawn together via an analytical thread or 'story-line' running through the report (or via some other analytical structure) may give the impression of technical competence but a lack of imagination in conceptual or theoretical terms.

Ideas from the literature may be helpful to Alex and Mark in this context, as may their ability to be reflexive about their research. Mark learned from the existing literature that lone mothers are a heterogeneous group of people; his research confirmed this but also brought home to him something that he was not expecting: the almost paradoxical mix of positive and negative aspects within his interviewees' lives. His dissertation report is therefore going to be structured in such a way as to emphasise the diverse, multidimensional and ambiguous natures of lone mothers' lives. Some of Alex's statistical analyses were disappointingly inconclusive. However, they collectively suggested to her that contextual factors were more important than individual students' own characteristics, something that she intends to contrast with the emphases in some of the existing literature and to use as a signpost to potentially valuable future research (perhaps within her own Master's degree). Neither Alex nor Mark is afraid to be explicitly self-critical with regard to their research, which seems appropriate, as research is rarely or never flawless.

Tying up loose ends

Once their dissertations are more or less written up, Mark and Alex can move on to check whether there are any flaws that can be eradicated, improvements in fluency and style that can be made, and things that can be done to create a more favourable impression on the reader. Using the spell-check facility in their word processors is obvious; less obvious is the need to proofread the whole document (since the spell-check facility cannot tell that Mark meant to type 'from' rather than 'form'). Reading through her whole dissertation report may make Alex realise that she could usefully add some short sentences signposting changes in direction, which otherwise may come across to the reader as abrupt and awkward. She may also realise that it would be useful for the reader to have her survey codebook to hand as an appendix, though she would need to check that this did not inadvertently take her beyond the specified word limit. Mark may not initially think to include title and contents pages and a paragraph acknowledging the contributions made by his respondents, tolerant housemates, etc. Both Alex and Mark are sensible enough to ensure that their submitted dissertation reports are consistent with the departmental guidelines supplied to them.

Mark may have turned out to be a surprisingly good interviewer, and Alex's survey data may be of a quality of which any researcher would justifiably be proud. However, the marks that they receive will be based on their written dissertation reports and will thus only indirectly reflect the research processes that generated these. The last lap of the research process is thus, in instrumental terms at least, the most crucial one. While they may be heartily sick of their research projects by the end of the year, it would be a shame if either Alex or Mark made a sow's ear out of a silk purse, especially since their written dissertation reports may conceivably be of value to them at some later stage, i.e. as something more than mementoes of the time when they were students.

Appendix A   **Ethical codes**

GUIDANCE NOTES

Statement of Ethical Practice

The British Sociological Association gratefully acknowledges the use made of the ethical codes produced by the American Sociological Association, the Association of Social Anthropologists of the Commonwealth and the Social Research Association.

Styles of sociological work are diverse and subject to change, not least because sociologists work within a wide variety of settings. Sociologists, in carrying out their work, inevitably face ethical, and sometimes legal, dilemmas which arise out of competing obligations and conflicts of interest. The following statement aims to alert the members of the Association to issues that raise ethical concerns and to indicate potential problems and conflicts of interest that might arise in the course of their professional activities. While they are not exhaustive, the statement points to a set of obligations to which members should normally adhere as principles for guiding their conduct. Departures from the principles should be the result of deliberation and not ignorance. The strength of this statement and its binding force rest ultimately on active discussion, reflection, and continued use by sociologists. In addition, the statement will help to communicate the professional position of sociologists to others, especially those involved in or affected by the activities of sociologists.

The statement is meant, primarily, to inform members' ethical judgements rather than to impose on them an external set of standards. The purpose is to make members aware of the ethical issues that may arise in their work, and to encourage them to educate themselves and their colleagues to behave ethically. The statement does not, therefore, provide a set of recipes for resolving ethical choices or dilemmas, but recognises that often it will be necessary to make such choices on the basis of principles and values, and the (often conflicting) interests of those involved.

Statement of Ethical Practice

PROFESSIONAL INTEGRITY

Members should strive to maintain the integrity of sociological enquiry as a discipline, the freedom to research and study, and to publish and promote the results of sociological research. Members have a responsibility both to safeguard the proper interests of those involved in or affected by their work, and to report their findings accurately and truthfully. They need to consider the effects of their involvements and the consequences of their work or its misuse for those they study and other interested parties.

While recognising that training and skill are necessary to the conduct of social research, members should themselves recognise the boundaries of their professional competence. They should not accept work of a kind that they are not qualified to carry out. Members should satisfy themselves that the research they undertake is worthwhile and that the techniques proposed are appropriate. They should be clear about the limits of their detachment from and involvement in their areas of study.

Members should be careful not to claim an expertise in areas outside those that would be recognised academically as their true fields of expertise. Particularly in their relations with the media, members should have regard for the reputation of the discipline and refrain from offering expert commentaries in a form that would appear to give credence to material which, as researchers, they would regard as comprising inadequate or tendentious evidence.

RELATIONS WITH AND RESPONSIBILITIES TOWARDS RESEARCH PARTICIPANTS

Sociologists, when they carry out research, enter into personal and moral relationships with those they study, be they individuals, households, social groups or corporate entities. Although sociologists, like other researchers are committed to the advancement of knowledge, that goal does not, of itself, provide an entitlement to override the rights of others. Members must satisfy themselves that a study is necessary for the furtherance of knowledge before embarking upon it. Members should be aware that they have some responsibility for the use to which their research may be put. Discharging that responsibility may on occasion be difficult, especially in situations of social conflict, competing social interests or where there is unanticipated misuse of the research by third parties.

1. Relationships with research participants
[a] Sociologists have a responsibility to ensure that the physical, social and psychological well-being of research participants is not adversely affected by the research. They should strive to protect the rights of those they study, their interests, sensitivities and privacy, while recognising the difficulty of balancing potentially conflicting interests. Because sociologists study the relatively powerless as well as those more powerful than themselves, research relationships are frequently characterised by disparities of power and status. Despite this, research relationships should be characterised, whenever possible, by trust. In some cases, where the public interest dictates otherwise and particularly where power is being abused, obligations of trust and protection may weigh less heavily. Nevertheless, these obligations should not be discarded lightly.
[b] As far as possible sociological research should be based on the freely given informed consent of those studied. This implies a responsibility on the sociologist to explain as fully as possible, and in terms meaningful to participants, what the research is about, who is undertaking and financing it, why it is being undertaken, and how it is to be promoted.
(i) Research participants should be made aware of their right to refuse participation whenever and for whatever reason they wish.
(ii) Research participants should understand how far they will be afforded anonymity and confidentiality and should be able to reject the use of data-gathering devices such as tape recorders and video cameras. Sociologists should be careful, on the one hand, not to give

Statement of Ethical Practice

unrealistic guarantees of confidentiality and, on the other, not to permit communication of research films or records to audiences other than those to which the research participants have agreed.

(iii) Where there is a likelihood that data may be shared with other researchers, the potential uses to which the data might be put may need to be discussed with research participants.

(iv) When making notes, filming or recording for research purposes, sociologists should make clear to research participants the purpose of the notes, filming or recording, and, as precisely as possible, to whom it will be communicated.

(v) It should also be borne in mind that in some research contexts, especially those involving field research, it may be necessary for the obtaining of consent to be regarded, not as a once-and-for-all prior event, but as a process, subject to renegotiation over time. In addition, particular care may need to be taken during periods of prolonged fieldwork where it is easy for research participants to forget that they are being studied.

(vi) In some situations access to a research setting is gained via a 'gatekeeper'. In these situations members should adhere to the principle of obtaining informed consent directly from the research participants to whom access is required, while at the same time taking account of the gatekeepers' interest. Since the relationship between the research participant and the gatekeeper may continue long after the sociologist has left the research setting, care should be taken not to disturb that relationship unduly.

[c] It is incumbent upon members to be aware of the possible consequences of their work. Wherever possible they should attempt to anticipate, and to guard against, consequences for research participants which can be predicted to be harmful. Members are not absolved from this responsibility by the consent given by research participants.

[d] In many of its guises, social research intrudes into the lives of those studied. While some participants in sociological research may find the experience a positive and welcome one, for others, the experience may be disturbing. Even if not exposed to harm, those studied may feel wronged by aspects of the research process. This can be particularly so if they perceive apparent intrusions into their private and personal worlds, or where research gives rise to false hopes, uncalled for self-knowledge, or unnecessary anxiety. Members should consider carefully the possibility that the research experience may be a disturbing one and, normally, should attempt to minimise disturbance to those participating in research. It should be borne in mind that decisions made on the basis of research may have effects on individuals as members of a group, even if individual research participants are protected by confidentiality and anonymity.

[e] Special care should be taken where research participants are particularly vulnerable by virtue of factors such as age, social status and powerlessness. Where research participants are ill or too young or too old to participate, proxies may need to be used in order to gather data. In these situations care should be taken not to intrude on the personal space of the person to whom the data ultimately refer, or to disturb the relationship between this person and the proxy. Where it can be inferred that the person about whom data are sought would object to supplying certain kinds of information, that material should not be sought from the proxy.

2. Covert Research

There are serious ethical dangers in the use of covert research but covert methods may avoid certain problems. For instance, difficulties arise when research participants change their behaviour because they know they are being studied. Researchers may also face problems when access to spheres of social life is closed to social scientists by powerful or secretive interests. However, covert methods violate the principles of informed consent and may invade the privacy of those being studied. Participant or non-participant observation in

Statement of Ethical Practice

4

non-public spaces or experimental manipulation of research participants without their knowledge should be resorted to only where it is impossible to use other methods to obtain essential data. In such studies it is important to safeguard the anonymity of research participants. Ideally, where informed consent has not been obtained prior to the research it should be obtained post-hoc.

3. Anonymity, privacy and confidentiality

[a] The anonymity and privacy of those who participate in the research process should be respected. Personal information concerning research participants should be kept confidential. In some cases it may be necessary to decide whether it is proper or appropriate even to record certain kinds of sensitive information.

[b] Where possible, threats to the confidentiality and anonymity of research data should be anticipated by researchers. The identities and research records of those participating in research should be kept confidential whether or not an explicit pledge of confidentiality has been given. Appropriate measures should be taken to store research data in a secure manner. Members should have regard to their obligations under the Data Protection Act. Where appropriate and practicable, methods for preserving the privacy of data should be used. These may include the removal of identifiers, the use of pseudonyms and other technical means for breaking the link between data and identifiable individuals such as 'broadbanding' or micro-aggregation. Members should also take care to prevent data being published or released in a form which would permit the actual or potential identification of research participants. Potential informants and research participants, especially those possessing a combination of attributes which make them readily identifiable, may need to be reminded that it can be difficult to disguise their identity without introducing an unacceptably large measure of distortion into the data.

[c] Guarantees of confidentiality and anonymity given to research participants must be honoured, unless there are clear and overriding reasons to do otherwise. Other people, such as colleagues, research staff or others, given access to the data must also be made aware of their obligations in this respect. By the same token, sociologists should respect the efforts taken by other researchers to maintain anonymity. Research data given in confidence do not enjoy legal privilege, that is they may be liable to subpoena by a court. Research participants may also need to be made aware that it may not be possible to avoid legal threats to the privacy of the data.

[d] There may be less compelling grounds for extending guarantees of privacy or confidentiality to public organisations, collectivities, governments, officials or agencies than to individuals or small groups. Nevertheless, where guarantees have been given they should be honoured, unless there are clear and compelling reasons not to do so.

4. During their research members should avoid, where they can, actions which may have deleterious consequences for sociologists who come after them or which might undermine the reputation of sociology as a discipline.

RELATIONS WITH & RESPONSIBILITIES TOWARDS SPONSORS AND/OR FUNDERS

A common interest exists between sponsor, funder and sociologist as long as the aim of the social inquiry is to advance knowledge, although such knowledge may only be of limited benefit to the sponsor and the funder. That relationship is best served if the atmosphere is conducive to high professional standards. Members should attempt to ensure that sponsors and/or funders appreciate the obligations that sociologists have not only to them, but also to society at large, research participants and professional colleagues and the sociological community. The relationship between sponsors or funders and social researchers should be such as to enable social inquiry to be undertaken as objectively as possible. Research should be undertaken with a view to providing information or explanation rather than being constrained to reach particular

Statement of Ethical Practice

5

conclusions or prescribe particular courses of action.

1. Clarifying obligations, roles and rights

[a] Members should clarify in advance the respective obligations of funders and researchers where possible in the form of a written contract. They should refer the sponsor or funder to the relevant parts of the professional code to which they adhere. Members should also be careful not to promise or imply acceptance of conditions which are contrary to their professional ethics or competing commitments. Where some or all of those involved in the research are also acting as sponsors and/or funders of research the potential for conflict between the different roles and interests should also be made clear to them.

[b] Members should also recognise their own general or specific obligations to the sponsors whether contractually defined or only the subject of informal and often unwritten agreements. They should be honest and candid about their qualifications and expertise, the limitations, advantages and disadvantages of the various methods of analysis and data, and acknowledge the necessity for discretion with confidential information obtained from sponsors. They should also try not to conceal factors which are likely to affect satisfactory conditions or the completion of a proposed research project or contract.

2. Pre-empting outcomes and negotiations about research

[a] Members should not accept contractual conditions that are contingent upon a particular outcome or set of findings from a proposed inquiry. A conflict of obligations may also occur if the funder requires particular methods to be used.

[b] Members should try to clarify, before signing the contract, that they are entitled to be able to disclose the source of their funds, its personnel, the aims of the institution, and the purposes of the project.

[c] Members should also try to clarify their right to publish and spread the results of their research.

[d] Members have an obligation to ensure sponsors grasp the implications of the choice between alternative research methods.

3. Guarding privileged information and negotiating problematic sponsorship

[a] Members are frequently furnished with information by the funder who may legitimately require it to be kept confidential. Methods and procedures that have been utilised to produce published data should not, however, be kept confidential unless otherwise agreed.

[b] When negotiating sponsorships members should be aware of the requirements of the law with respect to the ownership of and rights of access to data.

[c] In some political, social and cultural contexts some sources of funding and sponsorship may be contentious. Candour and frankness about the source of funding may create problems of access or co-operation for the social researcher but concealment may have serious consequences for colleagues, the discipline and research participants. The emphasis should be on maximum openness.

[d] Where sponsors and funders also act directly or indirectly as gatekeepers and control access to participants, researchers should not devolve their responsibility to protect the participants' interests onto the gatekeeper. Members should be wary of inadvertently disturbing the relationship between participants and gatekeepers since that will continue long after the researcher has left.

4. Obligations to sponsors and/or funders during the research process

[a] Members have a responsibility to notify the sponsor and/or funder of any proposed departure from the terms of reference of the proposed change in the nature of the contracted research.

[b] A research study should not be undertaken on the basis of resources known from the start to be inadequate, whether the work is of a sociological or inter-disciplinary kind.

[c] When financial support or sponsorship has been accepted, members must make every

Statement of Ethical Practice

6

reasonable effort to complete the proposed research on schedule, including reports to the funding source.

[d] Members should be prepared to take comments from sponsors or funders or research participants.

[e] Members should, wherever possible, spread their research findings.

[f] Members should normally avoid restrictions on their freedom to publish or otherwise broadcast research findings.

At its meeting in July 1994, the BSA Executive Committee approved a set of Rules for the Conduct of Enquiries into Complaints against BSA members under the auspices of this Statement, and also under the auspices of the BSA Guidelines on Professional Conduct. If you would like more details about the Rules, you should contact the BSA Office at the address/phone number given at the end of this statement.

☐

☐

APPROVED AGM 92; AMENDED AGM 93 (draft amendments added December 1996). bsamisc\ethgu2.doc

British Sociological Association
Units 3F/G, Mountjoy Research Centre, Stockton Road, Durham DH1 3UR [UK] telephone +44 (0) 191 383 0839, facsimile +44 (0) 191 383 0782
e-mail: britsoc@dial.pipex.com, Home Page: http://dspace.dial.pipex.com/britsoc/
The BSA is a charity registered in England, number 213577

bera BERA Ethical Guidelines

British Educational Research Association Ethical Guidelines

Introduction

The British Educational Research Association adopted the following set of ethical guidelines at its Annual General Meeting on 28 August 1992. These are based on guidelines developed at a BERA seminar in March 1988 (published in Research Intelligence, February 1989) and the proposed ethical standards of the American Educational Research Association as published in Educational Researcher, December 1991. (We are grateful to the AERA Committee on Standards for permission to adapt their guidelines.)

The Guidelines

1. The British Educational Research Association believes that all educational research should be conducted within an ethic of respect for persons, respect for knowledge, respect for democratic values, and respect for the quality of educational research.

Responsibility to the research profession

2. Educational researchers should aim to avoid fabrication, falsification, or misrepresentation of evidence, data, findings, or conclusions.

3. Educational researchers should aim to report their findings to all relevant stakeholders and so refrain from keeping secret or selectively communicating their findings.

4. Educational researchers should aim to report research conceptions, procedures, results, and analyses accurately and in sufficient detail to allow other researchers to understand and interpret them.

5. Educational researchers should aim to decline requests to review the work of others when strong conflicts of interest are involved or when such requests cannot be conscientiously fulfilled on time. Materials sent for review should be read in their entirety and considered carefully, with evaluative comments justified with explicit reasons.

6. Educational researchers should aim to conduct their professional lives in such a way that they do not jeopardize future research, the public standing of the field, or the publication of results.

Responsibility to the participants

7. Participants in a research study have the right to be informed about the aims, purposes and likely publication of findings involved in the research and of potential consequences for participants, and to give their informed consent before participating in research.

8. Care should be taken when interviewing children and students up to school leaving age; permission should be obtained from the school, and if they so suggest, the parents.

9. Honesty and openness should characterize the relationship between researchers, participants and institutional representatives.

10. Participants have the right to withdraw from a study at any time.

11. Researchers have a responsibility to be mindful of cultural, religious, gendered, and other significant differences within the research population in the planning, conducting, and reporting of their research.

Responsibility to the public

12. Educational researchers should communicate their findings and the practical significance of their research in clear, straightforward, and appropriate language to relevant research populations, institutional representatives, and other stakeholders.

13. Informants and participants have a right to remain anonymous. This right should be respected when no clear understanding to the contrary has been reached. Researchers are responsible for taking appropriate precautions to protect the confidentiality of both participants and data. However, participants should also be made aware that in certain situations anonymity cannot be achieved.

Relationship with funding agencies

14. The data and results of a research study belong to the researchers who designed and conducted the study unless alternative contractual arrangements have been made with respect to either the data or the results or both.

15. Educational researchers should remain free to interpret and publish their findings without censorship or approval from individuals or organizations, including sponsors, funding agencies, participants, colleagues, supervisors, or administrators. This understanding should be conveyed to participants as part of the responsibility to secure informed consent. This does not mean however that researchers should not take every care to ensure that agreements on publication are reached.

16. Educational researchers should not agree to conduct research that conflicts with academic freedom, nor should they agree to undue or questionable influence by government or other funding agencies. Examples of such improper influence include endeavours to interfere with the conduct of research, the analysis of findings, or the reporting of interpretations. Researchers should report to BERA attempts by sponsors or funding agencies to use any questionable influence, so that BERA may respond publicly as an association on behalf of its members thereby protecting any individual or contract.

17. The aims and sponsorship of research should be made explicit by the researcher. Sponsors or funders have the right to have disclaimers included in research reports to differentiate their sponsorship from the conclusions of the research.

18. Educational researchers should fulfil their responsibilities to agencies funding research, which are entitled to an account of the use of their funds, and to a report of the procedures, findings, and implications of the funded research.

19. The host institution should appoint staff in the light of its routine practices and according to its normal criteria. The funding agency may have an advisory role in this respect, but should not have control over appointments.

20. Sponsored research projects should have an advisory group consisting of representatives from those groups and agencies which have a legitimate interest in the area of inquiry. This advisory group should facilitate access of the researcher(s) to sources of data, other specialists in the field and the wider educational community.

21. The funding agency should respect the right of the researcher(s) to keep his or her sources of data confidential.

22. In the event of a dispute between the funding agency and researcher(s) over the conduct of the research, or threatened termination of contract, the terms of the dispute and/or grounds for termination should be made explicit by the funding agency or researcher and be open to scrutiny by the advisory group. If either party feels that grounds for termination are unreasonable then there should be recourse to arbitration by a body or individual acceptable to both parties.

Publication

23. Researcher(s) have a duty to report both to the funding agency and to the wider public, including educational practitioners and other interested parties. The right to publish is therefore entailed by this duty to report. Researchers conducting sponsored research should retain the right to publish the findings under their own names. The right to publish is essential to the long-term viability of any research activity, to the credibility of the researcher (and of the funding agency in seeking to use research findings) and in the interests of an open society. The methodological principle of maximising the dissemination of information to all interested parties is an integral part of research strategy aimed at testing on a continuous basis the relevance, accuracy and comprehensiveness of findings as they emerge within the process of inquiry.

24. The conditions under which the right to publish might be legitimately restricted are:

- general legislation (e.g. in the area of libel or race relations);
- undertakings given to participants concerning confidentiality and generally not to cause unnecessary harm to those affected by the research findings; and
- failure to report findings in a manner consistent with the values of inquiry i.e. to report findings honestly, accurately, comprehensively, in context, and without undue sensationalisation.

25. Publications should indicate whether or not they are subject to reporting restrictions.

26. The researcher(s) should have the right, as a last resort and following discussions with the funding agency and advisory group, to publicly dissociate themselves from misleadingly selective accounts of the research.

27. Funding bodies should not be allowed to exercise restrictions on publication by default, e.g. by failing to answer requests for permission to publish, or by undue delay.

28. Resources need to be made available for dissemination and publication and should be built in to funding.

29. In the event of a dispute over publication, the researcher should seek recourse first to the advisory group and secondly to an independent arbitration body or individual.

Intellectual ownership

30. Authorship should be determined on the basis that all those, regardless of status, who have made a substantive and/or creative contribution to the generation of an intellectual product are entitled to be listed as authors of that product. (Examples of creative contributions are: writing first drafts or substantial portions; significant rewriting or substantive editing; contributing generative ideas or basic conceptual schema or analytic categories; collecting data which requires significant interpretation or judgement; and interpreting data.)

31. First authorship and order of authorship should be the consequence of relative leadership and creative contribution.

Relationship with host institution

32. Institutions should both develop their own codes of practice which govern ethical principles and establish appropriate standards of academic freedom, including the freedom to disseminate research findings. While such codes should be observed within all research, including non-contract research, they are particularly important in respect of contract research. Such codes should be honoured by institutions and researchers in the negotiation of contractual arrangements put forward by funding agencies, and in the carrying out of these obligations once they have been agreed.

33. While academic staff should not engage in contract research without agreement by the institution, the latter should not be allowed to compel academic staff to engage in particular contract research.

34. It is assumed that contracts will in all cases be interpreted reasonably and with regard to due process. However, should a legitimate disagreement arise between the funding agency and the researchers engaged on it, then the researchers' institutions should give the researchers full and loyal support in resolving this disagreement.

Reproduced courtesy of the British Educational Research Association.

Critical values for test statistics/statistical notation

Critical values (at the 5% level of significance) of various test statistics

Degrees of freedom (n)	χ_n^2	t_n	$F_{1,n}$	$F_{2,n}$	$F_{3,n}$	$F_{5,n}$	$F_{10,n}$	$F_{20,n}$
1	3.84	12.71	161.45	199.50	215.71	230.16	241.88	248.01
2	5.99	4.30	18.51	19.00	19.16	19.30	19.40	19.45
3	7.82	3.18	10.13	9.55	9.28	9.01	8.79	8.66
4	9.49	2.78	7.71	6.94	6.59	6.26	5.96	5.80
5	11.07	2.57	6.61	5.79	5.41	5.05	4.74	4.56
6	12.59	2.45	5.99	5.14	4.76	4.39	4.06	3.87
7	14.07	2.37	5.59	4.74	4.35	3.97	3.63	3.44
8	15.51	2.31	5.32	4.46	4.07	3.69	3.35	3.15
9	16.92	2.26	5.12	4.26	3.86	3.48	3.14	2.94
10	18.31	2.23	4.97	4.10	3.71	3.33	2.98	2.77
20	31.41	2.09	4.35	3.49	3.10	2.71	2.35	2.12
30	43.77	2.04	4.17	3.32	2.92	2.53	2.16	1.93
40	55.76	2.02	4.09	3.23	2.84	2.45	2.08	1.84
60	79.08	2.00	4.00	3.15	2.76	2.37	1.99	1.75
120	146.57	1.98	3.92	3.07	2.68	2.29	1.91	1.66
∞	∞	1.96	3.84	3.00	2.60	2.21	1.83	1.57

Notes: The critical values of t_n correspond to a two-tailed test.
The values in the table were generated using SPSS for Windows.

Statistical notation

Symbol or notation	Meaning of symbol or notation
μ	Population mean (see Chapter 3)
$\bar{x}$	Sample mean (see Chapter 3)
σ	Population standard deviation (see Chapter 3)
s	Sample standard deviation (see Chapter 3)
n	Sample size (see Chapter 3)
y^2	The square of y, i.e. $y \times y$
$\sqrt{}$	Square root sign (i.e. $\sqrt{y} \times \sqrt{y} = y$)
$\sum$	Summation sign (i.e. stands for 'the sum of')
∞	Infinity
d.f.	Degrees of freedom (see Chapter 9)
P	Probability value (P-value; see Chapter 9)
z	z-statistic (see Chapter 3)
χ_n^2	Chi-square statistic, with n degrees of freedom (as used in the analysis of cross-tabulations; see Chapter 9)
t_n	t-statistic with n degrees of freedom (see Chapter 9)
$F_{m,n}$	F-statistic with m and n degrees of freedom (see Chapter 9)
O and E	Observed and Expected values (in the analysis of cross-tabulations; see Chapter 9)
r	Correlation coefficient (see Chapter 9; r-squared is the variation explained in linear regression)
B	The slope of a regression line (see Chapter 9)
[AB]	An interaction term corresponding to variables A and B within a log-linear model (see Chapter 9)
k	Suggested population mean (i.e. suggested value for μ) (see Chapter 3: notation specific to this text)
γ	The desired level of accuracy of an estimate (for an interval-level variable) (see Chapter 3: notation specific to this text)
δ	The desired level of accuracy of an estimate (for a proportion) (see Chapter 3: notation specific to this text)

Glossary

Discussions of many of the technical and sociological terms used in this book can be found within the relevant chapters and these discussions can be located via the index. The list that follows therefore contains a selection of terms that either are not defined in the body of the book or which our experience has shown that students find awkward. Some of the terms in the list have contested meanings; it should thus be noted that the entries reflect the authors' definitions and interpretations of the various terms. Readers may also find it useful to refer to sociological dictionaries such as Abercrombie *et al.* (2000), Jary and Jary (2000) and Marshall (1998). Terms in bold within the entries are included elsewhere in the glossary.

analytic induction An approach to theoretical development that involves the formulation and reformulation of hypotheses via the examination of a series of cases (see Bryman, 1988: 81–83). An initial hypothesis is derived from the characteristics of one or more cases; if the characteristics of further cases are found to be inconsistent with the hypothesis, then either the hypothesis is revised or a restriction is placed on the range of cases to which it applies. The Grounded Theory approach to qualitative research has close links to analytic induction (see Chapters 3 and 8).

case study A piece of research that focuses on a single setting, organisation, individual or instance of a phenomenon. An **ethnography** will typically take the form of a case study, but case studies can also be quantitative, as, for example, in a survey of the pupils within a particular school. In fact, case studies very often involve the use of multiple methods (e.g. observation, interviews and documentary analysis). Case studies are usually orientated towards the holistic description and analysis of the case in question rather than towards (potentially dangerous) generalisations to a wider set of cases. The case selected for study may be a typical one, or a deviant case may deliberately be chosen. Case studies can be used for exploratory purposes, for illustrative purposes, and for the assessment of the impact of a specific form of intervention; they have also been used for the development or evaluation of theories.

concept A building block of social theory. A concept is a label applied to a social phenomenon; there are concepts corresponding to a variety of types of social phenomena such as social institutions (e.g. 'the family'), the characteristics of individuals (e.g. 'health'), social processes (e.g. 'industrialisation') and sets of values (e.g. the 'Protestant ethic'). Theory is produced by relating concepts to each other (as, for example, in Weber's use of the 'Protestant ethic' to explain the development of 'capitalism'). The relevance and nature of concepts are often contested (as, for example, in the case of 'social class').

dependent variable Statistical analyses frequently involve an examination of the effect(s) of one or more explanatory or independent variables on another variable. This latter variable is the dependent variable. For example, an analysis might involve a consideration of the effects of gender, parental social class and year of birth (independent variables) on age at first marriage (the dependent variable). The designation of a particular variable as the dependent variable is a product of theorising on the part of the researcher; the independent and dependent variables thus collectively form a theoretical model. While the appropriate choice of dependent variable may sometimes appear obvious, the decision made by the researcher is nevertheless an inherently theoretical one.

discourse A set of ideas and terminology relating to some aspect of the social world. Discourses can be viewed as mechanisms for exercising power (e.g. in the work of Foucault), as well as or instead of simply describing social phenomena. Bodies such as the state or professions may use discourses in this way, and groups within society that are in conflict with each other may generate competing discourses (see Chapter 7).

empiricism A theory of knowledge that argues that all legitimate knowledge of the social world derives from direct experience and that knowledge is only valid if it can be tested via (empirical) observation. Empiricism is generally viewed as a component of a broader theory of knowledge, **positivism** (Bryman, 1988: 14). Empiricism is also sometimes used as a term of abuse, implying an atheoretical approach to the collection and analysis of data.

epistemology Theories of knowledge. A researcher's epistemological standpoint thus relates to the way in which they believe the social world can be known. For example, advocates of **empiricism** put forward the argument that all knowledge derives from direct experience of the world, whereas advocates of **rationalism** argue that knowledge can be derived via reason. Particular research approaches and methods are frequently argued to be tied to particular epistemological perspectives; however, arguments such as those which view quantitative research as inseparable from empiricism and/or **positivism** are often over-simplistic (see Bryman, 1988).

ethnography The observation and description of the social behaviour of a group within a setting, organisation or community. The roots of ethnography lie within social anthropology and underpin its core method: observation, while participating in the life of the group. Participant observation is, however, only one of the methods used by ethnographers, who utilise a range of other qualitative methods and may also use quantitative data to help document the group and its context. The ethnographer's immersion in the life of the group and their desire to understand it from the perspective(s) of group members provide links to epistemological approaches such as **phenomenology**, though such links are not clear-cut and should not be overstated. Meticulous fieldnotes are a key component of ethnography, since the approach involves the detailed description of the group and its setting.

ethnomethodology An approach, given its name by Garfinkel, which focuses on the ways in which **social actors** make sense of their social world. From an ethnomethodological perspective, social reality is created by this process (see **reflexivity**). Arguably this emphasis on the viewpoints of social actors means that ethnomethodologists' research is closer to **phenomenology** than is typically the case with qualitative research more generally. Research by ethnomethodologists often takes the form of the detailed analysis of conversations; ethnomethodologists sometimes subscribe to **relativism** and are often sceptical about the scope for generalising findings beyond specific times and settings.

feminist research Feminist researchers have often (though not always) argued that, if it is to be consistent with a feminist perspective, social research requires a distinctive **epistemological** position and **methodology**, and perhaps also the use of particular methods. Arguably, research which can be labelled as **positivist** or as **empiricist** corresponds to a masculine way of knowing about the social world. Consequently, many feminists have oriented themselves towards approaches and methods that prioritise (women's) subjective experiences and voices, and have thus engaged in qualitative research. However, the weakness of the link between epistemology and method means that some feminist researchers (and also the authors of this book) believe that a role exists for quantitative methods within feminist research.

frequency distribution The numbers of occurrences in a sample of each value of a variable. In a **random sample** the observed frequency distribution will approximately reflect the distribution in the **population** from which the sample was drawn; this underlying distribution may approximate to one of the key statistical distributions, such as the normal distribution (which is bell-shaped, with higher frequencies for values close to the average (mean) and lower frequencies for high and low values).

hypothesis testing A hypothesis is a theoretical statement about the relationship between a number of concepts. In the context of a statistical analysis, hypothesis testing requires that a precise statement be made of the hypothesised relationship between the variables concerned, so that a process of **significance testing** and **statistical inference** can take place. Hypothesis testing is the basis of one approach to theoretical development (the hypothetico-deductive method); an alternative approach is **analytic induction**.

independent variable See **dependent variable**.

informed consent This is obtained when respondents both explicitly agree to participate in a research study and also have an adequate knowledge of the nature, purposes and likely outcomes of the study. It is an inherently debatable concept, since it is not possible (and may not be desirable) for a respondent to have a full knowledge of what participation will entail until after they have participated, and it is not possible for the researcher to anticipate fully in advance the study's findings and consequences. As is the case for many ethical issues in social research, the researcher's judgement as to what constitutes adequately informed consent is crucial.

interpretative (or interpretive) approaches Approaches to social research which focus on the meanings of actions to **social actors**; the advocates of such approaches view these meanings as fundamental to a valid understanding of social reality. The actions and their meanings are seen as reflecting the actors' experiences and interpretations of their social worlds; the objective of a researcher working from an interpretative perspective is thus to develop theory that is based upon and consistent with the interpretations that individuals make of these worlds (see **symbolic interactionism**; **phenomenology**).

methodology While this term is sometimes applied to the methods and techniques used by social researchers, the methodological aspects of a study more accurately refer to the philosophy of science embedded both within these methods and also within the researcher's approach to data collection and analysis more generally. Since methodology thus relates to philosophical aspects of the way in which social research generates knowledge, it has close links to **epistemology**.

naturalism and naturalistic research Somewhat confusingly, this term has two distinct usages in relation to social research, which are close to being polar opposites. As used in this book, it relates to the extent to which social research is consistent with and respects the nature of the phenomenon that is being examined. Hence naturalistic research refers to social research which attempts to minimise the degree to which it interferes with the situations and processes being studied (limiting **reactivity**) and which attempts to produce findings which are consistent with the view of social reality of respondents or people within the research setting (see Bryman, 1988: 58–59).

The other common usage of the term naturalism relates to the suitability of natural science methods and methodology for social research, with the implication being that they are appropriate.

norm A commonly held belief within a group or society that people ought to behave in a particular way is a social norm. The sociological meaning of the term thus relates to expected behaviour rather than actual behaviour; however, the term norm is also sometimes used to describe the most common or typical form of behaviour. Social norms constrain individuals' behaviour; when an individual deviates from a norm they may be subjected to some form of sanction.

ontology Concerned with the existence of (and relationships between) different kinds of things. When social researchers discuss the social world they assume the existence of things such as **social actors**, cultural **norms** and **social structure**, and are thus making ontological assumptions. Thus ontology is concerned with the kinds of things that exist, and **epistemology** is concerned with how researchers can know about them.

operationalisation of concepts The process by which indicators are developed so that **concepts** can be measured (see Chapter 5). The operationalisation of concepts is the bridge between theory and data; for research to be successful the indicators developed must have an adequate degree of **validity** and level of **reliability**.

parameter A term frequently used to refer to a characteristic (usually a quantifiable one) that varies between a number of cases. However, a more specific usage of the term is found within statistical analyses, where a parameter is a quantity that a researcher wishes to estimate and which corresponds to the **population** of interest. For example, a researcher may wish to know the average (mean) age at retirement of university lecturers, in which case the parameter of interest is the mean age at retirement.

Another parameter of interest to the above researcher might be the difference between the mean ages of women and of men at retirement, i.e. the 'effect' of gender on retirement age. As implied

by this example, the 'parameter estimates' reported in statistical analyses are often estimates of the effects of **independent variables** on a **dependent variable**.

Statistical analyses often rely on assumptions about the spread of values of a characteristic in the **population**. These assumptions give rise to additional parameters that are estimated within the analyses. Hence the term parametric statistics refers to forms of **statistical inference** that involve assumptions about the shapes of the distributions of values for variables; non-parametric statistics do not rely on such assumptions.

phenomenology A term that relates to the study of human consciousness and experience. It is a broad philosophical approach, but its more specific relevance to social research has been demonstrated by researchers drawing upon the work of Schutz. His work makes a distinction between the physical and social worlds as objects of study by researchers; unlike **positivism**, phenomenology sees the application of natural science methods within social research as potentially problematic. The crucial point is that, from a phenomenological viewpoint, the researcher must grasp the **social actor**'s experience of the social world before she or he can understand it herself or himself. The 'thought objects' of the researcher must be consistent with the 'thought objects' of the researched (Schutz, cited in Bryman, 1988: 51). However, Bryman notes that the use of the term phenomenological simply to indicate attention to the actor's perspective ignores much of the complexity of phenomenology as a philosophical approach (1988: 53).

population In the statistical analysis of a sample, the overall set of items from which the sample of items was drawn: for example, a sample of teachers may have been drawn from the population consisting of all teachers employed by state schools in England and Wales. The researcher uses their statistical analysis to make inferences about this population, which in this case should ideally correspond to the set of teachers who are of substantive interest to the researcher.

positivism A philosophy of social science of which there are a range of variants but which typically involves support both for **empiricism**, which argues that knowledge needs to be based on direct experience of the social world, and also for the application within social research of various aspects of the methods of the natural sciences (Bryman, 1988: 14). Quantitative research has frequently been labelled (criticised) by some sub-groups of sociologists as being positivist (see Chapter 5). However, the relevance of this criticism is dependent both on the extent to which the label is accurate and also on the epistemological perspective of the researcher. In other words, not all quantitative researchers are positivists, and those who are would regard the criticism as irrelevant, since their own frame of reference implies that quantitative data constitute a valid form of knowledge.

postmodernism A body of ideas that, among other things, sees the contemporary world as fragmentary and fluid, views social reality as localised and resistant to universal generalisations, and sees truth (as might arguably be uncovered by empirical research) as a myth, with knowledge being more a function of language than a reflection of some underlying reality. Key writers in this area include Baudrillard and Lyotard. Clearly postmodernism poses challenges to many of the research approaches discussed in this book (see Chapter 6); however, the authors would in turn challenge the credibility of some aspects of the postmodern interpretation of contemporary society.

precision Sometimes simply refers to the level of detail of a variable. For example, the ages of a sample of students might be measured in years (rather than years and months). However, precision is also used to describe how close a researcher's estimate of a quantity is likely to be to the actual value of the quantity in the population, given that any estimate based on a sample cannot be expected to match the population value exactly. For example, the precision of a sample mean relates to how close its value is likely to be to that of the population mean (see Chapter 3). In this case the

precision is clearly dependent on how much 'noise' is inherent within the sampling process, i.e. on the likely quantity of **sampling error**.

random sampling It is not uncommon for the term random to be used incorrectly to refer to haphazard, opportunistic forms of sampling. When used correctly, the term random sampling refers to a form of sampling where all members of the **population** of interest have a known, non-zero probability of inclusion in the sample. Random sampling is a pre-requisite for most **statistical inference** and **significance testing**. Note that it is not necessary for the probabilities of inclusion of all the population members to be equal; this is a more specific form of sampling, i.e. simple random sampling (see Chapter 3), which is the most straightforward form of random sampling to deal with at the analysis stage.

rationalism The term has a number of related meanings. It is sometimes used to describe a belief in the superiority of reason and rational decision making as opposed to faith and instinct. However, the use of the term that is relevant to this text is one where it refers to a preference for generating knowledge via reason, rather than generating knowledge via experience of the world.

reactivity Refers to the response of research participants and settings to being researched. While formal interviews may on average lead to greater reactive effects than ethnographic fieldwork, most research approaches leave open to a greater or lesser extent the possibility that the data collected will be affected by the research instrument and thus will provide a distorted picture of the social phenomenon of interest. Thus all researchers need to assess the scope for and possible impacts of reactive effects within their research. For example, in Wallerstein's longitudinal study of the impact of divorce, participating in the first wave of interviews may feasibly have altered some children's perspectives on their situations, and may consequently have affected these children's lives and hence the data generated by later interviews.

reflexivity **Social actors'** accounts of social situations and processes not only describe these situations and processes but also to an extent create these social phenomena via their description and interpretation. This applies as much to social researchers as it does to other social actors; researchers therefore need to be aware that they play an active role in the creation of their research findings. Reflexivity as an issue in social research thus relates to the researcher's (need for an) understanding of their own contribution to the way in which data generation and data analysis shape the research outcomes.

relativism In the context of social research, (epistemological) relativism implies that different research **methodologies** simply constitute different ways of knowing, whose relative merits cannot be assessed with reference to some universally applicable notion of 'truth'. Acceptance of relativism (as by some **ethnomethodologists**) can also imply that knowledge is 'local', i.e. that the theories developed by researchers are researcher- and setting-specific.

reliability It is a desirable property of a research instrument that it should generate the same findings if applied more than once to the same individual, assuming that the individual has not changed in the interim. Reliability refers to the consistency of repeated measurements of the same quantity or property.

Sometimes researchers use measuring instruments such as scales which contain a number of different items intended to measure the same thing. The term reliability can also be used with reference to the consistency of such different forms of measurement.

The reliability of a scale based on a number of items can be quantified fairly easily by examining the consistency of the data generated by the different items (see Chapter 5). However, assessing the reliability of a single measure is more difficult; applying it to the same quantity on two occasions (the test–retest approach) does not necessarily tap the underlying variability of the measure, since the quantity may have changed and there is also scope for **reactivity**. (See also **validity**.)

respondent A participant within a research study, such as someone who completes a questionnaire in a postal survey, or who is interviewed by a researcher.

sampling distribution The **frequency distribution** of the values of a statistic that would be obtained if that statistic were calculated using data from each of an (infinite) series of samples. For example, the sampling distribution of the mean is the frequency distribution corresponding to the sample means that would be obtained from such a series of samples.

The shape of the sampling distribution of the mean usually corresponds approximately to the bell shape of the normal (or Gaussian) distribution (see Chapter 3). In other words, the frequency distribution corresponding to the sample means obtained from an (infinite) series of samples would contain a small proportion of sample means that were markedly lower or markedly higher than the population mean and a much greater proportion of sample means that were relatively close to the population mean.

sampling error When a sample is used as a way of estimating the characteristics of a **population**, a consequence of the process of sampling is that the sample is unlikely to be exactly representative of the population. Even when **random sampling** is used, a certain amount of sampling error will usually occur (see Chapter 3): for example, a random sample of women will usually be slightly taller or slightly shorter on average than the average height of women in the population. When the sampling process is not random, an additional source of potential error, i.e. bias, exists.

significance In a statistical analysis, the significance of an observed pattern is assessed using **significance testing**. However, statistical significance as assessed in this fashion only relates to the researcher's level of confidence that a pattern observed in a sample also exists in the **population**. Thus a statistically significant finding may or may not be of **substantive** significance: for example, a researcher may conclude on the basis of a signific-ance test applied to a large sample that the average (mean) earnings of female graduates is signific-antly lower than that of male graduates, but if the difference is only 50p per week it is arguably of negligible substantive significance.

significance testing This allows the researcher to decide whether it is plausible that an observed pat-tern or relationship in a sample is a reflection of a similar pattern or relationship in the **population** from which the sample was drawn. Significance testing is thus a foundation of **statistical inference**, and hence has **random sampling** as a pre-requisite.

The basis of a significance test is a comparison of an observed pattern or relationship in the sample with the pattern that would have been expected in the sample given a hypothesis stating that no such pattern or relationship exists in the popula-tion (the so-called null hypothesis). The prob-ability (P-value; see Chapter 3) that a difference as large as that found between the observed and expected patterns would have occurred simply as a consequence of **sampling error** is calculated. This probability is then compared with a pre-determined significance level, typically 0.05 (5%), 0.01 (1%) or 0.001 (0.1%), which is intended as an appropriate measure of rarity.

If the calculated probability is less than the significance level, then a difference of that mag-nitude between the observed and expected patterns would only rarely occur 'by chance' (i.e. simply as a consequence of sampling error), and the observed pattern or relationship is therefore deemed to be 'statistically significant'. A statistically significant relationship is thus one which the researcher is pre-pared to infer exists in the population as well as in the sample.

social actor Rather than describing a person who self-consciously 'plays a part' in their social inter-actions, the term simply describes anyone who carries out social actions. However, the term carries with it an emphasis on agency, i.e. the ability of people to act in a way that is voluntary rather than determined by the constraints of **social structure**.

Hence qualitative research, with its emphasis on the viewpoints and decision-making processes of individuals, typically focuses on social actors and their agency.

social structure This can be viewed as consisting of ongoing large-scale features of a society, such as social institutions (e.g. the church, the family, the legal system), the class structure and social **norms**. Sociological research into a social phe-nomenon (e.g. the process of selecting a marriage partner) often involves a consideration of the respective roles played by structural constraints and by agency (i.e. the voluntary actions of individual **social actors**). Giddens has attempted to marry together structure and agency within his structura-tion theory.

standard deviation Some **variables** take the form of a number of units (e.g. age in years, or income in pounds or euros). The standard deviation is a measure of dispersion (i.e. spread) applicable to such interval-level quantitative data (see Chapter 3). It summarises the range of values corresponding to a set of cases, and is calculated by taking the square root of the average of the squared differ-ences between each value and the mean (average) of all the values. Its principal advantages over other measures of spread are that it incorporates information from all the cases and that it is linked to standard techniques of statistical analysis and testing.

statistical inference The process by which researchers use a sample to learn (make infer-ences) about patterns and relationships in a cor-responding **population**. Statistical inference relies on **significance testing**, which in turn requires that **random sampling** is used, in order that the infer-ences made cannot be a reflection of biases in the sampling process.

substantive Social research studies apply research methods to data on substantive topics or issues in the context of particular epistemological frame-works. In other words, the term substantive relates to the social setting or phenomenon of interest rather than to the methods and **methodology** of the research.

symbolic interactionism Researchers utilising this approach view **social actors** as interpreting social situations and then acting in a way which depends on a self-conscious assessment of how others will view their actions. From this perspective the meaning of a situation is determined by an individual's social interactions with others, together with their own interpretation of the situation. Key figures in the development of this approach include G.H. Mead and Blumer; a link is often drawn between symbolic interactionism and participant observation (see the discussion in Bryman, 1988: 56).

taxonomy A term that relates to classifications and the process of classification. While it is most closely identified with biological classification, social researchers also develop classifications of societies, forms of behaviour and other social phenomena. Such classifications are usually inherently theoretical, either because they are intended as explanatory tools or because they reflect implicitly the researchers' theoretical frameworks.

triangulation Refers to the examination of a single substantive issue within a piece of social research by different researchers, and/or using different research methods, and/or using different theoretical approaches, and/or using different data sources. The term is most closely associated with Norman Denzin. The use of a number of different 'angles' is intended to enhance the **validity** of the research.

unit of analysis A researcher's analysis has as its focus of attention an individual case or set of individual cases. For example, a researcher may be interviewing stepmothers to uncover their experiences of step-parenthood. The unit of analysis in this example is the individual stepmother. On occasions the researcher may be interested in more than one level of analysis: for example, he/she may also be interested in contrasting different stepfamilies, in which case the unit of analysis is the stepfamily as a whole. Most statistical analyses involve a single unit of analysis: for example, in an analysis of the lifespan of small businesses, the unit of analysis is the business. However, multi-level models (see Chapter 9) involve more than one unit of analysis: as, for example, in an analysis of the GCSE results of pupils within schools.

validity As used in social research, the term refers to the extent to which a measure (indicator) measures properly the concept of interest to the researcher (or possibly to the extent to which a research approach is an appropriate way of generating the data that the researcher requires). There are a number of ways of assessing different aspects of a measure's validity, but there is always an element of subjectivity in assessments of validity, and the validity of a measure is thus often contested on theoretical and/or technical grounds. (See also **reliability**.)

variable A measurable characteristic which varies across a set of cases. For example, the age, sex and highest educational qualification of each member of a sample of adults constitute three different variables. The levels of measurement (see Chapter 9) of these three variables clearly differ: age can be measured on a continuous scale, sex is usually viewed as having two categories, and highest qualification is typically an ordered set of categories. Variables can also play different roles within theoretical models (see **dependent variable**).

weighting A process within which research findings from a sample are manipulated to take account of the sample design and/or response rates, in an attempt to increase the representativeness of the findings relative to the **population** (see Chapter 3). In essence, data corresponding to those sub-groups of the population which are underrepresented within the sample are counted more than once, whereas data corresponding to over-represented sub-groups are counted less than once.

References

Abberley, P. 1996. 'Disabled by Numbers'. In Levitas, R. and Guy, W. (eds) *Interpreting Official Statistics*. London: Routledge.

Abercrombie, N., Hill, S. and Turner, B. (eds) 2000. *The Penguin Dictionary of Sociology*. Harmondsworth: Penguin.

Agresti, A. 1990. *Categorical Data Analysis*. New York: Wiley.

Aitkin, M., Anderson, D., Francis, B. and Hinde, J. 1989. *Statistical Modelling in GLIM*. Oxford: Clarendon Press.

Allison, P.D. 1984. *Event History Analysis: Regression for Longitudinal Event Data* (QASS Series: No. 46). London: Sage.

Anderson, B., Silver, B. and Abramson, P. 1988. 'The Effects of the Race of the Interviewer on Race-Related Attitudes of Black Respondents in SRC/CPS National Election Studies', *Public Opinion Quarterly*, 52: 289–324.

Anderson, S., Auquier, A., Hauck, W., Oakes, D., Vandaele, W. and Weisberg, H. 1980. *Statistical Methods for Comparative Studies: Techniques for Bias Reduction*. New York: Wiley.

Annandale, E. and Hunt, K. 1990. 'Masculinity, Femininity and Sex: An Exploration of their Relative Contribution to Explaining Gender Differences in Health', *Sociology of Health and Illness*, 12.1: 24–46.

Arber, S. 1990. 'Revealing Women's Health: Re-analysing the General Household Survey'. In Roberts, H. (ed.) *Women's Health Counts*. London: Routledge.

Arendell, T. 1986. *Mothers and Divorce*. Berkeley: University of California Press.

Asher, H.B. 1976. *Causal Modeling* (QASS Series: No. 3). London: Sage.

Astin, M., Lawton, D. and Hirst, M. 1996. 'The Prevalence of Pain in a Disabled Population', *Social Science and Medicine*, 42.11: 1457–1464.

Atkinson, J.M. 1978. *Discovering Suicide: Studies in the Social Organization of Sudden Death*. London: Macmillan.

Atkinson, P. 1981. *The Clinical Experience: The Construction and Reconstruction of Medical Reality*. Farnborough: Gower.

Babbie, E. 1990. *Survey Research Methods* (2nd Edition). Belmont, CA: Wadsworth.

Bailey, S., Charlton, J., Dollamore, G. and Fitzpatrick, J. 2000. 'Families, Groups and Clusters of Local and Health Authorities: Revised for Authorities in 1999', *Population Trends*, 99 (Spring 2000): 37–52.

Ball, M. and Smith, G. 1992. *Analyzing Visual Data*. London: Sage.

Ball, S. 1981. *Beachside Comprehensive: A Case-Study of Secondary Schooling*. Cambridge: Cambridge University Press.

Barnes, J. 1979. *Who Should Know What? Social Science, Privacy and Ethics*. Cambridge: Cambridge University Press.

Barthes, R. 1967. *Elements of Semiology*. London: Jonathan Cape.

Bateson, N. 1984. *Data Construction in Social Surveys*. London: George Allen and Unwin.

Becker, H.S. (ed.) 1981. *Exploring Society Photographically*. Chicago: University of Chicago Press.

Becker, H.S. 1986. *Writing for Social Scientists: How to Start and Finish Your Thesis, Book, or Article*. Chicago: University of Chicago Press.

Becker, H.S., Geer, B., Hughes, E.C. and Strauss, A. 1961. *Boys in White*. Chicago: University of Chicago Press.

Becker, H.S., Geer, B. and Hughes, E.C. 1968. *Making the Grade*. New York: Wiley.

Bell, C. and Newby, H. (eds) 1977. *Doing Sociological Research*. London: Allen and Unwin.

Blalock, H.M. Jr. 1981. *Social Statistics* (Revised 2nd Edition). London: McGraw-Hill.

Blaxter, L., Hughes, C. and Tight, M. 1996. *How to Research*. Buckingham: Open University Press.

Blaxter, M. 1990. *Health and Lifestyles*. London: Routledge.

Boelen, W.A.M. 1992. 'Street Corner Society: Cornerville Revisited', *Journal of Contemporary Ethnography*, 21.1: 11–52.

Bogdan, R. 1974. *Being Different: The Autobiography of Jane Fry*. New York: Wiley.

Bogdan, R. and Biklen, S. 1982. *Qualitative Research for Education: An Introduction to Theory and Methods*. London: Allyn and Bacon.

Bourque, L. and Fielder, E. 1995. *How to Conduct Self-Administered and Mail Surveys* (Volume 3 of *The Survey Kit*). London: Sage.

Brannen, J. 1992. *Mixing Methods: Qualitative and Quantitative Research*. Aldershot: Avebury.

Brannen, J. and Collard, J. 1982. *Marriages in Trouble: The Process of Seeking Help*. London: Tavistock.

Brierley, P. 1988. 'Religion'. In Halsey, A.H. (ed.) *British Social Trends since 1900: A Guide to the Changing Social Structure of Britain*. London: Macmillan.

Brierley, P. (ed.) 1991. *Prospects for the Nineties. Trends and Tables from the 1989 English Church Census*. London: MARC Europe.

Brindle, D. 1999. 'Schools "Weak Link" in Plans to Cut Pregnancies', *Guardian*, 15 June, p. 11.

British Educational Research Association (BERA). 1992. *Ethical Guidelines for Educational Research*. Southwall: British Educational Research Association.

British Psychological Society (BPS). 2000. *Code of Conduct: Ethical Principles and Guidelines*. Leicester: British Psychological Society.

British Sociological Association (BSA). 1996. *Statement of Ethical Practice*. Durham: British Sociological Association.

Brook, L., Prior, G. and Taylor, B. 1992. *British Social Attitudes 1991 Survey: Technical Report*. London: Social and Community Planning Research.

Brownlow, K. 1997. *David Lean: A Biography*. London: Faber and Faber.

Bryman, A. 1988. *Quantity and Quality in Social Research*. London: Routledge.

Bryman, A. 1989. *Research Methods and Organization Studies*. London: Routledge.

Bryman, A. and Burgess, R. (eds) 1994. *Analyzing Qualitative Data*. London: Routledge.

Bryman, A. and Cramer, D. 1996. *Quantitative Data Analysis with Minitab: A Guide for Social Scientists*. London: Routledge.

Bryman, A. and Cramer, D. 1997. *Quantitative Data Analysis with SPSS for Windows: A Guide for Social Scientists*. London: Routledge.

Buck, N., Gershuny, J., Rose, D. and Scott, J. (eds) 1994. *Changing Households: The British Household Panel Study 1990–1992*. Colchester: Economic and Social Research Council Research Centre on Micro-Social Change.

Buford, B. 1992. *Among the Thugs*. London: Mandarin.

Bulmer, M. (ed.) 1979. *Censuses, Surveys and Privacy*. London: Macmillan.

Bulmer, M. 1980. 'Why Don't Sociologists Make More Use of Official Statistics?', *Sociology*, 14: 505–525. (Reprinted in Bulmer, M. (ed.) 1984. *Sociological Research Methods* (2nd Edition). London: Macmillan.)

Bulmer, M. (ed.) 1982. *Social Research Ethics*. London: Macmillan.

Bulmer, M. (ed.) 1984. *Sociological Research Methods* (2nd Edition). London: Macmillan.

Bulmer, M. 1992. *Overview of the ESRC Training Board Research into Training Programme*. London: London School of Economics and Political Science.

Burchell, B. 1994. 'The Effects of Labour Market Position, Job Insecurity, and Unemployment on Psychological Health'. In Gallie, D., Marsh, C. and Vogler, C. (eds) *Social Change and the Experience of Unemployment*. Oxford: Oxford University Press.

Burgess, R.G. 1983. *Experiencing Comprehensive Education: A Study of Bishop McGregor School*. London: Methuen.

Burgess, R.G. 1984. *In the Field*. London: Unwin Hyman.

Burgess, R.G. (ed.) 1986. *Key Variables in Social Investigation*. London: Routledge and Kegan Paul.

Burgess, R.G. 1988. 'Conversations with a Purpose: The Ethnographic Interview in Educational Research'. In Burgess, R. (ed.) *Conducting Qualitative Research*. Greenwich: JAI Press.

Burgess, R.G. 1993. *Research Methods*. Walton-on-Thames: Nelson.

Burgess, R.G. (ed.) 1994. *Postgraduate Education and Training in the Social Sciences: Processes and Products*. London: Jessica Kingsley.

Burgess, R.G., Hockey, J. and Pole, C.J. 1992. *Becoming a Postgraduate Student: The Organization of*

Postgraduate Training. ESRC Final Report. Swindon: Economic and Social Research Council.

Burgoyne, J. and Clark, D. 1984. *Making a Go of It: A Study of Stepfamilies in Sheffield*. London: Routledge and Kegan Paul.

Burholt, V. and Wenger, G.C. 1998. 'Differences over Time in Older People's Relationships with Children and Siblings', *Ageing and Society*, 18: 537–562.

Burnett, F.H. 1995 [1911]. *The Secret Garden*. Harmondsworth: Penguin.

Burnett, J., Vincent, D. and Mayall, D. (eds) 1984. *The Autobiography of the Working Class*. Brighton: Harvester Press.

Campbell, D. and Stanley, J. 1966. *Experimental and Quasi-Experimental Designs for Research*. Chicago: Rand McNally.

Cappell, C.L. and Guterbock, T.M. 1992. 'Visible Colleges: The Social and Conceptual Structure of Sociology Specialties', *American Sociological Review*, 57.2: 266–273.

Cartwright, A. and Seale, C. 1990. *The Natural History of a Survey: An Account of the Methodological Issues Encountered in a Study of Life before Death*. London: King Edward's Hospital Fund for London.

Catania, J., Binson, D., Canchola, J., Pollack, L., Hauck, W. and Coates, T. 1996. 'Effects of Interviewer Gender, Interviewer Choice and Item Wording on Responses to Questions Concerning Sexual Behaviour', *Public Opinion Quarterly*, 60.3: 345–375.

Cavendish, R. 1982. *Women on the Line*. London: Routledge and Kegan Paul.

Chapman, M. and Wykes, C. 1996. *Plain Figures* (2nd Edition). London: The Stationery Office.

Chatfield, C. 1996. *The Analysis of Time Series: An Introduction* (5th Edition). London: Chapman and Hall.

Chatfield, C. and Collins, A.J. 1980. *Introduction to Multivariate Analysis*. London: Chapman and Hall.

Cicourel, A. 1964. *Method and Measurement in Sociology*. New York: Free Press.

Clogg, C.C. and Shihadeh, E.S. 1994. *Statistical Models for Ordinal Variables*. London: Sage.

Coffey, A. and Atkinson, P. 1996. *Making Sense of Qualitative Data: Complementary Research Strategies*. London. Sage.

Cohen, L. and Manion, L. 1989. *Research Methods in Education* (2nd Edition). London: Routledge.

Colhoun, H. and Prescott-Clarke, P. (eds) 1996. *Health Survey for England, 1994* (Volume I: *Findings*) (Department of Health: Series HS No. 4). London: HMSO.

Converse, J. and Presser, S. 1986. *Survey Questions: Handcrafting the Standardized Questionnaire*. Beverly Hills: Sage.

Cook, J. and Fonow, M. 1990. 'Knowledge and Women's Interests: Issues of Epistemology and Methodology in Feminist Sociological Research'. In Nielsen, J. (ed.) *Feminist Research Methods: Exemplary Readings in the Social Sciences*. Oxford: Westview Press.

Cox, B.D. 1987. *The Health and Lifestyle Survey: Preliminary Report*. London: Health Promotion Research Trust.

Cox, D.R. and Oakes, D. 1984. *Analysis of Survival Data*. London: Chapman and Hall.

Cox, D.R. and Snell, E.J. 1989. *Analysis of Binary Data* (2nd Edition). London: Chapman and Hall.

Coxon, A.P.M. 1982. *The User's Guide to Multidimensional Scaling, With Special Reference to the MDS (X) Library of Computer Programs*. London: Heinemann Educational.

Croll, P. 1986. *Systematic Classroom Observation*. London: Falmer Press.

Crompton, R. 1993. *Class and Stratification: An Introduction to Current Debates*. Cambridge: Polity Press.

Cronbach, L.J. 1951. 'Coefficient Alpha and the Internal Consistency of Tests', *Psychometrika*, 16: 297–334.

Dale, A. and Davies, R.B. (eds) 1994. *Analyzing Social and Political Change: A Casebook of Methods*. London: Sage.

Dale, A. and Holdsworth, C. 1997. 'Issues in the Analysis of Ethnicity in the 1991 British Census: Evidence from Microdata', *Ethnic and Racial Studies*, 20.1: 160–181.

Dale, A. and Marsh, C. (eds) 1993. *The 1991 Census User's Guide*. London: HMSO.

Dale, A., Arber, S. and Procter, M. 1988. *Doing Secondary Analysis*. London: Unwin Hyman.

Dale, A., Fieldhouse, E. and Holdsworth, C. 1999. *Analysing Census Microdata*. London: Arnold.

De Vaus, D. 1996. *Surveys in Social Research* (4th Edition). London: UCL Press.

Delamont, S. 1992. *Fieldwork in Educational Settings: Methods, Pitfalls and Perspectives*. London: Falmer Press.

Delamont, S. and Galton, M. 1986. *Inside the Secondary Classroom*. London: Routledge and Kegan Paul.

DeLeuuw, E., Hox, J. and Snijkers, G. 1995. 'The Effect of Computer-Assisted Interviewing on Data Quality – A Review', *Journal of the Market Research Society*, 37.4: 325–344.

Denzin, N.K. 1970. *The Research Act in Sociology.* London: Butterworths.

Denzin, N.K. 1978. *The Research Act: A Theoretical Introduction to Sociological Methods* (2nd Edition). New York: McGraw-Hill.

Denzin, N.K. 1989. *The Research Act: A Theoretical Introduction to Sociological Methods* (3rd Edition). New Jersey: Prentice Hall.

Devine, F. and Heath, S. 1999. *Sociological Research Methods in Context.* Basingstoke: Macmillan.

Dey, I. 1993. *Qualitative Data Analysis: A User-Friendly Guide for Social Scientists.* London: Routledge.

Dibb, S., Simkin, L., Pride, W. and Ferrell, O. 1997. *Marketing: Concepts and Strategies* (3rd European Edition). New York: Houghton Mifflin.

Dobson, A. 1990. *An Introduction to Generalized Linear Models.* London: Chapman and Hall.

Dorling, D. and Simpson, S. (eds) 1999. *Statistics in Society: The Arithmetic of Politics.* London: Arnold.

Down, D. (ed.) (Office for National Statistics) 1999. *Family Spending: A Report on the 1998–99 Family Expenditure Survey.* London: The Stationery Office.

Draper, N.R. and Smith, H. 1981. *Applied Regression Analysis* (2nd Edition). New York: Wiley.

Dryler, H. 1999. 'The Impact of School and Classroom Characteristics on Educational Choices by Boys and Girls: A Multilevel Analysis', *Acta Sociologica*, 42.4: 299–318.

DSS (Department of Social Security). 1996. *Family Resources Survey: Great Britain 1994–95.* London: HMSO.

Durkheim, E. 1947. *The Division of Labour in Society.* New York: Macmillan.

Durkheim, E. 1951. *Suicide.* New York: Free Press.

Durkheim, E. 1952 [1897]. *Suicide.* London: Routledge and Kegan Paul.

Durkheim, E. 1966 [1895]. *The Rules of Sociological Method.* New York: Free Press.

Eco, U. 1988. *Foucault's Pendulum.* London: Pan Books.

Elliott, D. 1991. *Weighting for Non-Response: A Survey Researcher's Guide.* London: Office of Population Censuses and Surveys/HMSO.

Ellis, J. 1996. 'Revolutionary Spaces: Photographs of Working-Class Women by Esther Bubley 1940–1943', *Feminist Review*, 53: 74–94.

Ennis, J. 1992. 'The Social Organization of Sociological Knowledge: Modeling the Intersection of Specialties', *American Sociological Review*, 57.2: 259–265.

Erickson, B.H. and Nosanchuk, T.A. 1992. *Understanding Data* (2nd Edition). Buckingham: Open University Press.

Erikson, R. and Goldthorpe, J. 1993. *The Constant Flux: A Study of Class Mobility in Industrial Societies.* Oxford: Clarendon Press.

Everitt, B.S. 1984. *An Introduction to Latent Variable Models.* London: Chapman and Hall.

Everitt, B.S. 1992. *The Analysis of Contingency Tables* (2nd Edition). London: Chapman and Hall.

Everitt, B.S. 1993. *Cluster Analysis* (3rd Edition). London: Edward Arnold.

Everitt, B.S. and Dunn, G. 1991. *Applied Multivariate Data Analysis.* London: Edward Arnold.

Fairhurst, E. 1981. 'A Sociological Study of the Rehabilitation of Elderly Patients in an Urban Hospital' (unpublished Ph.D. thesis). Leeds: University of Leeds.

Fenton, S. 1996. 'Counting Ethnicity: Social Groups and Official Categories'. In Levitas, R. and Guy, W. (eds) *Interpreting Official Statistics.* London: Routledge.

Ferri, E. (ed.) 1993. *Life at 33: The Fifth Follow-Up of the National Child Development Study.* London: National Children's Bureau.

Fielding, J. and Gilbert, G.N. 2000. *Understanding Social Statistics.* London: Sage.

Fielding, N. and Lee, R. (eds) 1991. *Using Computers in Qualitative Research.* London: Sage.

Fienberg, S.E. 1980. *The Analysis of Cross-Classified Categorical Data* (2nd Edition). Cambridge, MA: MIT Press.

Finch, J. 1984. 'It's Great to Have Someone to Talk to: The Ethics and Politics of Interviewing Women'. In Bell, C. and Roberts, H. (eds) *Social Researching: Politics, Problems, Practice.* London: Routledge and Kegan Paul.

Finch, J. 1986. *Research and Policy: The Uses of Qualitative Methods in Social and Educational Research.* London: Falmer Press.

Finch, J. and Mason, J. 1993. *Negotiating Family Responsibilities.* London: Tavistock/Routledge.

Fine, G.A. 1987. *With the Boys: Little League Baseball and Preadolescent Culture.* Chicago: University of Chicago Press.

Fink, A. 1995. *The Survey Handbook* (Volume 1 of *The Survey Kit*). London: Sage.

Finnegan, R. 1996. 'Using Documents'. In Sapsford, R. and Jupp, V. (eds) *Data Collection and Analysis.* London: Sage.

Flood, J. 1983. *Barristers' Clerks: The Law's Middlemen.* Manchester: Manchester University Press.

Fonow, M.M. and Cook, J.A. (eds) 1991. *Beyond Methodology: Feminist Scholarship as Lived Research.* Bloomington: Indiana University Press.

Foster, J. 1990. *Villains: Crime and Community in the Inner City*. London: Routledge.

Foster, P. 1996. *Observing Schools: A Methodological Guide*. London: Paul Chapman.

Foucault, M. 1977. *Discipline and Punish*. London: Allen Unwin.

Foucault, M. 1979. *The History of Sexuality* (Volume 1). London: Allen Lane.

Foucault, M. 1980. *Power/Knowledge*. New York: Pantheon Books.

Fowler, F. 1993. *Survey Research Methods* (2nd Edition). London: Sage.

Fowler, F. 1995. *Improving Survey Questions: Design and Evaluation*. Thousand Oaks, CA: Sage.

Frankfort-Nachmias, C. and Nachmias, D. 1992. *Research Methods in the Social Sciences* (4th Edition). Sevenoaks: Edward Arnold.

Fraser, E.E. 1994. 'Reconciling Conceptual and Measurement Problems in the Comparative Study of Human Rights', *International Journal of Comparative Sociology*, 35.1–2: 1–18.

Frey, J. and Oishi, S. 1995. *How to Conduct Interviews by Telephone and in Person* (Volume 4 of *The Survey Kit*). London: Sage.

Frude, N. 1993. *A Guide to SPSS-PC+* (2nd Edition). London: Macmillan.

Gallie, D., Marsh, C. and Vogler, C. (eds) 1994. *Social Change and the Experience of Unemployment*. Oxford: Oxford University Press.

Gallup, G.H. 1947. 'The Quintamensional Plan of Question Design', *Public Opinion Quarterly*, 11: 385–393.

Galton, M. 1988. 'Structured Observation Techniques'. In Keeves, J. (ed.) *Educational Research, Methodology and Measurement: An International Handbook*. Oxford: Pergamon.

Galton, M., Hargreaves, L., Comber, C., Wall, D. with Pell, A. 1999. *Inside the Primary Classroom 20 Years On*. London: Routledge.

Gans, H.J. 1968. 'The Participant-Observer as a Human-Being: Observations on the Personal Aspects of Field Work'. In Becker, H.S., Geer, B., Riesman, D. and Weiss, R.S. (eds) *Institutions and the Person: Papers Presented to Everett C. Hughes*. Chicago: Aldine. (Reprinted in Burgess, R.G. (ed.) 1982. *Field Research: A Sourcebook and Field Manual*. London: Unwin Hyman, pp. 53–61.)

Gathorne-Hardy, J. 1984. *Doctors: The Lives and Work of GPs*. London: Weidenfeld and Nicolson.

Gelman, A., Carlin, J.B., Stern, H.S. and Rubin, D.B. 1995. *Bayesian Data Analysis*. London: Chapman and Hall.

Gibson, C. 1994. *Dissolving Wedlock*. London: Routledge.

Giddens, A. 1979. *Central Problems in Social Theory*. London: Macmillan.

Giddens, A. 1982. *New Rules of Sociological Method*. London: Hutchinson.

Gilbert, G.N. 1993a. *Analyzing Tabular Data: Loglinear and Logistic Models for Social Researchers*. London: UCL Press.

Gilbert, N. (ed.) 1993b. *Researching Social Life*. London: Sage.

Gilbert, N. and Doran, J. (eds) 1994. *Simulating Societies*. London: UCL Press.

Glaser, B.G. and Strauss, A.L. 1967. *The Discovery of Grounded Theory: Strategies for Qualitative Research*. New York: Aldine.

Goffman, E. 1959. *The Presentation of Self in Everyday Life*. Harmondsworth: Penguin.

Gold, R. 1958. 'Roles in Sociological Field Observation', *Social Forces*, 36.3: 217–223.

Goldberg, D. and Blackwell, B. 1970. 'Psychiatric Illness in General Practice: A Detailed Study Using a New Method of Case Identification', *British Medical Journal*, 2: 439–443.

Goldstein, H. 1995. *Multilevel Statistical Models* (2nd Edition). London: Edward Arnold.

Goldthorpe, J.H. 1983. 'Women and Class Analysis: In Defence of the Conventional View', *Sociology*, 17.4.

Goldthorpe, J.H. and Hope, K.E. 1974. *The Social Grading of Occupations: A New Approach and Scale*. Oxford: Clarendon Press.

Goldthorpe, J.H., Llewellyn, C. and Payne, C. 1987. *Social Mobility and Class Structure in Modern Britain* (2nd Edition). Oxford: Clarendon Press.

Goodson, I.F. (ed.) 1992. *Studying Teachers' Lives*. London: Routledge.

Gordon, T. 1994. *Single Women: On the Margins?* London: Macmillan.

Goyder, J. 1987. *The Silent Minority: Nonrespondents on Sample Surveys*. Cambridge: Polity Press.

Graham, H. 1982. 'Do Her Answers Fit His Questions? Women and the Survey Method'. In Gamarnikow, E. *et al.* (eds) *The Public and the Private*. London: Heinemann Educational.

Greene, G. and Kahn, C. (eds) 1985. *Making a Difference: Feminist Literary Criticism*. London: Routledge.

Griffin, J.H. 1977. *Black Like Me*. Boston: Houghton Mifflin.

Groves, R. 1989. *Survey Errors and Survey Costs*. New York: Wiley.

Guy, W. 1996. 'Health for All?'. In Levitas, R. and Guy, W. (eds) *Interpreting Official Statistics*. London: Routledge.

Hage, J. and Meeker, B.F. 1988. *Social Causality*. London: Unwin Hyman.

Hakim, C. 1987. *Research Design*. London: Unwin Hyman.

Halfpenny, P. 1992. *Positivism and Sociology: Explaining Social Life*. Aldershot: Gregg Revivals.

Halfpenny, P., Parthemore, J., Taylor, J. and Wilson, I. 1992. 'A Knowledge-Based System to Provide Intelligent Support for Writing Questionnaires'. In Westlake, A., Banks, R., Payne, C. and Orchard, T. (eds) *Survey and Statistical Computing*. Amsterdam: North-Holland.

Hammersley, M. and Atkinson, P. 1983. *Ethnography: Principles in Practice*. London: Tavistock.

Hammersley, M. and Atkinson, P. 1995. *Ethnography: Principles in Practice* (2nd Edition). London: Routledge.

Hantrais, L. and Mangen, S. (eds) 1996. *Cross-National Research Methods in the Social Sciences*. London: Pinter.

Harris, R. 1986. *Selling Hitler*. London: Faber.

Hatch, J.A. and Wisniewski, R. (eds) 1995. *Life History and Narrative*. London: Falmer Press.

Hays, W.L. 1973. *Statistics for the Social Sciences* (2nd Edition). New York: Holt, Rinehart and Winston.

Healy, M.J.R. 1988. *GLIM: An Introduction*. Oxford: Clarendon Press.

Heath, A., Jowell, R. and Curtice, J. 1985. *How Britain Votes*. Oxford: Pergamon Press.

Heath, A., Jowell, R. and Curtice, J. (eds) 1994. *Labour's Last Chance: The 1992 Election and Beyond*. Aldershot: Dartmouth.

Hedges, B. 1978. 'Sampling Minority Populations'. In Wilson, M. (ed.) *Social and Educational Research in Action*. Harlow: Longman.

Henry, G. 1995. *Graphing Data: Techniques for Display and Analysis*. London: Sage.

Hey, V. 1997. *The Company She Keeps. An Ethnography of Girls' Friendships*. Buckingham: Open University Press.

Hickman, M. 1998. 'Reconstructing Deconstructing "Race": British Political Discourses about the Irish in Britain', *Ethnic and Racial Studies*, 21.2: 288–307.

Hinde, A. 1998. *Demographic Methods*. London: Arnold.

Hindess, B. 1973. *The Use of Official Statistics in Sociology*. London: Macmillan.

Hinton, P. 1995. *Statistics Explained: A Guide for Social Science Students*. London: Routledge.

Hirst, M. 1992. 'Employment Patterns of Mothers with a Disabled Young Person', *Work, Employment and Society*, 6.1: 87–107.

Hobbs, D. 1988. *Doing the Business: Entrepreneurship, the Working Class, and Detectives in the East End of London*. Oxford: Oxford University Press.

Hobbs, D. and May, T. 1993. (eds) *Interpreting the Field: Accounts of Ethnography*. Oxford. Clarendon Press.

Hockey, J. 1986. *Squaddies: Portrait of a Subculture*. Exeter: University of Exeter Press.

Hoinville, G., Jowell, R. and Associates. 1977. *Survey Research Practice*. London: Heinemann Educational.

Holdaway, S. 1983. *Inside the British Police: A Force at Work*. Oxford: Basil Blackwell.

Holdsworth, C. and Dale, A. 1997. 'Ethnic Differences in Women's Employment', *Work, Employment and Society*, 11.3: 435–457.

Hollway, W. and Jefferson, T. 2000. *Doing Qualitative Research Differently: Free Association, Narrative and the Interview Method*. London: Sage.

Holsti, O. 1969. *Content Analysis for the Social Sciences and Humanities*. Reading, MA: Addison-Wesley.

Holt, T. 1998. 'National Statistics: Meeting New Challenges', *The Statistician* (Journal of the Royal Statistical Society: Series D), 47.4: 645–646.

Homan, R. 1991. *The Ethics of Social Research*. Harlow: Longman.

Horn, R.V. 1993. *Statistical Indicators for the Economic and Social Sciences*. Cambridge: Cambridge University Press.

Howard, J. 1996. *Michael Powell*. London: Batsford.

Huby, M. and Dix, G. 1992a. 'Merging Methods: Integrating Quantitative and Qualitative Approaches to Survey Design, Analysis and Interpretation'. In Westlake, A., Banks, R., Payne, C. and Orchard, T. (eds) 1992. *Survey and Statistical Computing*. London: North-Holland.

Huby, M. and Dix, G. 1992b. *Evaluating the Social Fund* (DSS Research Report Series No. 9). London: HMSO.

Huff, D. 1954. *How to Lie with Statistics*. London: Gollancz.

Hughes, C. 1991. *Stepparents: Wicked or Wonderful?* Aldershot: Avebury.

Hughes, E.C. 1960. 'Introduction: The Place of Fieldwork in Social Science'. In Junker, B.H. (ed.) *Field Work: An Introduction to the Social Sciences*. Chicago: University of Chicago Press.

Humphreys, L. 1970. *Tearoom Trade*. London: Duckworth.

ILO. 1990. *International Standard Classification of Occupations*. Geneva: International Labour Organization.

Jagger, E. 1998. 'Marketing the Self, Buying an Other: Dating in a Post Modern, Consumer Society', *Sociology*, 32.4: 795–814.

Jarvie, I.C. 1969. 'The Problem of Ethical Integrity in Participant Observation', *Current Anthropology*, 10.5: 505–508. (Reprinted in Burgess, R.G. (ed.) 1982. *Field Research: a Sourcebook and Field Manual*. London: Unwin Hyman, pp. 68–72.)

Jary, D. and Jary, J. (eds) 2000. *Dictionary of Sociology*. Glasgow: Harper Collins.

John, J.A. 1977. *Experiments: Design and Analysis* (2nd Edition). London: Griffin.

Johnson, A., Wadsworth, J., Wellings, K. and Field, J. 1994. *Sexual Attitudes and Lifestyles*. Oxford: Blackwell Scientific.

Jowell, R., Brook, L. and Prior, G. (eds) 1992. *British Social Attitudes: The 9th Report*. Aldershot: Dartmouth.

Jowell, R., Curtice, J., Park, A., Brook, L. and Thomson, K. (eds) 1996. *British Social Attitudes: The 13th Report*. Aldershot: Dartmouth.

Junker, B.H. (ed.) 1960. *Field Work: An Introduction to the Social Sciences*. Chicago: University of Chicago Press.

Jupp, V. 1989. *Methods of Criminological Research*. London: Unwin Hyman.

Jupp, V. and Norris, C. 1993. 'Traditions in Documentary Analysis'. In Hammersley, M. (ed.) *Social Research: Philosophy, Politics and Practice*. London: Sage.

Kalton, G. 1966. *Introduction to Statistical Ideas for Social Scientists*. London: Chapman and Hall.

Kalton, G. 1983. *Compensating for Missing Survey Data*. Ann Arbor, MI: Institute for Social Research.

Kalton, G. and Stowell, R. 1979. 'A Study of Coder Variability', *Applied Statistics*, 28: 276–289.

Kavanagh, S. and Knapp, M. 1999. 'Cognitive Disability and Direct Care Costs for Elderly People', *British Journal of Psychiatry*, 174: 539–546.

Keats, D. 2000. *Interviewing: A Practical Guide for Students and Professionals*. Buckingham: Open University Press.

Kiecker, P. and Nelson, J. 1996. 'Do Interviewers Follow Telephone Survey Instructions?', *Journal of the Market Research Society*, 38.2: 161–176.

Kiernan, K. 1992. 'The Impact of Family Disruption in Childhood on Transitions Made in Young Adult Life', *Population Studies*, 46.2: 213–234.

King, E. 1996. 'The Use of the Self in Qualitative Research'. In Richardson, J.T.E. (ed.) *Handbook of Qualitative Research Methods for Psychologists and the Social Sciences*. Leicester: BPS Books (British Psychological Society).

King, R. 1978. *All Things Bright and Beautiful? A Sociological Study of Infants' Classrooms*. Chichester: Wiley.

Kinnear, P.R. and Gray, C.D. 1994. *SPSS for Windows Made Simple*. Hove: Lawrence Erlbaum Associates.

Kitsuse, J. and Cicourel, A. 1963. 'A Note on the Uses of Official Statistics', *Social Problems*, 11: 131–139.

Kitzinger, J. and Barbour, S. 1999. 'The Challenge and Promise of Focus Groups'. In Barbour, S. and Kitzinger, J. (eds) *Developing Focus Group Research: Politics, Theory and Practice*. London: Sage.

Kleinman, S. and Copp, M. 1993. *Emotions and Fieldwork*. Newbury Park, CA: Sage.

Klockars, C.B. 1975. *The Professional Fence*. London: Tavistock.

Kotler, P. 1997. *Marketing Management: Analysis, Planning, Implementation and Control* (9th Edition). London: Prentice Hall International.

Krueger, R.A. 1994. *Focus Groups: A Practical Guide for Applied Research* (2nd Edition). London: Sage.

Lampard, R. 1994. 'An Examination of the Relationship between Marital Dissolution and Unemployment'. In Gallie, D., Marsh, C. and Vogler, C. (eds) *Social Change and the Experience of Unemployment*. Oxford: Oxford University Press.

Lampard, R. 1995. 'Parents' Occupations and their Children's Occupational Attainment: A Contribution to the Debate on the Class Assignment of Families', *Sociology* 29.4: 715–728.

Lampard, R. 1996. 'Might Britain Be a Meritocracy: A Comment on Saunders', *Sociology*, 30.2: 387–393.

Lampard, R. 1997. 'Party Political Homogamy in Great Britain', *European Sociological Review*, 13.1: 79–99.

Lampard, R. and Peggs, K. 1999. 'Repartnering: The Relevance of Parenthood and Gender to Cohabitation and Remarriage among the Formerly Married', *British Journal of Sociology*, 50.3: 443–465.

Lapsley, R. and Westlake, M. 1989. *Film Theory: An Introduction*. Manchester: Manchester University Press.

Lather, P.A. 1991. *Getting Smart: Feminist Research and Pedagogy With/in the Postmodern*. London: Routledge.

Lee, D. and Turner, B. (eds) 1996. *Conflicts about Class: Debating Inequality in Late Industrialism*. Harlow: Longman.

Lee, R. 1993. *Doing Research on Sensitive Topics*. London: Sage.

Leonard, P. 1996. 'Three Discourses on Practice: A Postmodern Re-appraisal', *Journal of Sociology and Social Welfare*, 23.2: 7–26.

Levitas, R. 1996a. 'Fiddling While Britain Burns? The "Measurement" of Unemployment'. In Levitas, R.

and Guy, W. (eds) *Interpreting Official Statistics*. London: Routledge.

Levitas, R. 1996b. 'The Legacy of Rayner'. In Levitas, R. and Guy, W. (eds) *Interpreting Official Statistics*. London: Routledge.

Levitas, R. and Guy, W. (eds) 1996. *Interpreting Official Statistics*. London: Routledge.

Lewis-Beck, M.S. (ed.) 1993. *Regression Analysis*. London: Sage.

Lincoln, Y.S. and Guba, E. 1985. *Naturalistic Inquiry*. Beverly Hills, CA: Sage.

Lindsey, J.K. 1995. *Introductory Statistics: A Modelling Approach*. Oxford: Clarendon Press.

Little, R.J.A. and Rubin, D.B. 1987. *Statistical Analysis with Missing Data*. New York: Wiley.

Llewellyn, M. 1980. 'Studying Girls at School: The Implications of Confusion'. In Deem, R. (ed.) *Schooling for Women's Work*. London: Routledge and Kegan Paul.

Loether, H.J. and McTavish, D.G. 1993. *Descriptive and Inferential Statistics: An Introduction* (4th Edition). London: Allyn and Bacon.

Lofland, J. and Lofland, L.H. 1995. *Analyzing Social Settings: A Guide to Qualitative Observation and Analysis* (3rd Edition). Belmont, CA: Wadsworth.

Lynn, P. and Lievesley, D. 1992. *Drawing General Population Samples in Great Britain*. London: Social and Community Planning Research.

Lyon, D. 1987. *The Information Society: Issues and Illusions*. Cambridge: Polity Press.

Mac an Ghaill, M. 1994. *The Making of Men: Masculinities, Sexualities and Schooling*. Buckingham: Open University Press.

MacMillan, K. and McLachlan, S. 1999. 'Theory-Building with NUD*IST: Using Computer-Assisted Qualitative Analysis in a Media Case Study', *Sociological Research Online*, 4.2: 135–151.

Magnusson, D. and Bergman, L. (eds) 1990. *Data Quality in Longitudinal Research*. Cambridge: Cambridge University Press.

Malinowski, B. 1922. *Argonauts of the Western Pacific: An Account of Native Enterprise and Adventure in the Archipelagoes of Melanesian New Guinea*. London: Routledge and Kegan Paul.

Manly, B.F.J. 1986. *Multivariate Statistical Methods: A Primer*. London: Chapman and Hall.

Marsh, C. 1982. *The Survey Method: The Contribution of Surveys to Sociological Explanation*. London: George Allen and Unwin.

Marsh, C. 1986. 'Social Class and Occupation'. In Burgess, R. (ed.) *Key Variables in Social Investigation*. London: Routledge and Kegan Paul.

Marsh, C. 1988. *Exploring Data: An Introduction to Data Analysis for Social Scientists*. Oxford: Polity Press.

Marsh, C., Skinner, C., Arber, S., Penhale, B., Openshaw, S., Hobcraft, J., Lievesley, D. and Walford, N. 1991. 'The Case for Samples of Anonymized Records from the 1991 Census', *Journal of the Royal Statistical Society (Series A)*, 154.2: 305–340.

Marshall, C. and Rossman, G.B. 1989. *Designing Qualitative Research*. London: Sage.

Marshall, G. (ed.) 1998. *The Oxford Dictionary of Sociology*. Oxford: Oxford University Press.

Marshall, G. and Swift, A. 1996. 'Merit and Mobility: A Reply to Saunders', *Sociology*, 30.2: 375–386.

Marshall, G., Rose, D., Newby, H. and Vogler, C. 1988. *Social Class in Modern Britain*. London: Unwin Hyman.

Martin, J. and Manners, T. 1995. 'Computer Assisted Personal Interviewing in Survey Research'. In Lee, R. (ed.) *Information Technology for the Social Scientist*. London: UCL Press.

Martin, J., Meltzer, H. and Elliott, D. 1988. 'The Prevalence of Disability among Adults', *OPCS Surveys of Disability in Britain*, Report 1. London: HMSO.

Mason, J. 1996. *Qualitative Researching*. London: Sage.

May, T. 1993. *Social Research: Issues, Methods and Process*. Buckingham: Open University Press.

Mayo, E. 1949. *Social Problems of Industrial Civilisation*. London: Routledge and Kegan Paul.

McCrossan, L. 1991. *A Handbook for Interviewers*. London: Office of Population Censuses and Surveys/HMSO.

McDonald, K. and Tipton, C. 1993. 'Using Documents'. In Gilbert, N. (ed.) *Researching Social Life*. London: Sage.

McNeill, P. 1990. *Research Methods* (2nd Edition). London: Routledge.

Merton, R. and Kendall, P. 1946. 'The Focused Interview', *American Journal of Sociology*, 51.6: 541–557.

Miles, I. and Irvine, J. 1979. 'The Critique of Official Statistics'. In Irvine, J., Miles, I. and Evans, J. (eds) *Demystifying Social Statistics*. London: Pluto.

Miles, M. and Huberman, A. 1984. *Qualitative Data Analysis*. London: Sage.

Miles, M. and Huberman, A. 1994. *Qualitative Data Analysis: An Expanded Sourcebook* (2nd Edition). London: Sage.

Mills, C.W. 1959. *The Sociological Imagination*. Harmondsworth: Penguin.

Mishler, E. 1986. *Research Interviewing*. Cambridge, MA: Harvard University Press.

Model, S. 1999. 'Ethnic Inequality in England: An Analysis Based on the 1991 Census', *Ethnic and Racial Studies*, 22.6: 966–990.

Mohr, W. 1999. 'Deconstructing the Language of Psychiatric Hospitalization', *Journal of Advanced Nursing*, 29.5: 1052–1059.

Morgan, D.L. and Spanish, M.T. 1984. 'Focus Groups: A New Tool for Qualitative Research', *Qualitative Sociology*, 7.3: 253–270.

Morrison, D.E. (ed.) 1998. *The Search for a Method: Focus Groups and the Development of Mass Communications Research*. Luton: University of Luton Press.

Morrison, M. and Galloway, S. 1996. 'Using Diaries to Research Supply Teachers' Lives'. In Busfield, J. and Lyon, E.S. (eds) *Methodological Imaginations*. London: Macmillan.

Morton-Williams, J. 1978. 'Unstructured Design Work'. In Hoinville, G., Jowell, R. and Associates. *Survey Research Practice*. Aldershot: Gower.

Morton-Williams, J. 1993. *Interviewing Approaches*. Aldershot: Dartmouth.

Moser, C. and Kalton, G. 1971. *Survey Methods in Social Investigation* (2nd Edition). London: Heinemann.

Neave, H.R. and Worthington, P.L. 1988. *Distribution-Free Tests*. London: Routledge.

Neill, S. 1991. *Classroom Nonverbal Communication*. London. Routledge.

Neill, S. and Caswell, C. 1993. *Body Language for Competent Teachers*. London: Routledge.

Nichols, T. 1996. 'Social Class: Official, Sociological and Marxist'. In Levitas, R. and Guy, W. (eds) *Interpreting Official Statistics*. London: Routledge.

Nieuwenhuys, O. 1994. *Children's Lifeworlds, Welfare and Labour in the Developing World*. London: Routledge.

Nieuwenhuys, O. 1996. *Action Research with Street Children: A Role for Street Educators* (Special Issue on Children's Participation, PLA Notes 25). London: International Institute for Environment and Development.

Norusis, M.J. (and SPSS Inc.) 1993. *SPSS for Windows: Base System User's Guide, Release 6.0*. Chicago: SPSS Inc.

Norusis, M.J. 1994a. *SPSS Advanced Statistics 6.1*. Chicago: SPSS Inc.

Norusis, M.J. 1994b. *SPSS Professional Statistics 6.1*. Chicago: SPSS Inc.

Oakley, A. 1981. 'Interviewing Women: A Contradiction in Terms'. In Roberts, H. (ed.) *Doing Feminist Research*. London: Routledge and Kegan Paul.

Oakley, A. 1985. *The Sociology of Housework*. Oxford: Blackwell.

O'Connell-Davidson, J. and Layder, D. 1994. *Methods, Sex and Madness*. London: Routledge.

ONS (Office for National Statistics). 1996a. *Guide to Official Statistics: 1996 Edition*. London: HMSO.

ONS. 1996b. *Harmonised Concepts and Questions for Government Social Surveys*. London: Government Statistical Service.

ONS. 1997. *Living in Britain: Results from the 1995 General Household Survey*. London: The Stationery Office.

ONS. 1999. *Cancer Survival Trends in England and Wales 1971–1995: Deprivation and NHS Region* (Series SMPS No. 61). London: The Stationery Office.

OPCS (Office of Population Censuses and Surveys). 1990a. *Labour Force Survey, 1989*. London: HMSO.

OPCS. 1990b. *Abortion Statistics: Legal Abortions Carried Out under the 1967 Abortion Act in England and Wales, 1990*. London: HMSO.

OPCS. 1991a. *General Household Survey, 1989*. London: HMSO.

OPCS. 1991b. *Standard Occupational Classification* (3 volumes). London: HMSO.

OPCS. 1993. *1991 Census: Household Composition (Great Britain)* CEN 91 HC. London: HMSO.

OPCS. 1994. *General Household Survey 1992* (OPCS Series GHS, No. 23). London: HMSO.

Oppenheim, A. 1992. *Questionnaire Design, Interviewing and Attitude Measurement*. New York: Basic Books.

Oyen, E. (ed.) 1990. *Comparative Methodology*. London: Sage.

Paige, R. 1973. *Down among the Dossers*. London: Davis-Poynter Ltd.

Pakulski, J. and Waters, M. 1996. *The Death of Class*. London: Sage.

Parry, O. 1987. 'Uncovering the Ethnographer'. In McKeganey, N. and Cunningham-Burley, S. (eds) *Enter the Sociologist*. Aldershot: Avebury.

Patton, M.Q. 1990. *Qualitative Evaluation and Research Methods* (2nd Edition). Newbury Park, CA: Sage.

Payne, C., Payne, J. and Heath, A. 1994. 'Modelling Trends in Multi-Way Tables'. In Dale, A. and Davies, R.B. (eds) *Analyzing Social and Political Change: A Casebook of Methods*. London: Sage.

Phoenix, A. 1991. *Young Mothers?* Cambridge: Polity Press.

Platt, J. 1981. 'Evidence and Proof in Documentary Research: 1. Some Specific Problems of Documentary Research', *Sociological Review*, 29.1: 31–52.

Plewis, I. 1997. *Statistics in Education*. London: Arnold.

Plummer, K. 1983. *Documents of Life: An Introduction to the Problems and Literature of a Humanistic Method*. London: George Allen and Unwin.

Pole, C.J. 1989. 'The Transfer from School to Non-School: A Study in Five Labour Markets' (unpublished Ph.D. thesis). Leicester: University of Leicester.

Pole, C.J. 1993. *Assessing and Recording Achievement: Implementing a New Approach in School*. Buckingham: Open University Press.

Pole, C.J. 1994. *Evaluation of Project Gemini*. Coventry: Centre for Educational Development, Appraisal and Research (CEDAR).

Pole, C.J. 1995. 'Don't Shoot the Messenger: A Study in the Politics and Control of Funded Research', *Evaluation and Research in Education*, 9.3: 135–149.

Pole, C.J. 1999. 'Black Teachers Giving Voice: Choosing and Experiencing Teaching.' *Teacher Development*, 3.3: 313–328.

Pole, C.J., Mizen, P. and Bolton, A. 1999. 'Realising Children's Agency in Research: Partners and Participants', *International Journal of Social Research Methodology*, 2.1: 39–54.

Pollard, A.H., Yusuf, F. and Pollard, G.N. 1981. *Demographic Techniques* (2nd Edition). Oxford: Pergamon.

Pollert, A. 1981. *Girls, Wives, Factory Lives*. London: Macmillan.

Potter, J. and Wetherell, M. 1994. 'Analyzing Discourse'. In Bryman, A. and Burgess, R.G. (eds) *Analyzing Qualitative Data*. London: Routledge.

Powell, M. 1986. *A Life in Movies: An Autobiography*. London: Heinemann.

Prandy, K. 1990. 'The Revised Cambridge Scale of Occupations', *Sociology*, 24.4: 629–655.

Pressat, R. 1978. *Statistical Demography*. London: Methuen.

Procter, I. and Padfield, M. 1995. 'Young Women's Career Aspirations: What Happens to Them?', *Youth and Society*, 47: 16–38.

Procter, I. and Padfield, M. 1998. *Young Adult Women, Work and Family: Living a Contradiction*. London: Mansell.

Procter, M. 1993. 'Measuring Attitudes'. In Gilbert, G.N. (ed.) *Researching Social Life*. London: Sage.

Prosser, J. (ed.) 1998. *Image-based Research: A Sourcebook for Qualitative Researchers*. London: Falmer Press.

Pryce, K. 1979. *Endless Pressure: A Study of West Indian Life-styles in Bristol*. Harmondsworth: Penguin.

Ragin, C. 1987. *The Comparative Method: Moving Beyond Qualitative and Quantitative Strategies*. Berkeley: University of California Press.

Reid, S. 1987. *Working with Statistics: An Introduction to Quantitative Methods for Social Scientists*. Cambridge: Polity Press.

Reiner, R. 1996. 'The Case of the Missing Crimes'. In Levitas, R. and Guy, W. (eds) *Interpreting Official Statistics*. London: Routledge.

Reinharz, S. 1992. *Feminist Methods in Social Research*. Oxford: Oxford University Press.

Richards, L. and Richards, T. 1991. 'The Transformation of Qualitative Method'. In Fielding, N.G. and Lee, R.M. (eds) *Using Computers in Qualitative Research*. London: Sage.

Richards, T. and Richards, L. 1994. 'Using Computers in Qualitative Analysis'. In Denzin, N. and Lincoln, Y. (eds) *Handbook of Qualitative Research*. Newbury Park, CA: Sage.

Richardson, J.T.E. (ed.) 1996. *Handbook of Qualitative Research Methods for Psychologists and the Social Sciences*. Leicester: BPS Books (British Psychological Society).

Roberts, H. (ed.) 1990. *Women's Health Counts*. London: Routledge.

Roberts, H. 1993. 'The Women and Class Debate'. In Morgan, D. and Stanley, L. (eds) *Debates in Sociology*. Manchester: Manchester University Press.

Rose, D. and Corti, L. (eds) 1998. *Researching Social and Economic Change*. London: UCL Press.

Rose, D. and O'Reilly, K. (eds) 1997. *Constructing Classes: Towards a New Social Classification for the UK*. Swindon: Economic and Social Research Council/ Office for National Statistics.

Rose, D. and Sullivan, O. 1996. *Introducing Data Analysis for Social Scientists* (2nd Edition). Buckingham: Open University Press.

Rose, G. 1982. *Deciphering Sociological Research*. London: Macmillan.

Rosenthal, R. 1984. *Meta-analytic Procedures for Social Research*. London: Sage.

Rowntree, D. 1981. *Statistics without Tears: A Primer for Non-Mathematicians*. Harmondsworth: Penguin.

Sapsford, R. 1996. 'Extracting and Presenting Statistics'. In Sapsford, R. and Jupp, V. (eds) *Data Collection and Analysis*. London: Sage.

Sapsford, R. and Jupp, V. (eds) 1996. *Data Collection and Analysis*. London: Sage.

Saris, W.E. 1991. *Computer Assisted Interviewing*. London: Sage.

Saris, W.E. and Stronkhorst, L.H. 1984. *Causal Modelling in Non-Experimental Research: An Introduction to the LISREL Approach*. Amsterdam: Sociometric Research Foundation.

Saunders, P. 1989. *Social Class and Stratification*. London: Routledge.

Saunders, P. 1995. 'Might Britain Be a Meritocracy?', *Sociology*, 29.1: 23–41.

Scheurich, J.J. 1997. *Research Method in the Postmodern*. London: Falmer Press.

Schratz, M. and Walker, R. 1995. *Research as Social Change: New Opportunities for Qualitative Research*. London: Routledge.

Scott, J. 1990. *A Matter of Record: Documentary Sources in Social Research*. Cambridge: Polity Press.

Scott, J. 1991. *Social Network Analysis: A Handbook*. London: Sage.

Seale, C. (ed.) 1998. *Researching Society and Culture*. London: Sage.

Seidel, J. 1991. 'Method and Madness in the Application of Computer Technology to Qualitative Data Analysis'. In Fielding, N.G. and Lee, R.M. (eds) *Using Computers in Qualitative Research*. London: Sage.

Seidel, J.V., Kjolseth, R. and Seymour, E. 1988. *The Ethnograph: A User's Guide*. Littleton, CO: Qualis Research Associates.

Sharples, M. 1998. *How We Write: Writing as Creative Design*. London: Routledge.

Shaw, C. 1930. *The Jack-Roller: A Delinquent Boy's Own Story*. Chicago: University of Chicago Press.

Sieber, J. (ed.) 1982. *The Ethics of Social Research: Surveys and Experiments*. New York: Springer-Verlag.

Siegel, S. 1956. *Nonparametric Statistics for the Behavioural Sciences*. London: McGraw-Hill.

Sikes, P.J., Measor, L. and Woods, P. 1985. *Teacher Careers: Crises and Continuities*. London: Falmer Press.

Silverman, D. 1993. *Interpreting Qualitative Data: Methods for Analysing Talk, Text and Interaction*. London: Sage.

Skeggs, B. 1994. 'Situating the Production of Feminist Ethnography'. In Maynard, M. and Purvis, J. (eds) *Researching Women's Lives from a Feminist Perspective*. London: Taylor and Francis.

Skinner, C.J., Holt, D. and Smith, T.M.F. (eds) 1989. *Analysis of Complex Surveys*. Chichester: Wiley.

Smart, C. 1984. *The Ties That Bind: Law, Marriage and the Reproduction of Patriarchal Relations*. London: Routledge and Kegan Paul.

Smith, D. 1977. *Racial Disadvantage in Britain*. Harmondsworth: Penguin.

Spradley, J. 1979. *The Ethnographic Interview*. New York: Holt, Rinehart and Winston.

Sprokkereef, A., Lakin, E., Pole, C.J. and Burgess, R.G. 1995. 'The Data, The Team, The Ethnograph'. In Burgess, R.G. (ed.) *Computing in Qualitative Research* (Studies in Qualitative Methodology: Volume 5). Greenwich: JAI Press.

SRA. 1996. 'Social Research Association Ethical Guidelines'. In the *Social Research Association Directory of Members 1996/7*. London: SRA (Social Research Association).

Stacey, J. 1994. *Star Gazing: Hollywood Cinema and Female Spectatorship*. London: Routledge.

Staines, A. 1999. 'Poverty and Health'. In Dorling, D. and Simpson, S. (eds) *Statistics in Society: The Arithmetic of Politics*. London: Arnold.

Stanley, L. 1995. *Sex Surveyed 1949–1994: From Mass-Observation's 'Little Kinsey' to the National Survey and the Hite Reports*. London: Taylor and Francis.

Stanley, L. and Wise, S. 1993. *Breaking Out Again: Feminist Ontology and Epistemology*. London: Routledge.

Stewart, D. 1984. *Secondary Research: Information Sources and Methods*. Beverly Hills, CA: Sage.

Strauss, A. 1987. *Qualitative Analysis for Social Scientists*. Cambridge: Cambridge University Press.

Strauss, A. and Corbin, J. 1990. *Basics of Qualitative Research: Grounded Theory Procedures and Techniques*. London: Sage.

Strauss, A. and Corbin, J. (eds) 1997. *Grounded Theory in Practice*. London: Sage.

Stronach, I. and MacLure, M. 1997. *Educational Research Undone: The Postmodern Embrace*. Buckingham: Open University Press.

Sudman, S. and Bradburn, N. 1982. *Asking Questions: A Practical Guide to Questionnaire Design*. San Francisco: Jossey-Bass.

Sullivan, M.A., Queen, S.A. and Patrick, R.C. 1958. 'Participant Observation as Employed in the Study of a Military Training Program', *American Sociological Review*, 23.6: 660–667.

Swaddle K.M.O. and Heath, A. 1989. 'Official and Reported Turnout in the British General Election of 1987', *British Journal of Political Science*, 19: 537–570.

Swinnerton-Dyer, P. 1982. *Report of the Working Party on Postgraduate Education*. London: HMSO.

Sykes, W. and Collins, M. 1988. 'Effects of Mode of Interview: Experiments in the UK'. In Groves, R., Biemer, P., Lyberg, L., Massey, J., Nicholls, W. and Waksberg, J. (eds) *Telephone Survey Methodology*. New York: Wiley.

Szreter, S. 1993. 'The Idea of Demographic Transition and the Study of Fertility Change: A Critical Intellectual History', *Population and Development Review*, 19.4: 659–701.

Tesch, R. 1990. *Qualitative Research: Analysis Types and Software Tools*. London: Falmer Press.

Tesch, R. 1991. 'Software for Qualitative Researchers: Analysis Needs and Programme Capabilities'. In Fielding, N.G. and Lee, R.M. (eds) *Using Computers in Qualitative Research*. London: Sage.

Thomas, W.I. and Znaniecki, F. 1958 [1918–20]. *The Polish Peasant in Europe and America*. New York: Dover Publications.

Thompson, P. 1988. *The Voice of the Past: Oral History* (2nd Edition). Oxford: Oxford University Press.

Thorne, B. 1993. *Gender Play: Girls and Boys in School*. New Brunswick, NJ: Rutgers University Press.

Townsend, P. 1996. 'The Struggle for Independent Statistics on Poverty'. In Levitas, R. and Guy, W. (eds) *Interpreting Official Statistics*. London: Routledge.

Townsend, P., Davidson, N. and Whitehead M. (eds) 1988. *Inequalities in Health: The Black Report and the Health Divide*. Harmondsworth: Penguin.

Tufte, E.R. 1983. *The Visual Display of Quantitative Information*. Cheshire, CO: Graphics Press.

Tukey, J.W. 1977. *Exploratory Data Analysis*. Reading, MA: Addison-Wesley.

Tull, D.S. and Hawkins, D.I. 1993. *Marketing Research: Measurement and Method – A Text with Cases* (6th Edition). New York: Macmillan.

Tuma, N. 1994. 'Event History Analysis: An Introduction'. In Dale, A. and Davies, R.B. (eds) *Analyzing Social and Political Change: A Casebook of Methods*. London: Sage.

Van Dijk, T. (ed.) 1985. *Handbook of Discourse Analysis* (Volumes 1 to 4). London: Academic Press.

Wadsworth, J., Field, J., Johnson, A., Bradshaw, S. and Wellings, K. 1993. 'Methodology of the National Survey of Sexual Attitudes and Lifestyles', *Journal of the Royal Statistical Society (Series A)*, 156.3: 407–421.

Walker, R., Dix, G. and Huby, M. 1992. *Working the Social Fund* (DSS Research Report Series No. 8). London: HMSO.

Wallerstein, J. and Blakeslee, S. 1989. *Second Chances: Men, Women and Children a Decade after Divorce*. London: Bantam Press.

Wallerstein, J. and Kelly, J. 1980. *Surviving the Breakup: How Children and Parents Cope with Divorce*. London: Grant McIntyre.

Walsh, A. 1990. *Statistics for the Social Sciences: With Computer Applications*. New York: Harper and Row.

Webb, E., Campbell, D.T., Schwartz, R.D. and Sechrest, L. 1966. *Unobtrusive Measures: Nonreactive Research in the Social Sciences*. Chicago: Rand McNally.

Weber, M. 1949. *The Methodology of the Social Sciences*. New York: Free Press.

Weber, R. 1990. *Basic Content Analysis* (2nd Edition). London: Sage.

Weller, S.C. and Romney, A.K. 1990. *Metric Scaling: Correspondence Analysis* (QASS Series: No. 75). London: Sage.

West, J. 1996. 'Figuring Out Working Women'. In Levitas, R. and Guy, W. (eds) *Interpreting Official Statistics*. London: Routledge.

Westwood, S. 1984. *All Day Every Day: Factory and Family in the Making of Women's Lives*. London: Pluto.

Whyte, W.F. 1943. *Street Corner Society: The Social Structure of an Italian Slum*. Chicago: University of Chicago Press.

Wilkinson, R.G. 1996. *Unhealthy Societies: The Afflictions of Inequality*. London: Routledge.

Williams, J., Dunning, E. and Murphy, P. 1984. *Hooligans Abroad*. London: Routledge and Kegan Paul.

Winfield, G. 1987. *The Social Science PhD: The ESRC Inquiry on Submission Rates*. London: Economic and Social Research Council.

Winter, M. and Short, C. 1993. 'Believing and Belonging – Religion in Rural England', *British Journal of Sociology*, 44.4: 635–651.

Wolcott, H.F. 1981. 'Confessions of a "Trained" Observer'. In Popkewitz, T.S. and Tabachnick, B.R. (eds) *The Study of Schooling: Field Based Methodologies in Educational Research and Evaluation*. New York: Praeger, pp. 247–263.

Wolcott, H.F. 1983. 'Adequate Schools and Inadequate Education: The Life Story of a Sneaky Kid', *Anthropology and Education Quarterly*, 14: 3–32.

Wolcott, H.F. 1994. *Transforming Qualitative Data: Description, Analysis and Interpretation*. London: Sage.

Wolcott, H.F. 1995. *The Art of Fieldwork*. London: AltaMira Press.

Wolf, F. 1986. *Meta-analysis: Quantitative Methods for Research Synthesis*. London: Sage.

Woolf, D. (ed.) 1996. *Feminist Dilemmas in Fieldwork*. Oxford: Westview Press.

Wright, D. 1997. *Understanding Statistics: An Introduction for the Social Sciences*. London: Sage.

Wright, E.O. 1985. *Classes*. London: Verso.

Author, person and organisation index

Abberley, P., 92, 93, 172–3, 180
Abercrombie, N., 288
Abramson, P., 296
Agresti, A., 245
Ahmad, W., 174
Aitkin, M., 243
Allison, P.D., 245
Althusser, L., 160
Anderson, B., 116
Anderson, D., 296
Anderson, S., 243, 245
Annandale, E., 100, 268
Arber, S., 170, 298, 303
Arendell, T., 41
Asher, H.B., 242
Ashworth, J., 263–4
Astin, M., 174
Atkinson, J.M., 167–8
Atkinson, P., 11, 69, 78, 79, 126, 128, 131, 139, 141, 162, 192, 198, 209
Auquier, A., 296

Babbie, E., 120
Bailey, S., 244
Ball, M., 154
Ball, S., 139
Banks, R., 301
Barbour, R.S., 132
Barnes, J., 84
Barthes, R., 160
Bateson, N., 103, 118, 121
Baudrillard, J., 292
Becker, H.S., 77, 154, 159, 247, 300
Bell, C., 84, 299
Bem, S., 100, 109, 268
Bergman, L., 115
Biemer, P., 306
Biklen, S., 126
Binson, D., 298

Blackwell, B., 101
Blakeslee, S., 29, 44
Blalock, H.M. Jr., 212, 242
Blaxter, L., 2, 14, 143, 145
Blaxter, M., 68, 101, 265
Blumer, H., 295
Boddy, F.A., 171
Boelen, W.A.M., 88
Bogdan, R., 126, 139
Bolton, A., xii, 23–4
Bourque, L., 124
Bradburn, N., 100, 124
Bradshaw, J., 263–5
Bradshaw, S., 307
Brannen, J., 30, 46
Brierley, P., 7
Brindle, D., 158
British Educational Research Association [BERA], 84, 282–5
British Psychological Society [BPS], 84
British Sociological Association [BSA], 24, 84, 113, 276–81
Brook, L., 105, 107, 109, 118, 213, 302
Brownlow, K., 156
Bryman, A., 19, 91, 93, 95, 120, 124, 132, 153, 191, 199–200, 207, 241, 243, 244, 288, 289, 290, 291, 292, 295
Buck, N., 29, 179
Buford, B., 85
Bulmer, M., 26, 84, 113, 136, 166, 168, 169, 170–2, 177
Burchell, B., 102
Burgess, R.G., xii, 17, 28–9, 37, 43, 69, 75, 97, 101, 126, 128, 136–7, 140–1, 170, 191, 195–9, 199–200, 300, 302, 306
Burgoyne, J., 41–2
Burholt, V., 245
Burnett, F.H., 192
Burnett, J., 153
Busfield, J., 304

Subject index

access, 24, 33, 40–1, 44–6, 69, 87, 155–6, 183, 266–7
accuracy in surveys, 63
actor's perspective, 91, 92–3, 94, 99, 100, 129, 131, 136–8, 162, 262, 268, 290, 291, 294, 295
aggregating categories, 221–2
alpha
    Cronbach's, 100–2
analysis
    as destruction, 192–3
    forms and stages of, 189–91
analysis of covariance [ANCOVA], 243
analysis of variance [ANOVA], 229, 232–5, 238
analytic induction, 37, 200, 205–6, 209, 288
anonymity, 23–4, 45–6, 84, 113–15, 277–9, 283
archives (documents), 155–6, 177–8
ASCII format, 120
association
    measures of, 221, 223–4, 242
assumptions in statistical tests, 229, 230–1, 234, 238, 241
Atlas-ti, 271
atomism, 95, 161
attitude measurement, 100, 109–10
attrition in longitudinal studies, 29, 115
audiences, 78–9, 159–60, 162, 247–9, 253–4
authenticity (of documents), 157
authors and authorship (of documents), 159–60, 162–3, 259
availability sampling, 35
average, 54–5
axial coding, 201, 271

B (regression slope), 237–8, 239
Bayesian statistics, 245
Bem Sex Role Inventory, 100, 109, 268
bias, 33–4, 69
bibliographies, 15–17, 251, 259–60, 265
bimodal distribution, 56
binomial distribution, 63

bivariate analysis, 214–24, 224, 229–38, 272
British Crime Survey, 170, 176
British General Election Study [BES], 109, 116, 129, 185–6
British Household Panel Study [BHPS], 29, 124, 179
British Social Attitudes Survey [BSAS], xiii, 67, 97, 105–6, 107–8, 109, 118–19, 130–1, 133, 178, 212–28

Cambridge scale of occupations, 244
canonical correlation analysis, 243–4
case study, 288
causality, 94–5, 241
Census, 32–3, 67–8, 101–2, 171–2, 172, 173–4, 175, 177, 244
    Samples of Anonymised Records [SARs], 113, 174, 177
central limit theorem, 59
change
    analysis of, 29
chi-square
    disaggregation of statistic, 222–3, 242
    distribution, 220
    likelihood ratio statistic, 227
    statistic, 215–22, 223, 227, 242
Chicago School (of Sociology), 153, 171
cluster analysis, 244
cluster sampling, 50–4, 246
codebooks, 117–20, 124, 250, 271, 274
coder variability, 122–3
codes
    conceptual development, 199–206
    types of, 200–1, 204, 205, 271
coding, 117–24, 129, 161, 194–206
    axial, 201, 271
    frame, 118–19, 121, 123–4, 271
    multiple-answer questions, 121
    open, 199
    of open-ended questions, 117, 121, 122, 123–4, 271